The Zoo On the Sea

(Noah and the Ark)

WRITTEN BY **Claudia West**

ILLUSTRATED BY **Elettra Cudignotto**

The Zoo on the Sea
(Noah and the Ark)

Heyer Publishing
Website: GrammyGiggles.com
Email: Claudia@GrammyGiggles.com

Library of Congress Control Number: data on file
print ISBN: 978-1-7338784-0-1

Book Consultant: Judith Briles, The Book Shepherd, The Book Shepherd.com
Cover and interior design : Rebecca Finkel, F + P Graphic Design, FPGD.com
Printed in United States of America

"For every child, everywhere...
Because God loves each one!"
— Grammy Giggles

Do you know a person 600 years old?
600 years old? Yes, 600 years old!
In Genesis 7, a man we are told,
was 600 years old, yes 600 years old!

This man's name was Noah.
He was a good man.
And one day God told him
His big and wet plan:
"Noah," He said,
"You're the man for my plan!"

I want it to rain and I want it to flood,

to rain and to storm till the Earth turns to mud.

Then more rain will come, so much there will be

no longer an Earth—just one great big sea.

It's because all the people have gotten so bad.

And at first I was sad but now I am mad.

Every thing that they do, every thought that they have,

every thing that they say is all bad, bad, BAD!

Now here is YOUR part: you'll build a huge boat,
a sea-worthy Ark that will float, float, FLOAT.
A great big ol' Ark so big it will be
gigantic enough for a Zoo on the Sea.

When the Ark is all done, 40 days it will rain.
It will rain, it won't drain, it will pour
rain, rain, RAIN!

So Noah and his sons,
Japheth, Shem, and Ham,
built a BIG Ark in the
midst of dry land.

BUT ...

Think of the food,

All the MOUNTAINS of food

to feed two of each kind

of all creatures on Earth

and seven of each kind of bird—oh my word!

They'd need bird seed, and corn,

bananas, potatoes,

and carrots and apples,

hay, straw, and tomatoes,

and mangoes and peaches,

pineapples and plums

to fill a whole Ark-full

of tummy tum tums!

And what do you think
that they had there to drink?

When the Ark was completed, the animals came.
The animals came when God called their names.
He had in mind to have two of each kind:
a female and male.
Then God said, "Let's sail!"

The storm clouds rolled in.
The food was all stored.

The people and creatures
were safely on board.
Then God, God Himself,
came and shut the Ark's door.

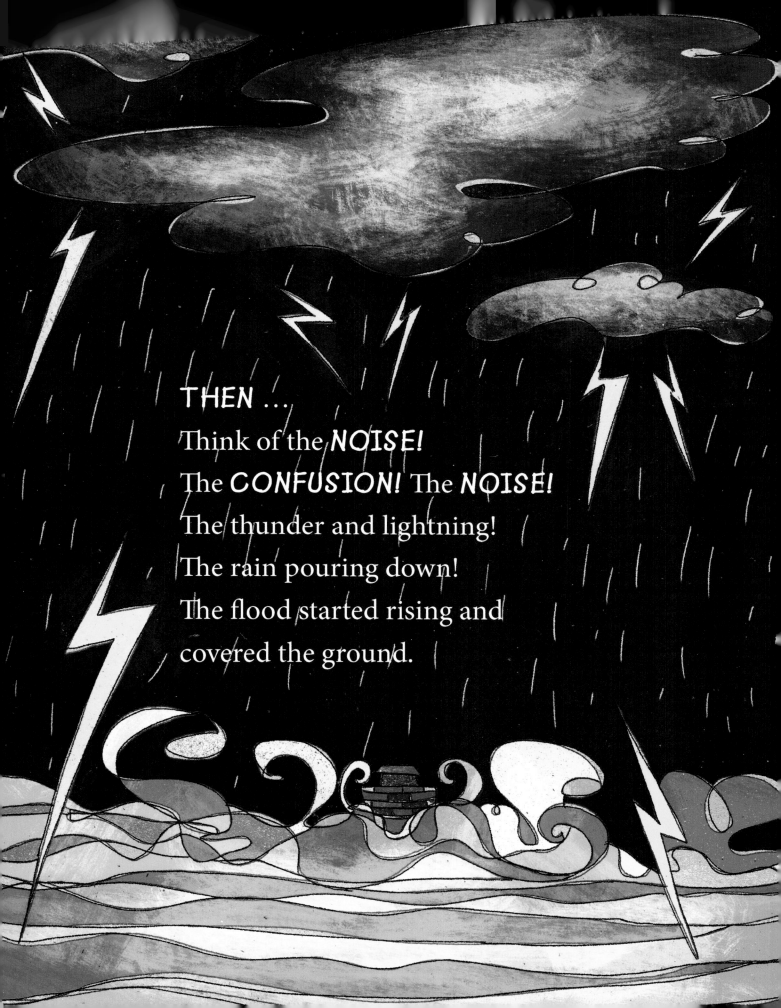

THEN ...

Think of the *NOISE!*

The *CONFUSION!* The *NOISE!*

The thunder and lightning!

The rain pouring down!

The flood started rising and

covered the ground.

And inside the Ark,
the stamping and pawing,
the bumping and clawing,
the hooting and tweeting,
the oinking and bleating,
the growling, the prowling,
the braying and neighing,
the barking, the howling,
and creaking of wood
as the Ark started
swaying!

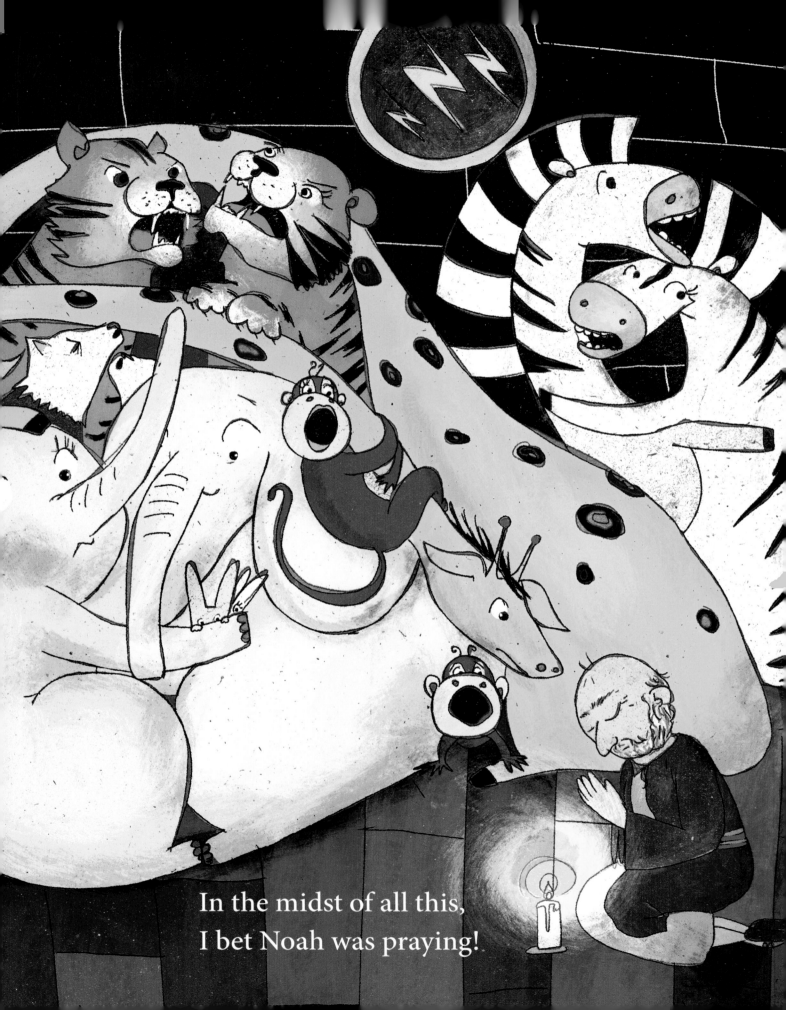

In the midst of all this,
I bet Noah was praying!

For the first 40 days the rain didn't stop,

so even with windows around the Ark's top,

without any sunshine it must've been dark

with no flashlights or lightbulbs to light up the Ark!

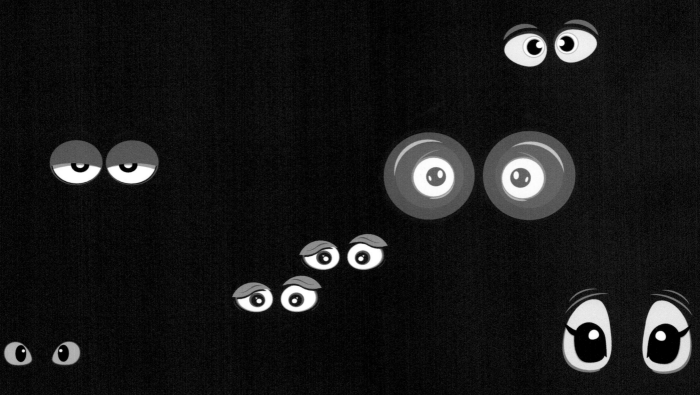

So what do you do
in an Ark in the dark?

AND ...
Think of the smell!
My, my, my what a smell!
Do you think that the smell aboard
would have been sweet
with thousands and thousands
of animals' feet?

And how 'bout the mess
that was down by their feet?
Just who would you guess
had to scoop and to sweep
all the POOP that was left
by the Zoo on the Deep?

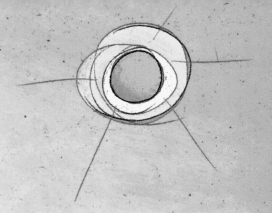

When God stopped the rain, water started to drain
from mountains and valleys and oceans and plains.

Then God sent the wind, and He made the wind blow.
That helped to dry up all the water below.

And after five months,

the Ark finally sat

on the side of a mountain

that's called Ararat.

That's where it was at.

That's where the Ark sat.

And for seven more months it just

SAT …

SAT …

SAT …

BUT ... think of the time ... all the hours of time!

Noah, his wife, his sons and their wives,

were inside that Ark for a year of their lives!

Do you think that they had lots of things there to do?

Do you think its a lot to take care of a zoo?

When nine months had passed
Noah wanted to know
if the land had dried up—
had things started to grow?

So out of a window
a raven was sent.
It never returned—
we don't know where it went!

Noah sent out a dove.
She returned to his hand.
There was still too much water
and no place to land.

So he sent her again
after waiting a week.
She returned to the Ark
with a leaf in her beak.

A third time he sent her.
She tweeted a tweet
and never returned—
her mission complete.

Two more months passed.
The hot sun in the sky
made plants start to grow
and mud start to dry.

And when it was dry
the LORD came to say,

You and the creatures can get out today!
I know you've been waiting to get off the Ark!
Today is the day that you all disembark!

THEN ...

Think of the joy!

The cheers, laughter, and joy!

I bet Noah's whole family

was clapping and dancing,

with animals happily

flapping and prancing

and braying and neighing

and hooting and tweeting

and flipping and skipping

and oinking and bleating

and jumping and running

in joyous stampeding

and hurrying, scurrying,

leaping with glee,

and twirling about

was that Zoo from the Sea.

Noah's mission was done.
He was six hundred and one!
He was so glad to be back on dry sod
that he built an altar and gave thanks to God.

The LORD said to Noah,
"Now look to the sky,
and hear this great promise
for I will not lie.
Never again will I flood
the whole world."
Then the sign of His promise
was grandly unfurled!

All the beautiful colors
painted the skies
in a RAINBOW—a sight
that delighted their eyes!

"When you see a rainbow
remember what's true:
God loves all His kiddos!
And that includes YOU!"

Grammy Giggles says,

"The storms of life seem so unfair
that you may think God doesn't care.
Nothing is farther from the truth!
His ark of love will carry you
like Noah's zoo!
That's what He'll do.
He's there for you.
He'll see you through!

Claudia West
also known as **Grammy Giggles**

Inspired by Dr. Seuss' books, she wrote a series of memorable and fun Bible stories when her two daughters, Rachel and Hannah, were little. Oodles of years drifted by, and her stories just sat, sat, sat on her computer. Now her granddaughter calls her Grammy and the kids at the Royal Family KIDS Camp call her Giggles. All love her stories as they sit, sit, sit listening and laughing. Now you can do the same with *The Zoo on the Sea.*

Calling Colorado home, she loves the beach when she vacations, enjoying the sights and sounds of the sea.

GrammyGiggles.com
Claudia@GrammyGiggles.com

Elettra Cudignotto
with her dog Giungla

Elettra lives in Vicenza, Italy and studied art at "IUAV" in Venice where in 2012 she graduated in Visual Arts and in 2014 she obtained a master degree in Economics and Management of Arts at "Ca Foscari."

She is talented in many genres of art, and specializes in book illustration. All her work is done in digital but her goal is to keep her drawings as much rough as possible because she loves textures, brushes, vivid colours and irregular lines.

To view more of her artwork and to contact her visit:

www.ElettraCudignotto.com

GRAMMY GIGGLES' BIBLE STORIES

THE ZOO ON THE SEA

FISH TUMMY SOUP

GOD'S PERFECTLY AWESOME IDEA

AND MORE TO COME...

Fish Tummy Soup

Told from the Fish's point of view, we learn about a happy fish who was minding his own business when God sent him on a mission. Just what was that secret mission? What happened when the Fish did his job? Grammy Giggles thinks that good things happen when people and fishes use their talents to do what God has in mind. Coming Christmas 2019.

God's Perfectly Awesome Idea

Cool ideas just kept popping up in God's mind, so He decided to create the Universe—including planet Earth and all its wonders! Grammy Giggles thinks that God had oodles of fun making everything there is! Coming Easter 2020.

There are many more stories to come! Discover them all!

PART 4 — PRESCRIPTIVE DESIGN METHODS, pg. C-183

CHAPTER 12 — VENEER, pg. C-183

CHAPTER 13 — GLASS UNIT MASONRY, pg. C-197

Building Code Requirements for Masonry Structures (TMS 402-13/ACI 530-13/ASCE 5-13)

SYNOPSIS

This Code covers the design and construction of masonry structures. It is written in such form that it may be adopted by reference in a legally adopted building code.

Among the subjects covered are: definitions; contract documents; quality assurance; materials; placement of embedded items; analysis and design; strength and serviceability; flexural and axial loads; shear; details and development of reinforcement; walls; columns; pilasters; beams and lintels; seismic design requirements; glass unit masonry; and veneers. An empirical design method applicable to buildings meeting specific location and construction criteria are also included.

The quality, inspection, testing, and placement of materials used in construction are covered by reference to TMS 602-13/ACI 530.1-13/ASCE 6-13 Specification for Masonry Structures and other standards.

Keywords: AAC, masonry, allowable stress design, anchors (fasteners); anchorage (structural); autoclaved aerated concrete masonry, beams; building codes; cements; clay brick; clay tile; columns; compressive strength; concrete block; concrete brick; construction; detailing; empirical design; flexural strength; glass units; grout; grouting; infills; joints; loads (forces); limit design; masonry; masonry cements; masonry load bearing walls; masonry mortars; masonry walls; modulus of elasticity; mortars; pilasters; prestressed masonry, quality assurance; reinforced masonry; reinforcing steel; seismic requirements; shear strength; specifications; splicing; stresses; strength design, structural analysis; structural design; ties; unreinforced masonry; veneers; walls.

This page is intentionally left blank.

PART 1: GENERAL

CHAPTER 1
GENERAL REQUIREMENTS

CODE

1.1 — Scope

1.1.1 *Minimum requirements*

This Code provides minimum requirements for the structural design and construction of masonry elements consisting of masonry units bedded in mortar.

1.1.2 *Governing building code*

This Code supplements the legally adopted building code and shall govern in matters pertaining to structural design and construction of masonry elements. In areas without a legally adopted building code, this Code defines the minimum acceptable standards of design and construction practice.

1.1.3 *SI information*

SI values shown in parentheses are not part of this Code. The equations in this document are for use with the specified inch-pound units only.

COMMENTARY

1.1 — Scope

1.1.1 *Minimum requirements*

This code governs structural design of both structural and non-structural masonry elements. Examples of non-structural elements are masonry veneer, glass unit masonry, and masonry partitions. Structural design aspects of non-structural masonry elements include, but are not limited to, gravity and lateral support, and load transfer to supporting elements.

Masonry structures may be required to have enhanced structural integrity as part of a comprehensive design against progressive collapse due to accident, misuse, sabotage or other causes. General design guidance addressing this issue is available in Commentary Section 1.4 of ASCE 7. Suggestions from that Commentary, of specific application to many masonry structures, include but are not limited to: consideration of plan layout to incorporate returns on walls, both interior and exterior; use of load-bearing interior walls; adequate continuity of walls, ties, and joint rigidity; providing walls capable of beam action; ductile detailing and the use of compartmentalized construction.

1.1.3 *SI information*

The equivalent equations for use with SI units are provided in the Equation Conversions table in Part 5.

CODE

1.2 — Contract documents and calculations

1.2.1   Show all Code-required drawing items on the project drawings, including:

(a) Name and date of issue of Code and supplement to which the design conforms.

(b) Loads used for the design of masonry structures.

(c) Specified compressive strength of masonry at stated ages or stages of construction for which masonry is designed, for each part of the structure, except for masonry designed in accordance with Part 4 or Appendix A.

(d) Size and location of structural elements.

(e) Details of anchorage of masonry to structural members, frames, and other construction, including the type, size, and location of connectors.

(f) Details of reinforcement, including the size, grade, type, lap splice length, and location of reinforcement.

(g) Reinforcing bars to be welded and welding requirements.

(h) Provision for dimensional changes resulting from elastic deformation, creep, shrinkage, temperature, and moisture.

(i) Size and permitted location of conduits, pipes, and sleeves.

1.2.2   Each portion of the structure shall be designed based on the specified compressive strength of masonry for that part of the structure, except for portions designed in accordance with Part 4 or Appendix A.

COMMENTARY

1.2 — Contract documents and calculations

The provisions for preparation of project drawings, project specifications, and issuance of permits are, in general, consistent with those of most legally adopted building codes and are intended as supplements to those codes.

This Code is not intended to be made a part of the contract documents. The contractor should not be required through contract documents to assume responsibility for design (Code) requirements, unless the construction entity is acting in a design-build capacity. A Commentary on TMS 602/ACI 530.1/ASCE 6 accompanies the Specification.

1.2.1   This Code lists some of the more important items of information that must be included in the project drawings or project specifications. This is not an all-inclusive list, and additional items may be required by the building official.

Masonry does not always behave in the same manner as its structural supports or adjacent construction. The designer should consider differential movements and the forces resulting from their restraint. The type of connection chosen should transfer only the loads planned. While some connections transfer loads perpendicular to the wall, other devices transfer loads within the plane of the wall. Figure CC-1.2-1 shows representative wall anchorage details that allow movement within the plane of the wall. While load transfer usually involves masonry attached to structural elements, such as beams or columns, the connection of nonstructural elements, such as door and window frames, should also be addressed.

Connectors are of a variety of sizes, shapes, and uses. In order to perform properly they should be identified on the project drawings.

1.2.2   Masonry design performed in accordance with engineered methods is based on the specified compressive strength of the masonry. For engineered masonry, structural adequacy of masonry construction requires that the compressive strength of masonry equals or exceeds the specified strength. Masonry design by prescriptive approaches relies on rules and masonry compressive strength need not be verified.

CODE

1.2.3   The contract documents shall be consistent with design assumptions.

1.2.4   Contract documents shall specify the minimum level of quality assurance as defined in Section 3.1, or shall include an itemized quality assurance program that equals or exceeds the requirements of Section 3.1.

COMMENTARY

1.2.3   The contract documents must accurately reflect design requirements. For example, joint and opening locations assumed in the design should be coordinated with locations shown on the drawings.

1.2.4   Verification that masonry construction conforms to the contract documents is required by this Code. A program of quality assurance must be included in the contract documents to satisfy this Code requirement.

Code and Commentary, C-3

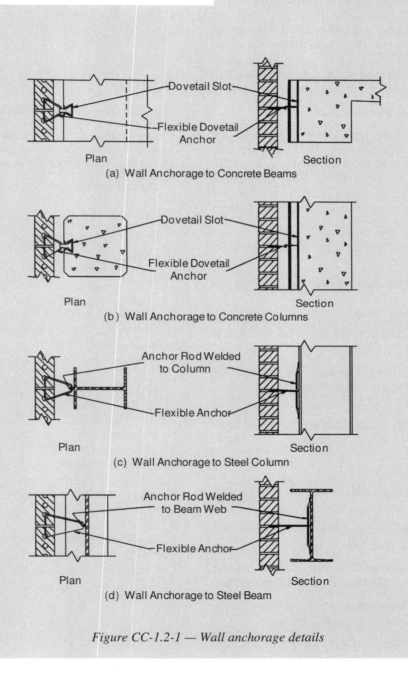

Figure CC-1.2-1 — Wall anchorage details

CODE

1.3 — Approval of special systems of design or construction

Sponsors of any system of design or construction within the scope of this Code, the adequacy of which has been shown by successful use or by analysis or test, but that does not conform to or is not addressed by this Code, shall have the right to present the data on which their design is based to a board of examiners appointed by the building official. The board shall be composed of licensed design professionals and shall have authority to investigate the submitted data, require tests, and formulate rules governing design and construction of such systems to meet the intent of this Code. The rules, when approved and promulgated by the building official, shall be of the same force and effect as the provisions of this Code.

1.4 — Standards cited in this Code

Standards of the American Concrete Institute, the American Society of Civil Engineers, ASTM International, the American Welding Society, and The Masonry Society cited in this Code are listed below with their serial designations, including year of adoption or revision, and are declared to be part of this Code as if fully set forth in this document.

TMS 602-13/ACI 530.1-13/ASCE 6-13 — Specification for Masonry Structures

ASCE 7-10 — Minimum Design Loads for Buildings and Other Structures

ASTM A416/A416M-12 — Standard Specification for Steel Strand, Uncoated Seven-Wire for Prestressed Concrete

ASTM A421/A421M-10 — Standard Specification for Uncoated Stress-Relieved Steel Wire for Prestressed Concrete

ASTM A706/A706M-09b — Standard Specification for Low-Alloy Steel Deformed and Plain Bars for Concrete Reinforcement

ASTM A722/A722M-12 — Standard Specification for Uncoated High-Strength Steel Bars for Prestressing Concrete

ASTM C34-12 — Standard Specification for Structural Clay Load-Bearing Wall Tile

ASTM C140-12a — Standard Test Methods for Sampling and Testing Concrete Masonry Units and Related Units

ASTM C426-10 — Standard Test Method for Linear Drying Shrinkage of Concrete Masonry Units

COMMENTARY

1.3 — Approval of special systems of design or construction

New methods of design, new materials, and new uses of materials must undergo a period of development before being specifically addressed by a code. Hence, valid systems or components might be excluded from use by implication if means were not available to obtain acceptance. This section permits proponents to submit data substantiating the adequacy of their system or component to a board of examiners.

1.4 — Standards cited in this Code

These standards are referenced in this Code. Specific dates are listed here because changes to the standard may result in changes of properties or procedures.

Contact information for these organizations is given below:

American Concrete Institute (ACI)
38800 Country Club Drive
Farmington Hills, MI 48331
www.aci-int.org

American Society of Civil Engineers (ASCE)
1801 Alexander Bell Drive
Reston, VA 20191
www.asce.org

ASTM International
100 Barr Harbor Drive
West Conshohocken, PA 19428-2959
www.astm.org

American Welding Society (AWS)
8669 NW 36th Street, Suite 130
Miami, Florida 33166-6672
www.aws.org

The Masonry Society (TMS)
105 South Sunset Street, Suite Q
Longmont, Colorado 80501-6172
www.masonrysociety.org

CODE

ASTM C476-10 — Standard Specification for Grout for Masonry

ASTM C482-02 (2009) — Standard Test Method for Bond Strength of Ceramic Tile to Portland Cement Paste

ASTM C1006-07 — Standard Test Method for Splitting Tensile Strength of Masonry Units

ASTM C1611/C1611M-09be1 — Standard Test Method for Slump Flow of Self-Consolidating Concrete

ASTM C1693-11 — Standard Specification for Autoclaved Aerated Concrete (AAC)

ASTM E111-04 (2010) — Standard Test Method for Young's Modulus, Tangent Modulus, and Chord Modulus

ASTM E488-96 (2003) — Standard Test Methods for Strength of Anchors in Concrete and Masonry Elements

AWS D 1.4/D1.4M: 2011 — Structural Welding Code — Reinforcing Steel

COMMENTARY

This page intentionally left blank

CHAPTER 2
NOTATION AND DEFINITIONS

CODE

2.1 — Notation

A_b = cross-sectional area of an anchor bolt, in.^{2} (mm^2)

A_{br} = bearing area, in.^{2} (mm^2)

A_g = gross cross-sectional area of a member, in.^{2} (mm^2)

A_n = net cross-sectional area of a member, in.^{2} (mm^2)

A_{nv} = net shear area, in.^{2} (mm^2)

A_{ps} = area of prestressing steel, in.^{2} (mm^2)

A_{pt} = projected tension area on masonry surface of a right circular cone, in.^{2} (mm^2)

A_{pv} = projected shear area on masonry surface of one-half of a right circular cone, in.^{2} (mm^2)

A_s = area of nonprestressed longitudinal tension reinforcement, in.^{2} (mm^2)

A_{sc} = area of reinforcement placed within the lap, near each end of the lapped reinforcing bars and transverse to them, in.^{2} (mm^2)

A_{st} = total area of laterally tied longitudinal reinforcing steel, in.^{2} (mm^2)

A_v = cross-sectional area of shear reinforcement, in.^{2} (mm^2)

A_1 = loaded area, in.^{2} (mm^2)

A_2 = supporting bearing area, in.^{2} (mm^2)

a = depth of an equivalent compression stress block at nominal strength, in. (mm)

B_a = allowable axial load on an anchor bolt, lb (N)

B_{ab} = allowable axial tensile load on an anchor bolt when governed by masonry breakout, lb (N)

B_{an} = nominal axial strength of an anchor bolt, lb (N)

B_{anb} = nominal axial tensile strength of an anchor bolt when governed by masonry breakout, lb (N)

B_{anp} = nominal axial tensile strength of an anchor bolt when governed by anchor pullout, lb (N)

B_{ans} = nominal axial tensile strength of an anchor bolt when governed by steel yielding, lb (N)

B_{ap} = allowable axial tensile load on an anchor bolt when governed by anchor pullout, lb (N)

B_{as} = allowable axial tensile load on an anchor bolt when governed by steel yielding, lb (N)

COMMENTARY

2.1 — Notation

Notations used in this Code are summarized here.

CODE

B_v = allowable shear load on an anchor bolt, lb (N)

B_{vb} = allowable shear load on an anchor bolt when governed by masonry breakout, lb (N)

B_{vc} = allowable shear load on an anchor bolt when governed by masonry crushing, lb (N)

B_{vn} = nominal shear strength of an anchor bolt, lb (N)

B_{vnb} = nominal shear strength of an anchor bolt when governed by masonry breakout, lb (N)

B_{vnc} = nominal shear strength of an anchor bolt when governed by masonry crushing, lb (N)

B_{vnpry} = nominal shear strength of an anchor bolt when governed by anchor pryout, lb (N)

B_{vns} = nominal shear strength of an anchor bolt when governed by steel yielding, lb (N)

B_{vpry} = allowable shear load on an anchor bolt when governed by anchor pryout, lb (N)

B_{vs} = allowable shear load on an anchor bolt when governed by steel yielding, lb (N)

b = width of section, in. (mm)

b_a = total applied design axial force on an anchor bolt, lb (N)

b_{af} = factored axial force in an anchor bolt, lb (N)

b_v = total applied design shear force on an anchor bolt, lb (N)

b_{vf} = factored shear force in an anchor bolt, lb (N)

b_w = width of wall beam, in. (mm)

C_d = deflection amplification factor

c = distance from the fiber of maximum compressive strain to the neutral axis, in. (mm)

D = dead load or related internal moments and forces

d = distance from extreme compression fiber to centroid of tension reinforcement, in. (mm)

d_b = nominal diameter of reinforcement or anchor bolt, in. (mm)

d_v = actual depth of a member in direction of shear considered, in. (mm)

E = load effects of earthquake or related internal moments and forces

E_{AAC} = modulus of elasticity of AAC masonry in compression, psi (MPa)

E_{bb} = modulus of elasticity of bounding beams, psi (MPa)

COMMENTARY

CODE

E_{bc} = modulus of elasticity of bounding columns, psi (MPa)

E_m = modulus of elasticity of masonry in compression, psi (MPa)

E_{ps} = modulus of elasticity of prestressing steel, psi (MPa)

E_s = modulus of elasticity of steel, psi (MPa)

E_v = modulus of rigidity (shear modulus) of masonry, psi (MPa)

e = eccentricity of axial load, in. (mm)

e_b = projected leg extension of bent-bar anchor, measured from inside edge of anchor at bend to farthest point of anchor in the plane of the hook, in. (mm)

e_u = eccentricity of P_{uf}, in. (mm)

F_a = allowable compressive stress available to resist axial load only, psi (MPa)

F_b = allowable compressive stress available to resist flexure only, psi (MPa)

F_s = allowable tensile or compressive stress in reinforcement, psi (MPa)

F_v = allowable shear stress, psi (MPa)

F_{vm} = allowable shear stress resisted by the masonry, psi (MPa)

F_{vs} = allowable shear stress resisted by the shear reinforcement, psi (MPa)

f_a = calculated compressive stress in masonry due to axial load only, psi (MPa)

f_b = calculated compressive stress in masonry due to flexure only, psi (MPa)

f'_{AAC} = specified compressive strength of AAC masonry, psi (MPa)

f'_g = specified compressive strength of grout, psi (MPa)

f'_m = specified compressive strength of clay masonry or concrete masonry, psi (MPa)

f'_{mi} = specified compressive strength of clay masonry or concrete masonry at the time of prestress transfer, psi (MPa)

f_{ps} = stress in prestressing tendon at nominal strength, psi (MPa)

f_{pu} = specified tensile strength of prestressing tendon, psi (MPa)

f_{py} = specified yield strength of prestressing tendon, psi (MPa)

f_r = modulus of rupture, psi (MPa)

COMMENTARY

CODE

f_{rAAC} = modulus of rupture of AAC, psi (MPa)

f_s = calculated tensile or compressive stress in reinforcement, psi (MPa)

f_{se} = effective stress in prestressing tendon after all prestress losses have occurred, psi (MPa)

f_{tAAC} = splitting tensile strength of AAC as determined in accordance with ASTM C1006, psi (MPa)

f_v = calculated shear stress in masonry, psi (MPa)

f_y = specified yield strength of steel for reinforcement and anchors, psi (MPa)

h = effective height of column, wall, or pilaster, in. (mm)

h_{inf} = vertical dimension of infill, in. (mm)

h_w = height of entire wall or of the segment of wall considered, in. (mm)

I_{bb} = moment of inertia of bounding beam for bending in the plane of the infill, in.^{4} (mm^4)

I_{bc} = moment of inertia of bounding column for bending in the plane of the infill, in.^{4} (mm^4)

I_{cr} = moment of inertia of cracked cross-sectional area of a member, in.^{4} (mm^4)

I_{eff} = effective moment of inertia, in.^{4} (mm^4)

I_g = moment of inertia of gross cross-sectional area of a member, in.^{4} (mm^4)

I_n = moment of inertia of net cross-sectional area of a member, in.^{4} (mm^4)

j = ratio of distance between centroid of flexural compressive forces and centroid of tensile forces to depth, d

K = dimension used to calculate reinforcement development, in. (mm)

K_{AAC} = dimension used to calculate reinforcement development for AAC masonry, in. (mm)

k_c = coefficient of creep of masonry, per psi (per MPa)

k_e = coefficient of irreversible moisture expansion of clay masonry

k_m = coefficient of shrinkage of concrete masonry

k_t = coefficient of thermal expansion of masonry per degree Fahrenheit (degree Celsius)

L = live load or related internal moments and forces

l = clear span between supports, in. (mm)

l_b = effective embedment length of headed or bent anchor bolts, in. (mm)

COMMENTARY

CODE

COMMENTARY

l_{be} = anchor bolt edge distance, in. (mm)

l_d = development length or lap length of straight reinforcement, in. (mm)

l_e = equivalent embedment length provided by standard hooks measured from the start of the hook (point of tangency), in. (mm)

l_{eff} = effective span length for a deep beam, in. (mm)

l_{inf} = plan length of infill, in. (mm)

l_p = clear span of the prestressed member in the direction of the prestressing tendon, in. (mm)

l_w = length of entire wall or of the segment of wall considered in direction of shear force, in. (mm)

M = maximum moment at the section under consideration, in.-lb (N-mm)

M_a = maximum moment in member due to the applied unfactored loading for which deflection is calculated, in.-lb (N-mm)

M_{cr} = nominal cracking moment strength, in.-lb (N-mm)

M_n = nominal moment strength, in.-lb (N-mm)

M_{ser} = service moment at midheight of a member, including P-delta effects, in.-lb (N-mm)

M_u = factored moment, magnified by second-order effects where required by the code, in.-lb (N-mm)

$M_{u,0}$ = factored moment from first-order analysis, in.-lb (N-mm)

n = modular ratio, E_s/E_m

N_u = factored compressive force acting normal to shear surface that is associated with the V_u loading combination case under consideration, lb (N)

N_v = compressive force acting normal to shear surface, lb (N)

P = axial load, lb (N)

P_a = allowable axial compressive force in a reinforced member, lb (N)

P_e = Euler buckling load, lb (N)

P_n = nominal axial strength, lb (N)

P_{ps} = prestressing tendon force at time and location relevant for design, lb (N)

P_u = factored axial load, lb (N)

P_{uf} = factored load from tributary floor or roof areas, lb (N)

CODE

COMMENTARY

P_{uw} = factored weight of wall area tributary to wall section under consideration, lb (N)

Q = first moment about the neutral axis of an area between the extreme fiber and the plane at which the shear stress is being calculated, in.^{3} (mm^3)

Q_E = the effect of horizontal seismic (earthquake-induced) forces

$q_{n\ inf}$ = nominal out-of-plane flexural capacity of infill per unit area, psf (Pa)

q_z = velocity pressure determined in accordance with ASCE 7, psf (kPa)

R = response modification coefficient

r = radius of gyration, in. (mm)

S = snow load or related internal moments and forces

S_n = section modulus of the net cross-sectional area of a member, in.^{3} (mm^3)

s = spacing of reinforcement, in. (mm)

s_l = total linear drying shrinkage of concrete masonry units determined in accordance with ASTM C426

t = nominal thickness of member, in. (mm)

t_{inf} = specified thickness of infill, in. (mm)

$t_{net\ inf}$ = net thickness of infill, in. (mm)

t_{sp} = specified thickness of member, in. (mm)

v = shear stress, psi (MPa)

V = shear force, lb (N)

V_{lim} = limiting base-shear strength, lb (N)

V_{nAAC} = nominal shear strength provided by AAC masonry, lb (N)

V_n = nominal shear strength, lb (N)

$V_{n\ inf}$ = nominal horizontal in-plane shear strength of infill, lb (N)

V_{nm} = nominal shear strength provided by masonry, lb (N)

V_{ns} = nominal shear strength provided by shear reinforcement, lb (N)

V_u = factored shear force, lb (N)

V_{ub} = base-shear demand, lb (N)

W = wind load or related internal moments and forces

W_S = dimension of the structural wall strip defined in Sections 14.3.2 and A.5.1 and shown in Figures 14.3.1-1 and A.5.1-1.

CODE

COMMENTARY

W_T = dimension of the tributary length of wall, defined in Sections 14.3.2 and A.5.1 and shown in Figures 14.3.1-1 and A.5.1-1.

w_{inf} = width of equivalent strut, in. (mm)

w_{strut} = horizontal projection of the width of the diagonal strut, in. (mm)

w_u = out-of-plane factored uniformly distributed load, lb/in. (N/mm)

z = internal lever arm between compressive and tensile forces in a deep beam, in. (mm)

α_{arch} = horizontal arching parameter for infill, $lb^{0.25}$ ($N^{0.25}$)

β_{arch} = vertical arching parameter for infill, $lb^{0.25}$ ($N^{0.25}$)

β_b = ratio of area of reinforcement cut off to total area of tension reinforcement at a section

γ = reinforcement size factor

γ_g = grouted shear wall factor

Δ = calculated story drift, in. (mm)

Δ_a = allowable story drift, in. (mm)

δ = moment magnification factor

δ_{ne} = displacements calculated using code-prescribed seismic forces and assuming elastic behavior, in. (mm)

δ_s = horizontal deflection at midheight under allowable stress design load combinations, in. (mm)

δ_u = deflection due to factored loads, in. (mm)

ε_{cs} = drying shrinkage of AAC

ε_{mu} = maximum usable compressive strain of masonry

ξ = lap splice confinement reinforcement factor

θ_{strut} = angle of infill diagonal with respect to the horizontal, degrees

λ_{strut} = characteristic stiffness parameter for infill, in.$^{-1}$ (mm^{-1})

μ_{AAC} = coefficient of friction of AAC

ρ = reinforcement ratio

ρ_{max} = maximum flexural tension reinforcement ratio

ϕ = strength-reduction factor

ψ = magnification factor for second-order effects

CODE

2.2 — Definitions

Anchor — Metal rod, wire, or strap that secures masonry to its structural support.

Anchor pullout — Anchor failure defined by the anchor sliding out of the material in which it is embedded without breaking out a substantial portion of the surrounding material.

Area, gross cross-sectional — The area delineated by the out-to-out dimensions of masonry in the plane under consideration.

Area, net cross-sectional — The area of masonry units, grout, and mortar crossed by the plane under consideration based on out-to-out dimensions.

Area, net shear — The net area of the web of a shear element.

Autoclaved aerated concrete — Low-density cementitious product of calcium silicate hydrates, whose material specifications are defined in ASTM C1693.

Autoclaved aerated concrete (AAC) masonry — Autoclaved aerated concrete units manufactured without reinforcement, set on a mortar leveling bed, bonded with thin-bed mortar, placed with or without grout, and placed with or without reinforcement.

Backing — Wall or surface to which veneer is attached.

Bed joint — The horizontal layer of mortar on which a masonry unit is laid.

COMMENTARY

2.2 — Definitions

For consistent application of this Code, terms are defined that have particular meanings in this Code. The definitions given are for use in application of this Code only and do not always correspond to ordinary usage. Other terms are defined in referenced documents and those definitions are applicable. If any term is defined in both this Code and in a referenced document, the definition in this Code applies. Referenced documents are listed in Section 1.4 and include ASTM standards. Terminology standards include ASTM C1232 Standard Terminology of Masonry and ASTM C1180 Standard Terminology of Mortar and Grout for Unit Masonry. Glossaries of masonry terminology are available from several sources within the industry (BIA TN 2, 1999; NCMA TEK 1-4, 2004; and IMI, 1981).

Area, net shear — The net shear area for a partially grouted flanged shear wall is shown in Figure CC-2.2-1.

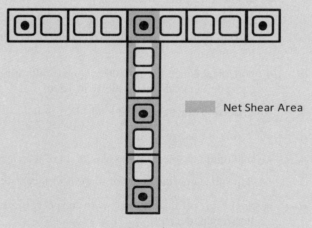

Figure CC-2.2-1 — Net shear area

CODE

Bond beam — A horizontal, sloped, or stepped element that is fully grouted, has longitudinal bar reinforcement, and is constructed within a masonry wall.

COMMENTARY

Bond beam – This reinforced member is usually constructed horizontally, but may be sloped or stepped to match an adjacent roof, for example, as shown in Figure CC-2.2-2.

Notes:

(1) Masonry wall
(2) Fully grouted bond beam with reinforcement
(3) Sloped top of wall
(4) Length of noncontact lap splice
(5) Spacing between bars in noncontact lap splice

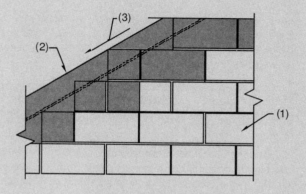

(a) Sloped Bond Beam
(not to scale)

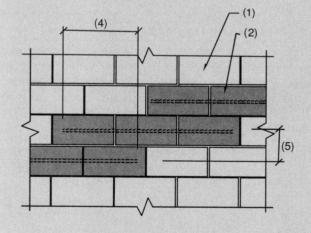

(b) Stepped Bond Beam
(not to scale)

Figure CC-2.2-2 — Sloped and stepped bond beams

CODE

Bonded prestressing tendon — Prestressing tendon encapsulated by prestressing grout in a corrugated duct that is bonded to the surrounding masonry through grouting.

Bounding frame — The columns and upper and lower beams or slabs that surround masonry infill and provide structural support.

Building official — The officer or other designated authority charged with the administration and enforcement of this Code, or the building official's duly authorized representative.

Cavity wall — A masonry wall consisting of two or more wythes, at least two of which are separated by a continuous air space; air space(s) between wythes may contain insulation; and separated wythes must be connected by wall ties.

Collar joint — Vertical longitudinal space between wythes of masonry or between masonry wythe and back-up construction, which is permitted to be filled with mortar or grout.

Column — A structural member, not built integrally into a wall, designed primarily to resist compressive loads parallel to its longitudinal axis and subject to dimensional limitations.

Composite action — Transfer of stress between components of a member designed so that in resisting loads, the combined components act together as a single member.

Composite masonry — Multiwythe masonry members with wythes bonded to produce composite action.

Compressive strength of masonry — Maximum compressive force resisted per unit of net cross-sectional area of masonry, determined by testing masonry prisms or a function of individual masonry units, mortar, and grout, in accordance with the provisions of TMS 602/ACI 530.1/ASCE 6.

Connector — A mechanical device for securing two or more pieces, parts, or members together, including anchors, wall ties, and fasteners.

Contract documents — Documents establishing the required work, and including in particular, the project drawings and project specifications.

Corbel — A projection of successive courses from the face of masonry.

Cover, grout — thickness of grout surrounding the outer surface of embedded reinforcement, anchor, or tie.

Cover, masonry — thickness of masonry units, mortar, and grout surrounding the outer surface of embedded reinforcement, anchor, or tie.

COMMENTARY

Column — Generally, a column spans vertically, though it may have another orientation in space.

CODE

Cover, mortar — thickness of mortar surrounding the outer surface of embedded reinforcement, anchor, or tie.

Deep beam — A beam that has an effective span-to-depth ratio, l_{eff}/d_v, less than 3 for a continuous span and less than 2 for a simple span.

Depth — The dimension of a member measured in the plane of a cross section perpendicular to the neutral axis.

Design story drift — The difference of deflections at the top and bottom of the story under consideration, taking into account the possibility of inelastic deformations as defined in ASCE 7. In the equivalent lateral force method, the story drift is calculated by multiplying the deflections determined from an elastic analysis by the appropriate deflection amplification factor, C_d, from ASCE 7.

Design strength — The nominal strength of an element multiplied by the appropriate strength-reduction factor.

Diaphragm — A roof or floor system designed to transmit lateral forces to shear walls or other lateral-force-resisting elements.

Dimension, nominal — The specified dimension plus an allowance for the joints with which the units are to be laid. Nominal dimensions are usually stated in whole numbers nearest to the specified dimensions.

Dimensions, specified — Dimensions specified for the manufacture or construction of a unit, joint, or element.

Effective height — Clear height of a member between lines of support or points of support and used for calculating the slenderness ratio of a member. Effective height for unbraced members shall be calculated.

Effective prestress — Stress remaining in prestressing tendons after all losses have occurred.

Foundation pier — A vertical foundation member, not built integrally into a foundation wall, empirically designed to support gravity loads and subject to dimensional limitations.

Glass unit masonry — Masonry composed of glass units bonded by mortar.

Grout — (1) A plastic mixture of cementitious materials, aggregates, and water, with or without admixtures, initially produced to pouring consistency without segregation of the constituents during placement. (2) The hardened equivalent of such mixtures.

COMMENTARY

Dimension, nominal — Nominal dimensions are usually used to identify the size of a masonry unit. The thickness or width is given first, followed by height and length. The permitted tolerances for units are given in the appropriate material standards. Permitted tolerances for joints and masonry construction are given in the Specification.

Dimensions, specified — Specified dimensions are most often used for design calculations.

CODE

Grout, self-consolidating — A highly fluid and stable grout typically with admixtures, that remains homogeneous when placed and does not require puddling or vibration for consolidation.

Head joint — Vertical mortar joint placed between masonry units within the wythe at the time the masonry units are laid.

Header (bonder) — A masonry unit that connects two or more adjacent wythes of masonry.

Infill — Masonry constructed within the plane of, and bounded by, a structural frame.

Infill, net thickness — Minimum total thickness of the net cross-sectional area of an infill.

Infill, non-participating — Infill designed so that in-plane loads are not imparted to it from the bounding frame.

Infill, participating — Infill designed to resist in-plane loads imparted to it by the bounding frame.

Inspection, continuous — The Inspection Agency's full-time observation of work by being present in the area where the work is being performed.

Inspection, periodic — The Inspection Agency's part-time or intermittent observation of work during construction by being present in the area where the work has been or is being performed, and observation upon completion of the work.

Laterally restrained prestressing tendon — Prestressing tendon that is not free to move laterally within the cross section of the member.

Laterally unrestrained prestressing tendon — Prestressing tendon that is free to move laterally within the cross section of the member.

COMMENTARY

Infill, net thickness – The net thickness is shown in Figure CC-2.2-3

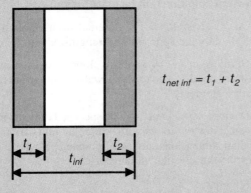

$$t_{net\,inf} = t_1 + t_2$$

Vertical Section through Hollow Unit in Infill Wall

Figure CC-2.2-3 — Thickness and net thickness of an infill

Inspection, continuous — The Inspection Agency is required to be on the project site whenever masonry tasks requiring continuous inspection are in progress.

Inspection, periodic — During construction requiring periodic inspection, the Inspection Agency is only required to be on the project site intermittently, and is required to observe completed work. The frequency of periodic inspections should be defined by the Architect/Engineer as part of the quality assurance plan, and should be consistent with the complexity and size of the project.

CODE

Licensed design professional — An individual who is licensed to practice design as defined by the statutory requirements of the professional licensing laws of the state or jurisdiction in which the project is to be constructed and who is in responsible charge of the design; in other documents, also referred to as *registered design professional.*

Load, dead — Dead weight supported by a member, as defined by the legally adopted building code.

Load, live — Live load specified by the legally adopted building code.

Load, service — Load specified by the legally adopted building code.

Longitudinal reinforcement — Reinforcement placed parallel to the longitudinal axis of the member.

Masonry breakout — Anchor failure defined by the separation of a volume of masonry, approximately conical in shape, from the member.

Masonry, partially grouted — Construction in which designated cells or spaces are filled with grout, while other cells or spaces are ungrouted.

Masonry unit, hollow — A masonry unit with net cross-sectional area of less than 75 percent of its gross cross-sectional area when measured in any plane parallel to the surface containing voids.

Masonry unit, solid — A masonry unit with net cross-sectional area of 75 percent or more of its gross cross-sectional area when measured in every plane parallel to the surface containing voids.

Modulus of elasticity — Ratio of normal stress to corresponding strain for tensile or compressive stresses below proportional limit of material.

Modulus of rigidity — Ratio of unit shear stress to unit shear strain for unit shear stress below the proportional limit of the material.

Nominal strength — The strength of an element or cross section calculated in accordance with the requirements and assumptions of the strength design methods of these provisions before application of strength-reduction factors.

Partition wall — An interior wall without structural function.

Pier —A reinforced, vertically spanning portion of a wall next to an opening, designed using strength design, and subject to dimensional limitations.

COMMENTARY

Licensed design professional — For convenience, the Commentary uses the term "designer" when referring to the licensed design professional.

Pier — The term "Pier" is used for convenience to define a portion of a wall, and only has meaning for certain reinforced members designed using strength design. The reinforcement requirements for piers are less severe than for columns because piers are part of a wall, have less slender geometry and more restrictive loading limits. A strength-designed member, not meeting the dimensional limits and requirements for a pier, should be designed as a wall or, if not built integrally with a wall, as a column.

CODE

Post-tensioning — Method of prestressing in which a prestressing tendon is tensioned after the masonry has been placed.

Prestressed masonry — Masonry in which internal compressive stresses have been introduced by prestressed tendons to counteract potential tensile stresses resulting from applied loads.

Prestressing grout — A cementitious mixture used to encapsulate bonded prestressing tendons.

Prestressing tendon — Steel elements such as wire, bar, or strand, used to impart prestress to masonry.

Pretensioning — Method of prestressing in which a prestressing tendon is tensioned before the transfer of stress into the masonry.

Prism — An assemblage of masonry units and mortar, with or without grout, used as a test specimen for determining properties of the masonry.

Project drawings — The drawings that, along with the project specifications, complete the descriptive information for constructing the work required by the contract documents.

Project specifications — The written documents that specify requirements for a project in accordance with the service parameters and other specific criteria established by the owner or the owner's agent.

Quality assurance — The administrative and procedural requirements established by the contract documents to assure that constructed masonry is in compliance with the contract documents.

Reinforcement — Nonprestressed steel reinforcement.

Required strength — The strength needed to resist factored loads.

Running bond — The placement of masonry units so that head joints in successive courses are horizontally offset at least one-quarter the unit length.

COMMENTARY

Running bond — This Code concerns itself only with the structural effect of the masonry bond pattern. Therefore, the only distinction made by this Code is between masonry laid in running bond and masonry that is not laid in running bond. For purposes of this Code, architectural bond patterns that do not satisfy the Code definition of running bond are classified as not running bond. Masonry laid in other bond patterns must be reinforced to provide continuity across the heads joints. Stack bond, which is commonly interpreted as a pattern with aligned heads joints, is one bond pattern that is required to be reinforced horizontally.

CODE

COMMENTARY

Shear wall — A wall, load-bearing or non-load-bearing, designed to resist lateral forces acting in the plane of the wall (sometimes referred to as a vertical diaphragm).

Shear wall, detailed plain (unreinforced) AAC masonry — An AAC masonry shear wall designed to resist lateral forces while neglecting stresses in reinforcement, although provided with minimum reinforcement and connections.

Shear wall, detailed plain (unreinforced) masonry — A masonry shear wall designed to resist lateral forces while neglecting stresses in reinforcement, although provided with minimum reinforcement and connections.

Shear wall, intermediate reinforced masonry — A masonry shear wall designed to resist lateral forces while considering stresses in reinforcement and to satisfy specific minimum reinforcement and connection requirements.

Shear wall, intermediate reinforced prestressed masonry — A prestressed masonry shear wall designed to resist lateral forces while considering stresses in reinforcement and to satisfy specific minimum reinforcement and connection requirements.

Shear wall, ordinary plain (unreinforced) AAC masonry — An AAC masonry shear wall designed to resist lateral forces while neglecting stresses in reinforcement, if present.

Shear wall, ordinary plain (unreinforced) masonry — A masonry shear wall designed to resist lateral forces while neglecting stresses in reinforcement, if present.

Shear wall, ordinary plain (unreinforced) prestressed masonry — A prestressed masonry shear wall designed to resist lateral forces while neglecting stresses in reinforcement, if present.

Shear wall, ordinary reinforced AAC masonry — An AAC masonry shear wall designed to resist lateral forces while considering stresses in reinforcement and satisfying prescriptive reinforcement and connection requirements.

Shear wall, ordinary reinforced masonry — A masonry shear wall designed to resist lateral forces while considering stresses in reinforcement and satisfying prescriptive reinforcement and connection requirements.

Shear wall, special reinforced masonry — A masonry shear wall designed to resist lateral forces while considering stresses in reinforcement and to satisfy special reinforcement and connection requirements.

Shear wall, special reinforced prestressed masonry — A prestressed masonry shear wall designed to resist lateral forces while considering stresses in reinforcement and to satisfy special reinforcement and connection requirements.

CODE

Slump flow — The circular spread of plastic self-consolidating grout, which is evaluated in accordance with ASTM C1611/C1611M.

Special boundary elements — In walls that are designed to resist in-plane load, end regions that are strengthened by reinforcement and are detailed to meet specific requirements, and may or may not be thicker than the wall.

Specified compressive strength of AAC masonry, f'_{AAC} — Minimum compressive strength, expressed as force per unit of net cross-sectional area, required of the AAC masonry used in construction by the contract documents, and upon which the project design is based. Whenever the quantity f'_{AAC} is under the radical sign, the square root of numerical value only is intended and the result has units of psi (MPa).

Specified compressive strength of masonry, f'_m — Minimum compressive strength, expressed as force per unit of net cross-sectional area, required of the masonry used in construction by the contract documents, and upon which the project design is based. Whenever the quantity f'_m is under the radical sign, the square root of numerical value only is intended and the result has units of psi (MPa).

Stirrup — Reinforcement used to resist shear in a flexural member.

Stone masonry — Masonry composed of field, quarried, or cast stone units bonded by mortar.

Stone masonry, ashlar — Stone masonry composed of rectangular units having sawed, dressed, or squared bed surfaces and bonded by mortar.

Stone masonry, rubble — Stone masonry composed of irregular-shaped units bonded by mortar.

Strength-reduction factor, ϕ — The factor by which the nominal strength is multiplied to obtain the design strength.

Tendon anchorage — In post-tensioning, a device used to anchor the prestressing tendon to the masonry or concrete member; in pretensioning, a device used to anchor the prestressing tendon during hardening of masonry mortar, grout, prestressing grout, or concrete.

Tendon coupler — A device for connecting two tendon ends, thereby transferring the prestressing force from end to end.

Tendon jacking force — Temporary force exerted by a device that introduces tension into prestressing tendons.

COMMENTARY

Special boundary elements — Requirements for longitudinal and transverse reinforcement have not been established in general and must be verified by testing. Research in this area is ongoing.

CODE

COMMENTARY

Thin-bed mortar — Mortar for use in construction of AAC unit masonry whose joints shall not be less than 1/16 in. (1.5 mm).

Tie, lateral — Loop of reinforcing bar or wire enclosing longitudinal reinforcement.

Tie, wall — Metal connector that connects wythes of masonry walls together.

Transfer — Act of applying to the masonry member the force in the prestressing tendons.

Transverse reinforcement — Reinforcement placed perpendicular to the longitudinal axis of the member.

Unbonded prestressing tendon — Prestressing tendon that is not bonded to masonry.

Unreinforced (plain) masonry — Masonry in which the tensile resistance of masonry is taken into consideration and the resistance of reinforcing steel, if present, is neglected.

Veneer, adhered — Masonry veneer secured to and supported by the backing through adhesion.

Veneer, anchored — Masonry veneer secured to and supported laterally by the backing through anchors and supported vertically by the foundation or other structural elements.

Veneer, masonry — A masonry wythe that provides the exterior finish of a wall system and transfers out-of-plane load directly to a backing, but is not considered to add strength or stiffness to the wall system.

Visual stability index (VSI) — An index, defined in ASTM C1611/C1611M, that qualitatively indicates the stability of self-consolidating grout

Wall — A vertical element with a horizontal length to thickness ratio greater than 3, used to enclose space.

Wall, load-bearing — Wall supporting vertical loads greater than 200 lb/linear ft (2919 N/m) in addition to its own weight.

Wall, masonry bonded hollow — A multiwythe wall built with masonry units arranged to provide an air space between the wythes and with the wythes bonded together with masonry units.

Width — The dimension of a member measured in the plane of a cross section parallel to the neutral axis.

Wythe — Each continuous vertical section of a wall, one masonry unit in thickness.

This page intentionally left blank

CHAPTER 3
QUALITY AND CONSTRUCTION

CODE

3.1 — Quality Assurance program

The quality assurance program shall comply with the requirements of this section, depending on the Risk Category, as defined in ASCE 7 or the legally adopted building code. The quality assurance program shall itemize the requirements for verifying conformance of material composition, quality, storage, handling, preparation, and placement with the requirements of TMS 602/ACI 530.1/ASCE 6.

3.1.1 *Level A Quality Assurance*
The minimum quality assurance program for masonry in Risk Category I, II, or III structures and designed in accordance with Part 4 or Appendix A shall comply with Table 3.1.1.

COMMENTARY

3.1 — Quality Assurance program

Masonry design provisions in this Code are valid when the quality of masonry construction meets or exceeds that described in the Specification. Therefore, in order to design masonry by this Code, verification of good quality construction is required. The means by which the quality of construction is monitored is the quality assurance program.

A quality assurance program must be defined in the contract documents, to answer questions such as "how to", "what method", "how often", and "who determines acceptance". This information is part of the administrative and procedural requirements. Typical requirements of a quality assurance program include review of material certifications, field inspection, and testing. The acts of providing submittals, inspecting, and testing are part of the quality assurance program.

Because the design and the complexity of masonry construction vary from project to project, so must the extent of the quality assurance program. The contract documents must indicate the testing, Special Inspection, and other measures that are required to assure that the Work is in conformance with the project requirements.

Section 3.1 establishes the minimum criteria required to assure that the quality of masonry construction conforms to the quality upon which the Code-permissible values are based. The scope of the quality assurance program depends on whether the structure is a Risk Category IV structure or not, as defined by ASCE 7 or the legally adopted building code. Because of their importance, Risk Category IV structures are subjected to more extensive quality assurance measures.

The level of required quality assurance depends on whether the masonry was designed in accordance with Part 3, Appendix B, or Appendix C (engineered) or in accordance with Part 4 or Appendix A (empirical or prescriptive).

CODE

3.1.2   Level B Quality Assurance

3.1.2.1   The minimum quality assurance program for masonry in Risk Category IV structures and designed in accordance with Chapter 12 or 13 shall comply with Table 3.1.2.

3.1.2.2   The minimum quality assurance program for masonry in Risk Category I, II, or III structures and designed in accordance with chapters other than those in Part 4 or Appendix A shall comply with Table 3.1.2.

3.1.3   Level C Quality Assurance

The minimum quality assurance program for masonry in Risk Category IV structures and designed in accordance with chapters other than those in Part 4 or Appendix A shall comply with Table 3.1.3.

3.1.4   Procedures

The quality assurance program shall set forth the procedures for reporting and review. The quality assurance program shall also include procedures for resolution of noncompliances.

COMMENTARY

3.1.2   Level B Quality Assurance

Implementation of testing and inspection requirements contained in Table 3.1.2 requires detailed knowledge of the appropriate procedures. Comprehensive testing and inspection procedures are available from recognized industry sources (Chrysler, 2010; NCMA, 2008; BIA, 2001; BIA 1988), which may be referenced for assistance in developing and implementing a Quality Assurance program. Certain applications, such as Masonry Veneer (Chapter 12), Masonry Partition Walls (Chapter 14) and Empirical Design of Masonry (Appendix A), do not require compressive strength verification of masonry as indicated in Table 3.1.2.

Installation techniques for AAC masonry and thin-bed mortar differ from concrete and clay masonry. Once it has been demonstrated in the field that compliance is attained for the installation of AAC masonry and thin-bed mortar, the frequency of Special Inspection may be revised from continuous to periodic. However, the frequency of Special Inspection should revert to continuous for the prescribed period whenever new AAC masonry installers work on the project.

3.1.3   Level C Quality Assurance

Premixed mortars and grouts are delivered to the project site as "trowel ready" or "pourable" materials, respectively. Preblended mortars and grouts are dry combined materials that are mixed with water at the project site. Verification of proportions of premixed or preblended mortars and grouts can be accomplished by review of manufacture's batch tickets (if applicable), a combination of preconstruction and construction testing, or other acceptable documentation.

3.1.4   Procedures

In addition to specifying testing and Special Inspection requirements, the quality assurance program must define the procedures for submitting the testing and inspection reports (that is, how many copies and to whom) and define the process by which those reports are to be reviewed.

Testing and evaluation should be addressed in the quality assurance program. The program should allow for the selection and approval of a testing agency, which agency should be provided with prequalification test information and the rights for sampling and testing of specific masonry construction materials in accordance with referenced standards. The evaluation of test results by the testing agency should indicate compliance or noncompliance with a referenced standard.

Further quality assurance evaluation should allow an appraisal of the testing program and the handling of nonconformance. Acceptable values for all test methods should be given in the contract documents.

Identification and resolution of noncomplying conditions should be addressed in the contract documents.

CODE

COMMENTARY

A responsible person should be identified to allow resolution of nonconformances. In agreement with others in the design/construct team, the resolutions should be repaired, reworked, accepted as is, or rejected. Repaired and reworked conditions should initiate a reinspection.

Records control should be addressed in the contract documents. The distribution of documents during and after construction should be delineated. The review of documents should persist throughout the construction period so that each party is informed and that records for documenting construction occurrences are available and correct after construction has been completed.

3.1.5 *Qualifications*

The quality assurance program shall define the qualifications for testing laboratories and for inspection agencies.

3.1.5 *Qualifications*

The entities verifying compliance must be competent and knowledgeable of masonry construction and the requirements of this Code. Therefore, minimum qualifications for those individuals must also be established by the quality assurance program in the contract documents.

The responsible party performing the quality control measures should document the organizational representatives who will be a part of the quality control segment, their qualifications, and their precise conduct during the performance of the quality assurance phase.

Laboratories that comply with the requirements of ASTM C1093 are more likely to be familiar with masonry materials and testing. Specifying that the testing agencies comply with the requirements of ASTM C1093 should improve the quality of the resulting masonry.

Table 3.1.1 — Level A Quality Assurance

MINIMUM VERIFICATION
Prior to construction, verify certificates of compliance used in masonry construction

Table 3.1.2 — Level B Quality Assurance

MINIMUM TESTS				
Verification of Slump flow and Visual Stability Index (VSI) as delivered to the project site in accordance with Specification Article 1.5 B.1.b.3 for self-consolidating grout				
Verification of f'_m and f'_{AAC} in accordance with Specification Article 1.4 B prior to construction, except where specifically exempted by this Code				

MINIMUM SPECIAL INSPECTION				
Inspection Task	**Frequency [a]**		**Reference for Criteria**	
	Continuous	Periodic	TMS 402/ ACI 530/ ASCE 5	TMS 602/ ACI 530.1/ ASCE 6
1. Verify compliance with the approved submittals		X		Art. 1.5
2. As masonry construction begins, verify that the following are in compliance:				
a. Proportions of site-prepared mortar		X		Art. 2.1, 2.6 A
b. Construction of mortar joints		X		Art. 3.3 B
c. Grade and size of prestressing tendons and anchorages		X		Art. 2.4 B, 2.4 H
d. Location of reinforcement, connectors, and prestressing tendons and anchorages		X		Art. 3.4, 3.6 A
e. Prestressing technique		X		Art. 3.6 B
f. Properties of thin-bed mortar for AAC masonry	X[b]	X[c]		Art. 2.1 C
3. Prior to grouting, verify that the following are in compliance:				
a. Grout space		X		Art. 3.2 D, 3.2 F
b. Grade, type, and size of reinforcement and anchor bolts, and prestressing tendons and anchorages		X	Sec. 6.1	Art. 2.4, 3.4
c. Placement of reinforcement, connectors, and prestressing tendons and anchorages		X	Sec. 6.1, 6.2.1, 6.2.6, 6.2.7	Art. 3.2 E, 3.4, 3.6 A
d. Proportions of site-prepared grout and prestressing grout for bonded tendons		X		Art. 2.6 B, 2.4 G.1.b
e. Construction of mortar joints		X		Art. 3.3 B

Continued on next page

Table 3.1.2 — Level B Quality Assurance (Continued)

MINIMUM SPECIAL INSPECTION				
Inspection Task	Frequency [a]		Reference for Criteria	
	Continuous	Periodic	TMS 402/ ACI 530/ ASCE 5	TMS 602/ ACI 530.1/ ASCE 6
4. Verify during construction:				
a. Size and location of structural elements		X		Art. 3.3 F
b. Type, size, and location of anchors, including other details of anchorage of masonry to structural members, frames, or other construction		X	Sec. 1.2.1(e), 6.1.4.3, 6.2.1	
c. Welding of reinforcement	X		Sec. 8.1.6.7.2, 9.3.3.4 (c), 11.3.3.4(b)	
d. Preparation, construction, and protection of masonry during cold weather (temperature below 40°F (4.4°C)) or hot weather (temperature above 90°F (32.2°C))		X		Art. 1.8 C, 1.8 D
e. Application and measurement of prestressing force	X			Art. 3.6 B
f. Placement of grout and prestressing grout for bonded tendons is in compliance	X			Art. 3.5, 3.6 C
g. Placement of AAC masonry units and construction of thin-bed mortar joints	X[b]	X[c]		Art. 3.3 B.9, 3.3 F.1.b
5. Observe preparation of grout specimens, mortar specimens, and/or prisms		X		Art. 1.4 B.2.a.3, 1.4 B.2.b.3, 1.4 B.2.c.3, 1.4 B.3, 1.4 B.4

(a) Frequency refers to the frequency of Special Inspection, which may be continuous during the task listed or periodic during the listed task, as defined in the table.
(b) Required for the first 5000 square feet (465 square meters) of AAC masonry.
(c) Required after the first 5000 square feet (465 square meters) of AAC masonry.

Table 3.1.3 — Level C Quality Assurance

MINIMUM TESTS
Verification of f'_m and f'_{AAC} in accordance with Specification Article 1.4 B prior to construction and for every 5,000 sq. ft (465 sq. m) during construction
Verification of proportions of materials in premixed or preblended mortar, prestressing grout, and grout other than self-consolidating grout, as delivered to the project site
Verification of Slump flow and Visual Stability Index (VSI) as delivered to the project site in accordance with Specification Article 1.5 B.1.b.3 for self-consolidating grout

MINIMUM SPECIAL INSPECTION				
Inspection Task	Frequency [(a)]		Reference for Criteria	
	Continuous	Periodic	TMS 402/ ACI 530/ ASCE 5	TMS 602/ ACI 530.1/ ASCE 6
1. Verify compliance with the approved submittals		X		Art. 1.5
2. Verify that the following are in compliance:				
a. Proportions of site-mixed mortar, grout and prestressing grout for bonded tendons		X		Art. 2.1, 2.6 A, 2.6 B, 2.6 C, 2.4 G.1.b
b. Grade, type, and size of reinforcement and anchor bolts, and prestressing tendons and anchorages		X	Sec. 6.1	Art. 2.4, 3.4
c. Placement of masonry units and construction of mortar joints		X		Art. 3.3 B
d. Placement of reinforcement, connectors, and prestressing tendons and anchorages	X		Sec. 6.1, 6.2.1, 6.2.6, 6.2.7	Art. 3.2 E, 3.4, 3.6 A
e. Grout space prior to grouting	X			Art. 3.2 D, 3.2 F
f. Placement of grout and prestressing grout for bonded tendons	X			Art. 3.5, 3.6 C
g. Size and location of structural elements		X		Art. 3.3 F
h. Type, size, and location of anchors including other details of anchorage of masonry to structural members, frames, or other construction	X		Sec. 1.2.1(e), 6.1.4.3, 6.2.1	
i. Welding of reinforcement	X		Sec. 8.1.6.7.2, 9.3.3.4 (c), 11.3.3.4(b)	
j. Preparation, construction, and protection of masonry during cold weather (temperature below 40°F (4.4°C)) or hot weather (temperature above 90°F (32.2°C))		X		Art. 1.8 C, 1.8 D
k. Application and measurement of prestressing force	X			Art. 3.6 B
l. Placement of AAC masonry units and construction of thin-bed mortar joints	X			Art. 3.3 B.9, 3.3 F.1.b
m. Properties of thin-bed mortar for AAC masonry	X			Art. 2.1 C.1
3. Observe preparation of grout specimens, mortar specimens, and/or prisms	X			Art. 1.4 B.2.a.3, 1.4 B.2.b.3, 1.4 B.2.c.3, 1.4 B.3, 1.4 B.4

(a) Frequency refers to the frequency of Special Inspection, which may be continuous during the task listed or periodic during the listed task, as defined in the table.

CODE

3.1.6 *Acceptance relative to strength requirements*

3.1.6.1 *Compliance with f $'_m$* — Compressive strength of masonry shall be considered satisfactory if the compressive strength of each masonry wythe and grouted collar joint equals or exceeds the value of f'_m.

3.1.6.2 *Determination of compressive strength* — Compressive strength of masonry shall be determined in accordance with the provisions of TMS 602/ACI 530.1/ASCE 6.

3.2 — Construction considerations

3.2.1 *Grouting, minimum spaces*

The minimum dimensions of spaces provided for the placement of grout shall be in accordance with Table 3.2.1. Grout pours with heights exceeding those shown in Table 3.2.1, cavity widths, or cell sizes smaller than those permitted in Table 3.2.1 or grout lift heights exceeding those permitted by Article 3.5 D of TMS 602/ACI 530.1/ASCE 6 are permitted if the results of a grout demonstration panel show that the grout spaces are filled and adequately consolidated. In that case, the procedures used in constructing the grout demonstration panel shall be the minimum acceptable standard for grouting, and the quality assurance program shall include inspection during construction to verify grout placement.

COMMENTARY

3.1.6 *Acceptance relative to strength requirements* Fundamental to the structural adequacy of masonry construction is the necessity that the compressive strength of masonry equals or exceeds the specified strength. Rather than mandating design based on different values of f'_m for each wythe of a multiwythe wall construction made of differing material, this Code requires the strength of each wythe and of grouted collar joints to equal or exceed f'_m for the portion of the structure considered. If a multiwythe wall is designed as a composite wall, the compressive strength of each wythe or grouted collar joint should equal or exceed f'_m.

3.2 — Construction considerations

The TMS 602/ACI 530.1/ASCE 6 Specification addresses material and construction requirements. It is an integral part of the Code in terms of minimum requirements relative to the composition, quality, storage, handling, and placement of materials for masonry structures. The Specification also includes provisions requiring verification that construction achieves the quality specified. The construction must conform to these requirements in order for the Code provisions to be valid.

3.2.1 *Grouting, minimum spaces*

Code Table 3.2.1 contains the least clear dimension for grouting between wythes and the minimum cell dimensions when grouting hollow units. Selection of units and bonding pattern should be coordinated to achieve these requirements. Vertical alignment of cells must also be considered. Projections or obstructions into the grout space and the diameter of horizontal reinforcement must be considered when calculating the minimum dimensions. See Figure CC-3.2-1.

Coarse grout and fine grout are differentiated by aggregate size in ASTM C476.

The grout space requirements of Code Table 3.2.1 are based on coarse and fine grouts as defined by ASTM C476, and cleaning practice to permit the complete filling of grout spaces and adequate consolidation using typical methods of construction. Grout spaces smaller than specified in Table 3.2.1 have been used successfully in some areas. When the designer is requested to accept a grouting procedure that does not comply with the limits in Table 3.2.1, construction of a grout demonstration panel is required. Destructive or non-destructive evaluation can confirm that filling and adequate consolidation have been achieved. The designer should establish criteria for the grout demonstration panel to assure that critical masonry elements included in the construction will be represented in the demonstration panel. Because a single grout demonstration panel erected prior to masonry construction cannot account for all conditions that may be encountered during construction, the designer should establish inspection procedures to verify grout placement

CODE

3.2.2 *Embedded conduits, pipes, and sleeves*
Conduits, pipes, and sleeves of any material to be embedded in masonry shall be compatible with masonry and shall comply with the following requirements.

3.2.2.1 Conduits, pipes, and sleeves shall not be considered to be structural replacements for the displaced masonry. The masonry design shall consider the structural effects of this displaced masonry.

3.2.2.2 Conduits, pipes, and sleeves in masonry shall be no closer than 3 diameters on center. Minimum spacing of conduits, pipes or sleeves of different diameters shall be determined using the larger diameter.

3.2.2.3 Vertical conduits, pipes, or sleeves placed in masonry columns or pilasters shall not displace more than 2 percent of the net cross section.

3.2.2.4 Pipes shall not be embedded in masonry, unless properly isolated from the masonry, when:

(a) Containing liquid, gas, or vapors at temperature higher than 150° F (66°C).

(b) Under pressure in excess of 55 psi (379 kPa).

(c) Containing water or other liquids subject to freezing.

COMMENTARY

during construction. These inspection procedures should include destructive or non-destructive evaluation to confirm that filling and adequate consolidation have been achieved.

3.2.2 *Embedded conduits, pipes, and sleeves*

3.2.2.1 Conduits, pipes, and sleeves not harmful to mortar and grout may be embedded within the masonry, but the masonry member strength should not be less than that required by design. Effects of reduction in section properties in the areas of conduit, pipe, or sleeve embedment should be considered.

For the integrity of the structure, conduit and pipe fittings within the masonry should be carefully positioned and assembled. The coupling size should be considered when determining sleeve size.

Aluminum should not be used in masonry unless it is effectively coated or otherwise isolated. Aluminum reacts with ions, and may also react electrolytically with steel, causing cracking, spalling of the masonry, or both. Aluminum electrical conduits present a special problem because stray electric current accelerates the adverse reaction.

Pipes and conduits placed in masonry, whether surrounded by mortar or grout or placed in unfilled spaces, need to allow unrestrained movement.

Table 3.2.1 — Grout space requirements

Grout type[1]	Maximum grout pour height, ft (m)	Minimum clear width of grout space,[2,3] in. (mm)	Minimum clear grout space dimensions for grouting cells of hollow units,[3,4,5] in. x in. (mm x mm)
Fine	1 (0.30)	$^3/_4$ (19.1)	$1^1/_2$ x 2 (38.1 x 50.8)
Fine	5.33 (1.63)	2 (50.8)	2 x 3 (50.8 x 76.2)
Fine	12.67 (3.86)	$2^1/_2$ (63.5)	$2^1/_2$ x 3 (63.5 x 76.2)
Fine	24 (7.32)	3 (76.2)	3 x 3 (76.2 x 76.2)
Coarse	1 (0.30)	$1^1/_2$ (38.1)	$1^1/_2$ x 3 (38.1 x 76.2)
Coarse	5.33 (1.63)	2 (50.8)	$2^1/_2$ x 3 (63.5 x 76.2)
Coarse	12.67 (3.86)	$2^1/_2$ (63.5)	3 x 3 (76.2 x 76.2)
Coarse	24 (7.32)	3 (76.2)	3 x 4 (76.2 x 102)

[1] Fine and coarse grouts are defined in ASTM C476.

[2] For grouting between masonry wythes.

[3] Minimum clear width of grout space and minimum clear grout space dimension are the net dimension of the space determined by subtracting masonry protrusions and the diameters of horizontal bars from the as-designed cross-section of the grout space. Grout type and maximum grout pour height shall be specified based on the minimum clear space.

[4] Area of vertical reinforcement shall not exceed 6 percent of the area of the grout space.

[5] Minimum grout space dimension for AAC masonry units shall be 3 in. (76.2 mm) x 3 in. (76.2 mm) or a 3-in. (76.2 mm) diameter cell.

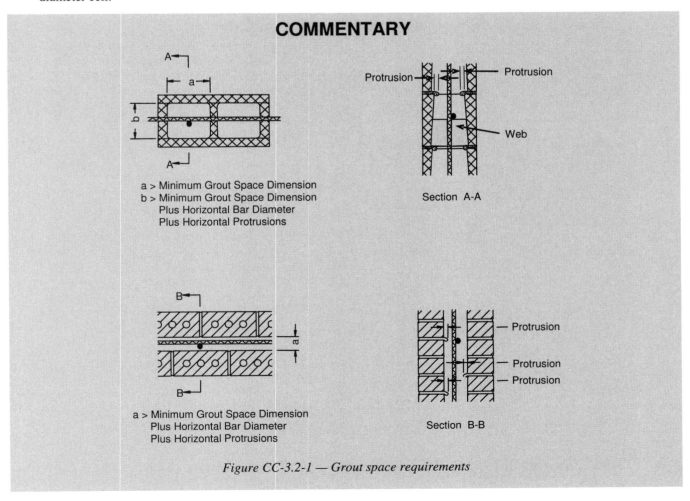

COMMENTARY

a > Minimum Grout Space Dimension
b > Minimum Grout Space Dimension
    Plus Horizontal Bar Diameter
    Plus Horizontal Protrusions

Section A-A

a > Minimum Grout Space Dimension
    Plus Horizontal Bar Diameter
    Plus Horizontal Protrusions

Section B-B

Figure CC-3.2-1 — Grout space requirements

This page intentionally left blank

PART 2: DESIGN REQUIREMENTS

CHAPTER 4
GENERAL ANALYSIS AND DESIGN CONSIDERATIONS

CODE

COMMENTARY

4.1 — Loading

4.1 — Loading

These provisions establish design load requirements. If the design loads specified by the legally adopted building code differ from those of ASCE 7, the legally adopted building code governs. The designer may decide to use the more stringent requirements.

4.1.1 *General*

Masonry shall be designed to resist applicable loads. A continuous load path or paths, with adequate strength and stiffness, shall be provided to transfer forces from the point of application to the final point of resistance.

4.1.2 *Load provisions*

Design loads shall be in accordance with the legally adopted building code of which this Code forms a part, with such live load reductions as are permitted in the legally adopted building code. In the absence of a legally adopted building code, or in the absence of design loads in the legally adopted building code, the load provisions of ASCE 7 shall be used, except as noted in this Code.

4.1.3 *Lateral load resistance*

Buildings shall be provided with a structural system designed to resist wind and earthquake loads and to accommodate the effect of the resulting deformations.

4.1.3 *Lateral load resistance*

Lateral load resistance must be provided by a braced structural system. Interior walls, infill panels, and similar elements may not be a part of the lateral-force-resisting system if isolated. However, when they resist lateral forces due to their rigidity, they should be considered in analysis.

4.1.4 *Load transfer at horizontal connections*

4.1.4.1 Walls, columns, and pilasters shall be designed to resist loads, moments, and shears applied at intersections with horizontal members.

4.1.4.2 Effect of lateral deflection and translation of members providing lateral support shall be considered.

4.1.4.3 Devices used for transferring lateral support from members that intersect walls, columns, or pilasters shall be designed to resist the forces involved.

4.1.4 *Load transfer at horizontal connections*

Masonry walls, pilasters, and columns may be connected to horizontal elements of the structure and may rely on the latter for lateral support and stability. The mechanism through which the interconnecting forces are transmitted may involve bond, mechanical anchorage, friction, bearing, or a combination thereof. The designer must assure that, regardless of the type of connection, the interacting forces are safely resisted.

In flexible frame construction, the relative movement (drift) between floors may generate forces within the members and the connections. This Code requires the effects of these movements to be considered in design.

CODE

4.1.5   *Other effects*

Consideration shall be given to effects of forces and deformations due to prestressing, vibrations, impact, shrinkage, expansion, temperature changes, creep, unequal settlement of supports, and differential movement.

4.1.6   *Lateral load distribution*

Lateral loads shall be distributed to the structural system in accordance with member stiffnesses and shall comply with the requirements of this section.

4.1.6.1   Flanges of intersecting walls designed in accordance with Section 5.1.1.2 shall be included in stiffness determination.

4.1.6.2   Distribution of load shall be consistent with the forces resisted by foundations.

4.1.6.3   Distribution of load shall include the effect of horizontal torsion of the structure due to eccentricity of wind or seismic loads resulting from the non-uniform distribution of mass.

COMMENTARY

4.1.5   *Other effects*

Service loads are not the sole source of stresses. The structure may also resist forces from the sources listed. The nature and extent of some of these forces may be greatly influenced by the choice of materials, structural connections, and geometric configuration.

4.1.6   *Lateral load distribution*

The design assumptions for masonry buildings include the use of a lateral-force-resisting system. The distribution of lateral loads to the members of the lateral-force-resisting system is a function of the rigidities of the structural system and of the horizontal diaphragms. The method of connection at intersecting walls and between walls and floor and roof diaphragms determines if the wall participates in the lateral-force-resisting system. Lateral loads from wind and seismic forces are normally considered to act in the direction of the principal axes of the structure. Lateral loads may cause forces in walls both perpendicular and parallel to the direction of the load. Horizontal torsion can be developed due to eccentricity of the applied load with respect to the center of rigidity.

The analysis of lateral load distribution should be in accordance with accepted engineering procedures. The analysis should rationally consider the effects of openings in shear walls and whether the masonry above the openings allows them to act as coupled shear walls. See Figure CC-4.1-1. The interaction of coupled shear walls is complex and further information may be obtained from ASCE, 1978.

Calculation of the stiffness of shear walls should consider shearing and flexural deformations. A guide for solid shear walls (that is, with no openings) is given in Figure CC-4.1-2. For nongrouted hollow unit shear walls, the use of equivalent solid thickness of wall in calculating web stiffness is acceptable.

COMMENTARY

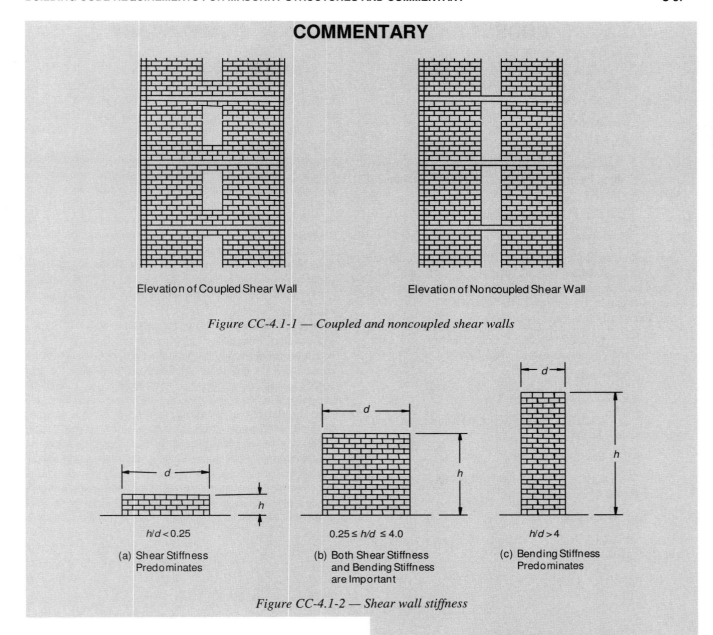

Elevation of Coupled Shear Wall

Elevation of Noncoupled Shear Wall

Figure CC-4.1-1 — Coupled and noncoupled shear walls

h/d < 0.25

(a) Shear Stiffness Predominates

0.25 ≤ h/d ≤ 4.0

(b) Both Shear Stiffness and Bending Stiffness are Important

h/d > 4

(c) Bending Stiffness Predominates

Figure CC-4.1-2 — Shear wall stiffness

<table>
<tr><td>

CODE

4.2 — Material properties

4.2.1 *General*

Unless otherwise determined by test, the following moduli and coefficients shall be used in determining the effects of elasticity, temperature, moisture expansion, shrinkage, and creep.

</td><td>

COMMENTARY

4.2 — Material properties

4.2.1 *General*

Proper evaluation of the building material movement from all sources is an important element of masonry design. Clay masonry and concrete masonry may behave quite differently under normal loading and weather conditions. The Committee has extensively studied available research information in the development of these material properties. The designer is encouraged to review industry standards for further design information and movement joint locations. Material properties can be determined by appropriate tests of the materials to be used.

</td></tr>
</table>

CODE

4.2.2   *Elastic moduli*

4.2.2.1 *Steel reinforcement* — Modulus of elasticity of steel reinforcement shall be taken as:

$$E_s = 29,000,000 \text{ psi } (200,000 \text{ MPa})$$

4.2.2.2 *Clay and concrete masonry*

4.2.2.2.1 The design of clay and concrete masonry shall be based on the following modulus of elasticity values:

$$E_m = 700 \, f'_m \text{ for clay masonry;}$$

$$E_m = 900 \, f'_m \text{ for concrete masonry;}$$

or the chord modulus of elasticity taken between 0.05 and 0.33 of the maximum compressive strength of each prism determined by test in accordance with the prism test method, Article 1.4 B.3 of TMS 602/ACI 530.1/ASCE 6, and ASTM E111.

4.2.2.2.2 Modulus of rigidity of clay masonry and concrete masonry shall be taken as:

$$E_v = 0.4 E_m$$

4.2.2.3 *AAC masonry*

4.2.2.3.1 Modulus of elasticity of AAC masonry shall be taken as:

$$E_{AAC} = 6500 \, (f'_{AAC})^{0.6}$$

4.2.2.3.2 Modulus of rigidity of AAC masonry shall be taken as:

$$E_v = 0.4 \, E_{AAC}$$

4.2.2.4 *Grout* — Modulus of elasticity of grout shall be taken as $500 \, f'_g$.

COMMENTARY

4.2.2   *Elastic moduli*

Modulus of elasticity for clay and concrete masonry has traditionally been taken as $1000 \, f'_m$ in previous masonry codes. Research (Wolde-Tinsae et al, 1993 and Colville et al, 1993) has indicated, however, that there is a large variation in the relationship of elastic modulus versus compressive strength of masonry, and that lower values may be more typical. However, differences in procedures between one research investigation and another may account for much of the indicated variation. Furthermore, the type of elastic moduli being reported (for example, secant modulus, tangent modulus, or chord modulus) is not always identified. The committee decided the most appropriate elastic modulus for allowable-stress design purposes is the slope of the stress-strain curve below a stress value of $0.33 f'_m$. The value of $0.33 f'_m$ was originally chosen because it was the allowable compressive stress prior to the 2011 Code. The committee did not see the need to change the modulus with the increase in allowable compressive stress to $0.45 f'_m$ in the 2011 Code because previous code editions also allowed the allowable compressive stress to be increased by one-third for load combinations including wind or seismic loads and the allowable moment capacity using allowable stress design is not significantly affected by the value of the masonry modulus of elasticity. Data at the bottom of the stress strain curve may be questionable due to the seating effect of the specimen during the initial loading phase if measurements are made on the testing machine platens. The committee therefore decided that the most appropriate elastic modulus for design purposes is the chord modulus from a stress value of 5 to 33 percent of the compressive strength of masonry (see Figure CC-4.2-1). The terms chord modulus and secant modulus have been used interchangeably in the past. The chord modulus, as used here, is defined as the slope of a line intersecting the stress-strain curve at two points, neither of which is the origin of the curve.

For clay and concrete masonry, the elastic modulus is determined as a function of masonry compressive strength using the relations developed from an extensive survey of modulus data by Wolde-Tinsae et al (1993) and results of a test program by Colville et al (1993). Code values for E_m are higher than indicated by a best fit of data relating E_m to the compressive strength of masonry. The higher Code values are based on the fact that actual compressive strength significantly exceeds the specified compressive strength of masonry, f'_m, particularly for clay masonry.

By using the Code values, the contribution of each wythe to composite action is more accurately accounted for in design calculations than would be the case if the elastic modulus of each part of a composite wall were based on one specified compressive strength of masonry.

CODE

COMMENTARY

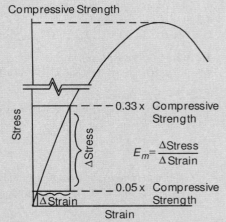

Figure CC-4.2-1 — Chord modulus of elasticity

The modulus of elasticity of autoclaved aerated concrete (AAC) masonry depends almost entirely on the modulus of elasticity of the AAC material itself. The relationship between modulus of elasticity and compressive strength is given in Tanner et al, 2005(a) and Argudo, 2003.

The modulus of elasticity of a grouted assemblage of clay or concrete masonry can usually be taken as a factor multiplied by the specified compressive strength, regardless of the extent of grouting, because the modulus of elasticity of the grout is usually close to that of the clay or concrete masonry. However, grout is usually much stiffer than the AAC material. While it is permissible and conservative to calculate the modulus of elasticity of a grouted assemblage of AAC masonry assuming that the modulus of elasticity of the grout is the same as that of the AAC material, it is also possible to recognize the greater modulus of elasticity of the grout by transforming the cross-sectional area of grout into an equivalent cross-sectional area of AAC, using the modular ratio between the two materials.

Because the inelastic stress-strain behavior of grout is generally similar to that of clay or concrete masonry, calculations of element resistance (whether based on allowable-stress or strength design) usually neglect possible differences in strength between grout and the surrounding masonry. For the same reasons noted above, the stress-strain behavior of grout usually differs considerably from that of the surrounding AAC material. It is possible that these differences in stress-strain behavior could also be considered in calculating element resistances. Research is ongoing to resolve this issue.

The relationship between the modulus of rigidity and the modulus of elasticity has historically been given as $0.4\,E_m$. No experimental evidence exists to support this relationship.

CODE

4.2.3 *Coefficients of thermal expansion*

4.2.3.1 *Clay masonry*

$k_t = 4 \times 10^{-6}$ in./in./°F (7.2×10^{-6} mm/mm/°C)

4.2.3.2 *Concrete masonry*

$k_t = 4.5 \times 10^{-6}$ in./in./°F (8.1×10^{-6} mm/mm/°C)

4.2.3.3 *AAC masonry*

$k_t = 4.5 \times 10^{-6}$ in./in./°F (8.1×10^{-6} mm/mm/°C)

4.2.4 *Coefficient of moisture expansion for clay masonry*

$k_e = 3 \times 10^{-4}$ in./in. (3×10^{-4} mm/mm)

4.2.5 *Coefficients of shrinkage*

4.2.5.1 *Concrete masonry*

$k_m = 0.5\ s_l$

4.2.5.2 *AAC masonry*

$k_m = 0.8\ \varepsilon_{cs}/100$

where ε_{cs} is determined in accordance with ASTM C1693.

4.2.6 *Coefficients of creep*

4.2.6.1 *Clay masonry*

$k_c = 0.7 \times 10^{-7}$, per psi (0.1×10^{-4}, per MPa)

4.2.6.2 *Concrete masonry*

$k_c = 2.5 \times 10^{-7}$, per psi (0.36×10^{-4}, per MPa)

4.2.6.3 *AAC masonry*

$k_c = 5.0 \times 10^{-7}$, per psi (0.72×10^{-4}, per MPa)

COMMENTARY

4.2.3 *Coefficients of thermal expansion*

Temperature changes cause material expansion and contraction. This material movement is theoretically reversible. These thermal expansion coefficients are slightly higher than mean values for the assemblage (Copeland, 1957; Plummer, 1962; Grimm, 1986).

Thermal expansion for concrete masonry varies with aggregate type (Copeland, 1957; Kalouseb, 1954).

Thermal expansion coefficients are given for AAC masonry in RILEM (1993).

4.2.4 *Coefficient of moisture expansion for clay masonry*

Fired clay products expand upon contact with moisture and the material does not return to its original size upon drying (Plummer, 1962; Grimm, 1986). This is a long-term expansion as clay particles react with atmospheric moisture. Continued moisture expansion of clay masonry units has been reported for 7½ years (Smith, 1973). Moisture expansion is not a design consideration for concrete masonry.

4.2.5 *Coefficients of shrinkage*

4.2.5.1 *Concrete masonry* — Concrete masonry is a cement-based material that shrinks due to moisture loss and carbonation (Kalouseb, 1954). The total linear drying shrinkage is determined in accordance with ASTM C426. The maximum shrinkage allowed by ASTM specifications for concrete masonry units (for example, ASTM C90), other than calcium silicate units, is 0.065%. Further design guidance for estimating the shrinkage due to moisture loss and carbonation is available (NCMA TEK 10-1A, 2005; NCMA TEK 10-2C, 2010; NCMA TEK 10-3, 2003, NCMA TEK18-02B, 2012). The shrinkage of clay masonry is negligible.

4.2.5.2 *AAC masonry* — At time of production, AAC masonry typically has a moisture content of about 30%. That value typically decreases to 15% or less within two to three months, regardless of ambient relative humidity. This process can take place during construction or prior to delivery. ASTM C1693 evaluates AAC material characteristics at moisture contents between 5% and 15%, a range that typifies AAC in service. The shrinkage coefficient of this section reflects the change in strain likely to be encountered within the extremes of moisture content typically encountered in service.

4.2.6 *Coefficients of creep*

When continuously stressed, these materials gradually deform in the direction of stress application. This movement is referred to as creep and is load and time dependent (Kalouseb, 1954; Lenczner and Salahuddin, 1976; RILEM, 1993). The values given are maximum values.

CODE

4.2.7 *Prestressing steel*

Modulus of elasticity of prestressing steel shall be determined by tests. For prestressing steels not specifically listed in ASTM A416/A416M, A421/A421M, or A722/A722M, tensile strength and relaxation losses shall be determined by tests.

4.3 — Section properties

4.3.1 *Stress calculations*

4.3.1.1 Members shall be designed using section properties based on the minimum net cross-sectional area of the member under consideration. Section properties shall be based on specified dimensions.

4.3.1.2 In members designed for composite action, stresses shall be calculated using section properties based on the minimum transformed net cross-sectional area of the composite member. The transformed area concept for elastic analysis, in which areas of dissimilar materials are transformed in accordance with relative elastic moduli ratios, shall apply.

COMMENTARY

4.2.7 *Prestressing steel*

The material and section properties of prestressing steels may vary with each manufacturer. Most significant for design are the prestressing tendon's cross section, modulus of elasticity, tensile strength, and stress-relaxation properties. Values for these properties for various manufacturers' wire, strand, and bar systems are given elsewhere (PTI, 2006). The modulus of elasticity of prestressing steel is often taken equal to 28,000 ksi (193,000 MPa) for design, but can vary and should be verified by the manufacturer. Stress-strain characteristics and stress-relaxation properties of prestressing steels must be determined by test, because these properties may vary between different steel forms (bar, wire, or strand) and types (mild, high strength, or stainless).

4.3 — Section properties

4.3.1 *Stress calculations*

Minimum net section is often difficult to establish in hollow unit masonry. The designer may choose to use the minimum thickness of the face shells of the units as the minimum net section. The minimum net section may not be the same in the vertical and horizontal directions.

For masonry of hollow units, the minimum cross-sectional area in both directions may conservatively be based on the minimum face-shell thickness (NCMA TEK 14-1B, 2007).

Solid clay masonry units are permitted to have coring up to a maximum of 25 percent of their gross cross-sectional area. For such units, the net cross-sectional area may be taken as equal to the gross cross-sectional area, except as provided in Section 8.1.4.2(c) for masonry headers. Several conditions of net area are shown in Figure CC-4.3-1.

Because the elastic properties of the materials used in members designed for composite action differ, equal strains produce different levels of stresses in the components. To calculate these stresses, a convenient transformed section with respect to the axis of resistance is considered. The resulting stresses developed in each fiber are related to the actual stresses by the ratio E_1 / E_x between the modulus of elasticity, E_1, of the most deformable material in the member and the modulus of elasticity, E_x, of the materials in the fiber considered. Thus, to obtain the transformed section, fibers of the actual section are conceptually widened by the ratio E_x/E_1. Stresses calculated based on the section properties of the transformed section, with respect to the axis of resistance considered, are then multiplied by E_x/E_1 to obtain actual stresses.

COMMENTARY

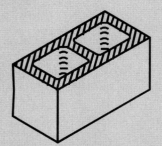

Brick More than 75% Solid
Net Area Equals Gross Area

Hollow Unit Full Mortar Bedding
(Requires Alignment of Crosswebs)

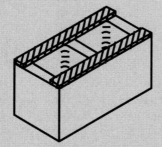

Hollow Unit Face Shell Mortar Bedding

Figure CC-4.3-1 — Net cross-sectional areas

CODE

4.3.2 *Stiffness*

Calculation of stiffness based on uncracked section is permissible. Use of the average net cross-sectional area of the member considered in stiffness calculations is permitted.

COMMENTARY

4.3.2 *Stiffness*

Stiffness is a function of the extent of cracking. Because unreinforced masonry is designed assuming it is uncracked, Code equations for design of unreinforced masonry are based on the member's uncracked moment of inertia and ignoring the effects of reinforcement, if present. Also, because the extent of tension cracking in shear walls is not known in advance, this Code allows the determination of stiffness to be based on uncracked section properties. For reinforced masonry, more accurate estimates may result if stiffness approximations are based on the cracked section.

The section properties of masonry members may vary from point to point. For example, in a single-wythe concrete masonry wall made of hollow ungrouted units, the cross-sectional area varies through the unit height. Also, the distribution of material varies along the length of the wall or unit. For stiffness calculations, an average value of the appropriate section property (cross-sectional area or moment of inertia) is considered adequate for design. The average net cross-sectional area of the member would in turn be based on average net cross-sectional area values of the masonry units and the mortar joints composing the member.

CODE

4.3.3   *Radius of gyration*

Radius of gyration shall be calculated using the average net cross-sectional area of the member considered.

4.3.4   *Bearing area*

The bearing area, A_{br}, for concentrated loads shall not exceed the following:

(a) $A_1\sqrt{A_2/A_1}$

(b) $2\,A_1$

The area, A_2, is the area of the lower base of the largest frustum of a right pyramid or cone that has the loaded area, A_1, as its upper base, slopes at 45 degrees from the horizontal, and is wholly contained within the support. For walls not laid in running bond, area A_2 shall terminate at head joints.

COMMENTARY

4.3.3   *Radius of gyration*

The radius of gyration is the square root of the ratio of bending moment of inertia to cross-sectional area. Because stiffness is based on the average net cross-sectional area of the member considered, this same area should be used in the calculation of radius of gyration.

4.3.4   *Bearing area*

When the supporting masonry area, A_2, is larger on all sides than the loaded area, A_1, this Code allows distribution of concentrated loads over a bearing area A_{br}, larger than A_1. The area A_2 is determined as illustrated in Figure CC-4.3-2. This is permissible because the confinement of the bearing area by surrounding masonry increases the bearing capacity of the masonry under the concentrated loads. When the edge of the loaded area, A_1, coincides with the face or edge of the masonry, the area A_2 is equal to the loaded area A_1.

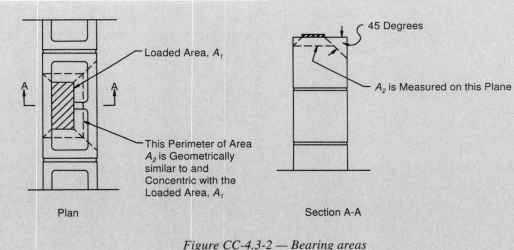

Figure CC-4.3-2 — Bearing areas

CODE

4.4 — Connection to structural frames

Masonry walls shall not be connected to structural frames unless the connections and walls are designed to resist design interconnecting forces and to accommodate calculated deflections.

COMMENTARY

4.4 — Connection to structural frames

Exterior masonry walls connected to structural frames are used primarily as non-load-bearing curtain walls. Regardless of the structural system used for support, there are differential movements between the structure and the wall. These differential movements may occur separately or in combination and may be due to the following:

1) Temperature increase or decrease of either the structural frame or the masonry wall.

2) Moisture and freezing expansion of brick or shrinkage of concrete block walls.

3) Elastic shortening of columns from axial loads, shrinkage, or creep.

4) Deflection of supporting beams.

5) Sidesway in multiple-story buildings.

6) Foundation movement.

Because the tensile strength of masonry is low, these differential movements must be accommodated by sufficient clearance between the frame and masonry and flexible or slip-type connections.

Structural frames and bracing should not be infilled with masonry to increase resistance to in-plane lateral forces without considering the differential movements listed above.

Wood, steel, or concrete columns may be surrounded by masonry serving as a decorative element. Masonry walls may be subject to forces as a result of their interaction with other structural components. Because the masonry element is often much stiffer, the load will be resisted primarily by the masonry. These forces, if transmitted to the surrounding masonry, should not exceed the allowable stresses of the masonry. Alternately, there should be sufficient clearance between the frame and masonry. Flexible ties should be used to allow for the deformations.

Beams or trusses supporting masonry walls are essentially embedded, and their deflections should be limited to the allowable deflections for the masonry being supported. See Section 5.2.1.4 for requirements.

CODE

4.5 — Masonry not laid in running bond

For masonry not laid in running bond, the minimum area of horizontal reinforcement shall be 0.00028 multiplied by the gross vertical cross-sectional area of the wall using specified dimensions. Horizontal reinforcement shall be placed at a maximum spacing of 48 in. (1219 mm) on center in horizontal mortar joints or in bond beams.

COMMENTARY

4.5 — Masonry not laid in running bond

The requirements for masonry laid in running bond are shown in Figure CC-4.5-1. The amount of horizontal reinforcement required in masonry not laid in running bond is a prescriptive amount to provide continuity across the head joints. Because lateral loads are reversible, reinforcement should either be centered in the element thickness by placement in the center of a bond beam, or should be symmetrically located by placing multiple bars in a bond beam or by using joint reinforcement in the mortar bed along each face shell. This reinforcement can be also used to resist load.

Although continuity across head joints in masonry not laid in running bond is a concern for AAC masonry as well as masonry of clay or concrete, the use of horizontal reinforcement to enhance continuity in AAC masonry is generally practical only by the use of bond beams.

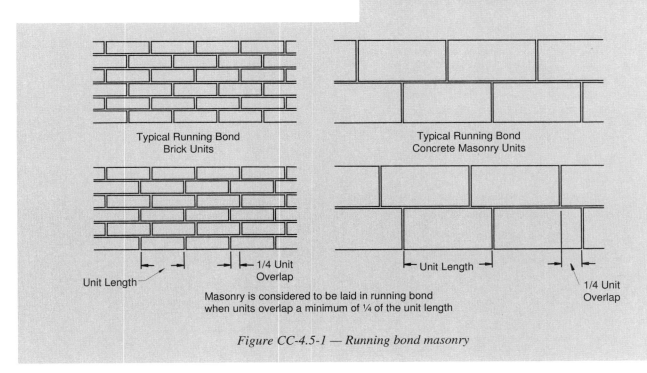

Figure CC-4.5-1 — Running bond masonry

This page intentionally left blank

CHAPTER 5
STRUCTURAL ELEMENTS

CODE

5.1 — Masonry assemblies

5.1.1 *Intersecting walls*

    5.1.1.1   Wall intersections shall meet one of the following requirements:

(a)   Design shall conform to the provisions of Section 5.1.1.2.

(b)   Transfer of shear between walls shall be prevented.

    5.1.1.2   *Design of wall intersection*

        5.1.1.2.1   Masonry shall be in running bond.

        5.1.1.2.2   Flanges shall be considered effective in resisting applied loads.

        5.1.1.2.3   The width of flange considered effective on each side of the web shall be the smaller of the actual flange on either side of the web wall or the following:

(a)   6 multiplied by the nominal flange thickness for unreinforced and reinforced masonry, when the flange is in compression

(b)   6 multiplied by the nominal flange thickness for unreinforced masonry, when the flange is in flexural tension

(c)   0.75 multiplied by the floor-to-floor wall height for reinforced masonry, when the flange is in flexural tension.

The effective flange width shall not extend past a movement joint.

        5.1.1.2.4   Design for shear, including the transfer of shear at interfaces, shall conform to the requirements of Section 8.2.6; or Section 8.3.5; or Section 9.2.6; or Section 9.3.4.1.2; or Section 10.6; or Section 11.3.4.1.2.

        5.1.1.2.5   The connection of intersecting walls shall conform to one of the following requirements:

(a)   At least fifty percent of the masonry units at the interface shall interlock.

(b)   Walls shall be anchored by steel connectors grouted into the wall and meeting the following requirements:

    (1)   Minimum size: $^1/_4$ in. x $1^1/_2$ in. x 28 in. (6.4 mm x 38.1 mm x 711 mm) including 2-in. (50.8-mm) long, 90-degree bend at each end to form a U or Z shape.

    (2)   Maximum spacing: 48 in. (1219 mm).

(c)   Intersecting reinforced bond beams shall be provided at a maximum spacing of 48 in. (1219 mm) on center. The area of reinforcement in each bond beam shall

COMMENTARY

5.1 — Masonry assemblies

5.1.1 *Intersecting walls*

Connections of webs to flanges of walls may be accomplished by running bond, metal connectors, or bond beams. Achieving stress transfer at a T intersection with running bond only is difficult. A running bond connection is shown in Figure CC-5.1-1 with a "T" geometry over their intersection.

The alternate method, using metal strap connectors, is shown in Figure CC-5.1-2. Bond beams, shown in Figure CC-5.1-3, are the third means of connecting webs to flanges.

When the flanges are connected at the intersection, they are required to be included in the design.

The effective width of the flange for compression and unreinforced masonry in flexural tension is based on shear-lag effects and is a traditional requirement. The effective width of the flange for reinforced masonry in flexural tension is based on the experimental and analytical work of He and Priestley (1992). They showed that the shear-lag effects are significant for uncracked walls, but become less severe after cracking. He and Priestley (1992) proposed that the effective width of the flange be determined as:

$$l_{ef} = \begin{cases} l_f & l_f/h \leq 1.5 \\ 0.75h + 0.5l_f & 1.5 < l_f/h \leq 3.5 \\ 2.5h & l_f/h > 3.5 \end{cases}$$

where l_{ef} is the effective flange width, l_f is the width of the flange, and h is height of the wall. These equations can result in effective flange widths greater than 1.5 times the height of the wall. However, a limit of the effective flange width of 1.5 times the wall height, or ¾ of the wall height on either side of the web, is provided in the code. This limit was chosen because the testing by He and Priestley (1992) was limited to a flange width of 1.4 times the wall height. Designers are cautioned that longitudinal reinforcement just outside the effective flange width specified by the code can affect the ductility and behavior of the wall. Any participation by the reinforcement in resisting the load can lead to other, more brittle, failure modes such as shear or crushing of the compression toe.

not be less than 0.1 in.^{2} per ft (211 mm^2/m) multiplied by the vertical spacing of the bond beams in feet (meters). Reinforcement shall be developed on each side of the intersection.

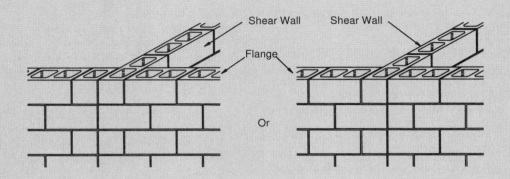

Figure CC-5.1-1 — Running bond lap at intersection

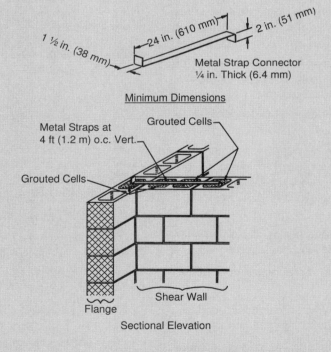

Figure CC-5.1-2 — Metal straps and grouting at wall intersections

COMMENTARY

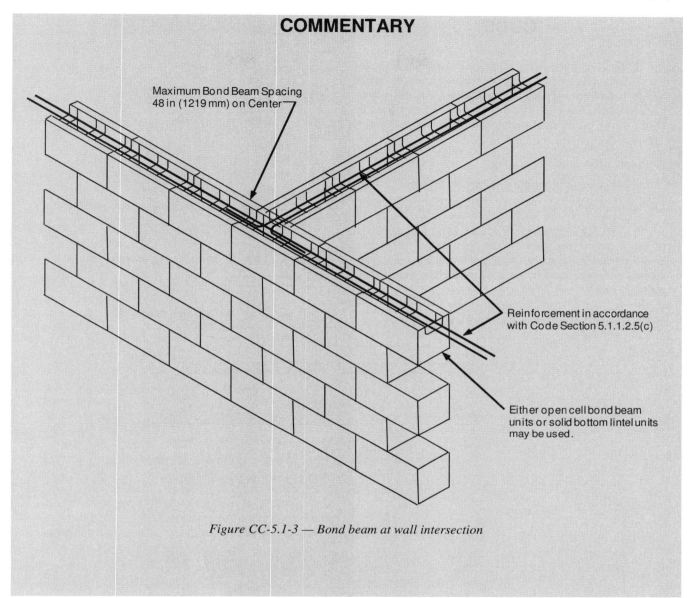

Maximum Bond Beam Spacing 48 in (1219 mm) on Center

Reinforcement in accordance with Code Section 5.1.1.2.5(c)

Either open cell bond beam units or solid bottom lintel units may be used.

Figure CC-5.1-3 — Bond beam at wall intersection

CODE

5.1.2   *Effective compressive width per bar*

5.1.2.1   For masonry not laid in running bond and having bond beams spaced not more than 48 in. (1219 mm) center-to-center, and for masonry laid in running bond, the width of the compression area used to calculate element capacity shall not exceed the least of:

(a) Center-to-center bar spacing.

(b) Six multiplied by the nominal wall thickness.

(c) 72 in. (1829 mm).

5.1.2.2   For masonry not laid in running bond and having bond beams spaced more than 48 in. (1219 mm) center-to-center, the width of the compression area used to calculate element capacity shall not exceed the length of the masonry unit.

COMMENTARY

5.1.2   *Effective compressive width per bar*

The effective width of the compressive area for each reinforcing bar must be established. Figure CC-5.1-4 depicts the limits for the conditions stated. Limited research (Dickey and MacIntosh, 1971) is available on this subject.

The limited ability of head joints to transfer stress when masonry is not laid in running bond is recognized by the requirements for bond beams. Open end masonry units that are fully grouted are assumed to transfer stress as indicated in Section 8.2.6.2(d), as for running bond.

The center-to-center bar spacing maximum is a limit to keep from overlapping areas of compressive stress. The 72-in. (1829-mm) maximum is an empirical choice of the committee.

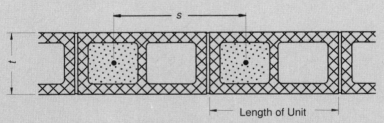

For masonry not laid in running bond with bond beams spaced less than or equal to 48 in. (1219 mm) and running bond masonry, *b* equals the lesser of:
   $b = s$
   $b = 6t$
   $b = 72$ in. (1829 mm)

For masonry not laid in running bond with bond beams spaced greater than 48 in. (1219 mm), *b* equals the lesser of:
   $b = s$
   $b = $ length of unit

Figure CC-5.1-4 — Width of compression area

CODE

5.1.3   *Concentrated loads*

5.1.3.1   Concentrated loads shall not be distributed over a length greater than the minimum of the following:

(a) The length of bearing area plus the length determined by considering the concentrated load to be dispersed along a 2 vertical: 1 horizontal line. The dispersion shall terminate at half the wall height, a movement joint, the end of the wall, or an opening, whichever provides the smallest length.

(b) The center-to-center distance between concentrated loads.

5.1.3.2   For walls not laid in running bond, concentrated loads shall not be distributed across head joints. Where concentrated loads acting on such walls are applied to a bond beam, the concentrated load is permitted to be distributed through the bond beam, but shall not be distributed across head joints below the bond beams.

COMMENTARY

5.1.3   *Concentrated loads*

Arora (1988) reports the results of tests of a wide variety of specimens under concentrated loads, including AAC masonry, concrete block masonry, and clay brick masonry specimens. Arora (1988) suggests that a concentrated load can be distributed at a 2:1 slope, terminating at half the wall height, where the wall height is from the point of application of the load to the foundation. Tests on the load dispersion through a bond beam on top of hollow masonry reported in Page and Shrive (1987) resulted in an angle from the horizontal of 59° for a 1-course CMU bond beam, 65° for a 2-course CMU bond beam, and 58° for a 2-course clay bond beam, or approximately a 2:1 slope. For simplicity in design, a 2:1 slope is used for all cases of load dispersion of a concentrated load.

Code provisions are illustrated in Figure CC-5.1-5. Figure CC-5.1-5a illustrates the dispersion of a concentrated load through a bond beam. A hollow wall would be checked for bearing under the bond beam using the effective length. Figure CC-5.1-5b illustrates the dispersion of a concentrated load in the wall. The effective length would be used for checking the wall under the axial force. A wall may have to be checked at several locations, such as under a bond beam and at midheight.

COMMENTARY

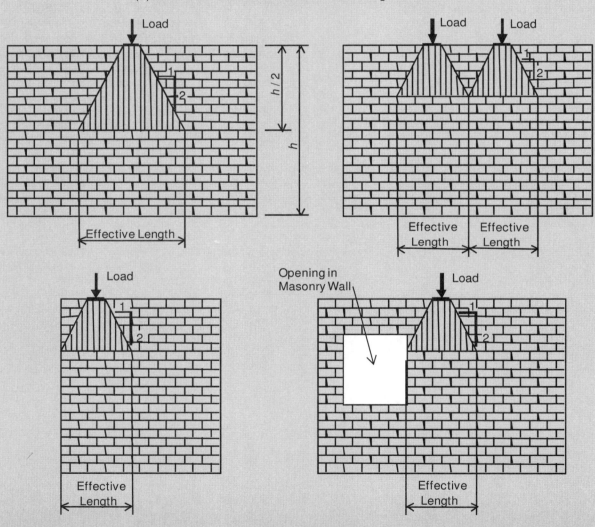

(a) Distribution of concentrated load through bond beam

(b) Distribution of concentrated load in wall

Figure CC-5.1-5. Distribution of concentrated loads

CODE

5.1.4 *Multiwythe masonry elements*

Design of masonry composed of more than one wythe shall comply with the provisions of Section 5.1.4.1, and either 5.1.4.2 or 5.1.4.3.

5.1.4.1 The provisions of Sections 5.1.4.2, and 5.1.4.3 shall not apply to AAC masonry units and glass masonry units.

5.1.4.2 *Composite action*

5.1.4.2.1 Multiwythe masonry designed for composite action shall have collar joints either:

(a) crossed by connecting headers, or

(b) filled with mortar or grout and connected by wall ties.

5.1.4.2.2 Headers used to bond adjacent wythes shall meet the requirements of either Section 8.1.4.2 or Section 9.1.7.2 and shall be provided as follows:

(a) Headers shall be uniformly distributed and the sum of their cross-sectional areas shall be at least 4 percent of the wall surface area.

(b) Headers connecting adjacent wythes shall be embedded a minimum of 3 in. (76.2 mm) in each wythe.

5.1.4.2.3 Wythes not bonded by headers shall meet the requirements of either Section 8.1.4.2 or Section 9.1.7.2 and shall be bonded by non-adjustable ties provided as follows:

Wire size	*Minimum number of ties required*
W1.7 (MW11)	one per $2^2/_3$ ft^2 (0.25 m^2) of masonry surface area
W2.8 (MW18)	one per $4^1/_2$ ft^2 (0.42 m^2) of masonry surface area

The maximum spacing between ties shall be 36 in. (914 mm) horizontally and 24 in. (610 mm) vertically.

The use of rectangular ties to connect masonry wythes of any type of masonry unit shall be permitted. The use of Z ties to connect to a masonry wythe of hollow masonry units shall not be permitted. Cross wires of joint reinforcement shall be permitted to be used instead of ties.

COMMENTARY

5.1.4.2 *Composite action* — Multiwythe masonry acts monolithically if sufficient shear transfer can occur across the interface between the wythes. See Figure CC-5.1-6. Shear transfer is achieved with headers crossing the collar joint or with mortar- or grout-filled collar joints. When mortar- or grout-filled collar joints are relied upon to transfer shear, ties are required to ensure structural integrity of the collar joint. Composite action requires that the shear stresses occurring at the interfaces are within the e limits prescribed.

Composite masonry walls generally consist of brick-to-brick, block-to-block, or brick-to-block wythes. The collar joint thickness ranges from $^3/_8$ to 4 in. (9.5 to 102 mm). The joint may contain either vertical or horizontal reinforcement, or reinforcement may be placed in either the brick or block wythe. Composite masonry is particularly advantageous for resisting high loads, both in-plane and out-of-plane.

5.1.4.2.2 Requirements for masonry headers (Figure CC-A.7-1) are empirical and taken from prior codes. The net area of the header should be used in calculating the stress even if a solid unit, which is allowed to have up to 25 percent coring, is used. Headers do not provide as much ductility as metal tied wythes with filled collar joints. The influence of differential movement is especially critical when headers are used. The committee does not encourage the use of headers.

5.1.4.2.3 The required size, number, and spacing of ties in composite masonry, shown in Figure CC-5.1-7, has been determined from past experience. The limitation of Z-ties to masonry of other than hollow units is also based on past experience.

COMMENTARY

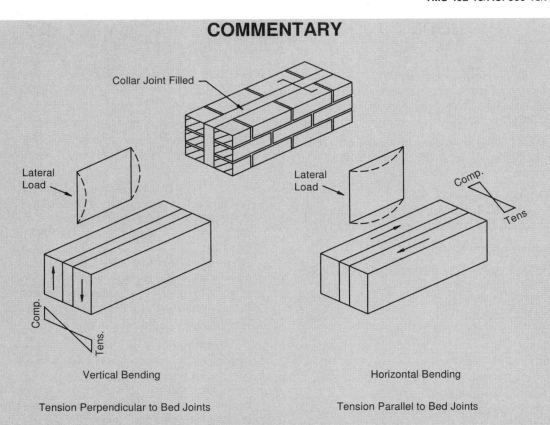

Vertical Bending

Tension Perpendicular to Bed Joints

Horizontal Bending

Tension Parallel to Bed Joints

Figure CC-5.1-6 — Stress distribution in composite multiwythe masonry

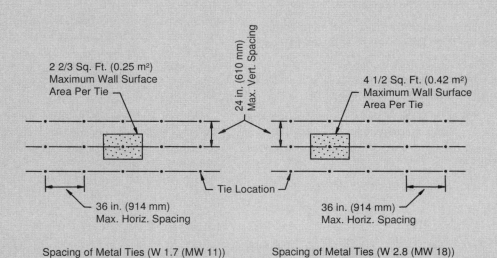

Figure CC-5.1-7 — Required tie spacing for composite multiwythe masonry

CODE

5.1.4.3 *Non-composite action* — The design of multiwythe masonry for non-composite action shall comply with Sections 5.1.4.3.1 and 5.1.4.3.2:

5.1.4.3.1 Each wythe shall be designed to resist individually the effects of loads imposed on it.

Unless a more detailed analysis is performed, the following requirements shall be satisfied:

(a) Collar joints shall not contain headers, grout, or mortar.

(b) Gravity loads from supported horizontal members shall be resisted by the wythe nearest to the center of span of the supported member. Any resulting bending moment about the weak axis of the masonry element shall be distributed to each wythe in proportion to its relative stiffness.

(c) Lateral loads acting parallel to the plane of the masonry element shall be resisted only by the wythe on which they are applied. Transfer of stresses from such loads between wythes shall be neglected.

(d) Lateral loads acting transverse to the plane of the masonry element shall be resisted by all wythes in proportion to their relative flexural stiffnesses.

(e) Specified distances between wythes shall not exceed 4.5 in. (114 mm) unless a detailed tie analysis is performed.

5.1.4.3.2 Wythes of masonry designed for non-composite action shall be connected by ties meeting the requirements of Section 5.1.4.2.3 or by adjustable ties. Where the cross wires of joint reinforcement are used as ties, the joint reinforcement shall be ladder-type or tab-type. Ties shall be without cavity drips.

Adjustable ties shall meet the following requirements:

(a) One tie shall be provided for each 1.77 ft^2 (0.16 m^2) of masonry surface area.

(b) Horizontal and vertical spacing shall not exceed 16 in. (406 mm).

(c) Adjustable ties shall not be used when the misalignment of bed joints from one wythe to the other exceeds $1^1/_4$ in. (31.8 mm).

(d) Maximum clearance between connecting parts of the tie shall be $^1/_{16}$ in. (1.6 mm).

(e) Pintle ties shall have at least two pintle legs of wire size W2.8 (MW18).

COMMENTARY

5.1.4.3 *Non-composite action* — Multiwythe masonry may be constructed so that each wythe is separated from the others by a space that may be crossed only by ties. The ties force compatible lateral deflection, but no composite action exists in the design.

5.1.4.3.1 Weak axis bending moments caused by either gravity loads or lateral loads are assumed to be distributed to each wythe in proportion to its relative stiffness. See Figure CC-5.1-8 for stress distribution in non-composite masonry. In non-composite masonry, the plane of the element is the plane of the space between wythes. Loads due to supported horizontal members are to be resisted by the wythe closest to center of span as a result of the deflection of the horizontal member.

In non-composite masonry, this Code limits the thickness of the cavity to 4½ in. (114 mm) to assure adequate performance. If cavity width exceeds 4½ in. (114 mm), the ties must be designed to resist the loads imposed upon them based on a rational analysis that takes into account buckling, tension, pullout, and load distribution.

The NCMA and Canadian Standards Association (NCMA TEK 12-1B, 2011; CSA, 1984) have recommendations for use in the design of ties for masonry with wide cavities.

5.1.4.3.2 The required size, number, and spacing of metal ties in non-composite masonry (Figure CC-5.1-7) have been determined from past experience. Requirements for adjustable ties are shown in Figure CC-5.1-9. They are based on the results in IIT (1963). Ladder-type or tab-type joint reinforcement is required because truss-type joint reinforcement restricts in-plane differential movement between wythes. However, the use of ties with drips (bends in ties to prevent moisture migration) has been eliminated because of their reduced strength.

COMMENTARY

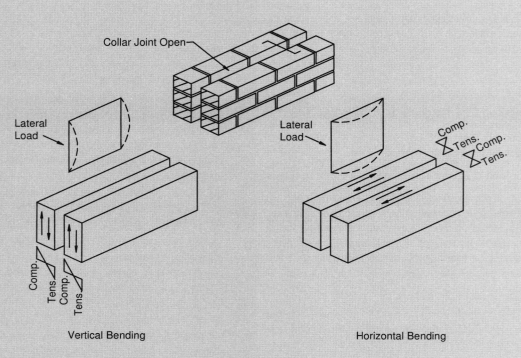

Figure CC-5.1-8 — Stress distribution in non-composite multiwythe masonry

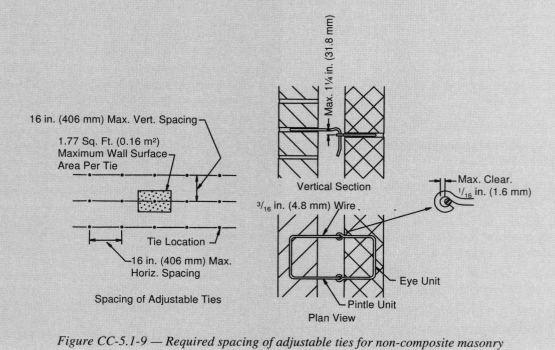

Figure CC-5.1-9 — Required spacing of adjustable ties for non-composite masonry

CODE

5.2 — Beams

Design of beams shall meet the requirements of Section 5.2.1 or Section 5.2.2. Design of beams shall also meet the requirements of Section 8.3, Section 9.3 or Section 11.3. Design requirements for masonry beams shall apply to masonry lintels.

5.2.1 *General beam design*
5.2.1.1 *Span length* — Span length shall be in accordance with the following:

5.2.1.1.1 Span length of beams not built integrally with supports shall be taken as the clear span plus depth of beam, but need not exceed the distance between centers of supports.

5.2.1.1.2 For determination of moments in beams that are continuous over supports, span length shall be taken as the distance between centers of supports.

5.2.1.2 *Lateral support* — The compression face of beams shall be laterally supported at a maximum spacing based on the smaller of:

(a) $32b$

(b) $120b^2/d$

5.2.1.3 *Bearing length* — Length of bearing of beams on their supports shall be a minimum of 4 in. (102 mm) in the direction of span.

5.2.1.4 *Deflections* — Masonry beams shall be designed to have adequate stiffness to limit deflections that adversely affect strength or serviceability.

5.2.1.4.1 The calculated deflection of beams providing vertical support to masonry designed in accordance with Section 8.2, Section 9.2, Section 11.2, Chapter 14, or Appendix A shall not exceed $l/600$ under unfactored dead plus live loads.

5.2.1 *General beam design*
5.2.1.1 *Span length*

5.2.1.2 *Lateral support* — To minimize lateral torsional buckling, the Code requires lateral bracing of the compression face. Hansell and Winter (1959) suggest that the slenderness ratios should be given in terms of ld/b^2. Revathi and Menon (2006) report on tests of seven under-reinforced slender concrete beams. In Figure CC-5.2-1, a straight line is fitted to the W_{test}/W_u ratio vs. ld/b^2, where W_{test} is the experimental capacity and W_u is the calculated capacity based on the full cross-sectional moment strength. W_{test}/W_u equals 1 where ld/b^2 equals 146. Based on this, the Code limit of 120 for ld/b^2 is reasonable and slightly conservative.

5.2.1.3 *Bearing length* — The minimum bearing length of 4 in. (102 mm) in the direction of span is considered a reasonable minimum to reduce concentrated compressive stresses at the edge of the support.

5.2.1.4 *Deflections* — The provisions of Section 5.2.1.4 address deflections that may occur at service load levels.

5.2.1.4.1 The deflection limits apply to beams and lintels of all materials that support unreinforced masonry. The deflection requirements may also be applicable to supported reinforced masonry that has vertical reinforcement only.

The deflection limit of $l/600$ should prevent long-term visible deflections and serviceability problems. In most cases, deflections of approximately twice this amount, or $l/300$, are required before the deflection becomes visible (Galambos and Ellingwood, 1986). This deflection limit is for immediate deflections. Creep will cause additional long-term deflections. A larger deflection limit of $l/480$ has been used when considering long-term deflections (CSA, 2004).

CODE

5.2.1.4.2 Deflection of masonry beams shall be calculated using the appropriate load-deflection relationship considering the actual end conditions. Unless stiffness values are obtained by a more comprehensive analysis, immediate deflections shall be calculated with an effective moment of inertia, I_{eff}, as follows.

$$I_{eff} = I_n\left(\frac{M_{cr}}{M_a}\right)^3 + I_{cr}\left[1-\left(\frac{M_{cr}}{M_a}\right)^3\right] \leq I_n$$

(Equation 5-1)

For continuous beams, I_{eff} shall be permitted to be taken as the average of values obtained from Equation 5-1 for the critical positive and negative moment regions.

For beams of uniform cross-section, I_{eff} shall be permitted to be taken as the value obtained from Equation 5-1 at midspan for simple spans and at the support for cantilevers. For masonry designed in accordance with Chapter 8, the cracking moment, M_{cr}, shall be calculated using the allowable flexural tensile stress taken from Table 8.2.4.2 multiplied by a factor of 2.5. For masonry designed in accordance with Chapter 9, the cracking moment, M_{cr}, shall be calculated using the value for the modulus of rupture, f_r, taken from Table 9.1.9.2. For masonry designed in accordance with Chapter 11, the cracking moment, M_{cr}, shall be calculated using the value for the modulus of rupture, f_{rAAC}, as given by Section 11.1.8.3.

5.2.1.4.3 Deflections of reinforced masonry beams need not be checked when the span length does not exceed 8 multiplied by the effective depth to the reinforcement, d, in the masonry beam.

COMMENTARY

5.2.1.4.2 The effective moment of inertia was developed to provide a transition between the upper and lower bounds of I_g and I_{cr} as a function of the ratio M_{cr}/M_a (Branson, 1965). This procedure was selected as being sufficiently accurate for use to control deflections (Horton and Tadros, 1990). Calculating a more accurate effective moment of inertia using a moment-curvature analysis may be desirable for some circumstances.

Most masonry beams have some end restraint due to being built integrally with a wall. Tests have shown that the end restraint from beams being built integrally with walls reduces the deflections from 20 to 45 percent of those of the simply supported specimens (Longworth and Warwaruk, 1983).

5.2.1.4.3 Reinforced masonry beams and lintels with span lengths of 8 times d have immediate deflections of approximately 1/600 of the span length (Bennett et al, 2007). Masonry beams and lintels with shorter spans should have sufficient stiffness to prevent serviceability problems and, therefore, deflections do not need to be checked.

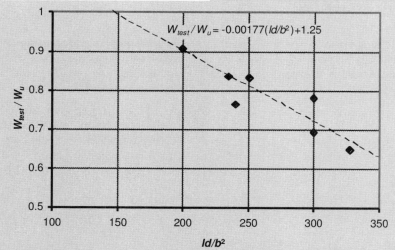

Figure CC-5.2-1 Beam capacity vs. beam slenderness (after Revathi and Menon (2006))

CODE

5.2.2 *Deep beams*

Design of deep beams shall meet the requirements of Section 5.2.1.2 and 5.2.1.3 in addition to the requirements of 5.2.2.1 through 5.2.2.5.

5.2.2.1 *Effective span length* — The effective span length, l_{eff}, shall be taken as the center-to-center distance between supports or 1.15 multiplied by the clear span, whichever is smaller.

COMMENTARY

5.2.2 *Deep beams*

Shear warping of the deep beam cross section and a combination of diagonal tension stress and flexural tension stress in the body of the deep beam require that these members be designed using deep beam theory when the span-to-depth ratio is within the limits given in the definition of deep beams. Background on the development of the deep beam provisions is given in Fonseca et al, 2011.

As per the definition in Section 2.2, a deep beam has an effective span-to-depth ratio, l_{eff}/d_v, less than 3 for a continuous span and less than 2 for a simple span. Sections of masonry over openings may be designed as deep beams if the span-to-depth ratio meets these limits. However, the depth of the beam need not be taken as the entire height of masonry above the opening. A shallower beam can be designed to support the remaining portion of the masonry above in addition to applied loads. This beam can be designed conventionally and need not meet the deep beam provisions if sufficiently shallow. (see Figure CC-5.2-2)

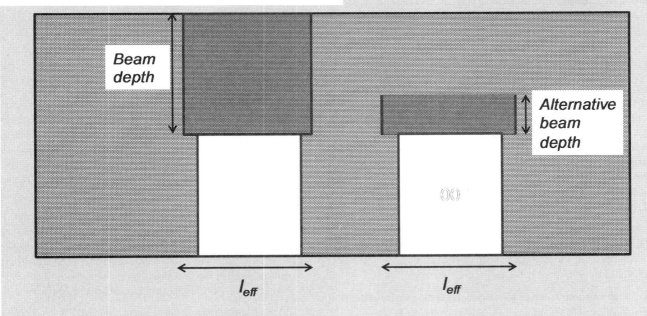

Figure CC-5.2-2 Possible depth of beams over openings in masonry walls

CODE

5.2.2.2 *Internal lever arm* — Unless determined by a more comprehensive analysis, the internal lever arm, z, shall be taken as:

(a) For simply supported spans.

(1) When $1 \le \dfrac{l_{eff}}{d_v} < 2$

$$z = 0.2\left(l_{eff} + 2d_v\right) \qquad \text{(Equation 5-2a)}$$

(2) When $\dfrac{l_{eff}}{d_v} < 1$

$$z = 0.6 l_{eff} \qquad \text{(Equation 5-2b)}$$

(b) For continuous spans

(1) When $1 \le \dfrac{l_{eff}}{d_v} < 3$

$$z = 0.2\left(l_{eff} + 1.5 d_v\right) \qquad \text{(Equation 5-3a)}$$

(2) When $\dfrac{l_{eff}}{d_v} < 1$

$$z = 0.5 l_{eff} \qquad \text{(Equation 5-3b)}$$

5.2.2.3 *Flexural reinforcement* — Distributed horizontal flexural reinforcement shall be provided in the tension zone of the beam for a depth equal to half of the beam depth, d_v. The maximum spacing of distributed horizontal flexural reinforcement shall not exceed one-fifth of the beam depth, d_v, nor 16 in. (406 mm). Joint reinforcement shall be permitted to be used as distributed horizontal flexural reinforcement in deep beams. Horizontal flexural reinforcement shall be anchored to develop the yield strength of the reinforcement at the face of supports.

5.2.2.4 *Minimum shear reinforcement* — The following provisions shall apply when shear reinforcement is required in accordance with Section 8.3.5, Section 9.3.4.1.2, or Section 11.3.4.1.2.

(a) The minimum area of vertical shear reinforcement shall be 0.0007 bd_v.

(b) Horizontal shear reinforcement shall have cross-sectional area equal to or greater than one half the area of the vertical shear reinforcement. Such reinforcement shall be equally distributed on both side faces of the beam when the nominal width of the beam is greater than 8 in. (203 mm).

(c) The maximum spacing of shear reinforcement shall not exceed one-fifth the beam depth, d_v, nor 16 in. (406 mm).

COMMENTARY

5.2.2.2 *Internal lever arm* — The theory used for design of beams has limited applicability to deep beams. Specifically, there will be a nonlinear distribution of strain in deep beams. The internal lever arm, z, between the centroid of the internal compressive forces and the internal tensile forces will be less than that calculated assuming a linear strain distribution. The Code equations for internal lever arm, z, can be used with either allowable stress design or strength design. For allowable stress design, z is commonly known as jd, and for strength design, z is commonly known as $d-(a/2)$. The internal lever arm provisions in the Code are based on CEB-FIP (1990).

5.2.2.3 *Flexural reinforcement* — The distribution of tensile stress in a deep beam is generally such that the lower one-half of the beam is required to have distributed flexural reinforcement. However, other loading conditions, such as uplift, and support conditions, such as continuous and fixed ends, should be considered in determining the portion of the deep beam that is subjected to tension. Distributed horizontal reinforcement resists tensile stress caused by shear as well as by flexure.

5.2.2.4 *Minimum shear reinforcement* – Distributed flexural reinforcement may be included as part of the provided shear reinforcement to meet the minimum distributed shear reinforcement ratio. The spacing of shear reinforcement is limited to restrain the width of the cracks.

Load applied along the top surface of a deep beam is transferred to supports mainly by arch action. Typically, deep beams do not need transverse reinforcement and it is sufficient to provide distributed flexural reinforcement (Park et al, 1975).

CODE

5.2.2.5 *Total reinforcement* — The sum of the cross-sectional areas of horizontal and vertical reinforcement shall be at least 0.001 multiplied by the gross cross-sectional area, bd_v, of the deep beam, using specified dimensions.

5.3 — Columns

Design of columns shall meet the requirements of Section 5.3.1 or Section 5.3.2. Design of columns shall also meet the requirements of Section 8.3, or Section 9.3, or Section 11.3.

5.3.1 *General column design*

5.3.1.1 *Dimensional limits* — Dimensions shall be in accordance with the following:

(a) The distance between lateral supports of a column shall not exceed 99 multiplied by the least radius of gyration, r.

(b) Minimum side dimension shall be 8 in. (203 mm) nominal.

5.3.1.2 *Construction* — Columns shall be fully grouted.

5.3.1.3 *Vertical reinforcement* — Vertical reinforcement in columns shall not be less than $0.0025A_n$ nor exceed $0.04A_n$. The minimum number of bars shall be four.

COMMENTARY

5.3 — Columns

Columns are defined in Section 2.2. They are isolated members usually under axial compressive loads and flexure. If damaged, columns may cause the collapse of other members; sometimes of an entire structure. These critical structural elements warrant the special requirements of this section.

5.3.1 *General column design*

5.3.1.1 *Dimensional limits* — The limit of 99 for the slenderness ratio, h/r, is judgment based. See Figure CC-5.3-1 for effective height determination. The minimum nominal side dimension of 8 in. (203 mm) results from practical considerations.

5.3.1.3 *Vertical reinforcement* — Minimum vertical reinforcement is required in masonry columns to prevent brittle failure. The maximum percentage limit in column vertical reinforcement was established based on the committee's experience. Four bars are required so ties can be used to provide a confined core of masonry.

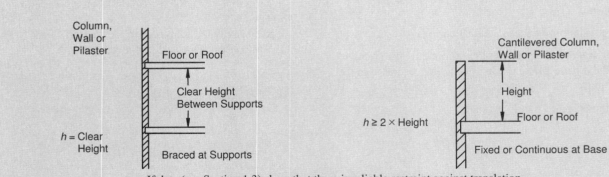

If data (see Section 1.3) show that there is reliable restraint against translation and rotation at the supports, the "effective height" may be taken as low as the distance between points of inflection for the loading case under consideration.

Figure CC-5.3-1 — Effective height, h, of column, wall, or pilaster

CODE

5.3.1.4 *Lateral ties* — Lateral ties shall conform to the following:

(a) Vertical reinforcement shall be enclosed by lateral ties at least $1/4$ in. (6.4 mm) in diameter.

(b) Vertical spacing of lateral ties shall not exceed 16 longitudinal bar diameters, 48 lateral tie bar or wire diameters, or least cross-sectional dimension of the member.

(c) Lateral ties shall be arranged so that every corner and alternate longitudinal bar shall have lateral support provided by the corner of a lateral tie with an included angle of not more than 135 degrees. No bar shall be farther than 6 in. (152 mm) clear on each side along the lateral tie from such a laterally supported bar. Lateral ties shall be placed in either a mortar joint or in grout. Where longitudinal bars are located around the perimeter of a circle, a complete circular lateral tie is permitted. Lap length for circular ties shall be 48 tie diameters.

(d) Lateral ties shall be located vertically not more than one-half lateral tie spacing above the top of footing or slab in any story, and shall be spaced not more than one-half a lateral tie spacing below the lowest horizontal reinforcement in beam, girder, slab, or drop panel above

5.3.2 *Lightly loaded columns*

Masonry columns used only to support light frame roofs of carports, porches, sheds or similar structures assigned to Seismic Design Category A, B, or C, which are subject to unfactored gravity loads not exceeding 2,000 lbs (8,900 N) acting within the cross-sectional dimensions of the column are permitted to be constructed as follows:

(a) Minimum side dimension shall be 8 in. (203 mm) nominal.

(b) Height shall not exceed 12 ft (3.66 m).

(c) Cross-sectional area of longitudinal reinforcement shall not be less than 0.2 in.^{2} (129 mm^2) centered in the column.

(d) Columns shall be fully grouted.

COMMENTARY

5.3.1.4 *Lateral ties* — Lateral reinforcement in columns performs two functions. It provides the required support to prevent buckling of longitudinal column reinforcing bars acting in compression and provides resistance to diagonal tension for columns acting in shear (Pfister, 1964). Ties may be located in the mortar joint, when the tie diameter does not exceed ½ the specified mortar joint thickness. For example, ¼ in. (6.4 mm) diameter ties may be placed in ½ in. (12.7 mm) thick mortar joints.

The requirements of this Code are modeled on those for reinforced concrete columns. Except for permitting ¼-in. (6.4-mm) ties in Seismic Design Category A, B, and C , they reflect the applicable provisions of the reinforced concrete code.

5.3.2 *Lightly loaded columns*

Masonry columns are often used to support roofs of carports, porches, sheds or similar light structures. These columns do not need to meet the detailing requirements of Section 5.3.1. The axial load limit of 2,000 pounds (8,900 N) was developed based on the flexural strength of a nominal 8 in. (203 mm) by 8 in. (203 mm) by 12 ft high (3.66 m) column with one No. 4 (M#13) reinforcing bar in the center and f'_m of 1350 psi (9.31 MPa). An axial load of 2,000 pounds (8,900 N) at the edge of the member will result in a moment that is approximately equal to the nominal flexural strength of this member.

CODE

5.4 — Pilasters

Walls interfacing with pilasters shall not be considered as flanges, unless the construction requirements of Sections 5.1.1.2.1 and 5.1.1.2.5 are met. When these construction requirements are met, the pilaster's flanges shall be designed in accordance with Sections 5.1.1.2.2 through 5.1.1.2.4.

5.5 — Corbels

5.5.1 *Load-bearing corbels*

Load-bearing corbels shall be designed in accordance with Chapter 8, 9 or 10.

5.5.2 *Non-load-bearing corbels*

Non-load-bearing corbels shall be designed in accordance with Chapter 8, 9 or 10 or detailed as follows:

(a) Solid masonry units or hollow units filled with mortar or grout shall be used.

(b) The maximum projection beyond the face of the wall shall not exceed:

    (1) one-half the wall thickness for multiwythe walls bonded by mortar or grout and wall ties or masonry headers, or

    (2) one-half the wythe thickness for single wythe walls, masonry bonded hollow walls, multiwythe walls with open collar joints, and veneer walls.

(c) The maximum projection of one unit shall not exceed:

    (1) one-half the nominal unit height.

    (2) one-third the nominal thickness of the unit or wythe.

(d) The back surface of the corbelled section shall remain within 1 in. (25.4 mm) of plane.

COMMENTARY

5.4 — Pilasters

Pilasters are masonry members that can serve several purposes. They may project from one or both sides of the wall, as shown in Figure CC-5.4-1. Pilasters contribute to the lateral load resistance of masonry walls and may resist vertical loads.

5.5 — Corbels

The provision for corbelling up to one-half of the wall or wythe thickness is theoretically valid only if the opposite side of the wall remains in its same plane. The addition of the 1-in. (25.4-mm) intrusion into the plane recognizes the impracticality of keeping the back surface plane. See Figure CC-5.5-1 and CC-5.5-2 for maximum permissible unit projection.

COMMENTARY

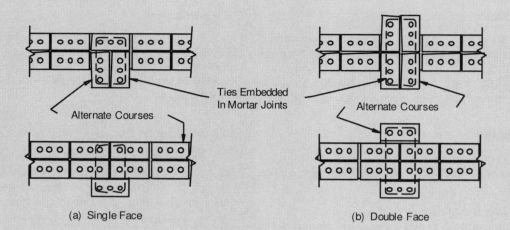

Brick Pilasters

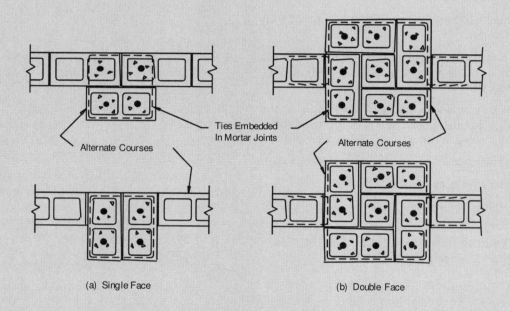

Block Pilasters

Figure CC-5.4-1 — Typical pilasters

COMMENTARY

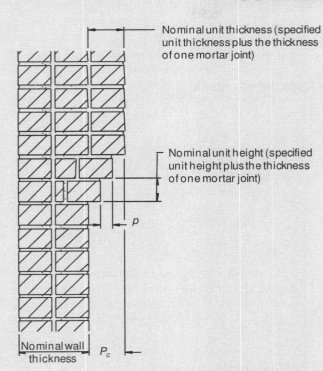

Limitations on Corbelling:

$P_c \leq$ one-half of nominal unit thickness

$p \leq$ one-half of nominal unit height

$p \leq$ one-third of nominal unit thickness

Where:

P_c = Allowable total horizontal projection of corbelling

p = Allowable projection of one unit

Note: Neither ties nor headers shown.

Figure CC-5.5-1 — Limits on corbelling in solid walls

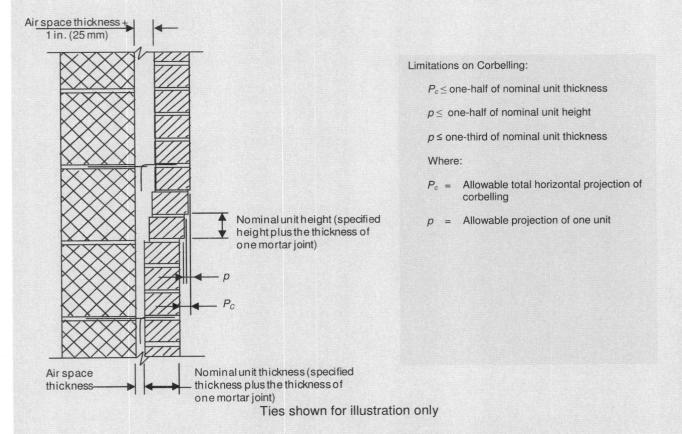

Limitations on Corbelling:

$P_c \leq$ one-half of nominal unit thickness

$p \leq$ one-half of nominal unit height

$p \leq$ one-third of nominal unit thickness

Where:

P_c = Allowable total horizontal projection of corbelling

p = Allowable projection of one unit

Ties shown for illustration only

Figure CC-5.5-2 – Limits on corbelling in walls with air space

This page intentionally left blank

CHAPTER 6
REINFORCEMENT, METAL ACCESSORIES, AND ANCHOR BOLTS

CODE

6.1 — Details of reinforcement and metal accessories

6.1.1 *Embedment*
Reinforcing bars shall be embedded in grout.

6.1.2 *Size of reinforcement*
6.1.2.1 The maximum size of reinforcement used in masonry shall be No. 11 (M #36).

6.1.2.2 The diameter of reinforcement shall not exceed one-half the least clear dimension of the cell, bond beam, or collar joint in which it is placed.

6.1.2.3 Longitudinal and cross wires of joint reinforcement shall have a minimum wire size of W1.1 (MW7) and a maximum wire size of one-half the joint thickness.

6.1.3 *Placement of reinforcement*
6.1.3.1 The clear distance between parallel bars shall not be less than the nominal diameter of the bars, nor less than 1 in. (25.4 mm).

6.1.3.2 In columns and pilasters, the clear distance between vertical bars shall not be less than one and one-half multiplied by the nominal bar diameter, nor less than $1\frac{1}{2}$ in. (38.1 mm).

6.1.3.3 The clear distance limitations between bars required in Sections 6.1.3.1 and 6.1.3.2 shall also apply to the clear distance between a contact lap splice and adjacent splices or bars.

COMMENTARY

6.1 — Details of reinforcement and metal accessories

When the provisions of this section were originally developed in the late 1980s, the Committee used the 1983 edition of the ACI 318 Code as a guide. Some of the requirements were simplified and others dropped, depending on their suitability for application to masonry.

6.1.2 *Size of reinforcement*
6.1.2.1 Limits on size of reinforcement are based on accepted practice and successful performance in construction. The No. 11 (M#36) limit is arbitrary, but Priestley and Bridgeman (1974) shows that distributed small bars provide better performance than fewer large bars. Properties of reinforcement are given in Table CC-6.1.2.

6.1.2.2 Adequate flow of grout necessary for good bond is achieved with this limitation. It also limits the size of reinforcement when combined with Section 3.2.1.

6.1.2.3 The function of joint reinforcement is to control the size and spacing of cracks caused by volume changes in masonry as well as to resist tension (Dickey, 1982). Joint reinforcement is commonly used in concrete masonry to minimize shrinkage cracking. The restriction on wire size ensures adequate performance. The maximum wire size of one-half the joint thickness allows free flow of mortar around joint reinforcement. Thus, a $\frac{3}{16}$-in. (4.8-mm) diameter wire can be placed in a $\frac{3}{8}$-in. (9.5-mm) joint.

6.1.3 *Placement of reinforcement*
Placement limits for reinforcement are based on successful construction practice over many years. The limits are intended to facilitate the flow of grout between bars. A minimum spacing between bars in a layer prevents longitudinal splitting of the masonry in the plane of the bars. Use of bundled bars in masonry construction is rarely required. Two bars per bundle is considered a practical maximum. It is important that bars be placed accurately. Reinforcing bar positioners are available to control bar position.

CODE

6.1.3.4 Groups of parallel reinforcing bars bundled in contact to act as a unit shall be limited to two in any one bundle. Individual bars in a bundle cut off within the span of a member shall terminate at points at least 40 bar diameters apart.

6.1.3.5 Reinforcement embedded in grout shall have a thickness of grout between the reinforcement and masonry units not less than $1/4$ in. (6.4 mm) for fine grout or $1/2$ in. (12.7 mm) for coarse grout.

6.1.4 *Protection of reinforcement and metal accessories*

6.1.4.1 Reinforcing bars shall have a masonry cover not less than the following:

(a) Masonry face exposed to earth or weather: 2 in. (50.8 mm) for bars larger than No. 5 (M #16); $1\frac{1}{2}$ in. (38.1 mm) for No. 5 (M #16) bars or smaller.

(b) Masonry not exposed to earth or weather: $1\frac{1}{2}$ in. (38.1 mm).

COMMENTARY

6.1.4 *Protection of reinforcement and metal accessories*

6.1.4.1 Reinforcing bars are traditionally not coated for corrosion resistance. The masonry cover retards corrosion of the steel. Cover is measured from the exterior masonry surface to the outermost surface of the reinforcement to which the cover requirement applies. It is measured to the outer edge of stirrups or ties, if transverse reinforcement encloses main bars. Masonry cover includes the thickness of masonry units, mortar, and grout. At bed joints, the protection for reinforcement is the total thickness of mortar and grout from the exterior of the mortar joint surface to outer-most surface of the reinforcement or metal accessory.

The condition "masonry face exposed to earth or weather" refers to direct exposure to moisture changes (alternate wetting and drying) and not just temperature changes.

Table CC-6.1.2 — Physical properties of steel reinforcing wire and bars

Designation	Diameter, in. (mm)	Area, in.^{2} (mm^2)	Perimeter, in. (mm)
Wire			
W1.1 (11 gage) (MW7)	0.121 (3.1)	0.011 (7.1)	0.380 (9.7)
W1.7 (9 gage) (MW11)	0.148 (3.8)	0.017 (11.0)	0.465 (11.8)
W2.1 (8 gage) (MW13)	0.162 (4.1)	0.020 (12.9)	0.509 (12.9)
W2.8 (3/16 in. wire) (MW18)	0.187 (4.8)	0.027 (17.4)	0.587 (14.9)
W4.9 (1/4 in. wire) (MW32)	0.250 (6.4)	0.049 (31.6)	0.785 (19.9)
Bars			
No. 3 (M#10)	0.375 (9.5)	0.11 (71.0)	1.178 (29.9)
No. 4 (M#13)	0.500 (12.7)	0.20 (129)	1.571 (39.9)
No. 5 (M#16)	0.625 (15.9)	0.31 (200)	1.963 (49.9)
No. 6 (M#19)	0.750 (19.1)	0.44 (284)	2.356 (59.8)
No. 7 (M#22)	0.875 (22.2)	0.60 (387)	2.749 (69.8)
No. 8 (M#25)	1.000 (25.4)	0.79 (510)	3.142 (79.8)
No. 9 (M#29)	1.128 (28.7)	1.00 (645)	3.544 (90.0)
No. 10 (M#32)	1.270 (32.3)	1.27 (819)	3.990 (101)
No. 11 (M#36)	1.410 (35.8)	1.56 (1006)	4.430 (113)

CODE

6.1.4.2 Longitudinal wires of joint reinforcement shall be fully embedded in mortar or grout with a minimum cover of $^5/_8$ in. (15.9 mm) when exposed to earth or weather and $^1/_2$ in. (12.7 mm) when not exposed to earth or weather. Joint reinforcement shall be stainless steel or protected from corrosion by hot-dipped galvanized coating or epoxy coating when used in masonry exposed to earth or weather and in interior walls exposed to a mean relative humidity exceeding 75 percent. All other joint reinforcement shall be mill galvanized, hot-dip galvanized, or stainless steel.

6.1.4.3 Wall ties, sheet-metal anchors, steel plates and bars, and inserts exposed to earth or weather, or exposed to a mean relative humidity exceeding 75 percent shall be stainless steel or protected from corrosion by hot-dip galvanized coating or epoxy coating. Wall ties, anchors, and inserts shall be mill galvanized, hot-dip galvanized, or stainless steel for all other cases. Anchor bolts, steel plates, and bars not exposed to earth, weather, nor exposed to a mean relative humidity exceeding 75 percent, need not be coated.

6.1.5 *Standard hooks*
Standard hooks shall consist of the following:

(a) 180-degree bend plus a minimum $4d_b$ extension, but not less than 2-1/2 in. (64 mm), at free end of bar;

(b) 90-degree bend plus a minimum $12d_b$ extension at free end of bar; or

(c) for stirrup and tie hooks for a No. 5 bar and smaller, either a 90-degree or 135-degree bend plus a minimum $6d_b$ extension, but not less than 2-1/2 in. (64 mm), at free end of bar.

6.1.6 *Minimum bend diameter for reinforcing bars*
The diameter of bend measured on the inside of reinforcing bars, other than for stirrups and ties, shall not be less than values specified in Table 6.1.6.

Table 6.1.6 — Minimum diameters of bend

Bar size and type	Minimum diameter
No. 3 through No. 7 (M #10 through #22) Grade 40 (Grade 280)	5 bar diameters
No. 3 through No. 8 (M #10 through #25) Grade 50 or 60 (Grade 350 or 420)	6 bar diameters
No. 9, No. 10, and No. 11 (M #29, #32, and #36) Grade 50 or 60 (Grade 350 or 420)	8 bar diameters

COMMENTARY

6.1.4.2 Because masonry cover protection for joint reinforcement is minimal, the protection of joint reinforcement in masonry is required in accordance with the Specification. Examples of interior walls exposed to a mean relative humidity exceeding 75 percent are natatoria and food processing plants.

6.1.4.3 Corrosion resistance requirements are included because masonry cover varies considerably for these items. The exception for anchor bolts is based on current industry practice.

6.1.5 *Standard hooks*
Standard hooks are shown in Figure CC-6.1-1.

6.1.6 *Minimum bend diameter for reinforcing bars*
Standard bends in reinforcing bars are described in terms of the inside diameter of bend because this is easier to measure than the radius of bend.

A broad survey of bending practices, a study of ASTM bend test requirements, and a pilot study of and experience with bending Grade 60 (Grade 420) bars were considered in establishing the minimum diameter of bend. The primary consideration was feasibility of bending without breakage. Experience has since established that these minimum bend diameters are satisfactory for general use without detrimental crushing of grout.

COMMENTARY

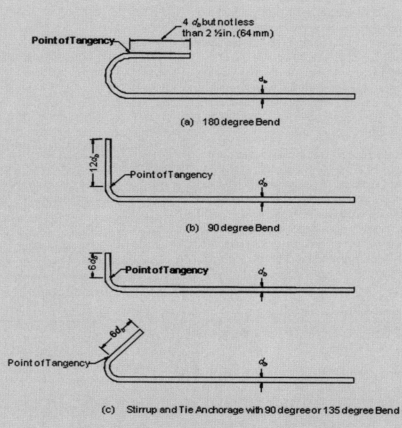

Figure CC-6.1-1 — Standard hooks

CODE

6.2 — Anchor bolts

Headed and bent-bar anchor bolts shall conform to the provisions of Sections 6.2.1 through 6.2.7.

6.2.1 *Placement*

Headed and bent-bar anchor bolts shall be embedded in grout. Anchor bolts of ¼ in. (6.4 mm) diameter are permitted to be placed in mortar bed joints that are at least ½ in. (12.7 mm) in thickness and, for purposes of application of the provisions of Sections 6.2, 8.1.3 and 9.1.6, are permitted to be considered as if they are embedded in grout.

Anchor bolts placed in the top of grouted cells and bond beams shall be positioned to maintain a minimum of ¼ in. (6.4 mm) of fine grout between the bolts and the masonry unit or ½ in. (12.7 mm) of coarse grout between the bolts and the masonry unit. Anchor bolts placed in drilled holes in the face shells of hollow masonry units shall be permitted to contact the masonry unit where the bolt passes through the face shell, but the portion of the bolt that is within the grouted cell shall be positioned to maintain a minimum of ¼ in. (6.4 mm) of fine grout between the head or bent leg of each bolt and the masonry unit or ½ in. (12.7 mm) of coarse grout between the head or bent leg of each bolt and the masonry unit.

The clear distance between parallel anchor bolts shall not be less than the nominal diameter of the anchor bolt, nor less than 1 in. (25.4 mm).

COMMENTARY

6.2 — Anchor bolts

These design values apply only to the specific types of bolts mentioned. These bolts are readily available and are depicted in Figure CC-6.2-1.

6.2.1 *Placement*

Most tests on anchor bolts in masonry have been performed on anchor bolts embedded in grout. Placement limits for anchor bolts are based on successful construction practice over many years. The limits are intended to facilitate the flow of grout between bolts and between bolts and the masonry unit.

Research at Portland State University (Rad and Mueller, 1998) and at Washington State University (Tubbs et al, 2000) has established that there is no difference in the performance of an anchor bolt installed through a tight-fitting hole in the face shell of a grouted hollow masonry unit and in an over-sized hole in the face shell of a grouted hollow masonry unit. Therefore, the clear distance requirement for grout to surround an anchor bolt is not needed where the bolt passes through the face shell. See Figure CC-6.2-2.

Quality/assurance/control (QA) procedures should ensure that there is sufficient clearance around the bolts prior to grout placement. These procedures should also require observation during grout placement to ensure that grout completely surrounds the bolts, as required by the QA Tables in Section 3.1.

Prior to the 2008 MSJC Code, provisions for the allowable shear load of anchors included explicit consideration of bolt edge distances. For edge distance less than 12 bolt diameters, the allowable load in shear was reduced by linear interpolation to zero at an edge distance of 1 in. (25 mm). Since publication of the 2008 MSJC Code, edge distance is considered in provisions for both allowable shear load and shear strength in the calculation of the projected area for shear, A_{pv} (Code Equation 6-2; also see Code and Commentary Section 6.2.3). The projected area is based on an assumed failure cone that originates at the bearing point of the anchor and radiates at 45° in the direction of the shear force towards the free edge of the masonry, thereby accounting for bolt edge distance. The portion of projected area overlapping an open cell, or open head joint, or that lies outside the masonry is deducted from the value of A_{pv}. No minimum edge distance is provided for the placement of anchor bolts. Placement of all anchors, including anchor bolts, must meet the minimum thickness of grout between the anchor and masonry units given in Code Section 6.2.1.

COMMENTARY

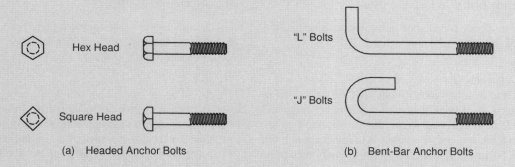

(a) Headed Anchor Bolts

(b) Bent-Bar Anchor Bolts

Figure CC-6.2-1 — Anchor bolts

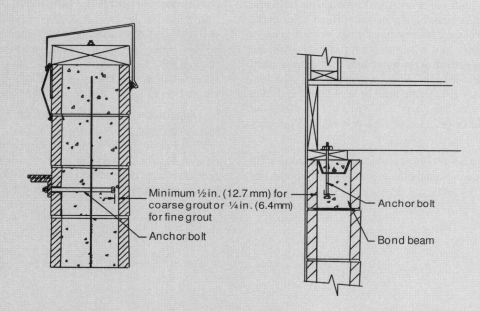

Minimum ½ in. (12.7 mm) for coarse grout or ¼ in. (6.4mm) for fine grout

Anchor bolt

Anchor bolt

Bond beam

Figure CC-6.2-2 — Anchor bolt clearance requirements for headed anchor bolts – bent-bars are similar

CODE

6.2.2 *Projected area for axial tension*

The projected area of headed and bent-bar anchor bolts loaded in axial tension, A_{pt}, shall be determined by Equation 6-1.

$$A_{pt} = \pi l_b^2 \qquad \text{(Equation 6-1)}$$

The portion of projected area overlapping an open cell, or open head joint, or that lies outside the masonry shall be deducted from the value of A_{pt} calculated using Equation 6-1. Where the projected areas of anchor bolts overlap, the value of A_{pt} calculated using Equation 6-1 shall be adjusted so that no portion of masonry is included more than once.

COMMENTARY

6.2.2 *Projected area for axial tension*

Results of tests (Brown and Whitlock, 1983; Allen et al, 2000) on headed anchor bolts in tension showed that anchor bolts often failed by breakout of a conically shaped section of masonry. The area, A_{pt}, is the projected area of the assumed failure cone. The cone originates at the compression bearing point of the embedment and radiates at 45° in the direction of the pull (See Figure CC-6.2-3). Other modes of tensile failure are possible. These modes include pullout (straightening of J- or L-bolts) and yield / fracture of the anchor steel.

When anchor bolts are closely spaced, stresses within the masonry begin to become additive, as shown in Figure CC-6.2-4. The Code requires that when projected areas of anchor bolts overlap, an adjustment be made so that the masonry is not overloaded. When the projected areas of two or more anchors overlap, the anchors with overlapping projected areas should be treated as an anchor group. The projected areas of the anchors in the group are summed, this area is adjusted for overlapping areas, and the capacity of the anchor group is calculated using the adjusted area in place of A_{pt}. See Figure CC-6.2-5 for examples of calculating adjusted values of A_{pt}. The equations given in Figure CC-6.2-5 are valid only when the projected areas of the bolts overlap.

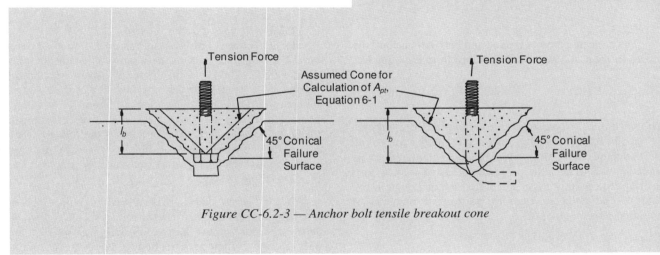

Figure CC-6.2-3 — Anchor bolt tensile breakout cone

COMMENTARY

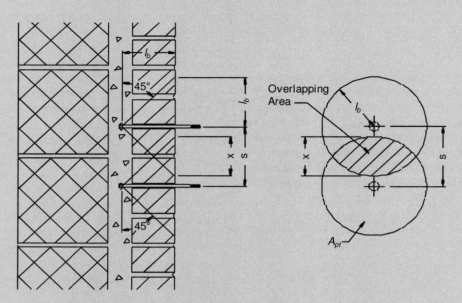

Figure CC-6.2-4 — Overlapping anchor bolt breakout cones

CODE

6.2.3   Projected area for shear

The projected area of headed and bent-bar anchor bolts loaded in shear, A_{pv}, shall be determined from Equation 6-2.

$$A_{pv} = \frac{\pi\, l_{be}^2}{2} \qquad\qquad \text{(Equation 6-2)}$$

The portion of projected area overlapping an open cell, or open head joint, or that lies outside the masonry shall be deducted from the value of A_{pv} calculated using Equation 6-2. Where the projected areas of anchor bolts overlap, the value of A_{pv} calculated using Equation 6-2 shall be adjusted so that no portion of masonry is included more than once.

COMMENTARY

6.2.3   Projected area for shear

Results of tests (Brown and Whitlock, 1983; Allen et al, 2000) on anchor bolts in shear showed that anchor bolts often failed by breakout of a conically shaped section of masonry. The area A_{pv} is the projected area of the assumed failure cone. The cone originates at the compression bearing point of the embedment and radiates at 45° in the direction of the shear force towards the free edge of the masonry (See Figure CC-6.2-6). Pryout (See Figure CC-6.2-7), masonry crushing, and yielding / fracture of the anchor steel are other possible failure modes.

When the projected areas of two or more anchors overlap, the shear design of these anchors should follow the same procedure as for the tension design of overlapping anchors. See Commentary Section 6.2.2.

COMMENTARY

A_{pt} at Top of Wall for Uplift

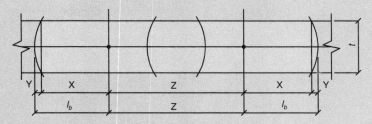

For $l_b \leq z \leq 2X$

$$X = \frac{1}{2}\sqrt{4(l_b)^2 - t^2}$$

$$Y = l_b - X = l_b - \frac{1}{2}\sqrt{4(l_b)^2 - t^2}$$

$$\therefore A_{pt} = (2X + Z)t + l_b^2\left(\frac{\pi\theta}{180} - \sin\theta\right) \quad \text{where } \theta = 2\arcsin\left(\frac{t/2}{l_b}\right) \text{ in degrees}$$

For $0 \leq z \leq l_b$

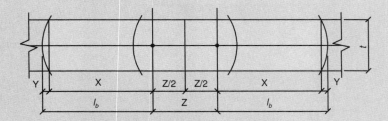

$$\therefore A_{pt} = (2X + Z)t + l_b^2\left(\frac{\pi\theta}{180} - \sin\theta\right) \quad \text{where } \theta = 2\arcsin\left(\frac{t/2}{l_b}\right) \text{ in degrees}$$

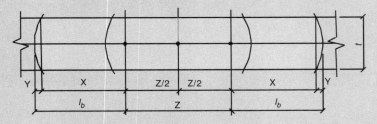

$$\therefore A_{pt} = (2X + Z)t + l_b^2\left(\frac{\pi\theta}{180} - \sin\theta\right) \quad \text{where } \theta = 2\arcsin\left(\frac{t/2}{l_b}\right) \text{ in degrees}$$

Figure CC-6.2-5 — Calculation of Adjusted Values of A_{pt} (Plan Views)

COMMENTARY

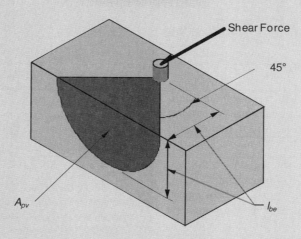

Figure CC-6.2-6 — Anchor bolt shear breakout

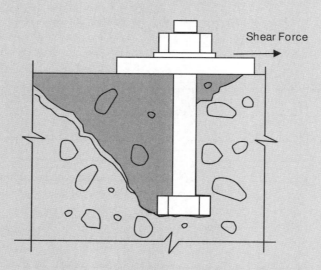

Figure CC-6.2-7 — Anchor bolt shear pryout

CODE

6.2.4 *Effective embedment length for headed anchor bolts*

The effective embedment length for a headed anchor bolt, l_b, shall be the length of the embedment measured perpendicular from the masonry surface to the compression bearing surface of the anchor head.

6.2.5 *Effective embedment length for bent-bar anchor bolts*

The effective embedment for a bent-bar anchor bolt, l_b, shall be the length of embedment measured perpendicular from the masonry surface to the compression bearing surface of the bent end, minus one anchor bolt diameter.

COMMENTARY

6.2.5 *Effective embedment length for bent-bar anchor bolts*

Tests (Brown and Whitlock, 1983) have shown that the pullout strength of bent-bar anchor bolts correlated best with a reduced embedment length. This may be explained with reference to Figure CC-6.2-8. Due to the radius of the bend, stresses are concentrated at a point less than the full embedment length.

COMMENTARY

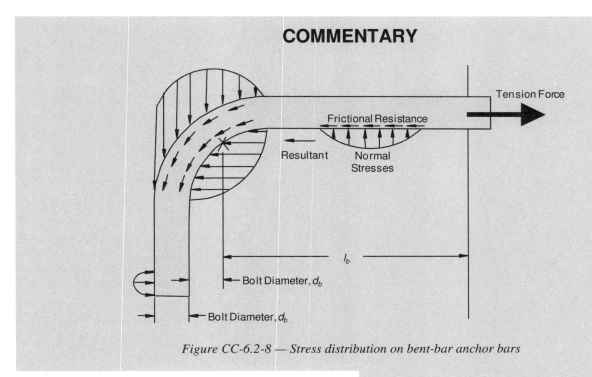

Figure CC-6.2-8 — Stress distribution on bent-bar anchor bars

CODE

6.2.6   *Minimum permissible effective embedment length*

The minimum permissible effective embedment length for headed and bent-bar anchor bolts shall be the greater of 4 bolt diameters or 2 in. (50.8 mm).

6.2.7   *Anchor bolt edge distance*

Anchor bolt edge distance, l_{be}, shall be measured in the direction of load from the edge of masonry to center of the cross section of anchor bolt.

COMMENTARY

6.2.6   *Minimum permissible effective embedment length*

The minimum embedment length requirement is considered a practical minimum based on typical construction methods for embedding anchor bolts in masonry. The validity of Code equations for shear and tension capacities of anchor bolts have not been verified by testing of anchor bolts with embedment lengths less than four bolt diameters.

This page intentionally left blank

CHAPTER 7
SEISMIC DESIGN REQUIREMENTS

CODE

7.1 — Scope

The seismic design requirements of Chapter 7 shall apply to the design and construction of masonry, except glass unit masonry and masonry veneer.

COMMENTARY

7.1 — Scope

The requirements in this section have been devised to improve performance of masonry construction when subjected to earthquake loads. Minimum seismic loading requirements are drawn from the legally adopted building code. In the event that the legally adopted building code does not contain appropriate criteria for the determination of seismic forces, the Code requires the use of ASCE 7, which represented the state-of-the-art in seismic design at the time these requirements were developed. Obviously, the seismic design provisions of this section may not be compatible with every edition of every building code that could be used in conjunction with these requirements. As with other aspects of structural design, the designer should understand the implications and limits of combining the minimum loading requirements of other documents with the resistance provisions of this Code.

Seismic design is not optional regardless of the assigned Seismic Design Category, the absolute value of the design seismic loads, or the relative difference between the design seismic loads and other design lateral forces such as wind. Unlike other design loads, seismic design of reinforced masonry elements permits inelastic response of the system, which in turn reduces the seismic design load. This reduction in load presumes an inherent level of inelastic ductility that may not otherwise be present if seismic design was neglected. When nonlinear response is assumed by reducing the seismic loading by an R factor greater than 1.5, the resulting seismic design load may be less than other loading conditions that assume a linear elastic model of the system. This is often misinterpreted by some to mean that the seismic loads do not 'control' the design and can be neglected. For the masonry system to be capable of achieving the ductility-related lower seismic loads, however, the minimum seismic design and detailing requirements of this section must be met.

The seismic design requirements are presented in a cumulative format. Thus, the provisions for Seismic Design Categories E and F include provisions for Seismic Design Category D, which include provisions for Seismic Design Category C, and so on.

This section does not apply to the design or detailing of masonry veneers or glass unit masonry systems. Seismic requirements for masonry veneers are provided in Chapter 12, Veneers. Glass unit masonry systems, by definition and design, are isolated, non-load-bearing elements and therefore cannot be used to resist seismic loads other than those induced by their own mass.

CODE

7.2 — General analysis

7.2.1 *Element interaction* — The interaction of structural and nonstructural elements that affect the linear and nonlinear response of the structure to earthquake motions shall be considered in the analysis.

7.2.2 *Load path* — Structural masonry elements that transmit forces resulting from earthquakes to the foundation shall comply with the requirements of Chapter 7.

7.2.3 *Anchorage design* — Load path connections and minimum anchorage forces shall comply with the requirements of the legally adopted building code. When the legally adopted building code does not prescribe minimum load path connection requirements and anchorage design forces, the requirements of ASCE 7 shall be used.

7.2.4 *Drift limits* — Under loading combinations that include earthquake, masonry structures shall be designed so the calculated story drift, Δ, does not exceed the allowable story drift, Δ_a, obtained from the legally adopted building code. When the legally adopted building code does not prescribe allowable story drifts, structures shall be designed so the calculated story drift, Δ, does not exceed the allowable story drift, Δ_a, obtained from ASCE 7.

It shall be permitted to assume that the following shear wall types comply with the story drift limits of ASCE 7: empirical, ordinary plain (unreinforced), detailed plain (unreinforced), ordinary reinforced, intermediate reinforced, ordinary plain (unreinforced) AAC masonry shear walls, and detailed plain (unreinforced) AAC masonry shear walls.

COMMENTARY

7.2 — General analysis

The designer is permitted to use any of the structural design methods presented in this Code to design to resist seismic loads. There are, however, limitations on some of the design methods and systems based upon the structure's assigned Seismic Design Category. For instance, empirical design (Appendix A) procedures are not permitted to be used in structures assigned to Seismic Design Categories D, E, or F. Further, empirically designed masonry elements can only be used as part of the seismic-force-resisting system in Seismic Design Category A.

7.2.1 *Element interaction* — Even if a nonstructural element is not part of the seismic-force-resisting system, it is possible for it to influence the structural response of the system during a seismic event. This may be particularly apparent due to the interaction of structural and nonstructural elements at displacements larger than those determined by linear elastic analysis.

7.2.2 *Load path* — This section clarifies load path requirements and alerts the designer that the base of the structure as defined in analysis may not necessarily correspond to the ground level.

7.2.3 *Anchorage design* — Previous editions of the Code contained minimum anchorage and connection design forces based upon antiquated service-level earthquake loads and velocity-related acceleration parameters. As these are minimum design loads, their values should be determined using load standards.

Experience has demonstrated that one of the chief causes of failure of masonry construction during earthquakes is inadequate anchorage of masonry walls to floors and roofs. For this reason, an arbitrary minimum anchorage based upon previously established practice has been set as noted in the referenced documents. When anchorage is between masonry walls and wood framed floors or roofs, the designer should avoid the use of wood ledgers in cross-grain bending.

7.2.4 *Drift limits* — Excessive deformation, particularly resulting from inelastic displacements, can potentially result in instability of the seismic-force-resisting system. This section provides procedures for the limitation of story drift. The term "drift" has two connotations:

1. "Story drift" is the maximum calculated lateral displacement within a story (the calculated displacement of one level relative to the level below caused by the effects of design seismic loads).

2. The calculated lateral displacement or deflection due to design seismic loads is the absolute displacement of any point in the structure relative to the base. This is not "story drift" and is not to be used for drift control or stability considerations because it may give a false impression of the effects in critical stories. However, it is important when considering seismic separation requirements.

CODE

COMMENTARY

Overall or total drift is the lateral displacement of the top of a building relative to the base. The overall drift ratio is the total drift divided by the building height. Story drift is the lateral displacement of one story relative to an adjacent story. The story drift ratio is the story drift divided by the corresponding story height. The overall drift ratio is usually an indication of moments in a structure and is also related to seismic separation demands. The story drift ratio is an indication of local seismic deformation, which relates to seismic separation demands within a story. The maximum story drift ratio could exceed the overall drift ratio.

There are many reasons for controlling drift in seismic design:

(a) To control the inelastic strain within the affected elements. Although the relationship between lateral drift and maximum nonlinear strain is imprecise, so is the current state of knowledge of what strain limitations should be.

(b) Under small lateral deformations, secondary stresses are normally within tolerable limits. However, larger deformations with heavy vertical loads can lead to significant secondary moments from P-delta effects in the design. The drift limits indirectly provide upper bounds for these effects.

(c) Buildings subjected to earthquakes need drift control to restrict damage to partitions, shaft and stair enclosures, glass, and other fragile nonstructural elements and, more importantly, to minimize differential movement demands on the seismic-force-resisting elements.

The designer must keep in mind that the allowable drift limits, Δ_a, correspond to story drifts and, therefore, are applicable to each story. They must not be exceeded in any story even though the drift in other stories may be well below the limit.

Although the provisions of this Code do not give equations for calculating building separations, the distance should be sufficient to avoid damaging contact under total calculated deflection for the design loading in order to avoid interference and possible destructive hammering between buildings. The distance should be equal to the total of the lateral deflections of the two units assumed deflecting toward each other (this involves increasing the separation with height). If the effects of hammering can be shown not to be detrimental, these distances may be reduced. For very rigid shear wall structures with rigid diaphragms whose lateral deflections are difficult to estimate, older code requirements for structural separations of at least 1 in. (25.4 mm) plus ½ in. (12.7 mm) for each 10 ft (3.1 m) of height above 20 ft (6.1 m) could be used as a guide.

Empirical, ordinary plain (unreinforced), detailed plain (unreinforced), ordinary reinforced, intermediate reinforced, ordinary plain (unreinforced) AAC, and detailed plain (unreinforced) AAC masonry shear walls are inherently

CODE

7.3 — Element classification

Masonry elements shall be classified in accordance with Section 7.3.1 and 7.3.2 as either participating or nonparticipating elements of the seismic-force-resisting system.

7.3.1 *Nonparticipating elements* — Masonry elements that are not part of the seismic-force-resisting system shall be classified as nonparticipating elements and shall be isolated in their own plane from the seismic-force-resisting system except as required for gravity support. Isolation joints and connectors shall be designed to accommodate the design story drift.

7.3.2 *Participating elements* — Masonry walls that are part of the seismic-force-resisting system shall be classified as participating elements and shall comply with the requirements of Section 7.3.2.1, 7.3.2.2, 7.3.2.3, 7.3.2.4, 7.3.2.5, 7.3.2.6, 7.3.2.7, 7.3.2.8, 7.3.2.9, 7.3.2.10, 7.3.2.11 or 7.3.2.12.

COMMENTARY

designed to have relatively low inelastic deformations under seismic loads. As such, the Committee felt that requiring designers to check story drifts for these systems of low and moderate ductility was superfluous.

7.3 — Element classification

Classifying masonry elements as either participating or nonparticipating in the seismic-force-resisting system is largely a function of design intent. Participating elements are those that are designed and detailed to actively resist seismic forces, including such elements as shear walls, columns, piers, pilasters, beams, and coupling elements. Nonparticipating elements can be any masonry assembly, but are not designed to collect and resist earthquake loads from other portions of the structure.

7.3.1 *Nonparticipating elements* — In previous editions of the Code, isolation of elements that were not part of the seismic-force-resisting system was not required in Seismic Design Categories A and B, rationalized, in part, due to the low hazard associated with these Seismic Design Categories. Non-isolated, nonparticipating elements, however, can influence a structure's strength and stiffness, and as a result the distribution of lateral loads. In considering the influence nonparticipating elements can inadvertently have on the performance of a structural system, the Committee opted to require that all nonparticipating elements be isolated from the seismic-force-resisting system. The Committee is continuing to discuss alternative design options that would allow non-isolated, nonparticipating elements with corresponding checks for strength, stiffness, and compatibility.

7.3.2 *Participating elements* — A seismic-force-resisting system must be defined for every structure. Most masonry buildings use masonry shear walls to serve as the seismic-force-resisting system, although other systems are sometimes used (such as concrete or steel frames with masonry infill). Such shear walls must be designed by the engineered methods in Part 3, unless the structure is assigned to Seismic Design Category A, in which case empirical provisions of Appendix A may be used.

Twelve shear wall types are defined by the Code. Depending upon the masonry material and detailing method used to design the shear wall, each wall type is intended to have a different capacity for inelastic response and energy dissipation in the event of a seismic event. These twelve shear wall types are assigned system design parameters such as response modification factors, *R*, based on their expected performance and ductility. Certain shear wall types are permitted in each seismic design category, and unreinforced shear wall types are not permitted in regions of intermediate and high seismic risk. Table CC-7.3.2-1 summarizes the requirements of each of the twelve types of masonry shear walls.

TABLE CC-7.3.2-1 Requirements for Masonry Shear Walls Based on Shear Wall Designation[1]

Shear Wall Designation	Design Methods	Reinforcement Requirements	Permitted In
Empirical Design of Masonry Shear Walls	Section A.3	None	SDC A
Ordinary Plain (Unreinforced) Masonry Shear Walls	Section 8.2 or Section 9.2	None	SDC A and B
Detailed Plain (Unreinforced) Masonry Shear Walls	Section 8.2 or Section 9.2	Section 7.3.2.3.1	SDC A and B
Ordinary Reinforced Masonry Shear Walls	Section 8.3 or Section 9.3	Section 7.3.2.3.1	SDC A, B, and C
Intermediate Reinforced Masonry Shear Walls	Section 8.3 or Section 9.3	Section 7.3.2.5	SDC A, B, and C
Special Reinforced Masonry Shear Walls	Section 8.3 or Section 9.3	Section 7.3.2.6	SDC A, B, C, D, E, and F
Ordinary Plain (Unreinforced) AAC Masonry Shear Walls	Section 11.2	Section 7.3.2.7.1	SDC A and B
Detailed Plain (Unreinforced) AAC Masonry Shear Walls	Section 11.2	Section 7.3.2.8.1	SDC A and B
Ordinary Reinforced AAC Masonry Shear Walls	Section 11.3	Section 7.3.2.9	SDC A, B, C, D, E, and F
Ordinary Plain (Unreinforced) Prestressed Masonry Shear Walls	Chapter 10	None	SDC A and B
Intermediate Reinforced Prestressed Masonry Shear Walls	Chapter 10	Section 7.3.2.11	SDC A, B, and C
Special Reinforced Prestressed Masonry Shear Walls	Chapter 10	Section 7.3.2.12	SDC A, B, C, D, E, and F

[1] Section and Chapter references in this table refer to Code Sections and Chapters.

CODE

7.3.2.1 *Empirical design of masonry shear walls* — Empirical design of shear walls shall comply with the requirements of Section A.3.

7.3.2.2 *Ordinary plain (unreinforced) masonry shear walls* — Design of ordinary plain (unreinforced) masonry shear walls shall comply with the requirements of Section 8.2 or Section 9.2.

7.3.2.3 *Detailed plain (unreinforced) masonry shear walls* — Design of detailed plain (unreinforced) masonry shear walls shall comply with the requirements of Section 8.2 or Section 9.2, and shall comply with the requirements of Section 7.3.2.3.1.

7.3.2.3.1 *Minimum reinforcement requirements* — Vertical reinforcement of at least 0.2 in.^{2} (129 mm^2) in cross-sectional area shall be provided at corners, within 16 in. (406 mm) of each side of openings, within 8 in. (203 mm) of each side of movement joints, within 8 in. (203 mm) of the ends of walls, and at a maximum spacing of 120 in. (3048 mm) on center.

Vertical reinforcement adjacent to openings need not be provided for openings smaller than 16 in. (406 mm), unless the distributed reinforcement is interrupted by such openings.

Horizontal reinforcement shall consist of at least two longitudinal wires of W1.7 (MW11) joint reinforcement spaced not more than 16 in. (406 mm) on center, or at least 0.2 in.^{2} (129 mm^2) in cross-sectional area of bond beam reinforcement spaced not more than 120 in. (3048 mm) on center. Horizontal reinforcement shall also be provided: at the bottom and top of wall openings and shall extend at least 24 in. (610 mm) but not less than 40 bar diameters past the opening; continuously at structurally connected roof and floor levels; and within 16 in. (406 mm) of the top of walls.

Horizontal reinforcement adjacent to openings need not be provided for openings smaller than 16 in. (406 mm), unless the distributed reinforcement is interrupted by such openings.

COMMENTARY

7.3.2.1 *Empirical design of masonry shear walls* — These shear walls are permitted to be used only in Seismic Design Category A. Empirical masonry shear walls are not designed or required to contain reinforcement.

7.3.2.2 *Ordinary plain (unreinforced) masonry shear walls* — These shear walls are permitted to be used only in Seismic Design Categories A and B. Plain masonry walls are designed as unreinforced masonry, although they may in fact contain reinforcement.

7.3.2.3 *Detailed plain (unreinforced) masonry shear walls* — These shear walls are designed as plain (unreinforced) masonry in accordance with the sections noted, but contain minimum reinforcement in the horizontal and vertical directions. Walls that are designed as unreinforced, but that contain minimum prescriptive reinforcement, have more favorable seismic design parameters, including higher response modification coefficients, R, than ordinary plain (unreinforced) masonry shear walls.

7.3.2.3.1 *Minimum reinforcement requirements* — The provisions of this section require a judgment-based minimum amount of reinforcement to be included in reinforced masonry wall construction. Tests reported in Gulkan et al (1979) have confirmed that masonry construction, reinforced as indicated, performs adequately considering the highest Seismic Design Category permitted for this shear wall type. This minimum required reinforcement may also be used to resist design loads.

CODE

7.3.2.4 *Ordinary reinforced masonry shear walls* — Design of ordinary reinforced masonry shear walls shall comply with the requirements of Section 8.3 or Section 9.3, and shall comply with the requirements of Section 7.3.2.3.1.

7.3.2.5 *Intermediate reinforced masonry shear walls* — Design of intermediate reinforced masonry shear walls shall comply with the requirements of Section 8.3 or Section 9.3. Reinforcement detailing shall also comply with the requirements of Section 7.3.2.3.1, except that the spacing of vertical reinforcement shall not exceed 48 in. (1219 mm).

7.3.2.6 *Special reinforced masonry shear walls* — Design of special reinforced masonry shear walls shall comply with the requirements of Section 8.3, Section 9.3, or Appendix C. Reinforcement detailing shall also comply with the requirements of Section 7.3.2.3.1 and the following:

(a) The maximum spacing of vertical reinforcement shall be the smallest of one-third the length of the shear wall, one-third the height of the shear wall, and 48 in. (1219 mm) for masonry laid in running bond and 24 in. (610 mm) for masonry not laid in running bond.

(b) The maximum spacing of horizontal reinforcement required to resist in-plane shear shall be uniformly distributed, shall be the smaller of one-third the length of the shear wall and one-third the height of the shear wall, and shall be embedded in grout. The maximum spacing of horizontal reinforcement shall not exceed 48 in. (1219 mm) for masonry laid in running bond and 24 in. (610 mm) for masonry not laid in running bond.

(c) The minimum cross-sectional area of vertical reinforcement shall be one-third of the required shear reinforcement. The sum of the cross-sectional area of horizontal and vertical reinforcement shall be at least 0.002 multiplied by the gross cross-sectional area of the wall, using specified dimensions.

COMMENTARY

7.3.2.4 *Ordinary reinforced masonry shear walls* — These shear walls are required to meet minimum requirements for reinforced masonry as noted in the referenced sections. Because they contain reinforcement, these walls can generally accommodate larger deformations and exhibit higher capacities than similarly configured plain (unreinforced) masonry walls. Hence, they are permitted in both areas of low and moderate seismic risk. Additionally, these walls have more favorable seismic design parameters, including higher response modification factors, R, than plain (unreinforced) masonry shear walls. To provide the minimum level of assumed inelastic ductility, however, minimum reinforcement is required as noted in Section 7.3.2.3.1.

7.3.2.5 *Intermediate reinforced masonry shear walls* — These shear walls are designed as reinforced masonry as noted in the referenced sections, and are also required to contain a minimum amount of prescriptive reinforcement. Because they contain reinforcement, their seismic performance is better than that of plain (unreinforced) masonry shear walls, and they are accordingly permitted in both areas of low and moderate seismic risk. Additionally, these walls have more favorable seismic design parameters including higher response modification factors, R, than plain (unreinforced) masonry shear walls and ordinary reinforced masonry shear walls.

7.3.2.6 *Special reinforced masonry shear walls* — These shear walls are designed as reinforced masonry as noted in the referenced sections and are also required to meet restrictive reinforcement and material requirements. Accordingly, they are permitted to be used as part of the seismic-force-resisting system in any Seismic Design Category. Additionally, these walls have the most favorable seismic design parameters, including the highest response modification factor, R, of any of the masonry shear wall types. The intent of Sections 7.3.2.6(a) through 7.3.2.6(f) is to provide a minimum level of in-plane shear reinforcement to improve ductility.

CODE

1. For masonry laid in running bond, the minimum cross-sectional area of reinforcement in each direction shall be at least 0.0007 multiplied by the gross cross-sectional area of the wall, using specified dimensions.

2. For masonry not laid in running bond, the minimum cross-sectional area of vertical reinforcement shall be at least 0.0007 multiplied by the gross cross-sectional area of the wall, using specified dimensions. The minimum cross-sectional area of horizontal reinforcement shall be at least 0.0015 multiplied by the gross cross-sectional area of the wall, using specified dimensions.

(d) Shear reinforcement shall be anchored around vertical reinforcing bars with a standard hook.

(e) Mechanical splices in flexural reinforcement in plastic hinge zones shall develop the specified tensile strength of the spliced bar.

(f) Masonry not laid in running bond shall be fully grouted and shall be constructed of hollow open-end units or two wythes of solid units.

7.3.2.6.1 *Shear capacity design*

7.3.2.6.1.1 When designing special reinforced masonry shear walls to resist in-plane forces in accordance with Section 9.3, the design shear strength, ϕV_n, shall exceed the shear corresponding to the development of 1.25 times the nominal flexural strength, M_n, of the element, except that the nominal shear strength, V_n, need not exceed 2.5 times required shear strength, V_u.

COMMENTARY

(e) In a structure undergoing inelastic deformations during an earthquake, the tensile stresses in flexural reinforcement in plastic hinge zones may approach the tensile strength of the reinforcement. This requirement is intended to avoid a splice failure in such reinforcement.

7.3.2.6.1 *Shear capacity design* — While different concepts and applications, the requirements of Code Section 7.3.2.6.1.1 and 7.3.2.6.1.2 are different methods of attempting to limit shear failures prior to nonlinear flexural behavior – or if one prefers – increase element ductility. The MSJC recognizes the slight discrepancy between the 2.5 design cap in Code Section 7.3.2.6.1.1 and the 1.5 load factor in Code Section 7.3.2.6.1.2. Given the historical precedence of each of these values, the Committee opted to maintain the two distinct values. When all factors and requirements for special reinforced masonry shear walls are considered, the resulting difference between the two requirements is small.

7.3.2.6.1.1 In previous editions of the Code, this design requirement was applied to all masonry elements designed by the strength design method (elements participating in the seismic-force-resisting system as well as those not participating in the seismic-force-resisting system, reinforced masonry elements, and unreinforced masonry elements) as well as all loading conditions. Upon further review, this design check was considered by the Committee to be related to inelastic ductility demand for seismic resistance and was therefore specifically applied to the seismic design requirements. Further, because unreinforced masonry systems by nature exhibit limited ductility, this check is required only for special reinforced masonry shear walls.

CODE

7.3.2.6.1.2 When designing special reinforced masonry shear walls in accordance with Section 8.3, the shear or diagonal tension stress resulting from in-plane seismic forces shall be increased by a factor of 1.5. The 1.5 multiplier need not be applied to the overturning moment.

7.3.2.7 *Ordinary plain (unreinforced) AAC masonry shear walls* — Design of ordinary plain (unreinforced) AAC masonry shear walls shall comply with the requirements of Section 11.2 and Section 7.3.2.7.1.

7.3.2.7.1 *Anchorage of floor and roof diaphragms in AAC masonry structures* — Floor and roof diaphragms in AAC masonry structures shall be anchored to a continuous grouted bond beam reinforced with at least two longitudinal reinforcing bars, having a total cross-sectional area of at least 0.4 in.^{2} (260 mm^2).

7.3.2.8 *Detailed plain (unreinforced) AAC masonry shear walls* — Design of detailed plain (unreinforced) AAC masonry shear walls shall comply with the requirements of Section 11.2 and Sections 7.3.2.7.1 and 7.3.2.8.1.

7.3.2.8.1 *Minimum reinforcement requirements* — Vertical reinforcement of at least 0.2 in.^{2} (129 mm^2) shall be provided within 24 in. (610 mm) of each side of openings, within 8 in. (203 mm) of movement joints, and within 24 in. (610 mm) of the ends of walls. Vertical reinforcement adjacent to openings need not be provided for openings smaller than 16 in. (406 mm), unless the distributed reinforcement is interrupted by such openings. Horizontal reinforcement shall be provided at the bottom and top of wall openings and shall extend at least 24 in. (610 mm) but not less than 40 bar diameters past the opening. Horizontal reinforcement adjacent to openings need not be provided for openings smaller than 16 in. (406 mm), unless the distributed reinforcement is interrupted by such openings.

COMMENTARY

7.3.2.6.1.2 The 1.5 load factor for reinforced masonry shear walls that are part of the seismic-force-resisting system designed by allowable stress design procedures is applied only to in-plane shear forces. It is not intended to be used for the design of in-plane overturning moments or out-of-plane overturning moments or shear. Increasing the design seismic load is intended to make the flexure mode of failure more dominant, resulting in better ductile performance.

7.3.2.7 *Ordinary plain (unreinforced) AAC masonry shear walls* – These shear walls are philosophically similar in concept to ordinary plain (unreinforced) masonry shear walls. As such, prescriptive mild reinforcement is not required, but may actually be present.

7.3.2.8 *Detailed plain (unreinforced) AAC masonry shear walls* — Prescriptive seismic requirements for AAC masonry shear walls are less severe than for conventional masonry shear walls, and are counterbalanced by more restrictive Code requirements for bond beams and additional requirements for floor diaphragms, contained in evaluation service reports and other documents dealing with floor diaphragms of various materials. AAC masonry shear walls and a full-scale, two-story assemblage specimen with prescriptive reinforcement meeting the requirements of this section have performed satisfactorily under reversed cyclic loads representing seismic excitation (Varela et al, 2006; Tanner, 2005(a)The maximum distance from the edge of an opening or end of a wall to the vertical reinforcement is set at 24 in. (610 mm) because the typical length of an AAC unit is 24 in. (610 mm).

CODE

7.3.2.9 *Ordinary reinforced AAC masonry shear walls* — Design of ordinary reinforced AAC masonry shear walls shall comply with the requirements of Section 11.3 and Sections 7.3.2.7.1 and 7.3.2.8.1.

7.3.2.9.1 *Shear capacity design* — The design shear strength, ϕV_n, shall exceed the shear corresponding to the development of 1.25 times the nominal flexural strength, M_n, of the element, except that the nominal shear strength, V_n, need not exceed 2.5 times required shear strength, V_u.

7.3.2.10 *Ordinary plain (unreinforced) prestressed masonry shear walls* — Design of ordinary plain (unreinforced) prestressed masonry shear walls shall comply with the requirements of Chapter 10.

7.3.2.11 *Intermediate reinforced prestressed masonry shear walls* — Intermediate reinforced prestressed masonry shear walls shall comply with the requirements of Chapter 10, the reinforcement detailing requirements of Section 7.3.2.3.1, and the following:

(a) Reinforcement shall be provided in accordance with Sections 7.3.2.6(a) and 7.3.2.6(b).

(b) The minimum area of horizontal reinforcement shall be $0.0007bd_v$.

(c) Shear walls subjected to load reversals shall be symmetrically reinforced.

(d) The nominal moment strength at any section along the shear wall shall not be less than one-fourth the maximum moment strength.

(e) The cross-sectional area of bonded tendons shall be considered to contribute to the minimum reinforcement in Sections 7.3.2.3.1, 7.3.2.6(a), and 7.3.2.6(b).

(f) Tendons shall be located in cells that are grouted the full height of the wall.

COMMENTARY

7.3.2.9 *Ordinary reinforced AAC masonry shear walls*

7.3.2.10 *Ordinary plain (unreinforced) prestressed masonry shear* walls — These shear walls are philosophically similar in concept to ordinary plain (unreinforced) masonry shear walls. As such, prescriptive mild reinforcement is not required, but may actually be present.

7.3.2.11 *Intermediate reinforced prestressed masonry shear* walls — These shear walls are philosophically similar in concept to intermediate reinforced masonry shear walls. To provide the intended level of inelastic ductility, prescriptive mild reinforcement is required. For consistency with 2003 IBC, intermediate reinforced prestressed masonry shear walls should include the detailing requirements from Section 7.3.2.6 (a) as well as Sections 3.2.3.5 and 3.2.4.3.2 (c) from the 2002 MSJC.

ASCE 7, Tables 12.2-1 and 12.14-1 conservatively combine all prestressed masonry shear walls into one category for seismic coefficients and structural system limitations on seismic design categories and height. The design limitations included in those tables are representative of ordinary plain (unreinforced) prestressed masonry shear walls. The criteria specific to intermediate reinforced prestressed shear walls have not yet been included from IBC 2003, Table 1617.6.2. To utilize the seismic criteria from IBC 2003, the structure would have to be accepted under Section 1.3, Approval of special systems of design and construction.

The seismic coefficients from IBC 2003, Table 1617.6.2 and the building height limitations based upon seismic design category are shown in Table CC-7.3.2-2.

CODE

7.3.2.12 *Special reinforced prestressed masonry shear walls* — Special reinforced prestressed masonry shear walls shall comply with the requirements of Chapter 10, the reinforcement detailing requirements of Sections 7.3.2.3.1 and 7.3.2.11 and the following:

(a) The cross-sectional area of bonded tendons shall be considered to contribute to the minimum reinforcement in Sections 7.3.2.3.1 and 7.3.2.11.

(b) Prestressing tendons shall consist of bars conforming to ASTM A722/A722M.

(c) All cells of the masonry wall shall be grouted.

(d) The requirements of Section 9.3.3.5 or 9.3.6.5 shall be met. Dead load axial forces shall include the effective prestress force, $A_{ps}f_{se}$.

(e) The design shear strength, ϕV_n, shall exceed the shear corresponding to the development of 1.25 times the nominal flexural strength, M_n, of the element, except that the nominal shear strength, V_n, need not exceed 2.5 times required shear strength, V_u.

COMMENTARY

7.3.2.12 *Special reinforced prestressed masonry shear walls* — These shear walls are philosophically similar in concept to special reinforced masonry shear walls. To provide the intended level of inelastic ductility, prescriptive mild reinforcement is required. For consistency with 2003 IBC, special reinforced prestressed masonry shear walls should include the detailing requirements from Sections 3.2.3.5 and 3.2.4.3.2 (c) from the 2002 MSJC.

ASCE 7, Table 12.2-1 and ASCE 7, Table 12.14-1 conservatively combine all prestressed masonry shear walls into one category for seismic coefficients and structural system limitations on seismic design categories and height. The design limitations included in those tables are representative of ordinary plain (unreinforced) prestressed masonry shear walls. The criteria specific to special reinforced prestressed shear walls have not yet been included from IBC 2003, Table 1617.6.2. To utilize the seismic criteria from IBC 2003, the structure would have to be accepted under Section 1.3, Approval of special systems of design and construction.

See Table CC-7.3.2-2. The data in this table is similar to ASCE 7, Table 12.2-1. Users that prefer to use the Simplified Design Procedure in ASCE 7 should interpret the table for use in lieu of ASCE 7, Table 12.14-1.

TABLE CC-7.3.2-2 2003 IBC Seismic Coefficients for Prestressed Masonry Shear Walls

	Response Modification Coefficient, R	System Overstrength Factor, Ω_o	Deflection Amplification Factor, C_d	SYSTEM LIMITATIONS AND BUILDING HEIGHT LIMITATIONS (FEET) BY SEISMIC DESIGN CATEGORY				
				A or B	C	D	E	F
Ordinary Plain Prestressed	1½	2½	1¼	NL	NP	NP	NP	NP
Intermediate Reinforced Prestressed	3 for Building Frame System and 2½ for Bearing Wall System	2½	2½	NL	35	NP	NP	NP
Special Reinforced Prestressed	4½	2½	4 for Building Frame System and 3½ for Bearing Wall System	NL	35	35	35	35

NL = no limit   NP = not permitted

CODE

7.4 — Seismic Design Category requirements

The design of masonry elements shall comply with the requirements of Sections 7.4.1 through 7.4.5 based on the Seismic Design Category as defined in the legally adopted building code. When the legally adopted building code does not define Seismic Design Categories, the provisions of ASCE 7 shall be used.

7.4.1 *Seismic Design Category A requirements —* Masonry elements in structures assigned to Seismic Design Category A shall comply with the requirements of Sections 7.1, 7.2, 7.4.1.1, and 7.4.1.2.

7.4.1.1 *Design of nonparticipating elements —* Nonparticipating masonry elements shall comply with the requirements of Section 7.3.1 and Chapter 8, 9, 10, 11, 14, Appendix A, or Appendix B.

7.4.1.2 *Design of participating elements —* Participating masonry elements shall be designed to comply with the requirements of Chapter 8, 9, 10, 11, Appendix A, or Appendix B. Masonry shear walls shall be designed to comply with the requirements of Section 7.3.2.1, 7.3.2.2, 7.3.2.3, 7.3.2.4, 7.3.2.5, 7.3.2.6, 7.3.2.7, 7.3.2.8, 7.3.2.9, 7.3.2.10, 7.3.2.11, or 7.3.2.12.

7.4.2 *Seismic Design Category B requirements —* Masonry elements in structures assigned to Seismic Design Category B shall comply with the requirements of Section 7.4.1 and with the additional requirements of Section 7.4.2.1.

7.4.2.1 *Design of participating elements —* Participating masonry elements shall be designed to comply with the requirements of Chapter 8, 9, 10, 11, or Appendix B. Masonry shear walls shall be designed to comply with the requirements of Section 7.3.2.2, 7.3.2.3, 7.3.2.4, 7.3.2.5, 7.3.2.6, 7.3.2.7, 7.3.2.8, 7.3.2.9, 7.3.2.10, 7.3.2.11, or 7.3.2.12.

COMMENTARY

7.4 — Seismic Design Category requirements

Every structure is assigned to a Seismic Design Category (SDC) in accordance with the legally adopted building code or per the requirements of ASCE 7, whichever govern for the specific project under consideration. Previous editions of the Code included requirements for Seismic Performance Categories and Seismic Zones, each of which is different than a Seismic Design Category.

7.4.1 *Seismic Design Category A requirements —* The general requirements of this Code provide for adequate performance of masonry construction assigned to Seismic Design Category A structures.

7.4.2 *Seismic Design Category B requirements —* Although masonry may be designed by the provisions of Chapter 8, Allowable Stress Design of Masonry; Chapter 9, Strength Design of Masonry; Chapter 10, Prestressed Masonry; Chapter 11, Strength Design of Autoclaved Aerated Concrete (AAC) Masonry; or Appendix A, Empirical Design of Masonry; or Appendix B, Design of Masonry Infill, the seismic-force-resisting system for structures assigned to Seismic Design Category B must be designed based on a structural analysis in accordance with Chapter 8, 9, 10 or 11, or Appendix B. The provisions of Appendix A cannot be used to design the seismic-force-resisting system of buildings assigned to Seismic Design Category B or higher.

CODE

7.4.3 *Seismic Design Category C requirements* — Masonry elements in structures assigned to Seismic Design Category C shall comply with the requirements of Section 7.4.2 and with the additional requirements of Section 7.4.3.1 and 7.4.3.2.

7.4.3.1 *Design of nonparticipating elements* — Nonparticipating masonry elements shall comply with the requirements of Section 7.3.1 and Chapter 8, 9, 10, 11, 14, Appendix A, or Appendix B. Nonparticipating masonry elements, except those constructed of AAC masonry, shall be reinforced in either the horizontal or vertical direction in accordance with the following:

(a) *Horizontal reinforcement* — Horizontal reinforcement shall consist of at least two longitudinal wires of W1.7 (MW11) bed joint reinforcement spaced not more than 16 in. (406 mm) on center for walls greater than 4 in. (102 mm) in width and at least one longitudinal W1.7 (MW11) wire spaced not more than 16 in. (406 mm) on center for walls not exceeding 4 in. (102 mm) in width or at least one No. 4 (M #13) bar spaced not more than 48 in. (1219 mm) on center. Where two longitudinal wires of joint reinforcement are used, the space between these wires shall be the widest that the mortar joint will accommodate. Horizontal reinforcement shall be provided within 16 in. (406 mm) of the top and bottom of these masonry walls.

(b) *Vertical reinforcement* — Vertical reinforcement shall consist of at least one No. 4 (M #13) bar spaced not more than 120 in. (3048 mm). Vertical reinforcement shall be located within 16 in. (406 mm) of the ends of masonry walls.

7.4.3.2 *Design of participating elements* — Participating masonry elements shall be designed to comply with the requirements of Section 8.3, 9.3, 11.3, or Appendix B. Masonry shear walls shall be designed to comply with the requirements of Section 7.3.2.4, 7.3.2.5, 7.3.2.6, 7.3.2.9, 7.3.2.11, or 7.3.2.12.

COMMENTARY

7.4.3 *Seismic Design Category C requirements* — In addition to the requirements of Seismic Design Category B, minimum levels of reinforcement and detailing are required. The minimum provisions for improved performance of masonry construction in Seismic Design Category C must be met regardless of the method of design. Shear walls designed as part of the seismic-force-resisting system in Seismic Design Category C and higher must be designed using reinforced masonry methods because of the increased risk and expected intensity of seismic activity. Ordinary reinforced masonry shear walls, ordinary reinforced AAC masonry shear walls, intermediate reinforced masonry shear walls, special reinforced masonry shear walls, or masonry infills are required to be used.

7.4.3.1 *Design of nonparticipating elements* — Reinforcement requirements of Section 7.4.3.1 are traditional for conventional concrete and clay masonry. They are prescriptive in nature. The intent of this requirement is to provide structural integrity for nonparticipating masonry walls. AAC masonry walls differ from concrete masonry walls and clay masonry walls in that the thin-bed mortar strength and associated bond strength is typically greater than that of the AAC units. Also, the unit weight of AAC masonry is typically less than one-third of the unit weight of clay or concrete masonry, reducing seismic inertial forces. This reduced load, combined with a tensile bond strength that is higher than the strength of the AAC material itself, provides a minimum level of structural integrity. Therefore, prescriptive reinforcement is not required. All masonry walls, including non-participating AAC masonry walls, are required to be designed to resist out-of-plane forces. If reinforcement is required, it must be provided in the direction of the span.

CODE

7.4.3.2.1 *Connections to masonry columns* — Where anchor bolts are used to connect horizontal elements to the tops of columns, anchor bolts shall be placed within lateral ties. Lateral ties shall enclose both the vertical bars in the column and the anchor bolts. There shall be a minimum of two No. 4 (M #13) lateral ties provided in the top 5 in. (127 mm) of the column.

7.4.3.2.2 *Anchorage of floor and roof diaphragms in AAC masonry structures* — Seismic load between floor and roof diaphragms and AAC masonry shear walls shall be transferred through connectors embedded in grout and designed in accordance with Section 4.1.4.

7.4.3.2.3 *Material requirements* — ASTM C34, structural clay load-bearing wall tiles, shall not be used as part of the seismic-force-resisting system.

7.4.3.2.4 *Lateral stiffness* — At each story level, at least 80 percent of the lateral stiffness shall be provided by seismic-force-resisting walls. Along each line of lateral resistance at a particular story level, at least 80 percent of the lateral stiffness shall be provided by seismic-force-resisting walls. Where seismic loads are determined based on a seismic response modification factor, R, not greater than 1.5, piers and columns shall be permitted to be used to provide seismic load resistance.

7.4.3.2.5 *Design of columns, pilasters, and beams supporting discontinuous elements* — Columns and pilasters that are part of the seismic-force-resisting system and that support reactions from discontinuous stiff elements shall be provided with transverse reinforcement spaced at no more than one-fourth of the least nominal dimension of the column or pilaster. The minimum transverse reinforcement ratio shall be 0.0015. Beams supporting reactions from discontinuous walls shall be provided with transverse reinforcement spaced at no more than one-half of the nominal depth of the beam. The minimum transverse reinforcement ratio shall be 0.0015.

COMMENTARY

7.4.3.2.1 *Connections to masonry columns* — Connections must be designed to transfer forces between masonry columns and horizontal elements in accordance with the requirements of Section 4.1.4. Experience has demonstrated that connections of structural members to masonry columns are vulnerable to damage during earthquakes unless properly anchored. Requirements are adapted from previously established practice developed as a result of the 1971 San Fernando earthquake.

7.4.3.2.2 *Anchorage of floor and roof diaphragms in AAC masonry structures* — Connectors are required to be placed in grout because of the relatively low strength of connectors embedded in AAC. Different detailing options are available, but often the connectors are placed in bond beams near the top of the wall.

7.4.3.2.3 *Material requirements* — The limitation on the use of ASTM C34 structural clay tile units in the seismic-force-resisting system is based on these units' limited ability to provide inelastic strength.

7.4.3.2.4 *Lateral stiffness* — In order to accurately distribute loads in a structure subjected to lateral loading, the lateral stiffness of all structural members should be considered. Although structures may be designed to use shear walls for lateral-load resistance, columns may also be incorporated for vertical capacity. The stipulation that seismic-force-resisting elements provide at least 80 percent of the lateral stiffness helps ensure that additional elements do not significantly contribute to the lateral stiffness. Based on typical design assumptions, the lateral stiffness of structural elements should be based on cracked section properties for reinforced masonry and uncracked section properties for unreinforced masonry.

The designer may opt to increase the percentage of lateral stiffness provided by piers and columns if the structure is designed to perform elastically under seismic loads.

7.4.3.2.5 *Design of columns, pilasters, and beams supporting discontinuous elements* — Discontinuous stiff members such as shear walls have global overturning forces at their edges that may be supported by columns, pilasters and beams. These vertical support elements are required to have a minimum level of confinement and shear detailing at the discontinuity level. The minimum detailing requirements in this section may be in excess of those requirements that are based on calculations using full-height relative stiffnesses of the elements of the seismic-force-resisting system.

A common example is a building with internal shear walls, such as interior corridor walls, that are discontinuous at the first story above grade or in a basement level. If this structure has a rigid diaphragm at all floor and roof levels; the global (full height) relative stiffnesses of the discontinuous elements is minor in comparison to the relative stiffnesses of the continuous elements at the

CODE

COMMENTARY

perimeter of the structure. All shear walls above the discontinuity, however, have a forced common interstory displacement. This forced interstory displacement induces overturning forces in the discontinuous shear walls at all levels having this forced story displacement. The accumulated overturning forces at the ends of the walls above the discontinuity in turn are likely to be supported by columns and pilasters in the discontinuous levels and the beams at the level above the discontinuity. This section specifies minimum detailing requirements for these columns, pilasters, and beams. The stiffness of the discontinuous element should be determined based on the relative stiffness of the discontinuous members above and below the discontinuity. If the interstory stiffness of the discontinuous wall below the discontinuity is less than 20% of the interstory stiffness above the discontinuity, the discontinuous element should be considered stiff.

7.4.4 *Seismic Design Category D requirements* — Masonry elements in structures assigned to Seismic Design Category D shall comply with the requirements of Section 7.4.3 and with the additional requirements of Sections 7.4.4.1 and 7.4.4.2.

Exception: Design of participating elements of AAC masonry shall comply with the requirements of 7.4.3.

7.4.4 *Seismic Design Category D requirements* — Masonry shear walls for structures assigned to Seismic Design Category D are required to meet the requirements of special reinforced masonry shear walls or ordinary reinforced AAC masonry shear walls because of the increased risk and expected intensity of seismic activity. The minimum amount of wall reinforcement for special reinforced masonry shear walls has been a long-standing, standard empirical requirement in areas of high seismic loading. It is expressed as a percentage of gross cross-sectional area of the wall. It is intended to improve the ductile behavior of the wall under earthquake loading and assist in crack control. Because the minimum required reinforcement may be used to satisfy design requirements, at least $1/3$ of the minimum amount is reserved for the lesser stressed direction in order to ensure an appropriate distribution of loads in both directions.

7.4.4.1 *Design of nonparticipating elements* — Nonparticipating masonry elements shall comply with the requirements of Chapter 8, 9, 10, 11, or Appendix B. Nonparticipating masonry elements, except those constructed of AAC masonry, shall be reinforced in either the horizontal or vertical direction in accordance with the following:

(a) *Horizontal reinforcement* — Horizontal reinforcement shall comply with Section 7.4.3.1(a).

(b) *Vertical reinforcement* — Vertical reinforcement shall consist of at least one No. 4 (M #13) bar spaced not more than 48 in. (1219 mm). Vertical reinforcement shall be located within 16 in. (406 mm) of the ends of masonry walls.

7.4.4.2 *Design of participating elements* — Masonry shear walls shall be designed to comply with the requirements of Section 7.3.2.6, 7.3.2.9, or 7.3.2.12.

CODE

7.4.4.2.1 *Minimum reinforcement for masonry columns* — Lateral ties in masonry columns shall be spaced not more than 8 in. (203 mm) on center and shall be at least 3/8 in. (9.5 mm) diameter. Lateral ties shall be embedded in grout.

7.4.4.2.2 *Material requirements* — Fully grouted participating elements shall be designed and specified with Type S or Type M cement-lime mortar, masonry cement mortar, or mortar cement mortar. Partially grouted participating elements shall be designed and specified with Type S or Type M cement-lime mortar or mortar cement mortar.

7.4.4.2.3 *Lateral tie anchorage* — Standard hooks for lateral tie anchorage shall be either a 135-degree standard hook or a 180-degree standard hook.

7.4.5 *Seismic Design Categories E and F requirements* — Masonry elements in structures assigned to Seismic Design Category E or F shall comply with the requirements of Section 7.4.4 and with the additional requirements of Section 7.4.5.1.

7.4.5.1 *Minimum reinforcement for nonparticipating masonry elements not laid in running bond* — Masonry not laid in running bond in nonparticipating elements shall have a cross-sectional area of horizontal reinforcement of at least 0.0015 multiplied by the gross cross-sectional area of masonry, using specified dimensions. The maximum spacing of horizontal reinforcement shall be 24 in. (610 mm). These elements shall be fully grouted and shall be constructed of hollow open-end units or two wythes of solid units.

COMMENTARY

7.4.4.2.1 *Minimum reinforcement for masonry columns* — Adequate lateral restraint is important for column reinforcement subjected to overturning forces due to earthquakes. Many column failures during earthquakes have been attributed to inadequate lateral tying. For this reason, closer spacing of ties than might otherwise be required is prudent. An arbitrary minimum spacing has been established through experience. Columns not involved in the seismic-force-resisting system should also be more heavily tied at the tops and bottoms for more ductile performance and better resistance to shear.

7.4.4.2.2 *Material requirements* — Based on numerous tests by several researchers, (Brown and Melander, 1999, Hamid et al, 1979, Minaie et al, 2009, Klingner et al, 2010) the behavior of fully grouted walls subjected to out-of-plane flexural and in-plane shear loads is dominated by grout and unaffected by mortar formulation. In tests by Minaie et al (2009) and Klingner et al (2010), fully grouted concrete masonry walls exhibited good in-plane response when subjected to seismic loads. For fully grouted participating elements in buildings assigned to Seismic Categories D or higher, no mortar material restrictions are necessary. Historical provisions requiring use of Type S or M cement-lime or mortar cement mortar are retained for partially grouted participating elements in buildings assigned to Seismic Design Categories D or higher.

7.4.5 *Seismic Design Categories E and F requirements* — See Commentary Sections 7.3.2.3.1 and 7.4.4. The ratio of minimum horizontal reinforcement is increased to reflect the possibility of higher seismic loads. Where fully grouted open end hollow units are used, part of the need for horizontal reinforcement is satisfied by the mechanical continuity provided by the grout core.

PART 3: ENGINEERED DESIGN METHODS

CHAPTER 8
ALLOWABLE STRESS DESIGN OF MASONRY

<table>
<tr><th>CODE</th><th>COMMENTARY</th></tr>
</table>

CODE

8.1 — General

8.1.1 *Scope*

This chapter provides requirements for allowable stress design of masonry. Masonry designed in accordance with this chapter shall comply with the requirements of Part 1, Part 2, Sections 8.1.2 through 8.1.6, and either Section 8.2 or 8.3.

8.1.2 *Design strength*

Calculated stresses shall not exceed the allowable stress requirements of this Chapter.

COMMENTARY

8.1 — General

8.1.1 *Scope*

Chapter 8 design procedures follow allowable stress design methodology, in which the calculated stresses resulting from nominal loads must not exceed permissible masonry and steel stresses.

For allowable stress design, linear elastic materials following Hooke's Law are assumed, that is, deformations (strains) are linearly proportional to the loads (stresses). All materials are assumed to be homogeneous and isotropic, and sections that are plane before bending remain plane after bending. These assumptions are adequate within the low range of working stresses under consideration. The allowable stresses are fractions of the specified compressive strength, resulting in conservative factors of safety.

Service load is the load that is assumed by the legally adopted building code to actually occur when the structure is in service. The stresses allowed under the action of service loads are limited to values within the elastic range of the materials.

Historically, a one-third increase in allowable stress had been permitted for load combinations that included wind or seismic loads. The origin and the reason for the one-third stress increase are unclear (Ellifritt, 1977). From a structural reliability standpoint, the one-third stress increase was a poor way to handle load combination effects. Therefore, the one-third stress increase was removed from this Code beginning with the 2011 edition. The allowable stresses of this Chapter should not be increased by one-third for wind and seismic load combinations.

8.1.2 *Design strength*

Calculated stresses designated by '*f* ' with subscript indicating stress type are required to be less than allowable stresses designated by '*F*' with subscript indicating the same stress type.

CODE

8.1.3 *Anchor bolts embedded in grout*
    8.1.3.1 *Design requirements* — Anchor bolts shall be designed using either the provisions of Section 8.1.3.2 or, for headed and bent-bar anchor bolts, by the provisions of Section 8.1.3.3.

    8.1.3.2 *Allowable loads determined by test*
    8.1.3.2.1 Anchor bolts shall be tested in accordance with ASTM E488, except that a minimum of five tests shall be performed. Loading conditions of the test shall be representative of intended use of the anchor bolt.

    8.1.3.2.2 Anchor bolt allowable loads used for design shall not exceed 20 percent of the average failure load from the tests.

    8.1.3.3 *Allowable loads determined by calculation for headed and bent-bar anchor bolts* — Allowable loads for headed and bent-bar anchor bolts embedded in grout shall be determined in accordance with the provisions of Sections 8.1.3.3.1 through 8.1.3.3.3.

    8.1.3.3.1 *Allowable axial tensile load of headed and bent-bar anchor bolts* — The allowable axial tensile load of headed anchor bolts shall be calculated using the provisions of Sections 8.1.3.3.1.1. The allowable axial tensile load of bent-bar anchor bolts shall be calculated using the provisions of Section 8.1.3.3.1.2.

    8.1.3.3.1.1 *Allowable axial tensile load of headed anchor bolts* — The allowable axial tensile load, B_a, of headed anchor bolts embedded in grout shall be the smaller of the values determined by Equation 8-1 and Equation 8-2.

$$B_{ab} = 1.25 A_{pt} \sqrt{f'_m} \qquad \text{(Equation 8-1)}$$

$$B_{as} = 0.6 A_b f_y \qquad \text{(Equation 8-2)}$$

COMMENTARY

8.1.3 *Anchor bolts embedded in grout*
Significant changes in the anchor bolt design provisions were incorporated into the 2008 MSJC Code. The changes included revising the safety factors for the Allowable Stress Design anchor bolt provisions to correspond to those used for the Strength Design anchor bolt provisions, and requiring consideration of additional failure modes in both the Allowable Stress Design and Strength Design provisions. The result of these changes in the 2008 Code is that the resulting anchor bolt designs produced using Allowable Stress Design or Strength Design should be approximately the same.

See Code Commentary 9.1.6 for additional discussion on the background and application of the anchor bolt design provisions.

8.1.3.3 *Allowable loads determined by calculation for headed and bent-bar anchor bolts* — The anchor provisions in this Code define bolt shear and tension capacities based on the bolt's specified yield strength. Anchors conforming to A307, Grade A specifications are allowed by the Code, but the ASTM A307, Grade A specification does not specify a yield strength. Use of a yield strength of 37 ksi in the Code design equations for A307 anchors will result in anchor capacities similar to those obtained using the American Institute of Steel Construction provisions.

    8.1.3.3.1.1 *Allowable axial tensile load of headed anchor bolts* — Equation 8-1 defines the allowable axial tensile load governed by masonry breakout. Equation 8-2 defines the allowable axial tensile load governed by steel yielding. The lower of these loads is the allowable axial tensile load on the anchor.

CODE

8.1.3.3.1.2 *Allowable axial tensile load of bent-bar anchor bolts* — The allowable axial tensile load, B_a, for bent-bar anchor bolts embedded in grout shall be the smallest of the values determined by Equation 8-3, Equation 8-4 , and Equation 8-5.

$$B_{ab} = 1.25 A_{pt} \sqrt{f'_m} \qquad \text{(Equation 8-3)}$$

$$B_{ap} = 0.6 f'_m e_b d_b + 120\pi (l_b + e_b + d_b) d_b$$
$$\text{(Equation 8-4)}$$

$$B_{as} = 0.6 A_b f_y \qquad \text{(Equation 8-5)}$$

8.1.3.3.2 *Allowable shear load of headed and bent-bar anchor bolts* — The allowable shear load, B_v, of headed and bent-bar anchor bolts embedded in grout shall be the smallest of the values determined by Equation 8-6 , Equation 8-7 , Equation 8-8, and Equation 8-9.

$$B_{vb} = 1.25 A_{pv} \sqrt{f'_m} \qquad \text{(Equation 8-6)}$$

$$B_{vc} = 350 \sqrt[4]{f'_m A_b} \qquad \text{(Equation 8-7)}$$

$$B_{vpry} = 2.0 B_{ab} = 2.5 A_{pt} \sqrt{f'_m} \qquad \text{(Equation 8-8)}$$

$$B_{vs} = 0.36 A_b f_y \qquad \text{(Equation 8-9)}$$

8.1.3.3.3 *Combined axial tension and shear* — Anchor bolts subjected to axial tension in combination with shear shall satisfy Equation 8-10.

$$\frac{b_a}{B_a} + \frac{b_v}{B_v} \leq 1 \qquad \text{(Equation 8-10)}$$

COMMENTARY

8.1.3.3.1.2 *Allowable axial tensile load of bent-bar anchor bolts* — Equation 8-3 defines the allowable axial tensile load governed by masonry breakout. Equation 8-4 defines the allowable axial tensile load governed by anchor pullout. Equation 8-5 defines the allowable axial tensile load governed by steel yielding. The lower of these loads is the allowable axial tensile load on the anchor.

8.1.3.3.2 *Allowable shear load of headed and bent-bar anchor bolts* — Equation 8-6 defines the allowable shear load governed by masonry breakout. Equation 8-7 defines the allowable shear load governed by masonry crushing. Equation 8-8 defines the allowable shear load governed by anchor pryout. Equation 8-9 defines the allowable shear load governed by steel yielding. The lower of these loads is the allowable shear load on the anchor.

CODE

8.1.4 *Shear stress in multiwythe masonry elements*

8.1.4.1 Design of multiwythe masonry for composite action shall meet the requirements of Section 5.1.4.2 and Section 8.1.4.2.

8.1.4.2 Shear stresses developed at the interfacess between wythes and collar joints or within headers shall not exceed the following:

(a)   mortared collar joints, 7 psi (48.3 kPa).

(b)   grouted collar joints, 13 psi (89.6 kPa).

(c)   headers,

$$1.3\sqrt{\text{specified unit compressive strength of header}}$$

psi (MPa) (over net area of header).

8.1.5   *Bearing stress*

Bearing stresses on masonry shall not exceed $0.33 f'_m$ and shall be calculated over the bearing area, A_{br}, as defined in Section 4.3.4.

COMMENTARY

8.1.4 *Shear stress in multiwythe masonry elements*

Limited test data (McCarthy et al, 1985; Williams and Geschwinder, 1982; Colville et al, 1987) are available to document shear strength of collar joints in masonry.

Test results (McCarthy et al, 1985; Williams and Geschwinder, 1982) show that shear bond strength of collar joints could vary from as low as 5 psi (34.5 kPa) to as high as 100 psi (690 kPa), depending on type and condition of the interface, consolidation of the joint, and type of loading. McCarthy et al (1985) reported an average value of 52 psi (359 kPa) with a coefficient of variation of 21.6 percent. An allowable shear stress value of 7 psi (48.3 kPa), which is four standard deviations below the average, is considered to account for the expected high variability of the interface bond. With some units, Type S mortar slushed collar joints may have better shear bond characteristics than Type N mortar. Results show that thickness of joints, unit absorption, and reinforcement have a negligible effect on shear bond strength. Grouted collar joints have higher allowable shear bond stress than the mortared collar joints (Williams and Geschwinder, 1982).

A strength analysis has been demonstrated by Porter et al (1986 and 1987) for composite masonry walls subjected to combined in-plane shear and gravity loads. In addition, these authors have shown adequate behavioral characteristics for both brick-to-brick and brick-to-block composite walls with a grouted collar joint (Wolde-Tinsae et al, 1985(a); Wolde-Tinsae et al, 1985(b); Ahmed et al, 1983(a); Ahmed et al, 1983(b)) . Finite element models for analyzing the interlaminar shearing stresses in collar joints of composite walls have been investigated (Anand and Young, 1982; Anand, 1985; Stevens and Anand, 1985; Anand and Rahman, 1986). They found that the shear stresses were principally transferred in the upper portion of the wall near the point of load application for the in-plane loads. Thus, below a certain distance, the overall strength of the composite masonry is controlled by the global strength of the wall, providing that the wythes are acting compositely.

CODE

8.1.6   *Development of reinforcement embedded in grout*

8.1.6.1   *General* — The calculated tension or compression in the reinforcement at each section shall be developed on each side of the section by development length, hook, mechanical device, or combination thereof. Hooks shall not be used to develop bars in compression.

8.1.6.2   *Development of wires in tension* — The development length of wire shall be determined by Equation 8-11, but shall not be less than 6 in. (152 mm).

$$l_d = 0.0015 d_b F_s \qquad \text{(Equation 8-11)}$$

Development length of epoxy-coated wire shall be taken as 150 percent of the length determined by Equation 8-11.

8.1.6.3   *Development of bars in tension or compression* — The required development length of reinforcing bars shall be determined by Equation 8-12, but shall not be less than 12 in. (305 mm).

$$l_d = \frac{0.13 \, d_b^{\,2} f_y \gamma}{K \sqrt{f_m'}} \qquad \text{(Equation 8-12)}$$

K shall not exceed the smallest of the following: the minimum masonry cover, the clear spacing between adjacent reinforcement splices, and $9d_b$.

γ = 1.0 for No. 3 (M#10) through No. 5 (M#16) bars;

γ = 1.3 for No. 6 (M#19) through No. 7 (M#22) bars;

and

γ = 1.5 for No. 8 (M#25) through No. 11 (M#36) bars.

Development length of epoxy-coated bars shall be taken as 150 percent of the length determined by Equation 8-12.

COMMENTARY

8.1.6   *Development of reinforcement embedded in grout*

8.1.6.1   *General* — From a point of peak stress in reinforcement, some length of reinforcement or anchorage is necessary through which to develop the stress. This development length or anchorage is necessary on both sides of such peak stress points, on one side to transfer stress into and on the other to transfer stress out of the reinforcement. Often the reinforcement continues for a considerable distance on one side of a critical stress point so that calculations need involve only the other side; for example, the negative moment reinforcement continuing through a support to the middle of the next span.

Bars and longitudinal wires must be deformed.

8.1.6.2   *Development of wires in tension* — Equation 8-11 can be derived from the basic development length expression and an allowable bond stress u for deformed bars in grout of 160 psi (1103 kPa) (Gallagher, 1935; Richart, 1949). Research (Treece and Jirsa, 1989) has shown that epoxy-coated reinforcing bars require longer development length than uncoated reinforcing bars. The 50 percent increase in development length does not apply to the 6 in. (152 mm) minimum.

$$l_d = d_b F_s / 4u = d_b F_s / 4(160) = 0.0015 d_b F_s$$

$$(\, l_d = 0.22 d_b F_s \text{ in SI units})$$

8.1.6.3   *Development of bars in tension or compression* —The 50 percent increase in development length does not apply to the 12 in. (305 mm) minimum.

CODE

8.1.6.4 *Embedment of flexural reinforcement*

8.1.6.4.1 *General*

8.1.6.4.1.1 Tension reinforcement is permitted to be developed by bending across the neutral axis of the member to be anchored or made continuous with reinforcement on the opposite face of the member.

8.1.6.4.1.2 Critical sections for development of reinforcement in flexural members are at points of maximum steel stress and at points within the span where adjacent reinforcement terminates or is bent.

8.1.6.4.1.3 Reinforcement shall extend beyond the point at which it is no longer required to resist flexure for a distance equal to the effective depth of the member or $12d_b$, whichever is greater, except at supports of simple spans and at the free end of cantilevers.

COMMENTARY

8.1.6.4 *Embedment of flexural reinforcement* — Figure CC-8.1-1 illustrates the embedment requirements of flexural reinforcement in a typical continuous beam. Figure CC-8.1-2 illustrates the embedment requirements in a typical continuous wall that is not part of the lateral-force-resisting system.

8.1.6.4.1 *General*

8.1.6.4.1.2 Critical sections for a typical continuous beam are indicated with a "c" or an "x" in Figure CC-8.1-1. Critical sections for a typical continuous wall are indicated with a "c" in Figure CC-8.1-2.

8.1.6.4.1.3 The moment diagrams customarily used in design are approximate. Some shifting of the location of maximum moments may occur due to changes in loading, settlement of supports, lateral loads, or other causes. A diagonal tension crack in a flexural member without stirrups may shift the location of the calculated tensile stress approximately a distance d toward a point of zero moment. When stirrups are provided, this effect is less severe, although still present.

To provide for shifts in the location of maximum moments, this Code requires the extension of reinforcement a distance d or $12d_b$ beyond the point at which it is theoretically no longer required to resist flexure, except as noted.

Cutoff points of bars to meet this requirement are illustrated in Figure CC-8.1-1.

When bars of different sizes are used, the extension should be in accordance with the diameter of bar being terminated. A bar bent to the far face of a beam and continued there may logically be considered effective in satisfying this section, to the point where the bar crosses the middepth of the member.

COMMENTARY

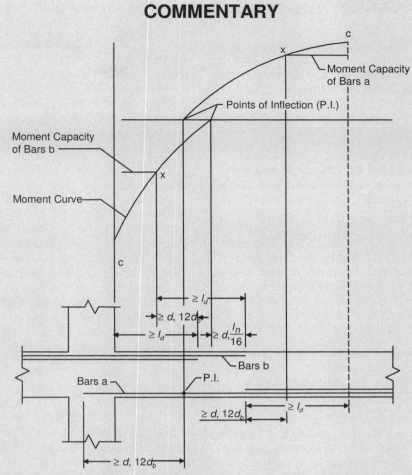

Figure CC-8.1-1 — Development of flexural reinforcement in a typical continuous beam

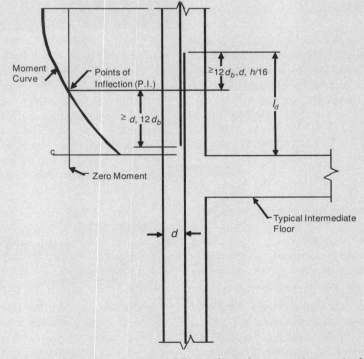

Figure CC-8.1-2 — Development of flexural reinforcement in a typical wall

CODE

8.1.6.4.1.4 Continuing reinforcement shall extend a distance l_d beyond the point where bent or terminated tension reinforcement is no longer required to resist flexure as required by Section 8.1.6.2 or 8.1.6.3.

8.1.6.4.1.5 Flexural reinforcement shall not be terminated in a tension zone unless one of the following conditions is satisfied:

(a) Shear at the cutoff point does not exceed two-thirds of the allowable shear at the section considered.

(b) Stirrup area in excess of that required for shear is provided along each terminated bar or wire over a distance from the termination point equal to three-fourths the effective depth of the member. Excess stirrup area, A_v, shall not be less than $60\, b_w s/f_y$. Spacing s shall not exceed $d/(8\,\beta_b)$.

(c) Continuous reinforcement provides double the area required for flexure at the cutoff point and shear does not exceed three-fourths the allowable shear at the section considered.

8.1.6.4.1.6 Anchorage complying with Section 8.1.6.2 or 8.1.6.3 shall be provided for tension reinforcement in corbels, deep flexural members, variable-depth arches, members where flexural reinforcement is not parallel with the compression face, and in other cases where the stress in flexural reinforcement does not vary linearly through the depth of the section.

8.1.6.4.2 *Development of positive moment reinforcement* — When a wall or other flexural member is part of the lateral-force-resisting system, at least 25 percent of the positive moment reinforcement shall extend into the support and be anchored to develop F_s in tension.

8.1.6.4.3 *Development of negative moment reinforcement*

8.1.6.4.3.1 Negative moment reinforcement in a continuous, restrained, or cantilever member shall be anchored in or through the supporting member in accordance with the provisions of Section 8.1.6.1.

8.1.6.4.3.2 At least one-third of the total reinforcement provided for moment at a support shall extend beyond the point of inflection the greater distance of the effective depth of the member or one-sixteenth of the span.

COMMENTARY

8.1.6.4.1.4 Peak stresses exist in the remaining bars wherever adjacent bars are cut off or bent in tension regions. In Figure CC-8.1-1 an "x" is used to indicate the peak stress points remaining in continuing bars after part of the bars have been cut off. If bars are cut off as short as the moment diagrams allow, these stresses become the full F_s, which requires a full embedment length as indicated. This extension may exceed the length required for flexure.

8.1.6.4.1.5 Evidence of reduced shear strength and loss of ductility when bars are cut off in a tension zone has been reported in Ferguson and Matloob (1959). As a result, the Code does not permit flexural reinforcement to be terminated in a tension zone unless special conditions are satisfied. Flexure cracks tend to open early wherever any reinforcement is terminated in a tension zone. If the stress in the continuing reinforcement and the shear strength are each near their limiting values, diagonal tension cracking tends to develop prematurely from these flexure cracks. Diagonal cracks are less likely to form where shear stress is low. A lower steel stress reduces the probability of such diagonal cracking.

8.1.6.4.1.6 In corbels, deep flexural members, variable-depth arches, members where the tension reinforcement is not parallel with the compression face, or other instances where the steel stress, f_s, in flexural reinforcement does not vary linearly in proportion to the moment, special means of analysis should be used to determine the peak stress for proper development of the flexural reinforcement.

8.1.6.4.2 *Development of positive moment reinforcement* — When a flexural member is part of the lateral-force-resisting system, loads greater than those anticipated in design may cause reversal of moment at supports. As a consequence, some positive reinforcement is required to be anchored into the support. This anchorage assures ductility of response in the event of serious overstress, such as from blast or earthquake. The use of more reinforcement at lower stresses is not sufficient. The full anchorage requirement need not be satisfied for reinforcement exceeding 25 percent of the total that is provided at the support.

8.1.6.4.3 Development of negative moment reinforcement — Negative reinforcement must be properly anchored beyond the support faces by extending the reinforcement ld into the support or by anchoring of the reinforcement with a standard hook or suitable mechanical device.

Section 8.1.6.4.3.2 provides for possible shifting of the moment diagram at a point of inflection, as discussed under Commentary Section 8.1.6.4.1.3. This requirement may exceed that of Section 8.1.6.4.1.3 and the more restrictive governs.

CODE

8.1.6.5 *Hooks*

8.1.6.5.1 Standard hooks in tension shall be considered to develop an equivalent embedment length, l_e, equal to 13 d_b.

8.1.6.5.2 The effect of hooks for bars in compression shall be neglected in design calculations.

8.1.6.6 *Development of shear reinforcement*

8.1.6.6.1 *Bar and wire reinforcement*

8.1.6.6.1.1 Shear reinforcement shall extend to a distance d from the extreme compression face and shall be carried as close to the compression and tension surfaces of the member as cover requirements and the proximity of other reinforcement permit. Shear reinforcement shall be anchored at both ends for its calculated stress.

8.1.6.6.1.2 The ends of single-leg or U-stirrups shall be anchored by one of the following means:

(a) A standard hook plus an effective embedment of 0.5 l_d. The effective embedment of a stirrup leg shall be taken as the distance between the middepth of the member, $d/2$, and the start of the hook (point of tangency).

(b) For No. 5 bar (M #16) and D31 (MD200) wire and smaller, bending around longitudinal reinforcement through at least 135 degrees plus an embedment of 0.33 l_d. The 0.33 l_d embedment of a stirrup leg shall be taken as the distance between middepth of member, $d/2$, and start of hook (point of tangency).

8.1.6.6.1.3 Between the anchored ends, each bend in the continuous portion of a transverse U-stirrup shall enclose a longitudinal bar.

8.1.6.6.1.4 Longitudinal bars bent to act as shear reinforcement, where extended into a region of tension, shall be continuous with longitudinal reinforcement and, where extended into a region of compression, shall be developed beyond middepth of the member, $d/2$.

8.1.6.6.1.5 Pairs of U-stirrups or ties placed to form a closed unit shall be considered properly spliced when length of laps are 1.7 l_d. In grout at least 18 in. (457 mm) deep, such splices with $A_v f_y$ not more than 9,000 lb (40030 N) per leg shall be permitted to be considered adequate if legs extend the full available depth of grout.

COMMENTARY

8.1.6.5 *Hooks*

8.1.6.5.1 Refer to Commentary Section 6.1.5 for more information on hooks.

8.1.6.5.2 In compression, hooks are ineffective and cannot be used as anchorage.

8.1.6.6 *Development of shear reinforcement*
Design and detailing of shear reinforcement locations and anchorage in masonry requires consideration of the masonry module and reinforcement cover and clearance requirements.

8.1.6.6.1 *Bar and wire reinforcement*

8.1.6.6.1.1 Stirrups must be carried as close to the compression face of the member as possible because near ultimate load, flexural tension cracks penetrate deeply.

8.1.6.6.1.2 The requirements for anchorage of U-stirrups for deformed reinforcing bars and deformed wire are illustrated in Figure CC-8.1-3.

(a) When a standard hook is used, 0.5 l_d must be provided between $d/2$ and the point of tangency of the hook.

This provision may require a reduction in size and spacing of web reinforcement, or an increase in the effective depth of the beam, for web reinforcement to be fully effective.

8.1.6.6.1.3 and 8.1.6.6.1.5 U-stirrups that enclose a longitudinal bar have sufficient pullout resistance in the tension zone of the masonry.

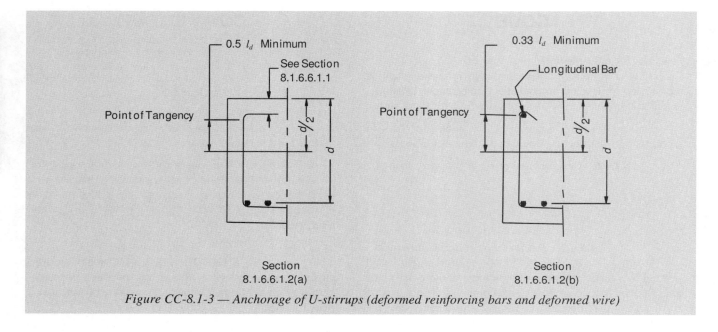

Figure CC-8.1-3 — Anchorage of U-stirrups (deformed reinforcing bars and deformed wire)

CODE

8.1.6.6.2 *Welded wire reinforcement*
8.1.6.6.2.1 For each leg of welded wire reinforcement forming simple U-stirrups, there shall be either:

(a) Two longitudinal wires at a 2-in. (50.8-mm) spacing along the member at the top of the U, or

(b) One longitudinal wire located not more than $d/4$ from the compression face and a second wire closer to the compression face and spaced at least 2 in. (50.8 mm) from the first wire. The second wire shall be located on the stirrup leg beyond a bend, or on a bend with an inside diameter of bend at least $8d_b$.

8.1.6.6.2.2 For each end of a single-leg stirrup of plain or deformed welded wire reinforcement, there shall be two longitudinal wires spaced a minimum of 2 in. (50.8 mm) with the inner wire placed at a distance at least $d/4$ or 2 in. (50.8 mm) from middepth of member, $d/2$. Outer longitudinal wire at tension face shall not be farther from the face than the portion of primary flexural reinforcement closest to the face.

8.1.6.7 *Splices of reinforcement* — Lap splices, welded splices, or mechanical splices are permitted in accordance with the provisions of this section.

COMMENTARY

8.1.6.6.2 *Welded wire reinforcement* — Although not often used in masonry construction, welded wire reinforcement provides a convenient means of placing reinforcement in a filled collar joint. See PCI (1980) for more information.

8.1.6.7 *Splices of reinforcement* — Continuity of reinforcement through proper splicing is necessary to provide force transfer. Effective splices can be provided through various forms: lap splices, welded splices or mechanical splices.

CODE

8.1.6.7.1 *Lap splices*

8.1.6.7.1.1 The minimum length of lap for bars in tension or compression shall be determined by Equation 8-12, but not less than 12 in. (305 mm).

8.1.6.7.1.2 Where reinforcement consisting of No. 3 (M#10) or larger bars is placed transversely within the lap, with at least one bar 8 in. (203 mm) or less from each end of the lap, the minimum length of lap for bars in tension or compression determined by Equation 8-12 shall be permitted to be reduced by multiplying by the confinement factor, ξ, determined in accordance with Equation 8-13. The clear space between the transverse bars and the lapped bars shall not exceed 1.5 in. (38 mm) and the transverse bars shall be fully developed in grouted masonry. The reduced lap splice length shall not be less than $36d_b$.

$$\xi = 1.0 - \frac{2.3 A_{sc}}{d_b^{2.5}} \qquad \text{(Equation 8-13)}$$

$$\text{Where}: \frac{2.3 A_{sc}}{d_b^{2.5}} \le 1.0$$

A_{sc} is the area of the transverse bars at each end of the lap splice and shall not be taken greater than 0.35 in.^{2} (226 mm^2).

8.1.6.7.1.3 Bars spliced by noncontact lap splices shall not be spaced transversely farther apart than one-fifth the required length of lap nor more than 8 in. (203 mm).

8.1.6.7.2 *Welded splices* — Welded splices shall have the bars butted and welded to develop in tension at least 125 percent of the specified yield strength of the bar. Welding shall conform to AWS D1.4/D1.4M. Reinforcement to be welded shall conform to ASTM A706, or shall be accompanied by a submittal showing its chemical analysis and carbon equivalent as required by AWS D1.4/D1.4M. Existing reinforcement to be welded shall conform to ASTM A706, or shall be analyzed chemically and its carbon equivalent determined as required by AWS D1.4/D1.4M.

COMMENTARY

8.1.6.7.1 *Lap splices* — The required length of the lap splice is based on developing a minimum reinforcing bar stress of 1.25 f_y. This requirement provides adequate strength while maintaining consistent requirements between lap, mechanical, and welded splices. Historically, the length of lap has been based on the bond stress that is capable of being developed between the reinforcing bar and the surrounding grout. Testing has shown that bond stress failure (or pull-out of the reinforcing bar) is only one possible mode of failure for lap splices. Other failure modes include rupture of the reinforcing bar and longitudinal splitting of masonry along the length of the lap. Experimental results of several independent research programs were combined and analyzed to provide insight into predicting the necessary lap lengths for reinforcing bar splices in masonry construction (Hogan et al, 1997). Equation 8-12 was fitted to the data and has a coefficient of determination, r^2, value of 0.93.

8.1.6.7.1.2 An extensive testing program conducted by the National Concrete Masonry Association (NCMA, 2009) and additional testing done by Washington State University (Mjelde et al, 2009) show that reinforcement provided transverse to lapped bars controls longitudinal tensile splitting of the masonry assembly. These tranverse bars increase the lap performance significantly, as long as there is at least one No. 3 (M#10) transverse reinforcing bar placed within 8 in. (203 mm) of each end of the splice. These bars must be fully developed and have a clear spacing between the transverse bars and the lapped bars not exceeding 1.5 in. (38 mm). Testing also indicated that the lap length must be at least $36d_b$ or the effect of the transverse reinforcement is minimal. As a result, this limit was applied to the lap length. The testing also showed that even when more transverse reinforcement area is provided, it becomes significantly less effective in quantities above 0.35 in.^{2} (226 mm^2). Thus, the transervse reinforcement area at each end of the lap, A_{sc}, is limited to 0.35 in.^{2} (226 mm^2), even if more is provided.

8.1.6.7.1.3 If individual bars in noncontact lap splices are too widely spaced, an unreinforced section is created, which forces a potential crack to follow a diagonal line. Lap splices may occur with the bars in adjacent grouted cells if the requirements of this section are met.

8.1.6.7.2 *Welded splices* — A full welded splice is primarily intended for large bars (No. 6 [M#19] and larger) in main members. The tensile strength requirement of 125 percent of specified yield strength is intended to ensure sound welding, adequate also for compression. It is desirable that splices be capable of developing the ultimate tensile strength of the bars spliced, but practical limitations make this ideal condition difficult to attain. The maximum reinforcement stress used in design under this Code is based upon yield strength. To ensure sufficient strength in splices so that brittle failure can be avoided, the 25 percent increase

CODE

COMMENTARY

above the specified yield strength was selected as both an adequate minimum for safety and a practicable maximum for economy.

When welding of reinforcing bars is required, the weldability of the steel and compatible welding procedures need to be considered. The provisions in AWS D1.4/D1.4M Welding Code cover aspects of welding reinforcing bars, including criteria to qualify welding procedures. Weldability of the steel is based on its chemical composition or carbon equivalent (CE). The Welding Code establishes preheat and interpass temperatures for a range of carbon equivalents and reinforcing bar sizes. Carbon equivalent is calculated from the chemical composition of the reinforcing bars. The Welding Code has two expressions for calculating carbon equivalent. A relatively short expression, considering only the elements carbon and manganese, is to be used for bars other than ASTM A706 material. A more comprehensive expression is given for ASTM A706 bars. The CE formula in the Welding Code for ASTM A706 bars is identical to the CE formula in ASTM A706.

The chemical analysis, for bars other than ASTM A706, required to calculate the carbon equivalent is not routinely provided by the producer of the reinforcing bars. For welding reinforcing bars other than ASTM A706 bars, the design drawings or project specifications should specifically require results of the chemical analysis to be furnished.

ASTM A706 covers low-alloy steel reinforcing bars intended for applications requiring controlled tensile properties or welding. Weldability is accomplished in ASTM A706 by limits or controls on chemical composition and on carbon equivalent (Gustafson and Felder, 1991). The producer is required by ASTM A706 to report the chemical composition and carbon equivalent.

The AWS D1.4/D1.4M Welding Code requires the contractor to prepare written welding procedure specifications conforming to the requirements of the Welding Code. Appendix A of the Welding Code contains a suggested form that shows the information required for such a specification for each joint welding procedure.

Welding to existing reinforcing bars is often necessary even though no mill test report of the existing reinforcement is available. This condition is particularly common in alterations or building expansions. AWS D1.4/D1.4M states for such bars that a chemical analysis may be performed on representative bars. If the chemical composition is not known or obtained, the Welding Code requires a minimum preheat. Welding of the particular bars should be performed in accordance with AWS D1.4/D1.4M, including their preheat. The designer should also determine if additional precautions are in order, based on other considerations such as stress level in the bars, consequences of failure, and heat damage to existing masonry due to welding operations.

CODE

COMMENTARY

Welding of wire to wire, and of wire or welded wire reinforcement to reinforcing bars or structural steel elements is not covered by AWS D1.4/D1.4M. If welding of this type is required on a project, the contract documents should specify requirements or performance criteria for this welding. If cold drawn wires are to be welded, the welding procedures should address the potential loss of yield strength and ductility achieved by the cold working process (during manufacture) when such wires are heated by welding. Machine and resistance welding as used in the manufacture of welded plain and deformed wire reinforcement is covered by ASTM A185 and ASTM A497, respectively, and is not part of this concern.

8.1.6.7.3 *Mechanical splices* — Mechanical splices shall have the bars connected to develop in tension or compression, as required, at least 125 percent of the specified yield strength of the bar.

8.1.6.7.3 *Mechanical splices* — Full mechanical splices are also required to develop 125 percent of the specified yield strength in tension or compression as required, for the same reasons discussed for full welded splices.

8.1.6.7.4 *End-bearing splices*
8.1.6.7.4.1 In bars required for compression only, the transmission of compressive stress by bearing of square cut ends held in concentric contact by a suitable device is permitted.

8.1.6.7.4 *End-bearing splices* — Experience with end-bearing splices has been almost exclusively with vertical bars in columns. If bars are significantly inclined from the vertical, special attention is required to ensure that adequate end-bearing contact can be achieved and maintained. The lateral tie requirements prevent end-bearing splices from sliding.

8.1.6.7.4.2 Bar ends shall terminate in flat surfaces within $1^1/_2$ degree of a right angle to the axis of the bars and shall be fitted within 3 degrees of full bearing after assembly.

8.1.6.7.4.3 End-bearing splices shall be used only in members containing closed ties, closed stirrups, or spirals.

8.1.6.7.5 *Splicing of wires in tension*
8.1.6.7.5.1 *Lap splices* — The minimum length of lap for wires in tension shall be determined by Equation 8-11, but shall not be less than 6 in. (152 mm).

8.1.6.7.5.2 *Welded splices* — Welded splices shall have the wires welded to develop at least 125 percent of the specified yield strength of the wire in tension.

8.1.6.7.5.2 *Welded splices* — If welded splices are required on a project, the contract documents should specify requirements or performance criteria for the welding. If cold drawn wires are to be welded, the welding procedures should address the potential loss of yield strength and ductility achieved by the cold working process (manufacturing) when such wires are heated by welding. Machine and resistance welding, as used in the manufacture of welded plain and deformed wire reinforcement, is covered by ASTM A185 and ASTM A497, respectively, and by ASTM A951 for joint reinforcement.

8.1.6.7.5.3 *Mechanical splices* — Mechanical splices shall have the wires connected to develop at least 125 percent of the specified yield strength of the wire in tension.

CODE

8.2 — Unreinforced masonry

8.2.1 *Scope*
This section provides requirements for the design of unreinforced masonry as defined in Section 2.2. Design of unreinforced masonry by the allowable stress method shall comply with the requirements of Part 1, Part 2, Section 8.1, and Section 8.2.

8.2.2 *Design criteria*
Unreinforced masonry members shall be designed in accordance with the principles of engineering mechanics and shall be designed to remain uncracked.

8.2.3 *Design assumptions*
The following assumptions shall be used in the design of unreinforced masonry members:

(a) Strain in masonry is directly proportional to the distance from the neutral axis.

(b) Flexural tensile stress in masonry is directly proportional to strain.

(c) Flexural compressive stress in combination with axial compressive stress in masonry is directly proportional to strain.

(d) Stresses in reinforcement, if present, are neglected when determining the resistance of masonry to design loads.

8.2.4 *Axial compression and flexure*
8.2.4.1 *Axial and flexural compression* — Members subjected to axial compression, flexure, or to combined axial compression and flexure shall be designed to satisfy Equation 8-14 and Equation 8-15.

$$\frac{f_a}{F_a} + \frac{f_b}{F_b} \le 1 \qquad \text{(Equation 8-14)}$$

$$P \le \left(\tfrac{1}{4}\right) P_e \qquad \text{(Equation 8-15)}$$

where:

(a) For members having an h/r ratio not greater than 99:

$$F_a = \left(\tfrac{1}{4}\right) f'_m \left[1 - \left(\frac{h}{140r}\right)^2\right] \qquad \text{(Equation 8-16)}$$

(b) For members having an h/r ratio greater than 99:

$$F_a = \left(\tfrac{1}{4}\right) f'_m \left(\frac{70r}{h}\right)^2 \qquad \text{(Equation 8-17)}$$

(c) $F_b = \left(\tfrac{1}{3}\right) f'_m$ \qquad (Equation 8-18)

COMMENTARY

8.2 — Unreinforced masonry

8.2.1 *Scope*
This section provides for the design of masonry members in which tensile stresses, not exceeding allowable limits, are resisted by the masonry. This has previously been referred to as unreinforced or plain masonry. Flexural tensile stresses may result from bending moments, from eccentric vertical loads, or from lateral loads.

8.2.2 *Design criteria*
A fundamental premise is that under the effects of design loads, masonry remains uncracked. Stresses due to restraint against differential movement, temperature change, moisture expansion, and shrinkage combine with the design load stresses. Stresses due to restraint should be controlled by joints or other construction techniques to ensure that the combined stresses do not exceed the allowable.

8.2.3 *Design assumptions*
Reinforcement may be placed in masonry walls to control the effects of movements from temperature changes or shrinkage, or as prescriptive seismic reinforcement. This reinforcement is not considered in calculating strength when using unreinforced masonry design.

8.2.4 *Axial compression and flexure*
8.2.4.1 *Axial and flexural compression* — Equation (8-14) is a unity interaction equation that is a simple proportioning of the available allowable stresses to the applied loads, and the equation is used to design masonry for combined axial and flexural compressive stresses. The unity equation can be expanded when biaxial bending is present by adding a third term for the bending stress quotient about the second axis of bending.

In this unity interaction equation, secondary bending effects resulting from the axial load are ignored. A more accurate equation would include the use of a moment magnifier applied to the flexure term, f_b/F_b. Although avoidance of a moment magnifier term can produce unconservative results in some cases, the committee decided not to include this term in Equation 8-14 for the following reasons:

- At larger h/r values, where moment magnification is more critical, the allowable axial load on the member is limited by Code Equation 8-15.

- For the practical range of h/r values, errors induced by ignoring the moment magnifier is relatively small, less than 15 percent.

CODE

(d) $P_e = \dfrac{\pi^2 E_m I_n}{h^2}\left(1 - 0.577\dfrac{e}{r}\right)^3$ (Equation 8-19)

COMMENTARY

- The overall safety factor of 4 included in the allowable stress equations is sufficiently large to allow this simplification in the design procedure.

The purpose of Equation 8-15 is to safeguard against a premature stability failure caused by eccentrically applied axial load. The equation is not intended to be used to check adequacy for combined axial compression and flexure. Therefore, in Equation 8-19, the value of the eccentricity "e" that is to be used to calculate P_e is the actual eccentricity of the applied compressive load. The value of "e" is not to be calculated as M_{max} divided by P where M_{max} is a moment caused by other than eccentric load.

Equation 8-15 is an essential check because the allowable compressive stress for members with an h/r ratio in excess of 99 has been developed assuming only a nominal eccentricity of the compressive load. Thus, when the eccentricity of the compressive load exceeds the minimum eccentricity of $0.1t$, Equation 8-17 will overestimate the allowable compressive stress and Equation 8-15 may control.

The allowable stress values for F_a presented in Equations 8-16 and 8-17 are based on an analysis of the results of axial load tests performed on clay and concrete masonry elements. A fit of an empirical curve to this test data, Figure CC-8.2-1, indicates that members having an h/r ratio not exceeding 99 fail under loads below the Euler buckling load at a stress level equal to:

$$f_m'\left[1 - (h/140r)^2\right]$$ (same with SI units)

Thus, for members having an h/r ratio not exceeding 99, this Code allows axial load stresses not exceeding $^1/_4$ of the aforementioned failure stress.

Applying the Euler theory of buckling to members having resistance in compression but not in tension, (Colville, 1978; Colville, 1979; Yokel, 1971) show that for a solid section, the critical compressive load for these members can be expressed by the formula

$$P_e = (\pi^2 E_m I_n / h^2)(1 - 2e/t)^3$$ (same with SI units)

in which

I_n =   uncracked moment of inertia

e =   eccentricity of axial compressive load with respect to the member longitudinal centroidal axis.

In the derivation of this buckling load equation, tension cracking is assumed to occur prior to failure.

For h/r values in excess of 99, the limited test data is approximated by the buckling load.

For a solid rectangular section, $r = \sqrt{t^2/12}$. Making this substitution into the buckling load equation gives

CODE

COMMENTARY

$$P_e = \frac{\pi^2 E_m I_n}{h^2}\left(1 - 0.577\frac{e}{r}\right)^3 \qquad \text{(Equation 8-19)}$$

Transforming the buckling equation using a minimum eccentricity of $0.1t$ (from Section 8.3.4.3) and an elastic modulus equal to $1000\,f'_m$, the axial compressive stress at buckling failure amounts approximately to $[70(r/h)]^2 f'_m$. At the time of the development of this equation, the committee had not developed a relationship between E_m and f'_m so the traditional relationship of $E_m = 1000\,f'_m$ was used (Colville, 1992). The same equation can be developed using $E_m = 667\,f'_m$ and an eccentricity of $0.05t$. Thus, for members having an h/r ratio in excess of 99, this Code allows an axial load compressive stress not exceeding $^1\!/_4$ of this failure stress (Equation 8-17).

Tests of masonry have shown (Hatzinikolas et al, 1978; Fattal and Cattaneo, 1976; Yokel and Dikkers, 1971; Yokel and Dikkers, 1973) that the maximum compressive stress at failure under flexural load is higher than the maximum compressive stress at failure under axial load. The higher stress under flexural load is attributed to the restraining effect of less highly strained compressive fibers on the fibers of maximum compressive strain. This effect is less pronounced in hollow masonry than solid masonry; however, the test data indicate that, calculated by the straight-line theory, the compressive stress at failure in hollow masonry subjected to flexure exceeds by $^1\!/_3$ that of the masonry under axial load. Thus, to maintain a factor of safety of 4 in design, the committee considered it conservative to establish the allowable compressive stress in flexure as:

$$F_b = {}^4\!/_3 \times ({}^1\!/_4)f'_m = ({}^1\!/_3)f'_m$$

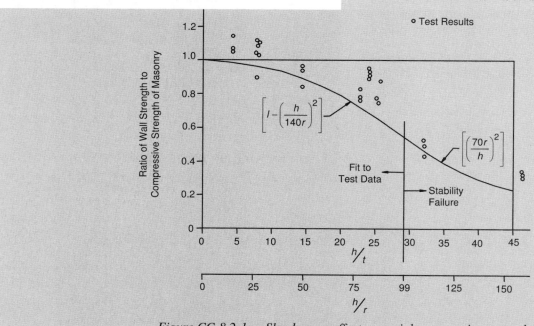

Figure CC-8.2-1 — Slenderness effects on axial compressive strength

CODE

8.2.4.2 *Flexural tension* — Allowable tensile stresses for masonry elements subjected to out-of-plane or in-plane bending shall be in accordance with the values in Table 8.2.4.2. For grouted masonry not laid in running bond, tension parallel to the bed joints shall be assumed to be resisted only by the minimum cross-sectional area of continuous grout that is parallel to the bed joints.

COMMENTARY

8.2.4.2 *Flexural tension* — Prior to the 2011 edition of the Code, allowable stresses were permitted to be increased by one-third when considering load combinations including wind or seismic loads. Unreinforced masonry walls designed under codes that permitted the one-third stress increase have had acceptable performance. However, rather than arbitrarily increasing the allowable flexural tensile stresses by one-third, the Committee assessed the allowable flexural tensile stresses using a reliability-based approach to see if an increase in allowable stresses is justified. Kim and Bennett (2002) performed a reliability analysis in which the flexural tensile stress was assumed to follow a lognormal distribution. They used a mean flexural tensile strength of the allowable flexural tensile stress in the 2008 Code multiplied by 5.1 based on the examination of 327 full-scale tests reported in the literature. Coefficients of variations for different data sets (e.g specific mortar type and direction of loading) ranged from 0.10 to 0.51, with a weighted average of 0.42. The coefficient of variation of 0.50 used by Kim and Bennett (2002) is greater than used in previous studies. For example, Ellingwood et al (1980) used a coefficient of variation of 0.24 and Stewart and Lawrence (2000) used a coefficient of variation of 0.30. Kim and Bennett felt, though, that a coefficient of variation of 0.50 is more representative of field conditions. The lognormal distribution was determined by comparing the Anderson-Darling statistic for normal, lognormal, and Weibull probability distributions. For unreinforced masonry walls subjected to wind loading and designed using the one-third stress increase, the reliability index was determined to be 2.66. This is slightly greater than the value of 2.5 that is typical for the design of other materials (Ellingwood et al, 1980). The reliability analysis by Kim and Bennett (2002) assumed the axial load was zero, which is the worst case. With increasing axial load (which has a lower coefficient of variation than 0.50), the reliability index would increase. Based on this reliability analysis, the Code committee felt justified in increasing the allowable flexural tensile stresses by a factor of 4/3 to compensate for the elimination of the previously permitted one-third stress increase.

The allowable tensile strength values are a function of the type of mortar being used. Mortar cement is a product that has bond strength requirements that have been established to provide comparable flexural bond strength to that achieved using portland cement-lime mortar (Melander and Ghosh, 1996; Hedstrom et al, 1991; Borchelt and Tann, 1996).

For masonry cement and air entrained portland-cement lime mortar, there are no conclusive research data and, hence, flexural tensile stresses are based on existing requirements in other codes.

Table 8.2.4.2 — Allowable flexural tensile stresses for clay and concrete masonry, psi (kPa)

Direction of flexural tensile stress and masonry type	Mortar types			
	Portland cement/lime or mortar cement		Masonry cement or air entrained portland cement/lime	
	M or S	N	M or S	N
Normal to bed joints				
Solid units	53 (366)	40 (276)	32 (221)	20 (138)
Hollow units[1]				
Ungrouted	33 (228)	25 (172)	20 (138)	12 (83)
Fully grouted	65 (448)	63 (434)	61 (420)	58 (400)
Parallel to bed joints in running bond				
Solid units	106 (731)	80 (552)	64 (441)	40 (276)
Hollow units				
Ungrouted and partially grouted	66 (455)	50 (345)	40 (276)	25 (172)
Fully grouted	106 (731)	80 (552)	64 (441)	40 (276)
Parallel to bed joints in masonry not laid in running bond				
Continuous grout section parallel to bed joints	133 (917)	133 (917)	133 (917)	133 (917)
Other	0 (0)	0 (0)	0 (0)	0 (0)

1 For partially grouted masonry, allowable stresses shall be determined on the basis of linear interpolation between fully grouted hollow units and ungrouted hollow units based on amount (percentage) of grouting.

CODE

COMMENTARY

The allowable tensile stresses are for tension stresses due to flexure under either out-of-plane or in-plane loading. While it is recognized that in-plane and out-of-plane strain gradients are different, for these low stress levels the effect due to any difference is small. Flexural tensile stress can be offset by axial compressive stress, but the net tensile stress due to combined bending and axial compression cannot exceed the allowable flexural tensile stress.

Variables affecting tensile bond strength of brick masonry normal to bed joints include mortar properties, unit initial rate of absorption, surface condition, workmanship, and curing condition. For tension parallel to bed joints, the strength and geometry of the units also affect tensile strength.

Historically, masonry not laid in running bond has been assumed to have no flexural bond strength across mortared head joints; thus the grout area alone is used to resist bending. Examples of continuous grout parallel to the bed joints are shown in Figure CC-8.2-2.

CODE

COMMENTARY

Test data using a bond wrench (Brown and Palm, 1982; Hamid, 1985) revealed tensile bond strength normal to bed joints ranging from 30 psi (207 kPa) to 190 psi (1,310 kPa). This wide range is attributed to the multitude of parameters affecting tensile bond strength.

Test results (Hamid, 1985; Ribar, 1982) show that masonry cement mortars and mortars with high air content generally have lower bond strength than portland cement-lime mortars.

Tests conducted by Hamid (1981) show the significant effect of the aspect ratio (height to least dimension) of the brick unit on the flexural tensile strength. The increase in the aspect ratio of the unit results in an increase in strength parallel to bed joints and a decrease in strength normal to bed joints.

Research work (Drysdale and Hamid, 1984) on flexural strength of concrete masonry has shown that grouting has a significant effect in increasing tensile strength over ungrouted masonry. A three-fold increase in tensile strength normal to bed joints was achieved using fine grout as compared to ungrouted masonry. The results also show that, within a practical range of strength, the actual strength of grout is not of major importance. For tension parallel to bed joints, a 133 percent increase in flexural strength was achieved by grouting the cells. Grout cores change the failure mode from stepped-wise cracking along the bed and head joints for hollow walls to a straight line path along the head joints and unit for grouted walls.

Research (Brown and Melander, 1999) has shown that flexural strength of unreinforced, grouted concrete and clay masonry is largely independent of mortar type or cementitious materials.

For partial grouting, the footnote to Table 8.2.4.2 permits interpolation between the fully grouted value and the hollow unit value based on the percentage of grouting. A concrete masonry wall with Type S portland cement-lime mortar grouted 50 percent and stressed normal to the bed joints would have an allowable stress midway between 86 psi (593 kPa) and 33 psi (228 kPa), hence an allowable stress of 59.5 psi (410 kPa).

The presence of flashing and other conditions at the base of the wall can significantly reduce the flexural bond. The values in Table 8.2.4.2 apply only to the flexural tensile stresses developed between masonry units, mortar, and grout.

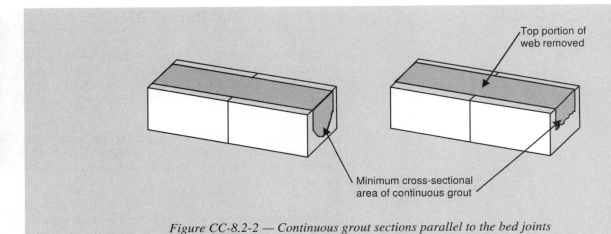

Figure CC-8.2-2 — Continuous grout sections parallel to the bed joints

Top portion of
web removed

Minimum cross-sectional
area of continuous grout

CODE

8.2.5 *Axial tension*
Axial tension resistance of unreinforced masonry shall
be neglected in design.

8.2.6 *Shear*

8.2.6.1 Shear stresses due to forces acting in the
direction considered shall be calculated in accordance with
Section 4.3.1 and determined by Equation 8-20.

$$f_v = \frac{VQ}{I_n b} \quad \text{(Equation 8-20)}$$

COMMENTARY

8.2.5 *Axial tension*
Net axial tension in unreinforced masonry walls due to
axially applied load is not permitted. If axial tension
develops in walls due to uplift of connected roofs or floors,
the walls must be reinforced to resist the tension.
Compressive stress from dead load can be used to offset
axial tension.

8.2.6 *Shear*
Three modes of shear failure in unreinforced masonry
are possible:

(a) Diagonal tension cracks form through the mortar and
masonry units.

(b) Sliding occurs along a straight crack at horizontal bed
joints.

(c) Cracks form, that stair-step from head joint to bed
joint.

In the absence of suitable research data, the committee
recommends that the allowable shear stress values given in
Code Section 8.2.6.2 be used for limiting out-of-plane shear
stresses.

8.2.6.1 A theoretical parabolic stress
distribution is used to define shear stress through the depth.
Some other codes use average shear stress so direct
comparison of allowable values is not valid. Effective area
requirements are given in Section 4.3.1. For rectangular
sections, Equation (8-20) produces a maximum shear stress
at mid-depth, that is equal to $^3/_2 \times V/A$. Equation (8-20) is
also used to calculate shear stresses for composite action
and shear stresses, resulting from out-of-plane loading, in
the connections between face shells of hollow units.

CODE

8.2.6.2 In-plane shear stresses shall not exceed any of:

(a) $1.5 \sqrt{f'_m}$

(b) 120 psi (0.827 MPa)

(c) For running bond masonry not fully grouted;

   $37 \text{ psi} + 0.45 \, N_v/A_n$

(d) For masonry not laid in running bond, constructed of open end units, and fully grouted;

   $37 \text{ psi} + 0.45 \, N_v/A_n$

(e) For running bond masonry fully grouted;

   $60 \text{ psi} + 0.45 \, N_v/A_n$

(f) For masonry not laid in running bond, constructed of other than open end units, and fully grouted;

   15 psi (103 kPa)

8.2.6.3 The minimum normalized web area of concrete masonry units, determined in accordance with ASTM C140, shall not be less than 27 in.^{2}/ft^2 (187,500 mm^2/m^2) or the calculated shear stresses in the webs shall not exceed the value given in Section 8.2.6.2(a).

COMMENTARY

8.2.6.2 Shear stress allowable values are applicable to shear walls without reinforcement. The values given are based on research (Woodward and Ranking, 1984; Pook, 1986; Nuss et al, 1978; Hamid et al, 1979). N_v is normally based on dead load.

8.2.6.3 Out-of-plane flexure causes horizontal and vertical shear stresses. Vertical shear stresses are resisted by the connection between the web and face shell of the unit. A normalized web area of 27 in.^{2}/ft^2 (187,500 mm^2/m^2) provides sufficient web area so that shear stresses between the web and face shell of a unit, resulting from out-of-plane loading, will not be critical.

CODE

8.3 — Reinforced masonry

8.3.1 *Scope*

This section provides requirements for the design of structures in which reinforcement is used to resist tensile forces in accordance with the principles of engineering mechanics and the contribution of the tensile strength of masonry is neglected, except as provided in Section 8.3.5. Design of reinforced masonry by the allowable stress method shall comply with the requirements of Part 1, Part 2, Section 8.1, and Section 8.3

8.3.2 *Design assumptions*

The following assumptions shall be used in the design of reinforced masonry:

(a) Strain compatibility exists between the reinforcement, grout, and masonry.

(b) Strains in reinforcement and masonry are directly proportional to the distances from the neutral axis.

(c) Stress is linearly proportional to the strain.

(d) The compressive resistance of steel reinforcement does not contribute to the axial and flexural strengths unless lateral reinforcement is provided in compliance with the requirements of Section 5.3.1.4.

(e) Stresses remain in the elastic range.

(f) Masonry in tension does not contribute to axial and flexural resistances. Axial and flexural tension stresses are resisted entirely by steel reinforcement.

8.3.3 *Steel reinforcement — Allowable stresses*

8.3.3.1 Tensile stress in bar reinforcement shall not exceed the following:

(a) Grade 40 or Grade 50 reinforcement: 20,000   psi (137.9 MPa)

(b) Grade 60 reinforcement: 32,000 psi (220.7 MPa)

8.3.3.2 Tensile stress in wire joint reinforcement shall not exceed 30,000 psi (206.9 MPa).

8.3.3.3 When lateral reinforcement is provided in compliance with the requirements of Section 5.3.1.4, the compressive stress in bar reinforcement shall not exceed the values given in Section 8.3.3.1.

8.3.4 *Axial compression and flexure*

8.3.4.1 Members subjected to axial compression, flexure, or combined axial compression and flexure shall be designed in compliance with Sections 8.3.4.2 through 8.3.4.4.

COMMENTARY

8.3 — Reinforced masonry

8.3.1 *Scope*

The requirements in this section pertain to the design of masonry in which flexural tension is assumed to be resisted by reinforcement alone, and the flexural tensile strength of masonry is neglected. Tension still develops in the masonry, but it is not considered to be effective in resisting design loads.

8.3.2 *Design assumptions*

The design assumptions listed have traditionally been used for allowable stress design of reinforced masonry members.

Although tension may develop in the masonry of a reinforced element, it is not considered effective in resisting axial and flexural design loads.

8.3.3 *Steel reinforcement — Allowable stresses —*
The allowable steel stresses have a sufficiently large factor of safety that second-order effects do not need to be considered in allowable stress design.

8.3.4 *Axial compression and flexure*
See Commentary for 8.2.4.1.

CODE

8.3.4.2 *Allowable forces and stresses*

8.3.4.2.1 The compressive force in reinforced masonry due to axial load only shall not exceed that given by Equation 8-21 or Equation 8-22:

(a) For members having an *h/r* ratio not greater than 99:

$$P_a = \left(0.25 f'_m A_n + 0.65 A_{st} F_s\right)\left[1 - \left(\frac{h}{140r}\right)^2\right]$$

(Equation 8-21)

(b) For members having an *h/r* ratio greater than 99:

$$P_a = \left(0.25 f'_m A_n + 0.65 A_{st} F_s\right)\left(\frac{70r}{h}\right)^2 \quad \text{(Equation 8-22)}$$

8.3.4.2.2 The compressive stress in masonry due to flexure or due to flexure in combination with axial load shall not exceed $0.45 f'_m$ provided that the calculated compressive stress due to the axial load component, f_a, does not exceed the allowable stress, F_a, in Section 8.2.4.1.

COMMENTARY

8.3.4.2 *Allowable forces and stresses* — This Code limits the compressive stress in masonry members based on the type of load acting on the member. The compressive force at the section resulting from axial loads or from the axial component of combined loads is calculated separately, and is limited to the values permitted in Section 8.3.4.2.1. Equation 8-21 or 8-22 controls the capacity of columns with large axial loads. The coefficient of 0.25 provides a factor of safety of about 4.0 against crushing of masonry. The coefficient of 0.65 was determined from tests of reinforced masonry columns and is taken from previous masonry codes (ACI 531, 1983; BIA, 1969). A second compressive stress calculation must be performed considering the combined effects of the axial load component and flexure at the section and should be limited to the values permitted in Section 8.3.4.2.2. (See Commentary for Section 8.2.4.)

8.3.4.2.2 Figure CC-8.3-1 shows the allowable moment (independent of member size and material strength) versus the ratio of steel reinforcement (Grade 60) multiplied by the steel yield strength and divided by the specified compressive strength of masonry (modified steel reinforcement ratio) for both clay and concrete masonry members subjected to pure flexure. When the masonry compressive stress controls the design, there is little increase in moment capacity with increasing steel reinforcement. This creates a limit on the amount of reinforcement that is practical to use in allowable stress design of masonry. Even when the masonry allowable compressive stress controls the design, the failure of the member will still be ductile. For clay masonry, the masonry stress begins to control the design at $0.39\rho_{bal}$ and for concrete masonry, the masonry stress begins to control the design at $0.38\rho_{bal}$, where ρ_{bal} is the reinforcement ratio at which the masonry would crush simultaneously with yielding of the reinforcement. The reinforcement ratio as a fraction of the balanced reinforcement ratio, ρ_{bal}, is also shown in Figure CC-8.3-1.

The interaction equation used in Section 8.2.4 is not applicable for reinforced masonry and is therefore not included in Section 8.3.

CODE

8.3.4.3 *Columns* — Design axial loads shall be assumed to act at an eccentricity at least equal to 0.1 multiplied by each side dimension. Each axis shall be considered independently.

COMMENTARY

8.3.4.3 *Columns* — The minimum eccentricity of axial load (Figure CC-8.3-2) results from construction imperfections not otherwise anticipated by analysis.

In the event that actual eccentricity exceeds the minimum eccentricity required by this Code, the actual eccentricity should be used. This Code requires that stresses be checked independently about each principal axis of the member (Figure CC-8.3-2).

Additional column design and detailing requirements are given in Section 5.3.

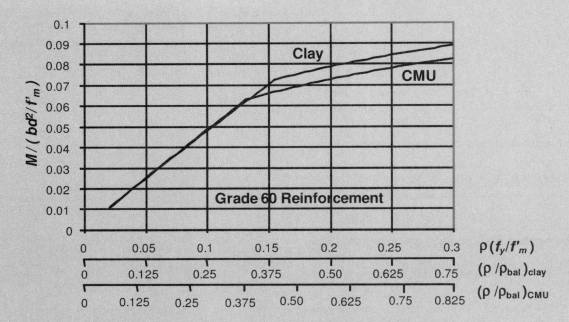

Figure CC-8.3-1 Allowable moment vs. modified steel reinforcement ratio

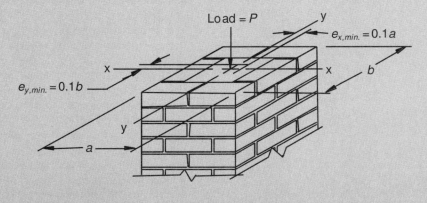

Load Acting at Centroid

Figure CC-8.3-2 — Minimum design eccentricity in columns

CODE

8.3.4.4 *Walls* — Special reinforced masonry shear walls having a shear span ratio, $M/(Vd_v)$, equal to or greater than 1.0 and having an axial load, P, greater than $0.05f'_m A_n$, which are subjected to in-plane forces, shall have a maximum ratio of flexural tensile reinforcement, ρ_{max}, not greater than that calculated as follows:

$$\rho_{max} = \frac{nf'_m}{2f_y\left(n+\dfrac{f_y}{f'_m}\right)} \qquad \text{(Equation 8-23)}$$

The maximum reinforcement ratio does not apply in the out-of-plane direction.

8.3.5 *Shear*

8.3.5.1 Members shall be designed in accordance with Sections 8.3.5.1.1 through 8.3.5.1.4.

8.3.5.1.1 Calculated shear stress in the masonry shall be determined by the relationship:

$$f_v = \frac{V}{A_{nv}} \qquad \text{(Equation 8-24)}$$

COMMENTARY

8.3.4.4 *Walls* — The balanced reinforcement ratio for a masonry element with a single layer of reinforcement designed by allowable stress design can be derived by applying principles of engineering mechanics to a cracked, transformed section. The resulting equation is:

$$\rho_b = \frac{nF_b}{2F_s\left(n+\dfrac{F_s}{F_b}\right)}$$

where ρ_b is the balanced reinforcement ratio resulting in a condition in which the reinforcement and the masonry simultaneously reach their specified allowable stresses. However, the ratio of allowable steel tensile stress to the specified yield strength of the reinforcement, and the ratio of allowable masonry compressive stress to the specified compressive strength of the masonry are not consistent (F_s can range from 40 percent to 53 percent of f_y while F_b is taken equal to $0.45f'_m$). Therefore, allowable stresses in the equation above are replaced with the corresponding specified strengths, as shown in Code Equation 8-23.

The equation is directly applicable for reinforcement concentrated at the end of the shear wall. For distributed reinforcement, the reinforcement ratio is obtained as the total area of tension reinforcement divided by bd.

8.3.5 *Shear*

Prior to the 2011 edition of the Code, the shear resistance provided by the masonry was not added to the shear resistance provided by the shear reinforcement (in allowable stress design). A recent study (Davis et al, 2010) examined eight different methods for predicting the in-plane shear capacity of masonry walls. The design provisions of Chapter 9 (strength design) of this Code were found to be the best predictor of shear strength. The 2008 MSJC's allowable stress design provisions had a greater amount of scatter. Therefore, the provisions of Chapter 9, which allow for the shear resistance provided by the masonry to be added to the shear resistance provided by the shear reinforcement, were appropriately modified and adopted for Chapter 8. See the flow chart for design of masonry members resisting shear shown in Figure CC-8.3-3.

CODE

8.3.5.1.2 The calculated shear stress, f_v, shall not exceed the allowable shear stress, F_v, where F_v shall be calculated using Equation 8-25 and shall not be taken greater than the limits given by Section 8.3.5.1.2 (a) through (c).

$$F_v = (F_{vm} + F_{vs})\gamma_g \qquad \text{(Equation 8-25)}$$

(a) Where $M/(Vd_v) \leq 0.25$:

$$F_v \leq \left(3\sqrt{f'_m}\right)\gamma_g \qquad \text{(Equation 8-26)}$$

(b) Where $M/(Vd_v) \geq 1.0$

$$F_v \leq \left(2\sqrt{f'_m}\right)\gamma_g \qquad \text{(Equation 8-27)}$$

γ_g = 0.75 for partially grouted shear walls and 1.0 otherwise.

(c) The maximum value of F_v for $M/(Vd_v)$ between 0.25 and 1.0 shall be permitted to be linearly interpolated.

8.3.5.1.3 The allowable shear stress resisted by the masonry, F_{vm}, shall be calculated using Equation 8-28 for special reinforced masonry shear walls and using Equation 8-29 for other masonry:

$$F_{vm} = \frac{1}{4}\left[\left(4.0 - 1.75\left(\frac{M}{Vd_v}\right)\right)\sqrt{f'_m}\right] + 0.25\frac{P}{A_n}$$

$$\text{(Equation 8-28)}$$

$$F_{vm} = \frac{1}{2}\left[\left(4.0 - 1.75\left(\frac{M}{Vd_v}\right)\right)\sqrt{f'_m}\right] + 0.25\frac{P}{A_n}$$

$$\text{(Equation 8-29)}$$

$M/(Vd_v)$ shall be taken as a positive number and need not be taken greater than 1.0.

8.3.5.1.4 The allowable shear stress resisted by the steel reinforcement, F_{vs}, shall be calculated using Equation 8-30:

$$F_{vs} = 0.5\left(\frac{A_v F_s d_v}{A_{nv} s}\right) \qquad \text{(Equation 8-30)}$$

8.3.5.2 Shear reinforcement shall be provided when f_v exceeds F_{vm}. When shear reinforcement is required, the provisions of Section 8.3.5.2.1 and 8.3.5.2.2 shall apply.

COMMENTARY

8.3.5.1.2 Allowable shear stress Equations 8-25 through 8-27 are based on strength design provisions, but reduced by a factor of safety of 2 to obtain allowable stress values. The provisions of this Section were developed through the study of and calibrated to cantilevered shear walls. The ratio $M/(Vd_v)$, can be difficult to interpret or apply consistently for other conditions such as for a uniformly loaded, simply supported beam. Concurrent values of M and Vd_v must be considered at appropriate locations along shear members, such as beams, to determine the critical $M/(Vd_v)$ ratio. To simplify the analytical process, designers are permitted to use $M/(Vd_v) = 1$. Commentary Section 9.3.4.1.2 provides additional information. Partially grouted shear walls can have lower strengths than predicted by the shear capacity equations using just the reduction of net area (Minaie et al, 2010; Nolph and ElGawady, 2011; Schultz, 1996a; Schultz, 1996b; Schultz and Hutchinson, 2001). The grouted shear wall factor, γ_g, is used to compensate for this reduced capacity until methods can be developed to more accurately predict the performance of these elements.

8.3.5.1.3 Equation 8-29 is based on strength design provisions with the masonry shear strength reduced by a factor of safety of 2 and service loads used instead of factored loads.

A reduced value is used for the allowable masonry shear stress in special reinforced masonry shear walls to account for degradation of masonry shear strength in plastic hinging regions. Davis et al (2010) proposed a factor with a value of 1.0 for wall ductility ratios of 2.0 or less, and a linear decrease to zero as the ductility ratio increases from 2.0 to 4.0. The committee chose a constant value of 0.5, resulting in the allowable stress being reduced by a factor of 2, for design convenience.

8.3.5.1.4 Commentary Section 9.3.4.1.2.2 provides additional information.

CODE

8.3.5.2.1 Shear reinforcement shall be provided parallel to the direction of applied shear force. Spacing of shear reinforcement shall not exceed the lesser of $d/2$ or 48 in. (1219 mm).

8.3.5.2.2 Reinforcement shall be provided perpendicular to the shear reinforcement and shall be at least equal to one-third A_v. The reinforcement shall be uniformly distributed and shall not exceed a spacing of 8 ft (2.44 m).

8.3.5.3 In composite masonry walls, shear stresses developed in the planes of interfaces between wythes and filled collar joints or between wythes and headers shall meet the requirements of Section 8.1.4.2.

8.3.5.4 In cantilever beams, the maximum shear shall be used. In noncantilever beams, the maximum shear shall be used except that sections located within a distance $d/2$ from the face of support shall be designed for the same shear as that calculated at a distance $d/2$ from the face of support when the following conditions are met:

(a) support reaction, in direction of applied shear force, introduces compression into the end regions of the beam, and

(b) no concentrated load occurs between face of support and a distance $d/2$ from face.

COMMENTARY

8.3.5.2.1 The assumed shear crack is at 45 degrees to the longitudinal reinforcement. Thus, a maximum spacing of $d/2$ is specified to assure that each crack is crossed by at least one bar. The 48-in. (1219-mm) maximum spacing is an arbitrary choice that has been in codes for many years.

8.3.5.3 Shear across collar joints in composite masonry walls is transferred by the mortar or grout in the collar joint. Shear stress in the collar joint or at the interface between the wythe and the collar joint is limited to the allowable stresses in Section 8.1.4.2. Shear transfer by wall ties or other reinforcement across the collar joint is not considered.

8.3.5.4 The beam or wall loading within $d/2$ of the support is assumed to be transferred in direct compression or tension to the support without increasing the shear force, provided no concentrated load occurs within the $d/2$ distance.

COMMENTARY

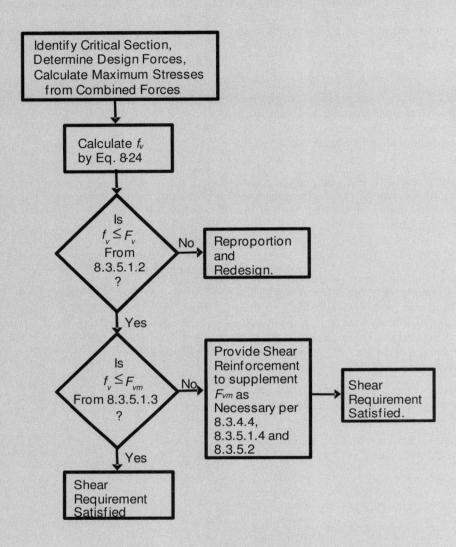

Figure CC-8.3-3 — Flow chart for shear design

CHAPTER 9
STRENGTH DESIGN OF MASONRY

CODE

9.1 — General

9.1.1 *Scope*

This Chapter provides minimum requirements for strength design of masonry. Masonry design by the strength design method shall comply with the requirements of Part 1, Part 2, Sections 9.1.2 through 9.1.9, and either Section 9.2 or 9.3.

9.1.2 *Required strength*

Required strength shall be determined in accordance with the strength design load combinations of the legally adopted building code. Members subject to compressive axial load shall be designed for the factored moment accompanying the factored axial load. The factored moment, M_u, shall include the moment induced by relative lateral displacement.

9.1.3 *Design strength*

Masonry members shall be proportioned so that the design strength equals or exceeds the required strength. Design strength is the nominal strength multiplied by the strength-reduction factor, ϕ, as specified in Section 9.1.4.

9.1.4 *Strength-reduction factors*

COMMENTARY

9.1 — General

9.1.1 *Scope*

Chapter 9 design procedures follow strength design methodology, in which internal forces resulting from application of factored loads must not exceed design strength (nominal member strength reduced by a strength-reduction factor ϕ).

Materials are assumed to be homogenous, isotropic, and exhibit nonlinear behavior. Under loads that exceed service levels, nonlinear material behavior, cracking, and reinforcing bar slip invalidate the assumption regarding the linearity of the stress-strain relation for masonry, grout, and reinforcing steel. If nonlinear behavior is modeled, however, nominal strength can be accurately predicted.

Much of the substantiating data for the strength design criteria in this Chapter was provided by research conducted by the Technical Coordinating Committee for Masonry Research (TCCMaR). This research program resulted in 63 research reports from 1985-1992. These reports are available from The Masonry Society, Longmont, CO. A summary of the TCCMaR program is found in Noland and Kingsley, 1995.

9.1.2 *Required strength*

9.1.3 *Design strength*

Nominal member strengths are typically calculated using minimum specified material strengths.

9.1.4 *Strength-reduction factors*

The strength-reduction factor accounts for the uncertainties in construction, material properties, calculated versus actual member strengths, as well as anticipated mode of failure. Strength-reduction (ϕ) factors are assigned values based on limiting the probability of failure to an acceptably small value, with some adjustment based on judgment and experience.

CODE

9.1.4.1 *Anchor bolts* — For cases where the nominal strength of an anchor bolt is controlled by masonry breakout, by masonry crushing, or by anchor bolt pryout, ϕ shall be taken as 0.50. For cases where the nominal strength of an anchor bolt is controlled by anchor bolt steel, ϕ shall be taken as 0.90. For cases where the nominal strength of an anchor bolt is controlled by anchor pullout, ϕ shall be taken as 0.65.

9.1.4.2 *Bearing* — For cases involving bearing on masonry, ϕ shall be taken as 0.60.

9.1.4.3 *Combinations of flexure and axial load in unreinforced masonry* — The value of ϕ shall be taken as 0.60 for unreinforced masonry subjected to flexure, axial load, or combinations thereof.

9.1.4.4 *Combinations of flexure and axial load in reinforced masonry* — The value of ϕ shall be taken as 0.90 for reinforced masonry subjected to flexure, axial load, or combinations thereof.

9.1.4.5 *Shear* — The value of ϕ shall be taken as 0.80 for masonry subjected to shear.

9.1.5 *Deformation requirements*

9.1.5.1 *Deflection of unreinforced (plain) masonry* — Deflection calculations for unreinforced (plain) masonry members shall be based on uncracked section properties.

9.1.5.2 *Deflection of reinforced masonry* — Deflection calculations for reinforced masonry members shall consider the effects of cracking and reinforcement on member stiffness. The flexural and shear stiffness properties assumed for deflection calculations shall not exceed one-half of the gross section properties, unless a cracked-section analysis is performed.

COMMENTARY

9.1.4.1 *Anchor bolts* — Because of the similarity between the behavior of anchor bolts embedded in grout and in concrete, and because available research data for anchor bolts in grout indicate similarity, the strength-reduction values associated with various controlling anchor bolt failures are derived from expressions based on research into the performance of anchor bolts embedded in concrete.

9.1.4.2 *Bearing* — The value of the strength-reduction factor used in bearing assumes that some degradation has occurred within the masonry material.

9.1.4.3 *Combinations of flexure and axial load in unreinforced masonry* — The same strength-reduction factor is used for the axial load and the flexural tension or compression induced by bending moment in unreinforced masonry elements. The lower strength-reduction factor associated with unreinforced elements (in comparison to reinforced elements) reflects an increase in the coefficient of variation of the measured strengths of unreinforced elements when compared to similarly configured reinforced elements.

9.1.4.4 *Combinations of flexure and axial load in reinforced masonry* — The same strength-reduction factor is used for the axial load and the flexural tension or compression induced by bending moment in reinforced masonry elements. The higher strength-reduction factor associated with reinforced elements (in comparison to unreinforced elements) reflects a decrease in the coefficient of variation of the measured strengths of reinforced elements when compared to similarly configured unreinforced elements.

9.1.4.5 *Shear* — The strength-reduction factor for calculating the design shear strength recognizes the greater uncertainty in calculating nominal shear strength than in calculating nominal flexural strength.

9.1.5 *Deformation requirements*

9.1.5.1 *Deflection of unreinforced (plain) masonry* — The deflection calculations of unreinforced masonry are based on elastic performance of the masonry assemblage as outlined in the design criteria of Section 9.2.2.

9.1.5.2 *Deflection of reinforced masonry* — Values of I_{eff} are typically about one-half of I_g for common configurations of elements that are fully grouted. Calculating a more accurate value using the cracked transformed section may be desirable for some circumstances (Abboud et al, 1993; Hamid et al, 1990).

CODE

9.1.6 *Anchor bolts embedded in grout*

9.1.6.1 *Design requirements* — Anchor bolts shall be designed using either the provisions of 9.1.6.2 or, for headed and bent-bar anchor bolts, by the provisions of Section 9.1.6.3.

9.1.6.2 *Nominal strengths determined by test*
9.1.6.2.1 Anchor bolts shall be tested in accordance with ASTM E488, except that a minimum of five tests shall be performed. Loading conditions of the test shall be representative of intended use of the anchor bolt.

9.1.6.2.2 Anchor bolt nominal strengths used for design shall not exceed 65 percent of the average failure load from the tests.

9.1.6.3 *Nominal strengths determined by calculation for headed and bent-bar anchor bolts* — Nominal strengths of headed and bent-bar anchor bolts embedded in grout shall be determined in accordance with the provisions of Sections 9.1.6.3.1 through 9.1.6.3.3.

9.1.6.3.1 *Nominal tensile strength of headed and bent-bar anchor bolts* — The nominal axial tensile strength of headed anchor bolts shall be calculated using the provisions of Sections 9.1.6.3.1.1. The nominal axial tensile strength of bent-bar anchor bolts shall be calculated using the provisions of Section 9.1.6.3.1.2.

COMMENTARY

9.1.6 *Anchor bolts embedded in grout*
Design of anchor bolts embedded in grout may be based on physical testing or, for headed and bent-bar anchor bolts, by calculation. Due to the wide variation in configurations of post-installed anchors, designers are referred to product literature published by manufacturers for these anchors.

9.1.6.1 *Design requirements*

9.1.6.2 *Nominal strengths determined by test* — Many types of anchor bolts, such as expansion anchors, toggle bolts, sleeve anchors, etc., are not addressed by Code Section 9.1.6.3 and, therefore, such anchors must be designed using test data. Testing may also be used to establish higher strengths than those calculated by Code Section 9.1.6.3. ASTM E488 requires only three tests. The variability of anchor bolt strength in masonry and the possibility that anchor bolts may be used in a non-redundant manner warrants an increase to the minimum of five tests stipulated by the Code. Assuming a normal probability distribution and a coefficient of variation of 20 percent for the test data, a fifth-percentile value for nominal strength is 67 percent, which is rounded to 65 percent of the average strength value. Failure modes obtained from testing should be reported and the associated ϕ factors should be used when establishing design strengths.

9.1.6.3 *Nominal strength determined by calculation for headed and bent-bar anchor bolts* — Design equations provided in the Code stem from research (Brown and Whitlock, 1983; Hatzinikolos et al, 1980; Rad et al, 1998; Tubbs et al, 1999; Allen et al, 2000; Brown et al, 2001; Weigel et al, 2002) conducted on headed anchor bolts and bent-bar anchor bolts (J- or L-bolts) embedded in grout.

The anchor provisions in this Code define bolt shear and tension capacities based on the bolt's specified yield strength. Anchors conforming to A307, Grade A specifications are allowed by the Code, but the ASTM A307, Grade A specification does not specify a yield strength. Use of a yield strength of 37 ksi in the Code design equations for A307 anchors will result in anchor capacities similar to those obtained using the American Institute of Steel Construction provisions.

9.1.6.3.1 *Nominal tensile strength of headed and bent-bar anchor bolts*

CODE

9.1.6.3.1.1 *Axial tensile strength of headed anchor bolts* — The nominal axial tensile strength, B_{an}, of headed anchor bolts embedded in grout shall be determined by Equation 9-1 (nominal axial tensile strength governed by masonry breakout) or Equation 9-2 (nominal axial tensile strength governed by steel yielding). The design axial tensile strength, ϕB_{an}, shall be the smaller of the values obtained from Equations 9-1 and 9-2 multiplied by the applicable ϕ value.

$$B_{anb} = 4A_{pt}\sqrt{f_m'} \qquad \text{(Equation 9-1)}$$

$$B_{ans} = A_b f_y \qquad \text{(Equation 9-2)}$$

9.1.6.3.1.2 *Axial tensile strength of bent-bar anchor bolts* – The nominal axial tensile strength, B_{an}, for bent-bar anchor bolts embedded in grout shall be determined by Equation 9-3 (nominal axial tensile strength governed by masonry breakout), Equation 9-4 (nominal axial tensile strength governed by anchor bolt pullout), or Equation 9-5 (nominal axial tensile strength governed by steel yielding). The design axial tensile strength, ϕB_{an}, shall be the smallest of the values obtained from Equations 9-3, 9-4 and 9-5 multiplied by the applicable ϕ value.

$$B_{anb} = 4A_{pt}\sqrt{f_m'} \qquad \text{(Equation 9-3)}$$

$$B_{anp} = 1.5f_m' e_b d_b + 300\pi(l_b + e_b + d_b)d_b$$

$$\text{(Equation 9-4)}$$

$$B_{ans} = A_b f_y \qquad \text{(Equation 9-5)}$$

9.1.6.3.2 *Shear strength of headed and bent-bar anchor bolts* — The nominal shear strength, B_{vn}, of headed and bent-bar anchor bolts shall be determined by Equation 9-6 (nominal shear strength governed by masonry breakout), Equation 9-7 (nominal shear strength governed by masonry crushing), Equation 9-8 (nominal shear strength governed by anchor bolt pryout) or Equation 9-9 (nominal shear strength governed by steel yielding). The design shear strength ϕB_{vn}, shall be the smallest of the values obtained from Equations 9-6, 9-7, 9-8 and 9-9 multiplied by the applicable ϕ value.

$$B_{vnb} = 4A_{pv}\sqrt{f_m'} \qquad \text{(Equation 9-6)}$$

$$B_{vnc} = 1050\sqrt[4]{f'_m A_b} \qquad \text{(Equation 9-7)}$$

$$B_{vnpry} = 2.0B_{anb} = 8A_{pt}\sqrt{f_m'} \qquad \text{(Equation 9-8)}$$

$$B_{vns} = 0.6A_b f_y \qquad \text{(Equation 9-9)}$$

COMMENTARY

9.1.6.3.1.1 *Axial tensile strength of headed anchor bolts* — Tensile strength of a headed anchor bolt is governed by yield of the anchor steel, Equation 9-2, or by breakout of an approximately conical volume of masonry starting at the anchor head and having a fracture surface oriented at approximately 45 degrees to the masonry surface, Equation 9-1. Steel strength is calculated using the effective tensile stress area of the anchor (that is, including the reduction in area of the anchor shank due to threads).

9.1.6.3.1.2 *Axial tensile strength of bent-bar anchor bolts* –- The tensile strength of a bent-bar anchor bolt (J- or L-bolt) is governed by yield of the anchor steel, Equation 9-5, by tensile cone breakout of the masonry, Equation 9-3, or by straightening and pullout of the anchor bolt from the masonry, Equation 9-4. Capacities corresponding to the first two failure modes are calculated as for headed anchor bolts. Code Equation 9-4 corresponds to anchor bolt pullout. The second term in Equation 9-4 is the portion of the anchor bolt capacity due to bond between bolt and grout. Accordingly, Specification Article 3.2A requires that precautions be taken to ensure that the shanks of the bent-bar anchor bolts are clean and free of debris that would otherwise interfere with the bond between anchor bolt and grout.

9.1.6.3.2 *Shear strength of headed and bent-bar anchor bolts* -- Shear strength of a headed or bent-bar anchor bolt is governed by yielding of the anchor steel, Equation 9-9, by masonry crushing, Equation 9-7, or by masonry shear breakout, Equation 9-6. Steel strength is calculated using the effective tensile stress area (that is, threads are conservatively assumed to lie in the critical shear plane). Pryout (see Figure CC-6.2-7) is also a possible failure mode. The pryout equation (Equation 9-8) is adapted from concrete research (Fuchs et al, 1995).

Under static shear loading, bent-bar anchor bolts do not exhibit straightening and pullout. Under reversed cyclic shear, however, available research (Malik et al, 1982) suggests that straightening and pullout may occur.

CODE

9.1.6.3.3 *Combined axial tension and shear* — Anchor bolts subjected to axial tension in combination with shear shall satisfy Equation 9-10.

$$\frac{b_{af}}{\phi\, B_{an}} + \frac{b_{vf}}{\phi\, B_{vn}} \leq 1 \qquad \text{(Equation 9-10)}$$

9.1.7 *Shear strength in multiwythe masonry elements*

9.1.7.1 Design of multiwythe masonry for composite action shall meet the requirements of Sections 5.1.4.2 and 9.1.7.2.

9.1.7.2 The nominal shear strength at the interfaces between wythes and collar joints or within headers shall be determined so that shear stresses shall not exceed the following:

(a) mortared collar joints, 14 psi (96.5 kPa).

(b) grouted collar joints, 26 psi (179.3 kPa).

(c) headers,

$$2.6\sqrt{\text{specified unit compressive strength of header}}$$

psi (MPa) (over net area of header).

9.1.8 *Nominal bearing strength*

The nominal bearing strength of masonry shall be calculated as $0.8\, f'_m$ multiplied by the bearing area, A_{br}, as defined in Section 4.3.4.

9.1.9 *Material properties*

9.1.9.1 *Compressive strength*

9.1.9.1.1 *Masonry compressive strength* — The specified compressive strength of masonry, f'_m, shall equal or exceed 1,500 psi (10.34 MPa). The value of f'_m used to determine nominal strength values in this chapter shall not exceed 4,000 psi (27.58 MPa) for concrete masonry and shall not exceed 6,000 psi (41.37 MPa) for clay masonry.

9.1.9.1.2 *Grout compressive strength* — For concrete masonry, the specified compressive strength of grout, f'_g, shall equal or exceed the specified compressive strength of masonry, f'_m, but shall not exceed 5,000 psi (34.47 MPa). For clay masonry, the specified compressive strength of grout, f'_g, shall not exceed 6,000 psi (41.37 MPa).

COMMENTARY

9.1.7 *Shear strength in multiwythe masonry elements*

The nominal shear strength is based on shear stresses that are twice the allowable shear stresses in allowable stress design. Commentary Section 8.1.4 provides additional information.

9.1.8 *Nominal bearing strength*

Commentary Section 4.3.4 provides further information.

9.1.9 *Material properties*

Commentary Section 4.2 provides additional information.

9.1.9.1 *Compressive strength*

9.1.9.1.1 *Masonry compressive strength* — Design criteria are based on TCCMaR research (Noland and Kingsley, 1995) conducted on structural masonry components having compressive strength in the range of 1,500 to 4,000 psi (10.34 to 27.58 MPa) for concrete masonry and 1,500 to 6,000 psi (10.34 to 41.37 MPa) for clay masonry. Thus, the upper limits given represent the upper values that were tested in the research.

9.1.9.1.2 *Grout compressive strength* — Because most empirically derived design equations calculate nominal strength as a function of the specified compressive strength of the masonry, the specified compressive strength of the grout is required to be at least equal to the specified compressive strength for concrete masonry. This requirement is an attempt to ensure that where the grout compressive strength controls the design (such as anchors embedded in grout), the nominal strength will not be affected. The limitation on the maximum grout compressive strength is due to the lack of available research using higher material strengths.

CODE

9.1.9.2 *Masonry modulus of rupture* — The modulus of rupture, f_r, for masonry elements subjected to out-of-plane or in-plane bending shall be in accordance with the values in Table 9.1.9.2. For grouted masonry not laid in running bond, tension parallel to the bed joints shall be assumed to be resisted only by the minimum cross-sectional area of continuous grout that is parallel to the bed joints.

COMMENTARY

9.1.9.2 *Masonry modulus of rupture* — The modulus of rupture values provided in Code Table 9.1.9.2 are directly proportional to the allowable stress values for flexural tension. In-plane and out-of-plane strain gradients are recognized as being different, but at these low stress levels this effect should be small.

Historically, masonry not laid in running bond has been assumed to have no flexural bond strength across mortared head joints; thus, the grout area alone is used to resist bending. Examples of a continuous grout section parallel to the bed joints are shown in Figure CC-8.2-2.

The presence of flashing and other conditions at the base of the wall can significantly reduce the flexural bond. The values in Table 9.1.9.2 apply only to the flexural tensile stresses developed between masonry units, mortar, and grout.

Table 9.1.9.2 — Modulus of rupture, f_r, psi (kPa)

Direction of flexural tensile stress and masonry type	Mortar types			
	Portland cement/lime or mortar cement		Masonry cement or air entrained portland cement/lime	
	M or S	N	M or S	N
Normal to bed joints				
Solid units	133 (919)	100 (690)	80 (552)	51 (349)
Hollow units[1]				
Ungrouted	84 (579)	64 (441)	51 (349)	31 (211)
Fully grouted	163 (1124)	158 (1089)	153 (1055)	145 (1000)
Parallel to bed joints in running bond				
Solid units	267 (1839)	200 (1379)	160 (1103)	100 (689)
Hollow units				
Ungrouted and partially grouted	167 (1149)	127 (873)	100 (689)	64 (441)
Fully grouted	267 (1839)	200 (1379)	160 (1103)	100 (689)
Parallel to bed joints in masonry not laid in running bond				
Continuous grout section parallel to bed joints	335 (2310)	335 (2310)	335 (2310)	335 (2310)
Other	0 (0)	0 (0)	0 (0)	0 (0)

[1] For partially grouted masonry, modulus of rupture values shall be determined on the basis of linear interpolation between fully grouted hollow units and ungrouted hollow units based on amount (percentage) of grouting.

CODE

9.1.9.3 *Reinforcement strengths*

9.1.9.3.1 *Reinforcement for in-plane flexural tension and flexural tension perpendicular to bed joints* — Masonry design shall be based on a reinforcement strength equal to the specified yield strength of reinforcement, f_y, which shall not exceed 60,000 psi (413.7 MPa). The actual yield strength shall not exceed 1.3 multiplied by the specified yield strength.

9.1.9.3.2 *Reinforcement for in-plane shear and flexural tension parallel to bed joints* — Masonry design shall be based on a specified yield strength, f_y, which shall not exceed 60,000 psi (413.7 MPa) for reinforcing bars and which shall not exceed 85,000 psi (586 MPa) for reinforcing wire.

COMMENTARY

9.1.9.3 *Reinforcement strengths*

9.1.9.3.1 *Reinforcement for in-plane flexural tension and flexural tension perpendicular to bed joints* — TCCMaR Research (Noland and Kingsley, 1995) conducted on reinforced masonry components used Grade 60 reinforcement. To be consistent with laboratory documented investigations, design is based on a nominal steel yield strength of 60,000 psi (413.7 MPa). The limitation on the flexural steel yield strength of 130 percent of the nominal yield strength is to minimize the over-strength unintentionally incorporated into a design.

9.1.9.3.2 *Reinforcement for in-plane shear and flexural tension parallel to bed joints* — Studies of minimum shear reinforcement requirements (Schultz, 1996a, Baenziger and Porter, 2011, Porter and Baenziger, 2007, Sveinsson et al, 1985, and Schultz and Hutchinson, 2001a) have shown that when sufficient area, strength, and strain elongation properties of reinforcement are provided to resist the load transferred from the masonry after cracking, then the reinforcement does not rupture upon cracking of the masonry. Equivalent performance of shear walls with bond beams and shear walls with bed joint reinforcement under simulated seismic loading was observed in the laboratory tests (Baenziger and Porter, 2011 and Schultz and Hutchinson, 2001a). Minimum Code requirements have been provided (Schultz, 1996a) to satisfy both strength and energy criteria. The limitation on steel yield strength of 130 percent of the nominal yield strength, in Section 9.1.9.3.1, does not apply to shear reinforcement because the risk of brittle shear failures is reduced with higher yield strength.

Joint reinforcement of at least 3/16 in. (4.8 mm) diameter longitudinal wire is deemed to have sufficient strain elongation and, thus, was selected as the minimum size when joint reinforcement is used as the primary shear and flexural reinforcement. The research (Baenziger and Porter, 2011) was for walls that contained a minimum of two 3/16 in. (4.8 mm) diameter longitudinal wires in a bed joint. Other research (Schultz and Hutchinson, 2001a) contained two No. 9 gage (0.148 in. (3.76 mm)) diameter longitudinal wires or two No. 5 gage (0.207 in. (5.26 mm)) diameter longitudinal wires in a bed joint. The No. 5 gage longitudinal wires exhibited similar ductility to the joint reinforcement in the Baenziger/Porter research.

CODE

9.2 — Unreinforced (plain) masonry

9.2.1 *Scope*

Design of unreinforced masonry by the strength design method shall comply with the requirements of Part 1, Part 2, Section 9.1, and Section 9.2.

9.2.2 *Design criteria*

Unreinforced masonry members shall be designed in accordance with the principles of engineering mechanics and shall be designed to remain uncracked.

9.2.3 *Design assumptions*

The following assumptions shall be used in the design of unreinforced masonry members:

(a) Strain in masonry shall be directly proportional to the distance from the neutral axis.

(b) Flexural tension in masonry shall be assumed to be directly proportional to strain.

(c) Flexural compressive stress in combination with axial compressive stress in masonry shall be assumed to be directly proportional to strain.

(d) Stresses in the reinforcement are not accounted for in determining the resistance to design loads.

9.2.4 *Nominal flexural and axial strength*

9.2.4.1 *Nominal strength* — The nominal strength of unreinforced (plain) masonry cross-sections for combined flexure and axial loads shall be determined so that:

(a) the compressive stress does not exceed $0.80\,f'_m$.

(b) the tensile stress does not exceed the modulus of rupture determined from Section 9.1.9.2.

9.2.4.2 *Nominal axial strength* — The nominal axial strength, P_n, shall not be taken greater than the following:

(a) For members having an h/r ratio not greater than 99:

$$P_n = 0.80 \left\{ 0.80\, A_n\, f'_m \left[1 - \left(\frac{h}{140\,r} \right)^2 \right] \right\}$$

(Equation 9-11)

COMMENTARY

9.2 — Unreinforced (plain) masonry

9.2.1 *Scope*

Commentary Section 8.2.1 provides further information.

9.2.2 *Design criteria*

The design of unreinforced masonry requires that the structure performs elastically under design loads. The system response factors used in the design of unreinforced masonry assume an elastic response. Commentary Section 8.2.2 provides further information.

9.2.3 *Design assumptions*

Commentary Section 8.2.3 provides further information.

9.2.4 *Nominal flexural and axial strength*

9.2.4.1 *Nominal strength* — This section gives requirements for constructing an interaction diagram for unreinforced masonry members subjected to combined flexure and axial loads. The requirements are illustrated in Figure CC-9.2-1. Also shown in Figure CC-9.2-1 are the requirements of Section 9.2.4.2, which give a maximum axial force.

9.2.4.2 *Nominal axial strength* — Commentary Section 9.3.4.1.1 gives additional information.

COMMENTARY

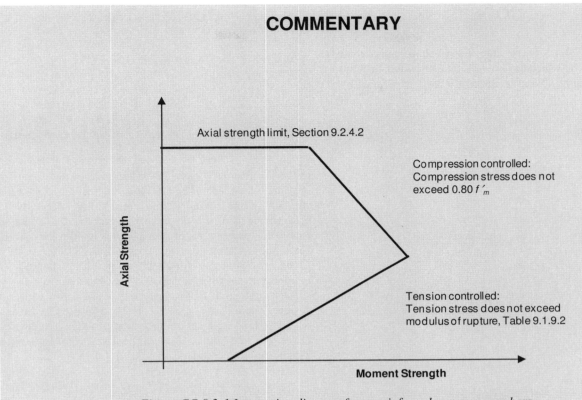

Figure CC-9.2-1 Interaction diagram for unreinforced masonry members

CODE

(b) For members having an *h/r* ratio greater than 99:

$$P_n = 0.80 \left[0.80 A_n f'_m \left(\frac{70r}{h} \right)^2 \right] \qquad \text{(Equation 9-12)}$$

9.2.4.3 *P-Delta effects*
9.2.4.3.1 Members shall be designed for the factored axial load, P_u, and the moment magnified for the effects of member curvature, M_u.

9.2.4.3.2 The magnified moment, M_u, shall be determined either by a second-order analysis, or by a first-order analysis and Equations 9-13 and 9-14.

$$M_u = \psi M_{u,0} \qquad \text{(Equation 9-13)}$$

$$\psi = \frac{1}{1 - \dfrac{P_u}{A_n f'_m \left(\dfrac{70r}{h} \right)^2}} \qquad \text{(Equation 9-14)}$$

9.2.4.3.3 A value of $\psi = 1$ shall be permitted for members in which $h/r \le 45$.

COMMENTARY

9.2.4.3 *P-delta effects* — P-delta effects are either determined by a second-order analysis, which includes *P*-delta effects, or a first-order analysis, which excludes *P*-delta effects and the use of moment magnifier. The moment magnifier is determined as:

$$\psi = \frac{C_m}{1 - \dfrac{P_u}{\phi_k P_{euler}}}$$

where ϕ_k is a stiffness reduction factor or a resistance factor to account for variability in stiffness, C_m is a factor relating the actual moment diagram to an equivalent uniform moment diagram, and P_{euler} is Euler's buckling load. For reinforced concrete design, a value of $\phi_k = 0.75$ is used (Mirza et al, 1987).

Euler's buckling load is obtained as $P_{euler} = \pi^2 E_m A_n r^2 / h^2$. Using $E_m = 700 f'_m$, which is the lower value of clay and concrete masonry, Euler's buckling load becomes:

CODE

9.2.4.3.4 A value of $\psi = 1$ shall be permitted for members in which $45 < h/r \leq 60$, provided that the nominal strength defined in Section 9.2.4.1 is reduced by 10 percent.

COMMENTARY

$$P_{euler} = \frac{\pi^2 E_m A_n r^2}{h^2}$$

$$= \frac{\pi^2 700 f'_m A_n r^2}{h^2} = A_n f'_m \left(\frac{83.1r}{h}\right)^2$$

Current design provisions calculate the axial strength of walls with $h/r > 99$ as $A_n f'_m (70r/h)^2$. Section 8.2.4.1 of the Commentary gives the background of this equation. It is based on using $E_m = 1000 f'_m$, neglecting the tensile strength of the masonry, and considering an accidental eccentricity of $0.10t$. In spite of the fact that this equation was developed using a higher modulus than in the current Code, the equation gives a strength of $(70/83.1)^2 = 0.71$ of Euler's buckling load for clay masonry. The value of 0.71 is approximately the value of ϕ_k that has been used as a stiffness reduction factor. For ease of use and because of designer's familiarity, a value of $(70\,r/h)$ is used for Euler's buckling load instead of an explicit stiffness reduction factor. For most walls, $C_m = 1$. The moment magnifier can thus be determined as:

$$\psi = \frac{1}{1 - \dfrac{P_u}{A_n f'_m \left(\dfrac{70r}{h}\right)^2}}$$

Figure CC-9.2-2 shows the ratio of the second-order stress, $\dfrac{P_u}{A_n} + \dfrac{\delta M_u}{S_n}$, divided by the first-order stress, $\dfrac{P_u}{A_n} + \dfrac{M_u}{S_n}$, when the second-order stress is at the strength design limit $\phi(0.8 f'_m)$. Typically slenderness effects are ignored if they contribute less than 5 percent (MacGregor et al, 1970). From Figure CC-9.2-2, slenderness effects contribute less than 5 percent for values of $h/r \leq 45$. An intermediate wall is one with a slenderness h/r greater than 45 but not greater than 60. Slenderness effects contribute about 10 percent to the design at $h/r = 60$. Intermediate walls can be designed using either the moment magnifier approach or a simplified method in which the nominal stresses are reduced by 10 percent. The Code requires walls with $h/r > 60$ to be designed using the moment magnifier approach.

9.2.5 *Axial tension* — Axial tension resistance of unreinforced masonry shall be neglected in design.

9.2.5 *Axial tension*
Commentary Section 8.2.5 provides further information.

CODE

9.2.6 *Nominal shear strength*

9.2.6.1 Nominal shear strength, V_n, shall be the smallest of (a), (b) and the applicable condition of (c) through (f):

(a) $3.8 A_{nv} \sqrt{f'_m}$

(b) $300 A_{nv}$

(c) For running bond masonry not fully grouted;

$56 A_{nv} + 0.45 N_u$

(d) For masonry not laid in running bond, constructed of open end units, and fully grouted;

$56 A_{nv} + 0.45 N_u$

(e) For running bond masonry fully grouted;

$90 A_{nv} + 0.45 N_u$

(f) For masonry not laid in running bond, constructed of other than open end units, and fully grouted;

$23 A_{nv}$

9.2.6.2 The minimum normalized web area of concrete masonry units, determined in accordance with ASTM C140, shall not be less than 27 in.^{2}/ft^2 (187,500 mm^2/m^2) or the nominal shear strength of the web shall not exceed $3.8 \sqrt{f'_m} I_n b / Q$.

COMMENTARY

9.2.6 *Nominal shear strength*

9.2.6.1 For a rectangular cross-section, the shear stress is assumed to follow a parabolic distribution. The Code is based on an average shear stress, which is two-thirds of the maximum shear stress for a parabolic shear stress distribution. Commentary Section 8.2.6 provides further information.

9.2.6.2 Out-of-plane flexure causes horizontal and vertical shear stresses. Vertical shear stresses are resisted by the connection between the web and face shell of the unit. A normalized web area of 27 in.^{2}/ft^2 (187,500 mm^2/m^2) provides sufficient web area so that shear stresses between the web and face shell of a unit, resulting from out-of-plane loading, will not be critical. For simplicity, the same nominal out-of-plane shear strength as for in-plane shear is conservatively used, although peak shear stresses instead of average shear stresses are being checked.

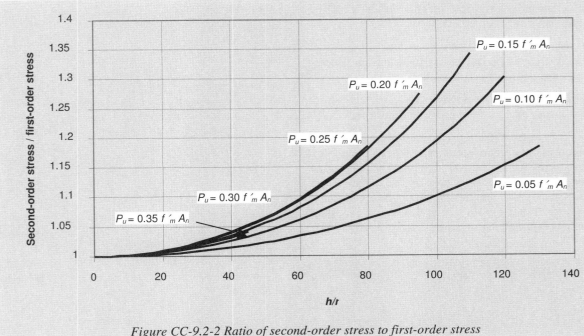

Figure CC-9.2-2 Ratio of second-order stress to first-order stress

CODE

9.3 — Reinforced masonry

9.3.1 *Scope*

This section provides requirements for the design of structures in which reinforcement is used to resist tensile forces in accordance with the principles of engineering mechanics and the contribution of the tensile resistance of the masonry is neglected except as provided in Section 9.3.4.1.2. Design of reinforced masonry by the strength design method shall comply with the requirements of Part 1, Part 2, Section 9.1, and Section 9.3.

9.3.2 *Design assumptions*

The following assumptions shall be used in the design of reinforced masonry:

(a) Strain compatibility exists between the reinforcement, grout, and masonry.

(b) The nominal strength of reinforced masonry cross-sections for combined flexure and axial load is based on applicable conditions of equilibrium.

(c) The maximum usable strain, ε_{mu}, at the extreme masonry compression fiber is 0.0035 for clay masonry and 0.0025 for concrete masonry.

(d) Strains in reinforcement and masonry are directly proportional to the distance from the neutral axis.

(e) Compression and tension stress in reinforcement is E_s multiplied by the steel strain, but not greater than f_y. Except as permitted in Section 9.3.3.5.1 (e) for determination of maximum area of flexural reinforcement, the compressive stress of steel reinforcement does not contribute to the axial and flexural resistance unless lateral restraining reinforcement is provided in compliance with the requirements of Section 5.3.1.4.

(f) Masonry in tension does not contribute to axial and flexural strengths. Axial and flexural tension stresses are resisted entirely by steel reinforcement.

(g) The relationship between masonry compressive stress and masonry strain is defined by the following:

Masonry stress of $0.80\, f'_m$ is uniformly distributed over an equivalent compression stress block bounded by edges of the cross section and a straight line located parallel to the neutral axis and located at a distance $a = 0.80\, c$ from the fiber of maximum compressive strain. The distance c from the fiber of maximum strain to the neutral axis shall be measured perpendicular to the neutral axis.

COMMENTARY

9.3 — Reinforced masonry

9.3.1 *Scope*

The high tensile strength of reinforcement complements the high compressive strength of masonry. Increased strength and greater ductility result from the use of reinforcement in masonry structures as compared with unreinforced masonry.

9.3.2 *Design assumptions*

The design assumptions listed have traditionally been used for strength design of reinforced masonry members.

The values for the maximum usable strain are based on research on masonry materials (Assis and Hamid, 1990; Brown, 1987). Concern has been raised as to the implied precision of the values. However, the Committee agrees that the reported values for the maximum usable strain reasonably represent those observed during testing.

Although tension may develop in the masonry of a reinforced element, it is not considered in calculating axial and flexural strengths.

CODE

9.3.3 *Reinforcement requirements and details*
  9.3.3.1 *Reinforcement size limitations*
(a) Reinforcing bars used in masonry shall not be larger than No. 9 (M#29). The nominal bar diameter shall not exceed one-eighth of the nominal member thickness and shall not exceed one-quarter of the least clear dimension of the cell, course, or collar joint in which the bar is placed. The area of reinforcing bars placed in a cell or in a course of hollow unit construction shall not exceed 4 percent of the cell area.

(b) Joint reinforcement longitudinal wire used in masonry as shear reinforcement shall be at least 3/16 in. (4.8 mm) diameter.

  9.3.3.2 *Standard hooks* — Standard hooks in tension shall be considered to develop an equivalent embedment length, l_e, as determined by Equation 9-15:

$$l_e = 13\,d_b \qquad \text{(Equation 9-15)}$$

  9.3.3.3 *Development* — The required tension or compression reinforcement shall be developed in accordance with the following provisions:

The required development length of reinforcement shall be determined by Equation 9-16, but shall not be less than 12 in. (305 mm).

$$l_d = \frac{0.13\,d_b^{\,2}\,f_y\gamma}{K\sqrt{f_m'}} \qquad \text{(Equation 9-16)}$$

K shall not exceed the smallest of the following: the minimum masonry cover, the clear spacing between adjacent reinforcement splices, and $9d_b$.

  γ = 1.0 for No. 3 (M#10) through No. 5 (M#16) bars;

  γ = 1.3 for No. 6 (M#19) through No. 7 (M#22) bars;

and

  γ = 1.5 for No. 8 (M#25) through No. 9 (M#29) bars.

Development length of epoxy-coated reinforcing bars shall be taken as 150 percent of the length determined by Equation 9-16.

COMMENTARY

9.3.3 *Reinforcement requirements and details*
  9.3.3.1 *Reinforcement size limitations*
(a) The limit of using a No. 9 (M #29) bar is motivated by the goal of having a larger number of smaller diameter bars to transfer stresses rather than a fewer number of larger diameter bars. Some TCCMaR research investigations (Noland and Kingsley, 1995) have concluded that in certain applications masonry reinforced with more uniformly distributed smaller diameter bars performs better than similarly configured masonry elements using fewer larger diameter bars. While not every investigation is conclusive, the Committee does agree that incorporating larger diameter reinforcement may dictate unreasonable cover distances or development lengths. The limitations on clear spacing and percentage of cell area are indirect methods of preventing problems associated with over-reinforcing and grout consolidation. At sections containing lap splices, the maximum area of reinforcement should not exceed 8 percent of the cell area.

(b) The limit of using at least 3/16 in. longitudinal wire in joint reinforcement used as shear reinforcement is to provide sufficient strain capacity to avoid rupture. The minimum wire size does not apply to wire reinforcement used to satisfy prescriptive seismic reinforcement.

  9.3.3.2 *Standard hooks* — Refer to Commentary Section 6.1.5 for further information.

  9.3.3.3 *Development* — The clear spacing between adjacent reinforcement does not apply to the reinforcing bars being spliced together. Refer to Commentary 8.1.6.7.1 for further information.

Schultz (2005) studied the performance of the 2005 MSJC formula for splice lengths in masonry relative to a database of splice tests. Schultz (2004, 2005) found that for clear cover in excess of $5d_b$, the 2005 MSJC lap splice formula gains accuracy, relative to the experimental database, when a $5d_b$ limit is not imposed on the coefficient. Additional testing and subsequent analysis by the National Concrete Masonry Association (2009) also found the $5d_b$ overly conservative and recommended that the limit on K be increased to 8.8 which is rounded to the current $9d_b$ limit.

The 50 percent increase in development length for epoxy-coated bars does not apply to the 12 in. (305 mm) minimum.

CODE

9.3.3.3.1 Reinforcement spliced by noncontact lap splices shall not be spaced farther apart than one-fifth the required length of lap nor more than 8 in. (203 mm).

9.3.3.3.2 Shear reinforcement shall extend the depth of the member less cover distances.

9.3.3.3.2.1 Except at wall intersections, the end of a horizontal reinforcing bar needed to satisfy shear strength requirements of Section 9.3.4.1.2 shall be bent around the edge vertical reinforcing bar with a 180-degree hook. The ends of single-leg or U-stirrups shall be anchored by one of the following means:

(a) A standard hook plus an effective embedment of $l_d/2$. The effective embedment of a stirrup leg shall be taken as the distance between the mid-depth of the member, $d/2$, and the start of the hook (point of tangency).

(b) For No. 5 (M #16) bars and smaller, bending around longitudinal reinforcement through at least 135 degrees plus an embedment of $l_d/3$. The $l_d/3$ embedment of a stirrup leg shall be taken as the distance between mid-depth of the member, $d/2$, and the start of the hook (point of tangency).

(c) Between the anchored ends, each bend in the continuous portion of a transverse U-stirrup shall enclose a longitudinal bar.

9.3.3.3.2.2 At wall intersections, horizontal reinforcing bars needed to satisfy shear strength requirements of Section 9.3.4.1.2 shall be bent around the edge vertical reinforcing bar with a 90-degree standard hook and shall extend horizontally into the intersecting wall a minimum distance at least equal to the development length.

9.3.3.3.2.3 Joint reinforcement used as shear reinforcement and needed to satisfy the shear strength requirements of Section 9.3.4.1.2 shall be anchored around the edge reinforcing bar in the edge cell, either by bar placement between adjacent cross-wires or with a 90-degree bend in longitudinal wires bent around the edge cell and with at least 3-in. (76-mm) bend extensions in mortar or grout.

9.3.3.3.3 *Development of wires in tension* — The development length of wire shall be determined by Equation 9-17, but shall not be less than 6 in. (152 mm).

$$l_d = 48\,d_b \qquad \text{(Equation 9-17)}$$

Development length of epoxy-coated wire shall be taken as 150 percent of the length determined by Equation 9-17.

COMMENTARY

9.3.3.3.1 If individual bars in noncontact lap splices are too widely spaced, an unreinforced section is created, which forces a potential crack to follow a zigzag line. Lap splices may occur with the bars in adjacent grouted cells if the requirements of this section are met.

9.3.3.3.2.1 In a wall without an intersecting wall at its end, the edge vertical bar is the bar closest to the end of the wall. When the wall has an intersecting wall at its end, the edge vertical bar is the bar at the intersection of walls. Hooking the horizontal reinforcement around a vertical bar located within the wall running parallel to the horizontal reinforcement would cause the reinforcement to protrude from the wall.

9.3.3.3.2.3 Wire reinforcement should be anchored around or beyond the edge reinforcing bar. Joint reinforcement longitudinal wires and wire bends are placed over masonry unit face shells in mortar and wire extensions can be placed in edge cell mortar or can extend into edge cell grout. Both joint reinforcement longitudinal wires and cross wires can be used to confine vertical reinforcing bars and grouted cells because wires are developed within a short length.

9.3.3.3.3 *Development of wires in tension* — Commentary 8.1.6.2. explains the development of wires as being $0.0015F_s d_b$. The term $F_s d_b$ is equivalent to 45 d_b since $F_s = 30,000$ psi. The value was rounded up to 48 d_b to be consistent with other sections of the Code.

CODE

9.3.3.4 *Splices* — Reinforcement splices shall comply with one of the following:

(a) The minimum length of lap for bars shall be 12 in. (305 mm) or the development length determined by Equation 9-16, whichever is greater.

(b) Where reinforcement consisting of No. 3 (M#10) or larger bars is placed within the lap, with at least one bar 8 in. (203 mm) or less from each end of the lap, the minimum length of lap for bars in tension or compression determined by Equation 9-16 shall be permitted to be reduced by multiplying the confinement reinforcement factor, ξ. The clear space between the transverse bars and the lapped bars shall not exceed 1.5 in. (38 mm) and the transverse bars shall be fully developed in grouted masonry. The reduced lap splice length shall not be less than $36d_b$.

$$\xi = 1.0 - \frac{2.3A_{sc}}{d_b^{2.5}} \qquad \text{(Equation 9-18)}$$

$$\text{Where}: \frac{2.3A_{sc}}{d_b^{2.5}} \le 1.0$$

A_{sc} is the area of the transverse bars at each end of the lap splice and shall not be taken greater than 0.35 in^2 (226 mm^2).

(c) A welded splice shall have the bars butted and welded to develop at least 125 percent of the yield strength, f_y, of the bar in tension or compression, as required. Welding shall conform to AWS D1.4/D1.4M. Reinforcement to be welded shall conform to ASTM A706, or shall be accompanied by a submittal showing its chemical analysis and carbon equivalent as required by AWS D1.4/D1.4M. Existing reinforcement to be welded shall conform to ASTM A706, or shall be analyzed chemically and its carbon equivalent determined as required by AWS D1.4/D1.4M.

(d) Mechanical splices shall have the bars connected to develop at least 125 percent of the yield strength, f_y, of the bar in tension or compression, as required.

(e) Where joint reinforcement is used as shear reinforcement, the splice length of the longitudinal wires shall be a minimum of $48d_b$.

COMMENTARY

9.3.3.4 *Splices* — Refer to Code Commentary Section 8.1.6.7.1 for information on splices.

(c) See Code Commentary Section 8.1.6.7.2 for additional information on welded splices.

(e) Research studies (Porter and Braun, 1998 and Porter and Braun, 1999) of gage length, embedment, and anchorage of joint reinforcement supports wire development lengths consistent with the traditional Code formula of 48 d_b. To avoid expanding the thickness of the bed joint, joint reinforcement wires should be lapped in the same bed joint without stacking longitudinal wires and cross wires. Where cells are fully grouted, interior longitudinal wires may be angled into the grout to accomplish the lap.

CODE

9.3.3.5 *Maximum area of flexural tensile reinforcement*

9.3.3.5.1 For masonry members where $M_u/(V_u d_v) \geq 1$, the cross-sectional area of flexural tensile reinforcement shall not exceed the area required to maintain axial equilibrium under the following conditions:

(a) A strain gradient shall be assumed, corresponding to a strain in the extreme tensile reinforcement equal to 1.5 multiplied by the yield strain and a maximum strain in the masonry as given by Section 9.3.2(c).

(b) The design assumptions of Section 9.3.2 shall apply.

(c) The stress in the tension reinforcement shall be taken as the product of the modulus of elasticity of the steel and the strain in the reinforcement, and need not be taken greater than f_y.

(d) Axial forces shall be taken from the loading combination given by $D + 0.75L + 0.525Q_E$.

(e) The effect of compression reinforcement, with or without lateral restraining reinforcement, shall be permitted to be included for purposes of calculating maximum flexural tensile reinforcement.

9.3.3.5.2 For intermediate reinforced masonry shear walls subject to in-plane loads where $M_u/(V_u d_v) \geq 1$, a strain gradient corresponding to a strain in the extreme tensile reinforcement equal to 3 multiplied by the yield strain and a maximum strain in the masonry as given by Section 9.3.2(c) shall be used. For intermediate reinforced masonry shear walls subject to out-of-plane loads, the provisions of Section 9.3.3.5.1 shall apply.

9.3.3.5.3 For special reinforced masonry shear walls subject to in-plane loads where $M_u/(V_u d_v) \geq 1$, a strain gradient corresponding to a strain in the extreme tensile reinforcement equal to 4 multiplied by the yield strain and a maximum strain in the masonry as given by Section 9.3.2(c) shall be used. For special reinforced masonry shear walls subject to out-of-plane loads, the provisions of Section 9.3.3.5.1 shall apply.

COMMENTARY

9.3.3.5 *Maximum area of flexural tensile reinforcement* — Longitudinal reinforcement in flexural members is limited to a maximum amount to ensure that masonry compressive strains will not exceed ultimate values. In other words, the compressive zone of the member will not crush before the tensile reinforcement develops the inelastic strain consistent with the curvature ductility implied by the R value used in design.

For masonry components that are part of the lateral-force-resisting system, maximum reinforcement is limited in accordance with a prescribed strain distribution based on a tensile strain equal to a factor times the yield strain for the reinforcing bar closest to the edge of the member, and a maximum masonry compressive strain equal to 0.0025 for concrete masonry or 0.0035 for clay-unit masonry. By limiting longitudinal reinforcement in this manner, inelastic curvature capacity is directly related to the strain gradient.

The tensile strain factor varies in accordance with the amount of curvature ductility expected, and ranges from 1.5 to 4 for specially reinforced masonry shear walls. Expected curvature ductility, controlled by the factor on tensile yield strain, is assumed to be associated directly with the displacement ductility, or the value of C_d as given for the type of component. For example, a strain factor of 3 for intermediate reinforced masonry shear walls corresponds to the slightly smaller C_d factor of 2.5, and a strain factor of 4 for specially reinforced walls corresponds to the slightly smaller C_d factor of 3.5.

The maximum reinforcement is determined by considering the prescribed strain distribution, determining the corresponding stress and force distribution, and using statics to sum axial forces.

For a fully grouted shear wall subjected to in-plane loads with uniformly distributed reinforcement, the maximum area of reinforcement per unit length of wall is determined as:

$$\frac{A_s}{d_v} = \frac{0.64 f'_m\, b \left(\dfrac{\varepsilon_{mu}}{\varepsilon_{mu} + \alpha \varepsilon_y} \right) - \dfrac{P}{d_v}}{f_y \left(\dfrac{\alpha \varepsilon_y - \varepsilon_{mu}}{\varepsilon_{mu} + \alpha \varepsilon_y} \right)}$$

CODE

9.3.3.5.4 For masonry members where $M_u/(V_u d_v) \leq 1$ and when designed using $R \leq 1.5$, there is no upper limit to the maximum flexural tensile reinforcement. For masonry members where $M_u/(V_u d_v) \leq 1$ and when designed using $R \geq 1.5$, the provisions of Section 9.3.3.5.1 shall apply.

COMMENTARY

For a fully grouted member with only concentrated tension reinforcement, the maximum reinforcement is:

$$\rho = \frac{A_s}{bd} = \frac{0.64 f_m' \left(\dfrac{\varepsilon_{mu}}{\varepsilon_{mu} + \alpha \varepsilon_y} \right) - \dfrac{P}{bd}}{f_y}$$

If there is concentrated compression reinforcement with an area equal to the concentrated tension reinforcement, A_s, the maximum reinforcement is:

$$\rho = \frac{A_s}{bd} = \frac{0.64 f_m' \left(\dfrac{\varepsilon_{mu}}{\varepsilon_{mu} + \alpha \varepsilon_y} \right) - \dfrac{P}{bd}}{f_y - \min\left\{ \varepsilon_{mu} - \dfrac{d'}{d}\left(\varepsilon_{mu} + \alpha \varepsilon_y \right), \varepsilon_y \right\} E_s}$$

where d' is the distance from the extreme compression fiber to the centroid of the compression reinforcement.

For partially grouted cross-sections subjected to out-of-plane loads, the maximum reinforcement is determined based on a fully grouted member with tension reinforcement only, provided that the neutral axis is in the flange. If the neutral axis is in the web, the maximum reinforcement is determined as:

$$\rho = \frac{A_s}{bd}$$

$$\rho = \frac{0.64 f_m' \left(\dfrac{\varepsilon_{mu}}{\varepsilon_{mu} + \alpha \varepsilon_y} \right)\left(\dfrac{b_w}{b} \right) + 0.80 f_m' \, t_{fs} \left(\dfrac{b - b_w}{bd} \right) - \dfrac{P}{bd}}{f_y}$$

where b_w is the width of the compression section minus the sum of the length of ungrouted cells, and t_{fs} is the specified face-shell thickness for hollow masonry units.

Because axial force is implicitly considered in the determination of maximum longitudinal reinforcement, inelastic curvature capacity can be relied on no matter what the level of axial compressive force. Thus, the strength-reduction factors, ϕ, for axial load and flexure can be the same as for flexure alone. Also, confinement reinforcement is not required because the maximum masonry compressive strain will be less than ultimate values.

The axial force is the expected load at the time of the design earthquake. It is derived from ASCE 7 Allowable Stress Load Combination 6 and consideration of the horizontal component of the seismic loading. The vertical component of the earthquake load, E_v, should not be included in calculating the axial force for purposes of determining maximum area of flexural tensile reinforcement.

CODE

COMMENTARY

For structures intended to undergo inelastic deformation, Sections 9.3.3.5.1, 9.3.3.5.2 and 9.3.3.5.3 are technically sound ways of achieving the design objective of inelastic deformation capacity. These provisions are, however, unnecessarily restrictive for those structures not required to undergo inelastic deformation under the design earthquake. Section 9.3.3.5.4 addresses a relaxation of the maximum reinforcement limits.

9.3.3.6 *Bundling of reinforcing bars* — Reinforcing bars shall not be bundled.

9.3.3.6 *Bundling of reinforcing bars* — This requirement stems from the lack of research on masonry with bundled bars.

9.3.3.7 *Joint reinforcement used as shear reinforcement* — Joint reinforcement used as shear reinforcement shall consist of at least two 3/16 in. (4.8 mm) diameter longitudinal wires located within a bed joint and placed over the masonry unit face shells. The maximum spacing of joint reinforcement used as shear reinforcement shall not exceed 16 in. (406 mm) for Seismic Design Categories (SDC) A and B and shall not exceed 8 in. (203 mm) in partially grouted walls for SDC C, D, E, and F. Joint reinforcement used as shear reinforcement in fully grouted walls for SDC C, D, E and F shall consist of four 3/16 in. (4.8 mm) diameter longitudinal wires at a spacing not to exceed 8 in. (203 mm).

9.3.3.7 *Joint reinforcement used as shear reinforcement* — The quantities of joint reinforcement indicated are minimums and the designer should evaluate whether additional reinforcement is required to satisfy specific seismic conditions. Research (Schultz, 1997) provides additional guidelines as to the strength and energy requirements of shear reinforcement. Other research (Schultz and Hutchinson, 2001a and Baenziger and Porter, 2011) provides additional perspective on the behavior of joint reinforcement under cyclic loading conditions.

9.3.4 *Design of beams, piers, and columns*

Member design forces shall be based on an analysis that considers the relative stiffness of structural members. The calculation of lateral stiffness shall include the contribution of all beams, piers, and columns. The effects of cracking on member stiffness shall be considered.

9.3.4 *Design of beams, piers, and columns*

9.3.4.1 *Nominal strength*

9.3.4.1.1 *Nominal axial and flexural strength* — The nominal axial strength, P_n, and the nominal flexural strength, M_n, of a cross section shall be determined in accordance with the design assumptions of Section 9.3.2 and the provisions of this Section. The nominal flexural strength at any section along a member shall not be less than one-fourth of the maximum nominal flexural strength at the critical section.

The nominal axial compressive strength shall not exceed Equation 9-19 or Equation 9-20, as appropriate.

(a) For members having an *h/r* ratio not greater than 99:

$$P_n = 0.80\left[0.80f'_m(A_n - A_{st}) + f_y A_{st}\right]\left[1-\left(\frac{h}{140r}\right)^2\right]$$

(Equation 9-19)

(b) For members having an *h/r* ratio greater than 99:

$$P_n = 0.80\left[0.80f'_m(A_n - A_{st}) + f_y A_{st}\right]\left(\frac{70r}{h}\right)^2$$

(Equation 9-20)

9.3.4.1 *Nominal strength*

9.3.4.1.1 *Nominal axial and flexural strength* — The nominal flexural strength of a member may be calculated using the assumption of an equivalent rectangular stress block as outlined in Section 9.3.2. Commentary Section 8.2.4 gives further information regarding slenderness effects on axial load strength as taken into account with the use of Equation 9-19 and Equation 9-20. Equation 9-19 and Equation 9-20 apply to simply supported end conditions, with or without transverse loading, which result in a symmetric deflection (curvature) about the midheight of the element. Where other support conditions or loading scenarios are known to exist, Equation 9-19 and Equation 9-20 should be modified accordingly to account for the effective height of the element or shape of the bending moment diagram over the clear span of the element. The weak-axis radius of gyration should be used in calculating slenderness-dependent reduction factors. The first coefficient, 0.80, in Equation 9-19 and Equation 9-20 accounts for unavoidable minimum eccentricity in the axial load.

CODE

9.3.4.1.2 *Nominal shear strength* — Nominal shear strength, V_n, shall be calculated using Equation 9-21, and shall not be taken greater than the limits given by 9.3.4.1.2 (a) through (c).

$$V_n = (V_{nm} + V_{ns})\gamma_g \qquad \text{(Equation 9-21)}$$

(a) Where $M_u/(V_u d_v) \le 0.25$:

$$V_n \le \left(6A_{nv}\sqrt{f'_m}\right)\gamma_g \qquad \text{(Equation 9-22)}$$

(b) Where $M_u/(V_u d_v) \ge 1.0$

$$V_n \le \left(4A_{nv}\sqrt{f'_m}\right)\gamma_g \qquad \text{(Equation 9-23)}$$

γ_g = 0.75 for partially grouted shear walls and 1.0 otherwise.

(c) The maximum value of V_n for $M_u/(V_u d_v)$ between 0.25 and 1.0 shall be permitted to be linearly interpolated.

9.3.4.1.2.1 *Nominal masonry shear strength* — Shear strength provided by the masonry, V_{nm}, shall be calculated using Equation 9-24:

$$V_{nm} = \left[4.0 - 1.75\left(\frac{M_u}{V_u d_v}\right)\right] A_{nv}\sqrt{f'_m} + 0.25 P_u$$

$$\text{(Equation 9-24)}$$

$M_u/(V_u d_v)$ shall be taken as a positive number and need not be taken greater than 1.0

9.3.4.1.2.2 *Nominal shear strength provided by reinforcement* — Nominal shear strength provided by shear reinforcement, V_{ns}, shall be calculated as follows:

$$V_{ns} = 0.5\left(\frac{A_v}{s}\right)f_y d_v \qquad \text{(Equation 9-25)}$$

COMMENTARY

9.3.4.1.2 *Nominal shear strength* — The shear strength equations in Section 9.3.4.1.2 are derived from research (Shing et al, 1990a; Shing et al, 1990b). The equations have been compared with results from fifty-six tests of masonry walls failing in in-plane shear (Davis et al, 2010). The test data encompassed both concrete masonry walls and clay masonry walls, all of which were fully grouted. The average ratio of the test strength to the calculated strength was 1.17 with a coefficient of variation of 0.15.

The limitations on maximum nominal shear strength are included to preclude critical (brittle) shear-related failures.

The provisions of this Section were developed through the study of and calibrated to cantilevered shear walls. The ratio $M_u/(V_u d_v)$ can be difficult to interpret or apply consistently for other conditions such as for a uniformly loaded, simply supported beam. Concurrent values of M_u and $V_u d_v$ must be considered at appropriate locations along shear members, such as beams, to determine the critical $M_u/(V_u d_v)$ ratio. To simplify the analytical process, designers are permitted to use $M_u/(V_u d_v) = 1$.

Partially grouted walls can produce lower strengths than predicted by the shear strength equations using just the reduction of net area (Minaie et al, 2010; Nolph and ElGawady, 2011; Schultz, 1996b; Schultz, 1996c; Schultz and Hutchinson, 2001b). The grouted shear wall factor is used to compensate for this reduced strength until methods can be developed to more accurately predict the performance of these elements.

9.3.4.1.2.1 *Nominal masonry shear strength* — Equation 9-24 is empirically derived from research (Shing et al, 1990a; Shing et al, 1990b).

9.3.4.1.2.2 *Nominal shear strength provided by reinforcement* — Equation 9-25 is empirically derived from research (Shing et al, 1990a; Shing et al, 1990b). The nominal shear strength provided by shear reinforcement, Equation 9-25, represents half the theoretical contribution. In other words, the nominal shear strength is determined as the full masonry contribution plus one-half the contribution from the shear reinforcement. Other coefficients were evaluated (0.6, 0.8, and 1.0), but the best fit to the experimental data was obtained using the 0.5 factor (Davis et al, 2010).

CODE

9.3.4.2 *Beams* — Design of beams shall meet the requirements of Section 5.2 and the additional requirements of Sections 9.3.4.2.1 through 9.3.4.2.4.

9.3.4.2.1 The factored axial compressive force on a beam shall not exceed $0.05 A_n f'_m$.

9.3.4.2.2 *Longitudinal reinforcement*

9.3.4.2.2.1 The variation in longitudinal reinforcing bars in a beam shall not be greater than one bar size. Not more than two bar sizes shall be used in a beam.

9.3.4.2.2.2 The nominal flexural strength of a beam shall not be less than 1.3 multiplied by the nominal cracking moment of the beam, M_{cr}. The modulus of rupture, f_r, for this calculation shall be determined in accordance with Section 9.1.9.2.

9.3.4.2.2.3 The requirements of Section 9.3.4.2.2.2 need not be applied if at every section the area of tensile reinforcement provided is at least one-third greater than that required by analysis.

9.3.4.2.3 *Transverse reinforcement* — Transverse reinforcement shall be provided where V_u exceeds ϕV_{nm}. The factored shear, V_u, shall include the effects of lateral load. When transverse reinforcement is required, the following provisions shall apply:

(a) Transverse reinforcement shall be a single bar with a 180-degree hook at each end.

(b) Transverse reinforcement shall be hooked around the longitudinal reinforcement.

(c) The minimum area of transverse reinforcement shall be $0.0007 bd_v$.

(d) The first transverse bar shall not be located more than one-fourth of the beam depth, d_v, from the end of the beam.

(e) The maximum spacing shall not exceed one-half the depth of the beam nor 48 in. (1219 mm).

COMMENTARY

9.3.4.2 *Beams* — This section applies to the design of lintels and beams.

9.3.4.2.2 *Longitudinal reinforcement*

9.3.4.2.2.1 Restricting the variation of bar sizes in a beam is included to increase the depth of the member compression zone and to increase member ductility. When incorporating two bars of significantly different sizes in a single beam, the larger bar requires a much higher force to reach yield strain, in effect "stiffening" the beam.

9.3.4.2.2.2 The requirement that the nominal flexural strength of a beam not be less than 1.3 multiplied by the nominal cracking moment is imposed to prevent brittle failures. This situation may occur where a beam is so lightly reinforced that the bending moment required to cause yielding of the reinforcement is less than the bending moment required to cause cracking.

9.3.4.2.2.3 This exception provides sufficient additional reinforcement in members in which the amount of reinforcement required by Section 9.3.4.2.2.2 would be excessive.

9.3.4.2.3 *Transverse reinforcement* — Beams recognized in this section of the Code are often designed to resist only shear forces due to gravity loads. Beams that are controlled by high seismic forces and lateral drift should be designed as ductile elements.

(a) Although some concerns have been raised regarding the difficulty in constructing beams containing a single bar stirrup, the Committee feels such spacing limitations within beams inhibits the construction of necessary lap lengths required for two-bar stirrups. Furthermore, the added volume of reinforcement as a result of lap splicing stirrups may prevent adequate consolidation of the grout.

(b) The requirement that shear reinforcement be hooked around the longitudinal reinforcement not only facilitates construction but also confines the longitudinal reinforcement and contributes to the development of the shear reinforcement.

(c) A minimum area of transverse reinforcement is established to prevent brittle shear failures.

(d) Although different codes contain different spacing requirements for the placement of transverse reinforcement, the Committee has conservatively established this requirement.

(e) The requirements of this section establish limitations on the spacing and placement of reinforcement in order to increase member ductility.

CODE

9.3.4.2.4 *Construction* — Beams shall be fully grouted.

9.3.4.3 *Piers*

9.3.4.3.1 The factored axial compression force on piers shall not exceed $0.3 A_n f'_m$.

9.3.4.3.2 *Longitudinal reinforcement* — A pier subjected to in-plane stress reversals shall be reinforced symmetrically about the neutral axis of the pier. Longitudinal reinforcement of piers shall comply with the following:

(a) At least one bar shall be provided in each end cell.

(b) The minimum area of longitudinal reinforcement shall be $0.0007 \, bd$.

9.3.4.3.3 *Dimensional limits* — Dimensions shall be in accordance with the following:

(a) The nominal thickness of a pier shall not exceed 16 in. (406 mm).

(b) The distance between lateral supports of a pier shall not exceed 25 multiplied by the nominal thickness of a pier except as provided for in Section 9.3.4.3.3(c).

(c) When the distance between lateral supports of a pier exceeds 25 multiplied by the nominal thickness of the pier, design shall be based on the provisions of Section 9.3.5.

(d) The nominal length of a pier shall not be less than three multiplied by its nominal thickness nor greater than six multiplied by its nominal thickness. The clear height of a pier shall not exceed five multiplied by its nominal length.

Exception: When the factored axial force at the location of maximum moment is less than $0.05 f'_m A_g$, the length of a pier shall be permitted to be equal to the thickness of the pier.

COMMENTARY

9.3.4.2.4 *Construction* — Although beams can physically be constructed of partially grouted masonry, the lack of research supporting the performance of partially grouted beams combined with the increased probability of brittle failure dictates this requirement.

9.3.4.3 *Piers*

9.3.4.3.1 Due to the less severe requirements imposed for the design of piers with respect to similar requirements for columns, the maximum axial force is arbitrarily limited to a relatively lower value.

9.3.4.3.2 *Longitudinal reinforcement* — These provisions are predominantly earthquake-related and are intended to provide ductility. Piers not subject to in-plane stress reversals are not required to comply with this section.

9.3.4.3.3 *Dimensional limits* — Judgment-based dimensional limits are established for piers to distinguish their design from walls and to prevent local instability or buckling modes.

CODE

9.3.5 *Wall design for out-of-plane loads*

9.3.5.1 *Scope* — The requirements of Section 9.3.5 shall apply to the design of walls for out-of-plane loads.

9.3.5.2 *Nominal axial and flexural strength* — The nominal axial strength, P_n, and the nominal flexural strength, M_n, of a cross-section shall be determined in accordance with the design assumptions of Section 9.3.2. The nominal axial compressive strength shall not exceed that determined by Equation 9-19 or Equation 9-20, as appropriate.

9.3.5.3 *Nominal shear strength* — The nominal shear strength shall be determined by Section 9.3.4.1.2.

9.3.5.4 P-*delta effects*

9.3.5.4.1 Members shall be designed for the factored axial load, P_u, and the moment magnified for the effects of member curvature, M_u. The magnified moment shall be determined either by Section 9.3.5.4.2 or Section 9.3.5.4.3.

9.3.5.4.2 Moment and deflection calculations in this section are based on simple support conditions top and bottom. For other support and fixity conditions, moments and deflections shall be calculated using established principles of mechanics.

The procedures set forth in this Section shall be used when the factored axial load stress at the location of maximum moment satisfies the requirement calculated by Equation 9-26.

COMMENTARY

9.3.5 *Wall design for out-of-plane loads*
9.3.5.1 *Scope*

9.3.5.2 *Nominal axial and flexural strength* — When the depth of the equivalent stress block is in the face shell of a wall that is fully or partially grouted, the nominal moment may be found from:

$$M_n = \left(P_u / \phi + A_s f_y\right)\left(\frac{t_{sp} - a}{2}\right) + A_s f_y\left(d - \frac{t_{sp}}{2}\right)$$

$$a = \frac{A_s f_y + P_u / \phi}{0.80 f_m' b}$$

The above equations are valid for both centered and noncentered flexural reinforcement. For centered flexural reinforcement, $d = t_{sp}/2$ and the nominal moment, M_n, is obtained as:

$$M_n = \left(P_u / \phi + A_s f_y\right)\left(d - \frac{a}{2}\right)$$

These equations take into account the effect of compressive vertical loads increasing the flexural strength of the section. In the case of axial tension, the flexural strength is decreased.

9.3.5.4.2 The provisions of this section are derived from results of tests on simply supported specimens. Because the maximum bending moment and deflection occur near the mid-height of those specimens, this section includes only design equations for that condition. When actual conditions are not simple supports, the curvature of a wall under out-of-plane lateral loading will be different than that assumed by these equations. Using the principles of mechanics, the points of inflection can be determined and actual moments and deflections can be calculated under different support conditions. The designer should examine all moment and deflection conditions to locate the critical section using the assumptions outlined in Section 9.3.5.

The criterion to limit vertical load on a cross section was included because the slender wall design method was based on data from testing with typical roof loads. For h/t ratios greater than 30, there is an additional limitation on the axial stress.

CODE

$$\left(\frac{P_u}{A_g}\right) \le 0.20 f'_m \qquad \text{(Equation 9-26)}$$

When the ratio of effective height to nominal thickness, h/t, exceeds 30, the factored axial stress shall not exceed $0.05f'_m$.

Factored moment and axial force shall be determined at the midheight of the wall and shall be used for design. The factored moment, M_u, at the midheight of the wall shall be calculated using Equation 9-27.

$$M_u = \frac{w_u h^2}{8} + P_{uf}\frac{e_u}{2} + P_u \delta_u \qquad \text{(Equation 9-27)}$$

Where:

$$P_u = P_{uw} + P_{uf} \qquad \text{(Equation 9-28)}$$

The deflection due to factored loads (δ_u) shall be obtained using Equations 9-29 and 9-30.

(a) Where $M_u < M_{cr}$

$$\delta_u = \frac{5M_u h^2}{48 E_m I_n} \qquad \text{(Equation 9-29)}$$

(b) Where $M_{cr} \le M_u \le M_n$

$$\delta_u = \frac{5M_{cr} h^2}{48 E_m I_n} + \frac{5(M_u - M_{cr})h^2}{48 E_m I_{cr}}$$

$$\text{(Equation 9-30)}$$

9.3.5.4.3 The factored moment, M_u, shall be determined either by a second-order analysis, or by a first-order analysis and Equations 9-31 through 9-33.

$$M_u = \psi M_{u,0} \qquad \text{(Equation 9-31)}$$

Where $M_{u,0}$ is the factored moment from first-order analysis.

$$\psi = \frac{1}{1 - \dfrac{P_u}{P_e}} \qquad \text{(Equation 9-32)}$$

Where:

$$P_e = \frac{\pi^2 E_m I_{eff}}{h^2} \qquad \text{(Equation 9-33)}$$

For $M_u < M_{cr}$, I_{eff} shall be taken as $0.75I_n$. For $M_u \ge M_{cr}$, I_{eff} shall be taken as I_{cr}. P_u/P_e cannot exceed 1.0.

COMMENTARY

The required moment due to lateral loads, eccentricity of axial load, and lateral deformations is assumed maximum at mid-height of the wall. In certain design conditions, such as large eccentricities acting simultaneously with small lateral loads, the design maximum moment may occur elsewhere. When this occurs, the designer should use the maximum moment at the critical section rather than the moment determined from Equation 9-27.

9.3.5.4.3 The moment magnifier provisions in this section were developed to provide an alternative to the traditional P-delta methods of Section 9.3.5.4.2. These provisions also allow other second-order analyses to be used.

The proposed moment magnification equation is very similar to that used for slender wall design for reinforced concrete. Concrete design provisions use a factor of 0.75 in the denominator of the moment magnifier to account for uncertainties in the wall stiffness. This factor is retained for uncracked walls. It is not used for cracked walls. Instead, the cracked moment of inertia is conservatively used for the entire wall height. Trial designs indicated that using this approach matches design using Section 9.3.5.4.2. If a 0.75 factor were included along with using the cracked moment of inertia for the entire height would result in design moments approximately 7% greater than using Section 9.3.5.4.2. The committee did not see any reason for the additional conservatism.

CODE	COMMENTARY

CODE

9.3.5.4.4 The cracking moment of the wall shall be calculated using the modulus of rupture, f_r, taken from Table 9.1.9.2.

9.3.5.4.5 The neutral axis for determining the cracked moment of inertia, I_{cr}, shall be determined in accordance with the design assumptions of Section 9.3.2. The effects of axial load shall be permitted to be included when calculating I_{cr}.

Unless stiffness values are obtained by a more comprehensive analysis, the cracked moment of inertia for a wall that is partially or fully grouted and whose neutral axis is in the face shell shall be obtained from Equation 9-34 and Equation 9-35.

$$I_{cr} = n\left(A_s + \frac{P_u}{f_y}\frac{t_{sp}}{2d}\right)(d-c)^2 + \frac{bc^3}{3} \quad \text{(Equation 9-34)}$$

$$c = \frac{A_s f_y + P_u}{0.64 f'_m b} \quad \text{(Equation 9-35)}$$

9.3.5.5 *Deflections* — The horizontal midheight deflection, δ_s, under allowable stress design load combinations shall be limited by the relation:

$$\delta_s \leq 0.007\ h \quad \text{(Equation 9-36)}$$

P-delta effects shall be included in deflection calculation using either Section 9.3.5.5.1 or Section 9.3.5.5.2.

9.3.5.5.1 For simple support conditions top and bottom, the midheight deflection, δ_s, shall be calculated using either Equation 9-29 or Equation 9-30, as applicable, and replacing M_u with M_{ser} and δ_u with δ_s.

COMMENTARY

9.3.5.4.4 The cracking moment, M_{cr}, is the calculated moment corresponding to first cracking. The Code permits the applied axial force to be included in the calculation of the cracking moment.

9.3.5.4.5 The Code requires that the neutral axis used to calculate the cracked moment of inertia be determined using the strain distribution at nominal strength. Amrhein and Lee (1984) used this condition to develop the original slender wall design provisions.

Equations 9-34 and 9-35 are valid for both centered and non-centered vertical reinforcement. The modification term of $(t_{sp}/2d)$ in Equation 9-34 accounts for a reduction in the contribution of the axial load to the cracked moment of inertia when the reinforcement is near the face of the wall.

9.3.5.5 *Deflections* — Historically, the recommendation has been to limit the deflection under allowable stress load combinations to $0.01h$. The committee has chosen a more stringent value of $0.007h$.

The Code limits the lateral deflection under allowable stress load combinations. A wall loaded in this range returns to its original vertical position when the lateral load is removed, because the stress in the reinforcement is within its elastic limit.

9.3.5.5.1 Equation 9-29 is for mid-height deflection of a simply supported wall for an uncracked section, and Equation 9-30 is for mid-height deflection for a cracked section. A wall is assumed to deflect as an uncracked section until the modulus of rupture is reached, after which it is assumed to deflect as a cracked section. The cracked moment of inertia is conservatively assumed to apply over the entire height of the wall. The cracked moment of inertia, I_{cr}, for a fully grouted or partially grouted cross section is usually the same as that for a hollow section because the compression stress block is generally within the thickness of the face shell.

These equations represent good approximations to test results, assuming that the wall is simply supported top and bottom, and is subjected to a uniformly distributed lateral load. If the wall is fixed at top, bottom, or both, other formulas should be developed considering the support conditions at the top or bottom and considering the possible deflection or rotation of the foundation, roof, or floor diaphragm.

CODE

9.3.5.5.2 The deflection, δ_s , shall be determined by a second-order analysis that includes the effects of cracking, or by a first-order analysis with the calculated deflections magnified by a factor of $1/(1-P/P_e)$, where P_e is determined from Equation (9-33).

9.3.6   *Wall design for in-plane loads*

9.3.6.1 *Scope* — The requirements of Section 9.3.6 shall apply to the design of walls to resist in-plane loads.

9.3.6.2 *Reinforcement* — Reinforcement shall be provided perpendicular to the shear reinforcement and shall be at least equal to one-third A_v. The reinforcement shall be uniformly distributed and shall not exceed a spacing of 8 ft (2.44 m).

9.3.6.3 *Flexural and axial strength* — The nominal flexural and axial strength shall be determined in accordance with Section 9.3.4.1.1.

9.3.6.4 *Shear strength* — The nominal shear strength shall be calculated in accordance with Section 9.3.4.1.2.

9.3.6.5 The maximum reinforcement requirements of Section 9.3.3.5 shall not apply if a shear wall is designed to satisfy the requirements of 9.3.6.5.1 through 9.3.6.5.5.

COMMENTARY

The Code requires that the neutral axis used to calculate the cracked moment of inertia be determined using the strain distribution at nominal strength. Amrhein and Lee (1984) used this condition to develop the original slender wall design provisions.

Equation 9-34 and 9-35 are valid for both centered and non-centered vertical reinforcement. The modification term of ($t_{sp}/2d$) in Equation 9-34 accounts for a reduction in the contribution of the axial load to the cracked moment of inertia when the reinforcement is near the face of the wall.

9.3.5.5.2 This section allows other second-order analyses to be used to predict wall deflections, including first-order deflections amplified using a moment magnification factor.

Less conservative estimation for first-order wall deformation can be obtained using an effective I value that accounts for partial cracking of the sections, such as that described in Section 5.2.1.4.2.

9.3.6   *Wall design for in-plane loads*

9.3.6.5 The maximum reinforcement requirements of Section 9.3.3.5 are intended to ensure that an intermediate or a special reinforced masonry shear wall has sufficient inelastic deformation capacity under the design-basis earthquake of ASCE 7 or the model building codes. Inelastic deformability is the ability of a structure or structural element to continue to sustain gravity loads as it deforms laterally under earthquake (or some other type of) excitation beyond the stage where the response of the structure or the structural element to that excitation is elastic (that is, associated with no residual displacement or damage). In the alternative shear wall design approach given in Sections 9.3.6.5.1 through 9.3.6.5.5, such inelastic deformability is sought to be ensured by means of specially confined boundary elements, making compliance with the maximum reinforcement requirements unnecessary. These requirements are therefore waived.

CODE

9.3.6.5.1 Special boundary elements need not be provided in shear walls meeting the following conditions:

1. $P_u \leq 0.10 A_g f'_m$ for geometrically symmetrical wall sections

    $P_u \leq 0.05 A_g f'_m$ for geometrically unsymmetrical wall sections; and either

2. $\dfrac{M_u}{V_u d_v} \leq 1.0$

    or

3. $V_u \leq 3A_{nv}\sqrt{f'_m}$ and $\dfrac{M_u}{V_u d_v} \leq 3.0$

9.3.6.5.2 The need for special boundary elements at the edges of shear walls shall be evaluated in accordance with Section 9.3.6.5.3 or 9.3.6.5.4. The requirements of Section 9.3.6.5.5 shall also be satisfied.

9.3.6.5.3 This Section applies to walls bending in single curvature in which the flexural limit state response is governed by yielding at the base of the wall. Walls not satisfying those requirements shall be designed in accordance with Section 9.3.6.5.4

(a) Special boundary elements shall be provided over portions of compression zones where:

$$c \geq \frac{l_w}{600\left(C_d \delta_{ne}/h_w\right)}$$

and c is calculated for the P_u given by ASCE 7 Strength Design Load Combination 5 ($1.2D + 1.0E + L + 0.2S$) or the corresponding strength design load combination of the legally adopted building code, and the corresponding nominal moment strength, M_n, at the base critical section. The load factor on L in Combination 5 is reducible to 0.5, as per exceptions to Section 2.3.2 of ASCE 7.

COMMENTARY

9.3.6.5.1 This subsection sets up some "screens" with the expectation that many, if not most, shear walls will go through the screens, in which case no special boundary elements would be required. This situation will be the case when a shear wall is lightly axially loaded and it is either short or is moderate in height and is subject to only moderate shear stresses.

The threshold values are adapted from the design procedure for special reinforced concrete shear walls in the 1997 Uniform Building Code (UBC). In the early 1990s, when this procedure of the 1997 UBC was first being developed, an ad hoc subcommittee within the Seismology Committee of the Structural Engineers Association of California had limited, unpublished parametric studies done, showing that a reinforced concrete shear wall passing through the "screens" could not develop sufficiently high compressive strains in the concrete to warrant special confinement. In the case of masonry, strains requiring special confinement would be values exceeding the maximum usable strains of Section 9.3.2 (c).

9.3.6.5.2 Two approaches for evaluating detailing requirements at wall boundaries are included in Section 9.3.6.5.2. Section 9.3.6.5.3 allows the use of displacement-based design of walls, in which the structural details are determined directly on the basis of the expected lateral displacements of the wall under the design-basis earthquake. The provisions of Section 9.3.6.5.4 are conservative for assessing required transverse reinforcement at wall boundaries for many walls. The requirements of Section 9.3.6.5.5 apply to shear walls designed by either Section 9.3.6.5.3 or 9.3.6.5.4.

9.3.6.5.3 Section 9.3.6.5.3 is based on the assumption that inelastic response of the wall is dominated by flexural action at a critical, yielding section – typically at the base. The wall should be proportioned so that the critical section occurs where intended (at the base).

(a) The following explanation, including Figure CC-9.3-3, is adapted from a paper by Wallace and Orakcal (2002). The relationship between the wall top displacement and wall curvature for a wall of uniform cross-section with a single critical section at the base is presented in Figure CC-9.3-3. The provisions of this Code are based on a simplified version of the model presented in Figure CC-9.3-3(a). The simplified model, shown in Figure CC-9.3-3(b), neglects the contribution of elastic deformations to the top displacement, and moves the center of the plastic hinge to the base of the wall. Based on the model of Figure CC-9.3-3, the relationship between the top displacement and the curvature at the base of the wall is:

$$C_d \delta_{ne} = \theta_p h_w = (\phi_u \ell_p)h_w = \left(\phi_u \frac{\ell_w}{2}\right)h_w$$

(Equation 1)

CODE

COMMENTARY

assuming that $\ell_p = \ell_w / 2$, as is permitted to be assumed by the 1997 UBC,

where $\quad \phi_u$ = ultimate curvature, and

$\qquad \theta_p$ = plastic rotation at the base of the wall.

If at the stage where the top deflection of the wall is δ_{ne}, the extreme fiber compressive strain at the critical section at the base does not exceed ε_{mu}, no special confinement would be required anywhere in the wall. Figure CC-9.3-4 illustrates such a strain distribution at the critical section. The neutral axis depth corresponding to this strain distribution is c_{cr}, and the corresponding ultimate curvature is $\phi_u = \varepsilon_{mu} / c_{cr}$. From Equation 1,

$$C_d \delta_{ne} = \left(\frac{\varepsilon_{mu}}{c_{cr}} \frac{\ell_w}{2} \right) h_w \qquad \text{(Equation 2a)}$$

or, $c_{cr} = \dfrac{\varepsilon_{mu}}{2} \dfrac{\ell_w}{(C_d \delta_{ne} / h_w)} \qquad \text{(Equation 2b)}$

From the equations above (see Figure CC-9.3-4), special detailing would be required if:

$$c \geq \frac{\varepsilon_{mu}}{2} \frac{\ell_w}{(C_d \delta_{ne} / h_w)} = \frac{0.003}{2} \frac{\ell_w}{(C_d \delta_{ne} / h_w)}$$

$$= \frac{\ell_w}{667 (C_d \delta_{ne} / h_w)} \approx \frac{\ell_w}{600 (C_d \delta_{ne} / h_w)}$$

because if the neutral axis depth exceeded the critical value, the extreme fiber compressive strain would exceed the maximum usable strain ε_{mu}. For purposes of this derivation, and to avoid having separate sets of drift-related requirements for clay and concrete masonry, a single useful strain of 0.003 is used, representing an average of the design values of 0.0025 for concrete masonry and 0.0035 for clay masonry.

(b) Where special boundary elements are required by Section 9.3.6.5.3 (a), the special boundary element reinforcement shall extend vertically from the critical section a distance not less than the larger of l_w or $M_u/4V_u$.

(b) These special extensions are intended to be an upper-bound estimate of the plastic hinge length for special reinforced masonry shear walls.

COMMENTARY

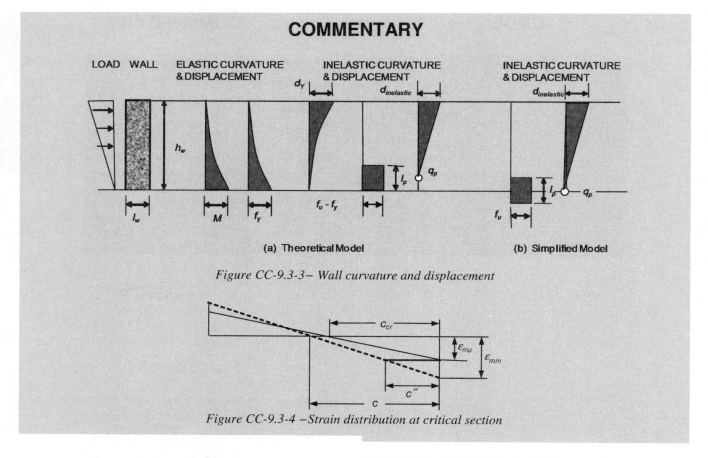

Figure CC-9.3-3– Wall curvature and displacement

Figure CC-9.3-4 –Strain distribution at critical section

CODE

9.3.6.5.4 Shear walls not designed by Section 9.3.6.5.3 shall have special boundary elements at boundaries and edges around openings in shear walls where the maximum extreme fiber compressive stress, corresponding to factored forces including earthquake effect, exceeds $0.2 f'_m$. The special boundary element shall be permitted to be discontinued where the calculated compressive stress is less than $0.15 f'_m$. Stresses shall be calculated for the factored forces using a linearly elastic model and gross section properties. For walls with flanges, an effective flange width as defined in Section 5.1.1.2.3 shall be used.

9.3.6.5.5 Where special boundary elements are required by Section 9.3.6.5.3 or 9.3.6.5.4, requirements (a) through (d) in this section shall be satisfied and tests shall be performed to verify the strain capacity of the element:

COMMENTARY

9.3.6.5.4 A stress-based approach is included to address wall configurations to which the application of displacement-based approach is not appropriate (for example, walls with openings, walls with setbacks, walls not controlled by flexure).

The Code has adopted the stress-based triggers of ACI 318-99 for cases where the displacement-based approach is not applicable, simply changing the threshold values of $0.2 f'_c$ and $0.15 f'_c$ for reinforced concrete walls to $0.2 f'_m$ and $0.15 f'_m$, respectively, for reinforced masonry walls. Other aspects of the ACI 318-99 approach are retained. Design for flexure and axial loads does not change depending on whether the neutral axis-based trigger or the stress-based trigger is used.

9.3.6.5.5 This Code requires that testing be done to verify that the detailing provided is capable of developing a strain capacity in the boundary element that would be in excess of the maximum imposed strain. Reasonably extensive tests need to be conducted to develop prescriptive detailing requirements for specially confined boundary elements of intermediate as well as special reinforced masonry shear walls.

CODE

(a) The special boundary element shall extend horizontally from the extreme compression fiber a distance not less than the larger of $(c - 0.1l_w)$ and $c/2$.

COMMENTARY

(a) Figure CC-9.3-4 shows that when the neutral axis depth c exceeds the critical neutral axis depth c_{cr}, the extreme compression fiber strain in the masonry reaches a value ε_{mm} in excess of the maximum usable strain ε_{mu}. The corresponding ultimate curvature ϕ is ε_{mu}/c. Based on the model of Figure CC-9.3-3(b),

$$C_d \delta_{ne} = \theta_p h_w = (\phi_u \ell_p) h_w = \left(\frac{\varepsilon_{mm}}{c} \frac{\ell_w}{2}\right) h_w$$

(Equation 3)

From Equation 3:

$$\varepsilon_{mm} = 2\left(\frac{C_d \delta_{ne}}{h_w}\right)\left(\frac{c}{\ell_w}\right)$$ (Equation 4)

The wall length over which the strains exceed the limiting value of ε_{mu}, denoted as c'', can be determined using similar triangles from Figure CC-9.3-4:

$$c'' = c\left(1 - \frac{\varepsilon_{mu}}{\varepsilon_{mm}}\right)$$ (Equation 5)

An expression for the required length of confinement can be developed by combining Equations 2 and 3:

$$\frac{c''}{\ell_w} = \frac{c}{\ell_w} - \frac{(\varepsilon_{mu}/2)}{(C_d \delta_{ne}/h_w)}$$ (Equation 6)

The term c/ℓ_w in Equation 4 accounts for the influence of material properties (f'_m, f_y), axial load, geometry, and quantities and distribution of reinforcement, whereas the term $(\varepsilon_{mu}/2)/(C_d \delta_{ne}/h_w)$ accounts for the influence of system response (roof displacement) and the maximum usable strain of masonry.

The wall length over which special transverse reinforcement is to be provided is based on Equation 6, with a value of $C_d \delta_{ne}/h_w = 0.015$:

$$\frac{c''}{\ell_w} = \frac{c}{\ell_w} - \frac{(0.003/2)}{0.015} = \frac{c}{\ell_w} - 0.1 \geq \frac{c}{2}$$ (Equation 7)

The value of $C_d \delta_{ne}/h_w$ was selected to provide an upper-bound estimate of the mean drift ratio of typical shear wall buildings constructed in the United States of America (Wallace and Moehle, 1992). Thus, the length of the wall that must be confined is conservative for many buildings. The value of $c/2$ represents a minimum length of confinement, is adopted from ACI 318-99, and is arbitrary.

CODE

(b) In flanged sections, the special boundary element shall include the effective flange width in compression and shall extend at least 12 in. (305 mm) into the web.

(c) Special boundary element transverse reinforcement at the wall base shall extend into the support a minimum of the development length of the largest longitudinal reinforcement in the boundary element unless the special boundary element terminates on a footing or mat, where special boundary element transverse reinforcement shall extend at least 12 in. (305 mm) into the footing or mat.

(d) Horizontal shear reinforcement in the wall web shall be anchored to develop the specified yield strength, f_y, within the confined core of the boundary element.

COMMENTARY

(b) This requirement originated in the 1997 UBC. Where flanges are highly stressed in compression, the web-to-flange interface is likely to be highly stressed and may sustain local crushing failure unless special boundary element reinforcement extends into the web.

(c) The same extension is required for special boundary element transverse reinforcement in special reinforced concrete shear walls and for special transverse reinforcement in reinforced concrete columns supporting reactions from discontinued stiff members in buildings assigned to high seismic design categories.

(d) Because horizontal reinforcement is likely to act as web reinforcement in walls requiring boundary elements, it needs to be fully anchored in boundary elements that act as flanges. Achievement of this anchorage is difficult when large transverse cracks occur in the boundary elements. Standard 90-degree hooks or mechanical anchorage schemes, instead of straight bar development are recommended.

CHAPTER 10
PRESTRESSED MASONRY

CODE

10.1 — General

10.1.1 *Scope*

This chapter provides requirements for design of masonry walls that are prestressed with bonded or unbonded prestressing tendons.

10.1.2 Walls shall be designed for strength requirements and checked for service load requirements.

10.1.3 The wall provisions of Part 1, Part 2, and Section 8.1 shall apply to prestressed masonry walls.

10.1.4 The provisions of Section 10.4.3 shall apply for the calculation of nominal moment strength.

10.1.5 Masonry shall be laid in running bond unless a bond beam or other technique is used to distribute anchorage forces.

COMMENTARY

10.1 — General

10.1.1 *Scope*

Prestressing forces are used in masonry walls to reduce or eliminate tensile stresses due to externally applied loads by using controlled precompression. The precompression is generated by prestressing tendons, either bars, wires, or strands, that are contained in openings in the masonry, which may be grouted. The prestressing tendons can be pre-tensioned (stressed against external abutments prior to placing the masonry), or post-tensioned (stressed against the masonry after it has been placed). Because most research and applications to date have focused on walls, the chapter applies only to walls, not columns, beams, nor lintels. (Provisions for columns, beams, and lintels will be developed in future editions of the Code.)

Most construction applications to date have involved post-tensioned, ungrouted masonry for its ease of construction and overall economy. Consequently, these code provisions primarily focus on post-tensioned masonry. Although not very common, pre-tensioning has been used to construct prefabricated masonry panels. A more detailed review of prestressed masonry systems and applications is given elsewhere (Schultz and Scolforo, 1991).

Throughout this Code and Specification, references to "reinforcement" apply to non-prestressed reinforcement. These references do not apply to prestressing tendons, except as explicitly noted in Chapter 10. Requirements for prestressing tendons use the terms "prestressing tendon" or "tendon." The provisions of Chapter 10 do not require a mandatory quantity of reinforcement or bonded prestressing tendons for prestressed masonry walls.

Anchorage forces are distributed within a wall similar to the way in which concentrated loads are distributed (as described in Section 5.1.3; see Figure CC-5.1-5). However, research (Woodham and Hamilton, 2003) has indicated that prestress losses can distribute to adjacent tendons as far laterally from the anchorage as the height of the wall.

CODE

10.1.6 For prestressed masonry members, the prestressing force shall be added to load combinations, except as modified by Section 10.4.2.

10.2 — Design methods

10.2.1 *General*
Prestressed masonry members shall be designed by elastic analysis using loading and load combinations in accordance with the provisions of Sections 4.1.2, except as noted in Section 10.4.3.

10.2.2 *After transfer*
Immediately after the transfer of prestressing force to the masonry, limitations on masonry stresses given in this chapter shall be based upon f'_{mi}.

10.3 — Permissible stresses in prestressing tendons

10.3.1 *Jacking force*
The stress in prestressing tendons due to the jacking force shall not exceed $0.94 f_{py}$, nor $0.80 f_{pu}$, nor the maximum value recommended by the manufacturer of the prestressing tendons or anchorages.

10.3.2 *Immediately after transfer*
The stress in the prestressing tendons immediately after transfer of the prestressing force to the masonry shall not exceed $0.82 f_{py}$ nor $0.74 f_{pu}$.

10.3.3 *Post-tensioned masonry members*
At the time of application of prestress, the stress in prestressing tendons at anchorages and couplers shall not exceed $0.78 f_{py}$ nor $0.70 f_{pu}$.

COMMENTARY

10.2 — Design methods

Originally, prestressed masonry was designed using allowable stress design with a moment strength check for walls with laterally restrained tendons. The British code for prestressed masonry (BSI, 1985; Phipps, 1992) and extensive research on the behavior of prestressed masonry were considered. Summaries of prestressed masonry research and proposed design criteria are available in the literature (Schultz and Scolforo, 1992(a and b); VSL, 1990; Curtin et al, 1988; Phipps and Montague, 1976). Design methods are now based upon strength provisions with serviceability checks.

A masonry wall is typically prestressed prior to 28 days after construction, sometimes within 24 hours after construction. The specified compressive strength of the masonry at the time of prestressing (f'_{mi}) is used to determine allowable prestressing levels. This strength will likely be a fraction of the 28-day specified compressive strength. Assessment of masonry compressive strength immediately before the transfer of prestress should be by testing of masonry prisms or by a record of strength gain over time of masonry prisms constructed of similar masonry units, mortar, and grout, when subjected to similar curing conditions.

10.3 — Permissible stresses in prestressing tendons

Allowable prestressing-tendon stresses are based on criteria established for prestressed concrete (ACI 318, 2011). Allowable prestressing-tendon stresses are for jacking forces and for the state of stress in the prestressing tendon immediately after the prestressing has been applied, or transferred, to the masonry. When calculating the prestressing-tendon stress immediately after transfer of prestress, consider all sources of short term prestress losses. These sources include such items as anchorage seating loss, elastic shortening of masonry, and friction losses.

CODE

10.3.4 *Effective prestress*

The calculated effective stress in the prestressing tendons under service loads, f_{se}, shall include the effects of the following:

(a) anchorage seating losses,

(b) elastic shortening of masonry,

(c) creep of masonry,

(d) shrinkage of concrete masonry,

(e) relaxation of prestressing tendon stress,

(f) friction losses,

(g) irreversible moisture expansion of clay masonry, and

(h) thermal effects.

COMMENTARY

10.3.4 *Effective prestress*

The state of stress in a prestressed masonry wall must be checked for each stage of loading. For each loading condition, the effective level of prestress should be used in the calculation of stresses and wall strength. Effective prestress is not a fixed quantity over time. Research on the loss and gain of prestress in prestressed masonry is extensive and includes testing of time-dependent phenomena such as creep, shrinkage, moisture expansion, and prestressing-tendon stress relaxation (PCI, 1975; Lenczner, 1985; Lenczner, 1987; Shrive, 1988) .

Instantaneous deformation of masonry due to the application of prestress may be calculated by the modulus of elasticity of masonry given in Section 4.2.2. Creep, shrinkage, and moisture expansion of masonry may be calculated by the coefficients given in Section 4.2. Change in effective prestress due to elastic deformation, creep, shrinkage, and moisture expansion should be based on relative modulus of elasticity of masonry and prestressing steel.

The stressing operation and relative placement of prestressing tendons should be considered in calculating losses. Elastic shortening during post-tensioning can reduce the stress in adjacent tendons that have already been stressed. Consequently, elastic shortening of the wall should be calculated considering the incremental application of post-tensioning. That elastic shortening should then be used to estimate the total loss of prestress. Alternatively, post-tensioning tendons can be prestressed to compensate for the elastic shortening caused by the incremental stressing operation.

Prestressing steel that is stressed to a large fraction of its yield strength and held at a constant strain will relax, requiring less stress to maintain a constant strain. The phenomenon of stress relaxation is associated with plastic deformation and its magnitude increases with steel stress as a fraction of steel strength. ASTM A416 (2006), A421 (2005), and A722 (2007) prestressing steels are stabilized for low relaxation losses during production. Other steel types that do not have this stabilization treatment may exhibit considerably higher relaxation losses. Their relaxation losses must be carefully assessed by testing. The loss of effective prestress due to stress relaxation of the prestressing tendon is dependent upon the level of prestress, which changes with time-dependent phenomenon such as creep, shrinkage, and moisture expansion of the masonry. An appropriate formula for predicting prestress loss due to relaxation has been developed (Lenczner, 1985; Lenczner, 1987; Shrive, 1988). Alternately, direct addition of the steel stress-relaxation value provided by the manufacturer can be used to calculate prestress losses and gains.

Friction losses are minimal or nonexistent for most post-tensioned masonry applications, because prestressing tendons are usually straight and contained in cavities. For anchorage losses, manufacturers' information should be used to calculate prestress losses. Changes in prestress due to

CODE

COMMENTARY

thermal fluctuations may be neglected if masonry is prestressed with high-strength prestressing steels. Loss of prestressing should be calculated for each design to determine effective prestress. Calculations should be based on the particular construction materials and methods as well as the climate and environmental conditions. Committee experience, research, and field experience with post-tensioned wall designs from Switzerland, Great Britain, Australia, and New Zealand has indicated that prestress losses are expected to be in the following ranges (Woodham and Hamilton, 2003; Hamilton and Badger, 2000; Biggs and Ganz, 1998; NCMA TEK 14-20A, 2002):

(a) Initial loss after jacking –5% to 10%

(b) Total losses after long-term service for concrete masonry – 30% to 35%

(c) Total losses after long-term service for clay masonry – 20% to 25%

The values in (b) and (c) include both the short-term and long-term losses expected for post-tensioning. The Committee believes these ranges provide reasonable estimates for typical wall applications, unless calculations, experience, or construction techniques indicate different losses are expected.

10.4 — Axial compression and flexure

10.4.1 General

10.4.1.1 Walls subjected to axial compression, flexure, or to combined axial compression and flexure shall be designed according to the provisions of Section 8.2.4, except as noted in Section 10.4.1.2, 10.4.1.3, 10.4.2, and 10.4.3.

10.4.1.2 The allowable compressive stresses due to axial loads, F_a, and flexure, F_b, and the allowable axial force in Equation 8-15 shall be permitted to be increased by 20 percent for the stress condition immediately after transfer of prestress.

10.4.1.3 Masonry shall not be subjected to flexural tensile stress from the combination of prestressing force and dead load.

10.4 — Axial compression and flexure

10.4.1 General

The requirements for prestressed masonry walls subjected to axial compression and flexure are separated into those with laterally unrestrained prestressing tendons and those with laterally restrained prestressing tendons. This separation was necessary because the flexural behavior of a prestressed masonry wall significantly depends upon the lateral restraint of the prestressing tendon. Lateral restraint of a prestressing tendon is typically provided by grouting the cell or void containing the tendon before or after transfer of prestressing force to the masonry. Lateral restraint may be provided by placing the masonry in contact with the tendon or the protective sheathing of the tendon at periodic intervals along the length of the prestressing tendon.

Allowable compressive stresses for prestressed masonry address two distinct loading stages; stresses immediately after transfer of prestressing force to the masonry wall and stresses after all prestress losses and gains have taken place. The magnitude of allowable axial compressive stress and bending compressive stress after all prestress losses and gains are consistent with those for unreinforced masonry in Section 8.2. Immediately after transfer of prestressing, allowable compressive stresses and applied axial load should be based upon f'_{mi} and may be increased by 20 percent. This means that the factors of safety at the time of the transfer of prestress may be lower than those after prestress losses and gains occur. The first reason for this is that the effective precompression stress at the time of transfer of prestressing almost certainly decreases over time and masonry

CODE

10.4.2 *Service load requirements*

10.4.2.1 For walls with laterally unrestrained prestressing tendons, the prestressing force, P_{ps}, shall be included in the calculation of the axial load, P, in Equation 8-15 and in the calculation of the eccentricity of the axial load, e, in Equation 8-19.

10.4.2.2 For walls with laterally restrained prestressing tendons, the prestressing force, P_{ps}, shall not be considered for the calculation of the axial load, P, in Equation 8-15. The prestressing force, P_{ps}, shall be considered for the calculation of the eccentricity of the axial resultant load, e, in Equation 8-19.

COMMENTARY

compressive strength most likely increases over time. Second, loads at the time of transfer of prestressing, namely prestress force and dead loads, are known more precisely than loads throughout the remainder of service life.

Cracking of prestressed masonry under permanent loads is to be avoided. The prestressing force and the dead weight of the wall are permanent loads. Cracking under permanent loading conditions is not desirable due to the potential for significant water penetration, which may precipitate corrosion of the prestressing tendons and accessories and damage to interior finishes. Masonry provides a significant flexural tensile resistance to cracking, as reflected by the allowable flexural tensile stress values stated in Section 8.2. Consequently, elimination of tensile stress under prestressing force and dead loads alone is a conservative measure, but one the committee deemed reasonable and reflective of current practice for prestressed masonry members.

10.4.2 *Service load requirements*

10.4.2.1 Because masonry walls with laterally unrestrained prestressing tendons are equivalent to masonry walls subjected to applied axial loads, the design approach for unreinforced masonry in Section 8.2 has been adopted for convenience and consistency. Buckling of masonry walls under prestressing force must be avoided for walls with laterally unrestrained prestressing tendons. The prestressing force, P_{ps}, is to be added to the design axial load, P, for stress and load calculations and in the calculation of the eccentricity of the axial resultant, e.

10.4.2.2 Lateral restraint of a prestressing tendon is typically provided by grouting the cell or void containing the tendon before or after transfer of prestressing force to the masonry. Lateral restraint may also be provided by placing the masonry in contact with the tendon or the tendon's protective sheath at periodic intervals along the length of the prestressing tendon (Stierwalt and Hamilton, 2000). In general, three intermediate contacts within a laterally unsupported wall length or height can be considered to provide full lateral support of the tendon but the analysis and decision are the responsibility of the designer.

Prestressed masonry walls with laterally restrained prestressing tendons require a modified design approach from the criteria in Section 8.2. If the prestressing tendon is laterally restrained, the wall cannot buckle under its own prestressing force. Any tendency to buckle under prestressing force induces a lateral deformation that is resisted by an equal and opposite restraining force provided by the prestressing tendon. Such walls are susceptible to buckling under axial loads other than prestressing, however, and this loading condition must be checked (Scolforo and Borchelt, 1992). For this condition, with both concentrically and eccentrically prestressed masonry walls, the prestressing force must be considered in the calculation of the eccentricity of this axial resultant, e, in Equation 8-19 of the Code. The flexural stress induced by eccentric prestressing causes an increase or decrease in the axial buckling load, depending

CODE

10.4.3 *Strength requirements*

10.4.3.1 Required strength shall be determined in accordance with the factored load combinations of the legally adopted building code. When the legally adopted building code does not provide factored load combinations, structures and members shall be designed to resist the combination of loads specified in ASCE 7 for strength design. Walls subject to compressive axial load shall be designed for the factored design moment and the accompanying factored axial load. The factored moment, M_u, shall include the moment induced by relative lateral displacement.

10.4.3.2 Values of the response modification coefficient (R) and the deflection amplification factor (C_d), indicated in ASCE 7 Table 12.2-1 for ordinary plain (unreinforced) masonry shear walls shall be used in determining base shear and design story drift.

10.4.3.3 The design moment strength shall be taken as the nominal moment strength, M_n, multiplied by a strength-reduction factor (ϕ) of 0.8.

10.4.3.4 For cross sections with uniform width, b, over the depth of the compression zone, the depth of the equivalent compression stress block, a, shall be determined by the following equation:

$$a = \frac{f_{ps} A_{ps} + f_y A_s + P_u / \phi}{0.80 \, f'_m \, b} \quad \text{(Equation 10-1)}$$

For other cross sections, Equation 10-1 shall be modified to consider the variable width of compression zone.

10.4.3.5 For walls with (a) uniform width, b, (b) concentric reinforcement and prestressing tendons, and (c) concentric axial load, the nominal moment strength, M_n, shall be calculated by the following equation:

$$M_n = \left(f_{ps}A_{ps} + f_y A_s + P_u / \phi\right)\left(d - \frac{a}{2}\right) \quad \text{(Equation 10-2)}$$

10.4.3.5.1 The quantity a shall be calculated according to Section 10.4.3.4 and f_{ps} shall be calculated according to Section 10.4.3.7.

10.4.3.5.2 The nominal moment strength for other conditions shall be based on static moment equilibrium principles.

10.4.3.5.3 The distance d shall be calculated as the actual distance from the centerline of the tendon to the compression face of the member. For walls with laterally unrestrained prestressing tendons and loaded out of plane, d shall not exceed the face-shell thickness plus one-half the tendon diameter plus 0.375 in. (9.5 mm).

COMMENTARY

upon the location and magnitude of the applied axial load relative to the prestressing force.

10.4.3 *Strength requirements*

Calculation of the moment strength of prestressed masonry walls is similar to the method for prestressed concrete (ACI 318, 2011). For bonded tendons, the simplification of taking the tendon stress at nominal moment strength equal to the yield strength can be more conservative for bars than for strands because the yield strength of a prestressing bar is a smaller percentage of the ultimate strength of the tendon.

The equation for the unbonded prestressing tendon stress, f_{ps}, at the moment strength condition (Equation 10-3) is based on tests of prestressed masonry walls, which were loaded out-of-plane. Equation 10-3 is used for calculating unbonded tendon stress at nominal moment strength for members loaded out-of-plane containing either laterally restrained or laterally unrestrained tendons. This equation provides improved estimates of the tendon stresses over previous equations in the Code (Schultz et al, 2003; Bean Popehn and Schultz, 2003; Bean Popehn and Schultz, 2010; Bean Popehn, 2007). Equation 10-3 can be solved iteratively for f_{ps}. For the first iteration, f_{ps} in the parenthetical term can be taken equal to f_{se}.

The equation for the nominal moment strength, M_n, is for the general case of a masonry wall with concentrically applied axial load and concentric tendons and reinforcement. This is representative of most prestressed masonry applications to date. For other conditions, the designer should refer to first principles of structural mechanics to determine the nominal moment strength of the wall.

The depth of the equivalent compression stress block must be determined with consideration of the cross section of the wall, the tensile resistance of tendons and reinforcement, and the factored design axial load, P_u. P_u is an additive quantity in Code Equations 10-1 and 10-2. Prestressing adds to the resistance for ultimate strength evaluations and is used with a load factor of 1.0. Equation 10-1 defining the depth of the equivalent compression stress block, a, is modified to match the value for the equivalent uniform stress parameter specified in Chapter 9 (Strength Design of Masonry) of the Code ($0.80f'_m$). A review of existing tests of post-tensioned masonry walls indicates that the flexural strength of the walls is more accurately calculated using uniform stresses smaller than the value specified in previous editions of the Code ($0.85 f'_m$) (Schultz et al, 2003; Bean Popehn and Schultz, 2003).

The ratio, a/d, is limited to assure ductile performance in flexure when using tendons fabricated from steel with yield strengths between 60 ksi (420 MPa) and 270 ksi (1865 MPa). As with reinforced masonry designed in accordance with Chapters 8 and 9, the calculated depth in compression should be compared to the depth available to resist compressive stresses. For sections with uniform width, the

CODE

10.4.3.5.4 When tendons are not placed in the center of the wall, d shall be calculated in each direction for out-of-plane bending.

10.4.3.6 The ratio a/d shall not exceed 0.38.

10.4.3.7 *Calculation of f_{ps} for out-of-plane bending*

10.4.3.7.1 For walls with bonded prestressing tendons, f_{ps} shall be calculated based on strain compatibility or shall be taken equal to f_{py}.

10.4.3.7.2 For walls with laterally restrained or laterally unrestrained unbonded prestressing tendons, the following equation shall be permitted to be used instead of a more accurate determination of f_{ps}:

$$f_{ps} = f_{se} + 0.03\left(\frac{E_{ps}d}{l_p}\right)\left(1 - 1.56\frac{A_{ps}f_{ps} + P}{f'_m bd}\right)$$

(Equation 10-3)

10.4.3.7.3 In Equation 10-3, the value of f_{ps} shall be not less than f_{se}, and not larger than f_{py}.

10.4.3.8 *Calculation of f_{ps} for shear walls* — For walls with bonded prestressing tendons, f_{ps} shall be calculated based on strain compatibility or shall be taken equal to f_{py}. Instead of a more accurate determination, f_{ps} for members with unbonded prestressing tendons shall be f_{se}.

10.5 — Axial tension

Axial tension shall be resisted by reinforcement, prestressing tendons, or both.

10.6 — Shear

10.6.1 For walls without bonded mild reinforcement, nominal shear strength, V_n, shall be calculated in accordance with Sections 9.2.6a, 9.2.6b, 9.2.6c, and 9.2.6e. N_u shall include the effective prestress force, $A_{ps}f_{se}$.

10.6.2 For walls with bonded mild reinforcement, nominal shear strength, V_n, shall be calculated in accordance with Section 9.3.4.1.2.

10.6.2.1 Nominal masonry shear strength, V_{nm}, shall be calculated in accordance with Section 9.3.4.1.2.1. P_u shall include the effective prestress force, $A_{ps}f_{se}$.

10.6.2.2 Nominal shear strength provided by reinforcement, V_{ns}, shall be calculated in accordance with Section 9.3.4.1.2.

COMMENTARY

value of the compression block depth, a, should be compared to the solid bearing depth available to resist compressive stresses. For hollow sections that are ungrouted or partially-grouted, the available depth may be limited to the face shell thickness of the masonry units, particularly if the webs are not mortared. The a/d limitation is intended to ensure significant yielding of the prestressing tendons prior to masonry compression failure. In such a situation, the nominal moment strength is determined by the strength of the prestressing tendon, which is the basis for a strength-reduction factor equal to 0.8. This ductility limit was determined for sections with bonded tendons, and when more experimental and field data are available on the ductility of both unbonded and bonded systems, this limit will again be reviewed.

The calculation of this limit assumes that the effective prestressing stress is equivalent to $0.65 f_y$. If the magnitude of the initial effective prestress (i.e., f_{se}) is less than $0.65 f_y$, then the strain in the steel at ultimate strength ε_s should be compared to the yield strain (i.e., $\varepsilon_y = f_y / E_s$). The steel strain at ultimate strength ε_s can be approximated by assuming the strain in the steel is equal to an initial strain due to the effective prestressing ($\varepsilon_{s,i} = f_{se}/E_s$) plus additional strain due to flexure ($\varepsilon_{s,flex} = 0.003\times((d - 1.25a)/1.25a)$).

10.5 — Axial tension

The axial tensile strength of masonry in a prestressed masonry wall is to be neglected, which is a conservative measure. This requirement is consistent with that of Section 8.3. If axial tension develops, for example due to wind uplift on the roof structure, the axial tension must be resisted by reinforcement, tendons, or both.

10.6 — Shear

This section applies to both in-plane and out-of-plane shear.

The shear strength of prestressed walls is calculated using the provisions of the Chapter 9. Calculation of shear strength is dictated by the presence or absence of bonded mild reinforcement. While the MSJC acknowledges that prestressed masonry walls are reinforced, for walls without bonded mild reinforcement, the unreinforced (plain) masonry shear provisions of Chapter 9 are used to calculate shear strength. When bonded mild reinforcement is provided, then the reinforced masonry shear provisions of Chapter 9 are used to calculate shear strength.

No shear strength enhancement due to arching action of the masonry is recognized in this Code for prestressed masonry walls. The formation of compression struts and tension ties in prestressed masonry is possible, but this phenomenon has not been considered.

CODE

10.7 — Deflection

Calculation of member deflection shall include camber, the effects of time-dependent phenomena, and P-delta effects.

10.8 — Prestressing tendon anchorages, couplers, and end blocks

10.8.1 Prestressing tendons in masonry construction shall be anchored by either:

(a) mechanical anchorage devices bearing directly on masonry or placed inside an end block of concrete or fully grouted masonry, or

(b) bond in reinforced concrete end blocks or members.

10.8.2 Anchorages and couplers for prestressing tendons shall develop at least 95 percent of the specified tensile strength of the prestressing tendons when tested in an unbonded condition, without exceeding anticipated set.

10.8.3 Reinforcement shall be provided in masonry members near anchorages if tensile stresses created by bursting, splitting, and spalling forces induced by the prestressing tendon exceed the capacity of the masonry.

10.8.4 *Bearing stresses*
10.8.4.1 In prestressing tendon anchorage zones, local bearing stress on the masonry shall be calculated based on the contact surface between masonry and the mechanical anchorage device or between masonry and the end block.

10.8.4.2 Bearing stresses on masonry due to maximum jacking force of the prestressing tendon shall not exceed $0.50 f'_{mi}$.

COMMENTARY

10.7 — Deflection

In accordance with Section 4.3.2, prestressed masonry wall deflection should be calculated based on uncracked section properties. Calculation of wall deflection must include the effect of time-dependent phenomenon such as creep and shrinkage of masonry and relaxation of prestressing tendons. There are no limits for the out-of-plane deflection of prestressed masonry walls. This is because appropriate out-of-plane deflection limits are project-specific. The designer should consider the potential for damage to interior finishes, and should limit deflections accordingly.

10.8 — Prestressing tendon anchorages, couplers, and end blocks

The provisions of this section of the Code are used to design the tendon anchorages, couplers, and end blocks to withstand the prestressing operation and effectively transfer prestress force to the masonry wall without distress to the masonry or the prestressing accessories. Anchorages are designed for adequate pull-out strength from their foundations.

Because the actual stresses are quite complicated around post-tensioning anchorages, experimental data, or a refined analysis should be used whenever possible. Appropriate formulas from the references (PTI, 1990) should be used as a guide to size prestressing tendon anchorages when experimental data or more refined analysis are not available. Additional guidance on design and details for post-tensioning anchorage zones is given in the references (Sanders et al, 1987).

In most cases, f'_{mi} is equal to or greater than $0.75 f'_m$ for prestressed masonry. At $0.75 f'_m$, the prestressed bearing stress of $0.50 f'_{mi}$ is equivalent to $0.375 f'_m$. If f'_{mi} is specified as equal to f'_m, the maximum permitted bearing stress would be the equivalent of $0.50 f'_m$.

CODE

10.9 — Protection of prestressing tendons and accessories

10.9.1 Prestressing tendons, anchorages, couplers, and end fittings in exterior walls exposed to earth or weather, or walls exposed to a mean relative humidity exceeding 75 percent, shall be corrosion-protected.

10.9.2 Corrosion protection of prestressing tendons shall not rely solely on masonry cover.

10.9.3 Parts of prestressing tendons not embedded in masonry shall be provided with mechanical and fire protection equivalent to that of the embedded parts of the tendon.

10.10 — Development of bonded tendons

Development of bonded prestressing tendons in grouted corrugated ducts, anchored in accordance with Section 10.8.1, does not need to be calculated.

COMMENTARY

10.9 — Protection of prestressing tendons and accessories

Corrosion protection of the prestressing tendon and accessories is required in masonry walls subject to a moist and corrosive environment. Methods of corrosion protection are addressed in the Specification. Masonry and grout cover is not considered adequate protection due to variable permeability and the sensitivity of prestressing tendons to corrosion. The methods of corrosion protection given in the Specification provide a minimum level of corrosion protection. The designer may wish to impose more substantial corrosion protection requirements, especially in highly corrosive environments.

10.10 — Development of bonded tendons

Consistent with design practice in prestressed concrete, development of post-tensioned tendons away from the anchorage does not need to be calculated.

This page intentionally left blank

CHAPTER 11
STRENGTH DESIGN OF AUTOCLAVED AERATED CONCRETE (AAC) MASONRY

CODE

11.1 — General

11.1.1 *Scope*

This Chapter provides minimum requirements for design of AAC masonry.

11.1.1.1 Except as stated elsewhere in this Chapter, design of AAC masonry shall comply with the requirements of Part 1 and Part 2, excluding Sections 5.5.1, 5.5.2(d) and 5.3.2.

11.1.1.2 Design of AAC masonry shall comply with Sections 11.1.2 through 11.1.9, and either Section 11.2 or 11.3.

11.1.2 *Required strength*

Required strength shall be determined in accordance with the strength design load combinations of the legally adopted building code. Members subject to compressive axial load shall be designed for the maximum design moment accompanying the axial load. The factored moment, M_u, shall include the moment induced by relative lateral displacement.

11.1.3 *Design strength*

AAC masonry members shall be proportioned so that the design strength equals or exceeds the required strength. Design strength is the nominal strength multiplied by the strength-reduction factor, ϕ, as specified in Section 11.1.5.

11.1.4 *Strength of joints*

AAC masonry members shall be made of AAC masonry units. The tensile bond strength of AAC masonry joints shall not be taken greater than the limits of Section 11.1.8.3. When AAC masonry units with a maximum height of 8 in. (203 mm) (nominal) are used, head joints shall be permitted to be left unfilled between AAC masonry units laid in running bond, provided that shear capacity is calculated using the formulas of this Code corresponding to that condition. Open head joints shall not be permitted in AAC masonry not laid in running bond.

COMMENTARY

11.1 — General

11.1.1 *Scope*

Design procedures in Chapter 11 are strength design methods in which internal forces resulting from application of factored loads must not exceed design strength (nominal member strength reduced by a strength-reduction factor ϕ).

Refer to Section 11.1.10 for requirements for corbels constructed of AAC masonry.

11.1.4 *Strength of joints*

Design provisions of Chapter 11 and prescriptive seismic reinforcement requirements of Chapter 7 are based on monolithic behavior of AAC masonry. The reduction in shear strength of AAC masonry shear walls laid in running bond with unfilled head joints is accounted for in Equation 11-13b. AAC masonry walls constructed with AAC masonry units greater in height than 8 in. (203 mm) (nominal) with unfilled head joints and AAC masonry walls not laid in running bond with unfilled head joints do not have sufficient test data to develop design provisions and thus are not permitted at this time.

CODE

11.1.5 *Strength-reduction factors*

11.1.5.1 *Anchor bolts* — For cases where the nominal strength of an anchor bolt is controlled by AAC masonry breakout, ϕ shall be taken as 0.50. For cases where the nominal strength of an anchor bolt is controlled by anchor bolt steel, ϕ shall be taken as 0.90. For cases where the nominal strength of an anchor bolt is controlled by anchor pullout, ϕ shall be taken as 0.65.

11.1.5.2 *Bearing* — For cases involving bearing on AAC masonry, ϕ shall be taken as 0.60.

11.1.5.3 *Combinations of flexure and axial load in unreinforced AAC masonry* — The value of ϕ shall be taken as 0.60 for unreinforced AAC masonry designed to resist flexure, axial load, or combinations thereof.

11.1.5.4 *Combinations of flexure and axial load in reinforced AAC masonry* — The value of ϕ shall be taken as 0.90 for reinforced AAC masonry designed to resist flexure, axial load, or combinations thereof.

11.1.5.5 *Shear* — The value of ϕ shall be taken as 0.80 for AAC masonry designed to resist shear.

11.1.6 *Deformation requirements*
11.1.6.1 *Deflection of unreinforced (plain) AAC masonry* — Deflection calculations for unreinforced (plain) AAC masonry members shall be based on uncracked section properties.

COMMENTARY

11.1.5 *Strength-reduction factors*
The strength-reduction factor incorporates the difference between the nominal strength provided in accordance with the provisions of Chapter 11 and the expected strength of the as-built AAC masonry. The strength-reduction factor also accounts for the uncertainties in construction, material properties, calculated versus actual member strengths, and anticipated mode of failure.

11.1.5.1 *Anchor bolts* — Anchor bolts embedded in grout in AAC masonry behave like those addressed in Chapter 9 and are designed identically. Anchors for use in AAC masonry units are available from a variety of manufacturers, and nominal resistance should be based on tested capacities.

11.1.5.2 *Bearing* — The value of the strength-reduction factor used in bearing assumes that some degradation has occurred within the masonry material.

11.1.5.3 *Combinations of flexure and axial load in unreinforced AAC masonry* — The same strength-reduction factor is used for the axial load and the flexural tension or compression induced by bending moment in unreinforced masonry elements. The lower strength-reduction factor associated with unreinforced elements (in comparison to reinforced elements) reflects an increase in the coefficient of variation of the measured strengths of unreinforced elements when compared to similarly configured reinforced elements.

11.1.5.4 *Combinations of flexure and axial load in reinforced AAC masonry* — The same strength-reduction factor is used for the axial load and the flexural tension or compression induced by bending moment in reinforced AAC masonry elements. The higher strength-reduction factor associated with reinforced elements (in comparison to unreinforced elements) reflects a decrease in the coefficient of variation of the measured strengths of reinforced elements when compared to similarly configured unreinforced elements.

11.1.5.5 *Shear* — Strength-reduction factors for calculating the design shear strength are commonly more conservative than those associated with the design flexural strength. However, the capacity design provisions of Chapter 11 require that shear capacity significantly exceed flexural capacity. Hence, the strength-reduction factor for shear is taken as 0.80, a value 33 percent larger than the historical value.

11.1.6 *Deformation requirements*
11.1.6.1 *Deflection of unreinforced (plain) AAC masonry* — The deflection calculations of unreinforced masonry are based on elastic performance of the masonry assemblage as outlined in the design criteria of Section 9.2.2.

CODE

11.1.6.2 *Deflection of reinforced AAC masonry* — Deflection calculations for reinforced AAC masonry members shall be based on cracked section properties including the reinforcement and grout. The flexural and shear stiffness properties assumed for deflection calculations shall not exceed one-half of the gross section properties unless a cracked-section analysis is performed.

11.1.7 *Anchor bolts*

Headed and bent-bar anchor bolts shall be embedded in grout, and shall be designed in accordance with Section 9.1.6 using f'_g instead of f'_m and neglecting the contribution of AAC to the edge distance and embedment depth. Anchors embedded in AAC without grout shall be designed using nominal capacities provided by the anchor manufacturer and verified by an independent testing agency.

11.1.8 *Material properties*

11.1.8.1 *Compressive strength*

11.1.8.1.1 *Masonry compressive strength* — The specified compressive strength of AAC masonry, f'_{AAC}, shall equal or exceed 290 psi (2.0 MPa).

11.1.8.1.2 *Grout compressive strength* — The specified compressive strength of grout, f'_g, shall equal or exceed 2,000 psi (13.8 MPa) and shall not exceed 5,000 psi (34.5 MPa).

11.1.8.2 *Masonry splitting tensile strength* — The splitting tensile strength f_{tAAC} shall be determined by Equation 11-1.

$$f_{tAAC} = 2.4\sqrt{f'_{AAC}}$$ (Equation 11-1)

COMMENTARY

11.1.6.2 *Deflection of reinforced AAC masonry* — Values of I_{eff} are typically about one-half of I_g for common configurations of elements that are fully grouted. Calculating a more accurate effective moment of inertia using a moment curvature analysis may be desirable for some circumstances. Historically, an effective moment of inertia has been calculated using net cross-sectional area properties and the ratio of the cracking moment strength based on appropriate modulus of rupture values to the applied moment resulting from unfactored loads as shown in the following equation. This equation has successfully been used for estimating the post-cracking flexural stiffness of both concrete and masonry.

$$I_{eff} = I_n \left(\frac{M_{cr}}{M_a}\right)^3 + I_{cr}\left[1 - \left(\frac{M_{cr}}{M_a}\right)^3\right] \leq I_n \leq 0.5I_g$$

11.1.7 *Anchor bolts*

Headed and bent-bar anchor bolts embedded in grout in AAC masonry behave like those addressed in Chapter 9 and are designed identically. Anchors for use in AAC masonry units are available from a variety of manufacturers.

11.1.8 *Material properties*

11.1.8.1 *Compressive strength*

11.1.8.1.1 *Masonry compressive strength* — Research (Varela et al, 2006; Tanner et al, 2005(a), Tanner et al, 2005(b); Argudo, 2003) has been conducted on structural components of AAC masonry with a compressive strength of 290 to 1,500 psi (2.0 to 10.3 MPa). Design criteria are based on these research results.

11.1.8.1.2 *Grout compressive strength* — Because most empirically derived design equations relate the calculated nominal strength as a function of the specified compressive strength of the masonry, the specified compressive strength of the grout is required to be at least equal to the specified compressive strength. Additionally, due to the hydrophilic nature of AAC masonry, care should be taken to control grout shrinkage by pre-wetting cells to be grouted or by using other means, such as non-shrink admixtures. Bond between grout and AAC units is equivalent to bond between grout and other masonry units (Tanner et al, 2005(a), Tanner et al, 2005(b); Argudo, 2003).

11.1.8.2 *Masonry splitting tensile strength* — The equation for splitting tensile strength is based on ASTM C1006 tests (Tanner et al, 2005(b); Argudo, 2003).

CODE

11.1.8.3 *Masonry modulus of rupture* — The modulus of rupture, f_{rAAC}, for AAC masonry elements shall be taken as twice the masonry splitting tensile strength, f_{tAAC}. If a section of AAC masonry contains a Type M or Type S horizontal leveling bed of mortar, the value of f_{rAAC} shall not exceed 50 psi (345 kPa) at that section. If a section of AAC masonry contains a horizontal bed joint of thin-bed mortar and AAC, the value of f_{rAAC} shall not exceed 80 psi (552 kPa) at that section.

11.1.8.4 *Masonry direct shear strength* — The direct shear strength, f_v, across an interface of AAC material shall be determined by Equation 11-2, and shall be taken as 50 psi (345 kPa) across an interface between grout and AAC material.

$$f_v = 0.15 f'_{AAC} \qquad \text{(Equation 11-2)}$$

11.1.8.5 *Coefficient of friction* — The coefficient of friction between AAC and AAC shall be 0.75. The coefficient of friction between AAC and thin-bed mortar or between AAC and leveling-bed mortar shall be 1.0.

11.1.8.6 *Reinforcement strength* — Masonry design shall be based on a reinforcement strength equal to the specified yield strength of reinforcement, f_y, which shall not exceed 60,000 psi (413.7 MPa). The actual yield strength shall not exceed 1.3 multiplied by the specified yield strength.

11.1.9 *Nominal bearing strength*

11.1.9.1 The nominal bearing strength of AAC masonry shall be calculated as f'_{AAC} multiplied by the bearing area, A_{br}, as defined in Section 4.3.4.

11.1.9.2 *Bearing for simply supported precast floor and roof members on AAC masonry shear walls* — The following minimum requirements shall apply so that after the consideration of tolerances, the distance from the edge of the supporting wall to the end of the precast member in the direction of the span is at least:

For AAC floor panels	2 in. (51 mm)
For solid or hollow-core slabs	2 in. (51 mm)
For beams or stemmed members	3 in. (76 mm)

COMMENTARY

11.1.8.3 *Masonry modulus of rupture* — The modulus of rupture is based on tests conducted in accordance with ASTM C78 (2002) on AAC masonry with different compressive strengths (Tanner et al, 2005(b); Argudo, 2003; Fouad, 2002). Modulus of rupture tests show that a thin-bed mortar joint can fail before the AAC material indicating that the tensile-bond strength of the thin-bed mortar is less than the modulus of rupture of the AAC. This critical value is 80 psi (552 kPa). The data are consistent with the formation of cracks in thin-bed mortar joints observed in AAC shear wall tests (Tanner et al, 2005(b); Argudo, 2003). Shear wall tests (Tanner et al, 2005(b)) show that when a leveling bed is present, flexural cracking capacity may be controlled by the tensile bond strength across the interface between the AAC and the leveling mortar, which is usually less than the modulus of rupture of the AAC material itself.

11.1.8.4 *Masonry direct shear strength* — The equation for direct shear strength is based on shear tests (Tanner et al, 2005(b); Argudo, 2003). Based on tests by Kingsley et al (1985), interface shear strength between grout and conventional masonry units varies from 100 to 250 psi (689 to 1,723 kPA). Based on tests by Forero and Klingner (2011), interface shear strength between grout and AAC material had a 5% fractile (lower characteristic) value of 50 psi (345 kPa).

11.1.8.5 *Coefficient of friction* — The coefficient of friction between AAC and AAC is based on direct shear tests performed at The University of Texas at Austin and. the coefficient of friction between AAC and leveling mortar is based on tests on shear walls at the same institution.

11.1.8.6 *Reinforcement strength* — Research[3.11] conducted on reinforced masonry components used Grade 60 steel. To be consistent with laboratory documented investigations, design is based on a nominal steel yield strength of 60,000 psi (413.7 MPa). The limitation on the steel yield strength of 130 percent of the nominal yield strength limits the over-strength that may be present in the construction.

11.1.9 *Nominal bearing strength*

11.1.9.1 Commentary Section 4.3.4 gives further information.

11.1.9.2 *Bearing for simply supported precast floor and roof members on AAC shear walls* — Bearing should be checked wherever floor or roof elements rest on AAC walls. The critical edge distance for bearing and the critical section for shear to be used in this calculation are shown in Figure CC-11.1-1.

CODE

11.1.10 *Corbels* — Load-bearing corbels of AAC masonry shall not be permitted. Non-load-bearing corbels of AAC masonry shall conform to the requirements of Section 5.5.2(a) through 5.5.2(c). The back section of the corbelled section shall remain within ¼ in. (6.4 mm) of plane.

COMMENTARY

11.1.10 *Corbels* — Load-bearing corbels of AAC masonry are not permitted due to the possibility of a brittle shear failure. Non-load-bearing corbels of AAC masonry are permitted, provided that the back section of the corbelled wall remains plane within the code limits. The relative ease in which AAC masonry can be cut and shaped makes this requirement practical.

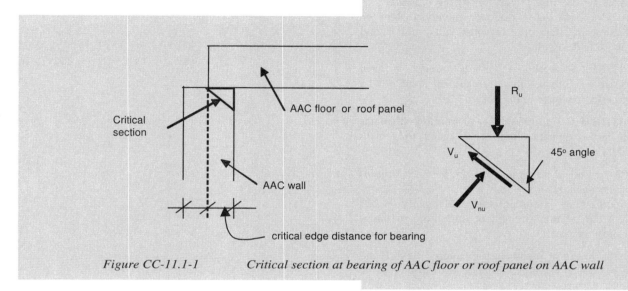

Figure CC-11.1-1   Critical section at bearing of AAC floor or roof panel on AAC wall

CODE

11.2 — Unreinforced (plain) AAC masonry

11.2.1 *Scope*

The requirements of Section 11.2 are in addition to the requirements of Part 1, Part 2, and Section 11.1, and govern masonry design in which AAC masonry is used to resist tensile forces.

11.2.1.1 *Strength for resisting loads* — Unreinforced (plain) AAC masonry members shall be designed using the strength of masonry units, mortar, and grout in resisting design loads.

11.2.1.2 *Strength contribution from reinforcement* — Stresses in reinforcement shall not be considered effective in resisting design loads.

11.2.1.3 *Design criteria* — Unreinforced (plain) AAC masonry members shall be designed to remain uncracked.

11.2.2 *Flexural strength of unreinforced (plain) AAC masonry members*

The following assumptions shall apply when determining the flexural strength of unreinforced (plain) AAC masonry members:

(a) Strength design of members for factored flexure and axial load shall be in accordance with principles of engineering mechanics.

(b) Strain in masonry shall be directly proportional to the distance from the neutral axis.

(c) Flexural tension in masonry shall be assumed to be directly proportional to strain.

(d) Flexural compressive stress in combination with axial compressive stress in masonry shall be assumed to be directly proportional to strain. Nominal compressive strength shall not exceed a stress corresponding to 0.85 f'_{AAC}.

(e) The nominal flexural tensile strength of AAC masonry shall be determined from Section 11.1.8.3.

COMMENTARY

CODE

11.2.3 *Nominal axial strength of unreinforced (plain) AAC masonry members*

Nominal axial strength, P_n, shall be calculated using Equation 11-3 or Equation 11-4.

(a)   For members having an *h/r* ratio not greater than 99:

$$P_n = 0.80 \left\{ 0.85 A_n \, f'_{AAC} \left[1 - \left(\frac{h}{140r} \right)^2 \right] \right\}$$

(Equation 11-3)

(b)   For members having an *h/r* ratio greater than 99:

$$P_n = 0.80 \left[0.85 A_n \, f'_{AAC} \left(\frac{70\,r}{h} \right)^2 \right] \quad \text{(Equation 11-4)}$$

11.2.4 *Axial tension*

The tensile strength of unreinforced AAC masonry shall be neglected in design when the masonry is subjected to axial tension forces.

11.2.5 *Nominal shear strength of unreinforced (plain) AAC masonry members*

The nominal shear strength of AAC masonry, V_{nAAC}, shall be the least of the values calculated by Sections 11.3.4.1.2.1 through 11.3.4.1.2.3. In evaluating nominal shear strength by Section 11.3.4.1.2.3, effects of reinforcement shall be neglected. The provisions of 11.3.4.1.2 shall apply to AAC shear walls not laid in running bond. The provisions of Section 11.3.4.1.2.4 shall apply to AAC walls loaded out-of-plane.

11.2.6 *Flexural cracking*

The flexural cracking strength shall be calculated in accordance with Section 11.3.6.5.

COMMENTARY

11.2.4 *Axial tension*

Commentary Section 8.2.5 provides further information.

CODE

11.3 — Reinforced AAC masonry

11.3.1 *Scope*

The requirements of this section are in addition to the requirements of Part 1, Part 2, and Section 11.1 and govern AAC masonry design in which reinforcement is used to resist tensile forces.

11.3.2 *Design assumptions*

The following assumptions apply to the design of reinforced AAC masonry:

(a) There is strain compatibility between the reinforcement, grout, and AAC masonry.

(b) The nominal strength of reinforced AAC masonry cross sections for combined flexure and axial load shall be based on applicable conditions of equilibrium.

(c) The maximum usable strain, ε_{mu}, at the extreme AAC masonry compression fiber shall be assumed to be 0.0012 for Class 2 AAC masonry and 0.003 for Class 4 AAC masonry and higher.

(d) Strain in reinforcement and AAC masonry shall be assumed to be directly proportional to the distance from the neutral axis.

(e) Tension and compression stresses in reinforcement shall be calculated as the product of steel modulus of elasticity, E_s, and steel strain, ε_s, but shall not be greater than f_y. Except as permitted in Section 11.3.3.5 for determination of maximum area of flexural reinforcement, the compressive stress of steel reinforcement shall be neglected unless lateral restraining reinforcement is provided in compliance with the requirements of Section 5.3.1.4.

(f) The tensile strength of AAC masonry shall be neglected in calculating axial and flexural strength.

(g) The relationship between AAC masonry compressive stress and masonry strain shall be assumed to be defined by the following: AAC masonry stress of $0.85 f'_{AAC}$ shall be assumed uniformly distributed over an equivalent compression stress block bounded by edges of the cross section and a straight line parallel to the neutral axis and located at a distance $a = 0.67\,c$ from the fiber of maximum compressive strain. The distance c from the fiber of maximum strain to the neutral axis shall be measured perpendicular to the neutral axis.

11.3.3 *Reinforcement requirements and details*

COMMENTARY

11.3 — Reinforced AAC masonry

Provisions are identical to those of concrete or clay masonry, with a few exceptions. Only those exceptions are addressed in this Commentary.

11.3.2 *Design assumptions*

For AAC, test results indicate that ε_{mu} for Class 4 AAC masonry and higher is 0.003 and the value of the stress in the equivalent rectangular stress block is $0.85 f'_{AAC}$ with $a = 0.67c$ (Argudo, 2003 and Tanner et al, 2005a). Additional testing has indicated a ε_{mu} of 0.0012 for Class 2 AAC masonry (Cancino, 2003 and Tanner et al, 2011).

11.3.3 *Reinforcement requirements and details*

CODE

11.3.3.1 *Reinforcing bar size limitations* — Reinforcing bars used in AAC masonry shall not be larger than No. 9 (M#29). The nominal bar diameter shall not exceed one-eighth of the nominal member thickness and shall not exceed one-quarter of the least clear dimension of the grout space in which it is placed. In plastic hinge zones, the area of reinforcing bars placed in a grout space shall not exceed 3 percent of the grout space area. In other than plastic hinge zones, the area of reinforcing bars placed in a grout space shall not exceed 4.5 percent of the grout space area.

11.3.3.2 *Standard hooks* — The equivalent embedment length to develop standard hooks in tension, l_e, shall be determined by Equation 11-5:

$$l_e = 13d_b \qquad \text{(Equation 11-5)}$$

11.3.3.3 *Development*

11.3.3.3.1 *Development of tension and compression reinforcement* — The required tension or compression reinforcement shall be developed in accordance with the following provisions:

The required development length of reinforcement shall be determined by Equation 11-6, but shall not be less than 12 in. (305 mm).

$$l_d = \frac{0.13 \, d_b{}^2 f_y \gamma}{K_{AAC}\sqrt{f'_g}} \qquad \text{(Equation 11-6)}$$

K_{AAC} shall not exceed the smallest of the following: the minimum grout cover, the clear spacing between adjacent reinforcement splices, and $9d_b$.

$\gamma = 1.0$ for No. 3 (M#10) through No. 5 (M#16) bars;

$\gamma = 1.3$ for No. 6 (M#19) through No. 7 (M#22) bars; and

$\gamma = 1.5$ for No. 8 (M#25) through No. 9 (M#29) bars.

11.3.3.3.2 *Development of shear reinforcement* — Shear reinforcement shall extend the depth of the member less cover distances.

11.3.3.3.2.1 Except at wall intersections, the end of a horizontal reinforcing bar needed to satisfy shear strength requirements of Section 11.3.4.1.2, shall be bent around the edge vertical reinforcing bar with a 180-degree hook. The ends of single-leg or U-stirrups shall be anchored by one of the following means:

(a) A standard hook plus an effective embedment of $l_d/2$. The effective embedment of a stirrup leg shall be taken as the distance between the mid-depth of the member, $d/2$, and the start of the hook (point of tangency).

COMMENTARY

11.3.3.1 *Reinforcing bar size limitations* — Grout spaces may include, but are not limited to, cores, bond beams, and collar joints. At sections containing lap splices, the maximum area of reinforcement specified in the Code may be doubled.

11.3.3.3.1 *Development of tension and compression reinforcement* — Development and lap splice detailing provisions for conventional masonry are calibrated to the masonry assembly strength, f'_m, which includes the contribution of each constituent material (unit, grout, and mortar). Due to the low compressive strength of AAC, however, the AAC masonry component is ignored and the calibration is based on f'_g.

CODE

(b) For No. 5 (M #16) bars and smaller, bending around longitudinal reinforcement through at least 135 degrees plus an embedment of $l_d/3$. The $l_d/3$ embedment of a stirrup leg shall be taken as the distance between mid-depth of the member, $d/2$, and the start of the hook (point of tangency).

(c) Between the anchored ends, each bend in the continuous portion of a transverse U-stirrup shall enclose a longitudinal bar.

11.3.3.3.2.2 At wall intersections, horizontal reinforcing bars needed to satisfy shear strength requirements of Section 11.3.4.1.2 shall be bent around the edge vertical reinforcing bar with a 90-degree standard hook and shall extend horizontally into the intersecting wall a minimum distance at least equal to the development length.

11.3.3.4 *Splices* — Reinforcement splices shall comply with one of the following:

(a) The minimum length of lap for bars shall be 12 in. (305 mm) or the development length determined by Equation 11-6, whichever is greater.

(b) A welded splice shall have the bars butted and welded to develop at least 125 percent of the yield strength, f_y, of the bar in tension or compression, as required. Welding shall conform to AWS D1.4. Reinforcement to be welded shall conform to ASTM A706, or shall be accompanied by a submittal showing its chemical analysis and carbon equivalent as required by AWS D1.4. Existing reinforcement to be welded shall conform to ASTM A706, or shall be analyzed chemically and its carbon equivalent determined as required by AWS D1.4.

(c) Mechanical splices shall have the bars connected to develop at least 125 percent of the yield strength, f_y, of the bar in tension or compression, as required.

11.3.3.5 *Maximum reinforcement percentages* — The ratio of reinforcement, ρ, shall be calculated in accordance with Section 9.3.3.5 with the following exceptions:

The maximum usable strain, ε_{mu}, at the extreme masonry compression fiber shall be in accordance with Section 11.3.2.c.

The strength of the compression zone shall be calculated as 85 percent of f'_{AAC} multiplied by 67 percent of the area of the compression zone.

11.3.3.6 *Bundling of reinforcing bars* — Reinforcing bars shall not be bundled.

COMMENTARY

11.3.3.4 *Splices* — See Code Commentary Section 8.1.6.7.2 for additional information on welded splices.

CODE

11.3.4 *Design of beams, piers, and columns*
Member design forces shall be based on an analysis that considers the relative stiffness of structural members. The calculation of lateral stiffness shall include the contribution of beams, piers, and columns. The effects of cracking on member stiffness shall be considered.

11.3.4.1 *Nominal strength*
11.3.4.1.1 *Nominal axial and flexural strength* — The nominal axial strength, P_n, and the nominal flexural strength, M_n, of a cross section shall be determined in accordance with the design assumptions of Section 11.3.2 and the provisions of Section 11.3.4.1. For any value of nominal flexural strength, the corresponding calculated nominal axial strength shall be modified for the effects of slenderness in accordance with Equation 11-7 or 11-8. The nominal flexural strength at any section along a member shall not be less than one-fourth of the maximum nominal flexural strength at the critical section.

The nominal axial compressive strength shall not exceed Equation 11-7 or Equation 11-8, as appropriate.

(a) For members having an h/r ratio not greater than 99:

$$P_n = 0.80 \left[0.85 f'_{AAC} \left(A_n - A_{st} \right) + f_y A_{st} \right] \left[1 - \left(\frac{h}{140r} \right)^2 \right]$$

(Equation 11-7)

(b) For members having an h/r ratio greater than 99:

$$P_n = 0.80 \left[0.85 f'_{AAC} \left(A_n - A_{st} \right) + f_y A_{st} \right] \left(\frac{70r}{h} \right)^2$$

(Equation 11-8)

11.3.4.1.2 *Nominal shear strength* — Nominal shear strength, V_n, shall be calculated using Equation 11-9 through Equation 11-12, as appropriate.

$$V_n = V_{nAAC} + V_{ns} \qquad \text{(Equation 11-9)}$$

where V_n shall not exceed the following:

(a) $V_n = \mu_{AAC} P_u$ \qquad (Equation 11-10)

At an interface of AAC and thin-bed mortar or leveling-bed mortar, the nominal sliding shear strength shall be calculated using Equation 11-10 and using the coefficient of friction from Section 11.1.8.5.

(b) Where $M_u/(V_u d_v) \leq 0.25$:

$$V_n \leq 6 A_{nv} \sqrt{f'_{AAC}} \qquad \text{(Equation 11-11)}$$

(c) Where $M_u/(V_u d_v) \geq 1.0$

$$V_n \leq 4 A_{nv} \sqrt{f'_{AAC}} \qquad \text{(Equation 11-12)}$$

(d) The maximum value of V_n for $M_u/(V_u d_v)$ between 0.25 and 1.0 shall be permitted to be linearly interpolated.

COMMENTARY

11.3.4.1.2 *Nominal shear strength* — The nominal shear strength of AAC walls is based on testing at UT Austin (Tanner et al, 2005(b); Argudo, 2003). Test results show that factory-installed, welded-wire reinforcement is developed primarily by bearing of the cross-wires on the AAC material, which normally crushes before the longitudinal wires develop significant stress. Therefore, the additional shear strength provided by the horizontal reinforcement should be neglected. Joint-type reinforcement will probably behave similarly and is not recommended. In contrast, deformed reinforcement placed in grouted bond beams is effective and should be included in calculating V_{ns}.

The upper limit on V_n, defined by Equation 11-10, is based on sliding shear. Flexural cracking can result in an unbonded interface, which typically occurs at a horizontal joint in a shear wall. For this reason, the shear capacity of an AAC bed joint is conservatively limited to the frictional resistance, without considering initial adhesion. The sliding shear capacity should be based on the frictional capacity consistent with the perpendicular force on the compressive stress block, including the compressive force required to

CODE

The nominal masonry shear strength shall be taken as the least of the values calculated using Section 11.3.4.1.2.1 and 11.3.4.1.2.2.

11.3.4.1.2.1 *Nominal masonry shear strength as governed by web-shear cracking* — Nominal masonry shear strength as governed by web-shear cracking, V_{nAAC}, shall be calculated using Equation 11-13a for AAC masonry with mortared head joints, and Equation 11-13b for masonry with unmortared head joints:

$$V_{nAAC} = 0.95\, l_w\, t\, \sqrt{f'_{AAC}}\, \sqrt{1 + \frac{P_u}{2.4\sqrt{f'_{AAC}}\; l_w\, t}}$$

(Equation 11-13a)

$$V_{nAAC} = 0.66\, l_w\, t\, \sqrt{f'_{AAC}}\, \sqrt{1 + \frac{P_u}{2.4\sqrt{f'_{AAC}}\; l_w\, t}}$$

(Equation 11-13b)

For AAC masonry not laid in running bond, nominal masonry shear strength as governed by web-shear cracking, V_{nAAC}, shall be calculated using Equation 11-13c:

$$V_{nAAC} = 0.9\, \sqrt{f'_{AAC}}\; A_{nv} + 0.05 P_u$$ (Equation 11-13c)

11.3.4.1.2.2 *Nominal shear strength as governed by crushing of diagonal compressive strut* — For walls with $M_u/(V_u\, d_v) < 1.5$, nominal shear strength, V_{nAAC}, as governed by crushing of a diagonal strut, shall be calculated as follows:

$$V_{nAAC} = 0.17 f'_{AAC} t \frac{h \cdot l_w^{\,2}}{h^2 + (\frac{3}{4} l_w)^2}$$ (Equation 11-14)

For walls with $M_u/(V_u\, d_v)$ equal to or exceeding 1.5, capacity as governed by crushing of the diagonal compressive strut need not be calculated.

11.3.4.1.2.3 *Nominal shear strength provided by shear reinforcement* — Nominal shear strength provided by reinforcement, V_{ns}, shall be calculated as follows:

$$V_{ns} = 0.5 \left(\frac{A_v}{s} \right) f_y d_v$$ (Equation 11-15)

Nominal shear strength provided by reinforcement, V_{ns}, shall include only deformed reinforcement embedded in grout for AAC shear walls.

COMMENTARY

equilibrate the tensile force in the flexural reinforcement. Dowel action should not be included.

11.3.4.1.2.1 *Nominal masonry shear strength as governed by web-shear cracking* —Equations 11-13a and 11-13b were developed based on observed web shear cracking in shear walls tested at the University of Texas at Austin (Tanner et al, 2005(b); Argudo, 2003) and Hebel AG (Vratsanou and Langer, 2001) in Germany. Independent testing has validated these equations (Costa et al, 2011; Tanner et al, 2011). During testing at the University of Texas at Austin, flexur-shear cracking of AAC shear walls was observed, as predicted, in 6 shear wall tests (Varela et al, 2006; Tanner et al, 2005(a); Tanner et al, 2005(b)). The presence of flexur-shear cracks did not reduce the strength or stiffness of tested AAC shear walls. Another AAC shear wall tested by Cancino (2003) performed in a similar manner. The results in both testing efforts indicate the hysteretic behavior was not changed after the formation of flexure-shear cracks. Thus, flexure-shear cracking does not constitute a limit state in AAC masonry and design equations are not provided.

Masonry units not laid in running bond may exhibit discontinuities at head joints. The nominal masonry shear strength calculation for AAC masonry not laid in running bond considers the likelihood of vertical discontinuities at head joints and is based on test results for AAC walls made of vertical panels with open vertical joints between some panels.

11.3.4.1.2.2 *Nominal shear strength as governed by crushing of diagonal compressive strut* — This mechanism limits the shear strength at large levels of axial load. It was based on test results (Tanner et al, 2005(b)), using a diagonal strut width of $0.25 l_w$ based on test observations.

11.3.4.1.2.3 *Nominal shear strength provided by shear reinforcement* — Equation 11-15 is based on Equation 9-24. Equation 9-24 was developed based on results of reversed cyclic load tests on masonry wall segments with horizontal reinforcement distributed over their heights. The reason for the 0.5 efficiency factor is the non-uniform distribution of tensile strain in the horizontal reinforcement over the height of the element. The formation of an inclined diagonal compressive strut from one corner of the wall segment to the diagonally opposite corner creates a strain field in which the horizontal shear reinforcement at the top and bottom of the segment may not yield. For that reason, not all of the horizontal shear reinforcement in the wall may be fully effective or

CODE

COMMENTARY

efficient in resisting shear forces.

AAC masonry walls differ from concrete masonry walls and clay masonry walls in that horizontal joint reinforcement is not used for horizontal shear reinforcement. For reasons of constructability, AAC walls are traditionally reinforced horizontally with deformed steel reinforcing bars in grout-filled bond beams. In addition, the strength of the thin set AAC mortar exceeds the strength of the AAC masonry units, which would suggest that AAC walls will behave in a manner similar to reinforced concrete. Assemblage testing conducted on AAC masonry walls also suggested that horizontal joint reinforcement provided in concrete bond beams could be fully effective in resisting shear. For this reason, earlier additions of the Code presented Equation 11-15 without the 0.5 efficiency factor, mimicking the reinforced concrete design equation for strength provided by shear reinforcement.

Although this appeared reasonable in the original judgment of the committee, no tests have been performed with AAC masonry walls having deformed horizontal reinforcement in concrete bond beams Until such testing is performed, the 0.5 efficiency factor is being included in Equation 11-15 to be consistent with design procedures associated with concrete masonry and clay masonry, and to provide a conservative design approach.

11.3.4.1.2.4 Nominal shear strength for beams and for out-of-plane loading of other members shall be calculated as follows:

$$V_{nAAC} = 0.8 \sqrt{f'_{AAC}} \ bd \qquad \text{(Equation 11-16)}$$

11.3.4.2 *Beams* — Design of beams shall meet the requirements of Section 5.2 and the additional requirements of Sections 11.3.4.2.1 through 11.3.4.2.5.

11.3.4.2.1 The factored axial compressive force on a beam shall not exceed $0.05 \ A_n f'_{AAC}$.

11.3.4.2.2 *Longitudinal reinforcement*
11.3.4.2.2.1 The variation in longitudinal reinforcing bars shall not be greater than one bar size. Not more than two bar sizes shall be used in a beam.

11.3.4.2.2.2 The nominal flexural strength of a beam shall not be less than 1.3 multiplied by the nominal cracking moment of the beam, M_{cr}. The modulus of rupture, f_{rAAC}, for this calculation shall be determined in accordance with Section 11.1.8.3.

11.3.4.2.2.2 Section 9.3.4.2.2.3 permits reducing the minimum tensile reinforcement requirement of 1.3 multiplied by the nominal cracking moment of the beam, M_{cr} to one-third greater than that required by analysis. Because AAC masonry beams tend to be lightly reinforced, this reduction is not appropriate in AAC masonry design.

CODE

11.3.4.2.3 *Transverse reinforcement* — Transverse reinforcement shall be provided where V_u exceeds ϕV_{nAAC}. The factored shear, V_u, shall include the effects of lateral load. When transverse reinforcement is required, the following provisions shall apply:

(a) Transverse reinforcement shall be a single bar with a 180-degree hook at each end.

(b) Transverse reinforcement shall be hooked around the longitudinal reinforcement.

(c) The minimum area of transverse reinforcement shall be 0.0007 bd_v.

(d) The first transverse bar shall not be located more than one-fourth of the beam depth, d_v, from the end of the beam.

(e) The maximum spacing shall not exceed the lesser of one-half the depth of the beam or 48 in. (1219 mm).

11.3.4.2.4 *Construction* — Beams shall be fully grouted.

11.3.4.2.5 *Dimensional limits* — The nominal depth of a beam shall not be less than 8 in. (203 mm).

11.3.4.3 *Piers*

11.3.4.3.1 The factored axial compression force on the piers shall not exceed 0.3 $A_n f'_{AAC}$.

11.3.4.3.2 *Longitudinal reinforcement* — A pier subjected to in-plane stress reversals shall be reinforced symmetrically about the geometric center of the pier. The longitudinal reinforcement of piers shall comply with the following:

(a) At least one bar shall be provided in each end cell.

(b) The minimum area of longitudinal reinforcement shall be 0.0007 bd.

11.3.4.3.3 *Dimensional limits* — Dimensions shall be in accordance with the following:

(a) The nominal thickness of a pier shall not be less than 6 in. (152 mm) and shall not exceed 16 in. (406 mm).

(b) The distance between lateral supports of a pier shall not exceed 25 multiplied by the nominal thickness of a pier except as provided for in Section 11.3.4.3.3(c).

(c) When the distance between lateral supports of a pier exceeds 25 multiplied by the nominal thickness of the pier, design shall be based on the provisions of Section 11.3.5.

COMMENTARY

CODE

(d) The nominal length of a pier shall not be less than three multiplied by its nominal thickness nor greater than six multiplied by its nominal thickness. The clear height of a pier shall not exceed five multiplied by its nominal length.

Exception: When the factored axial force at the location of maximum moment is less than $0.05 f'_{AAC} A_g$, the length of a pier shall be permitted to be taken equal to the thickness of the pier.

11.3.5 *Wall design for out-of-plane loads*

11.3.5.1 *Scope* — The requirements of Section 11.3.5 shall apply to the design of walls for out-of-plane loads.

11.3.5.2 *Maximum reinforcement* — The maximum reinforcement ratio shall be determined by Section 11.3.3.5.

11.3.5.3 *Nominal axial and flexural strength* — The nominal axial strength, P_n, and the nominal flexural strength, M_n, of a cross-section shall be determined in accordance with the design assumptions of Section 11.3.2. The nominal axial compressive strength shall not exceed that determined by Equation 11-7 or Equation 11-8, as appropriate.

11.3.5.4 *Nominal shear strength* — The nominal shear strength shall be determined by Section 11.3.4.1.2.

11.3.5.5 *P-delta effects*

11.3.5.5.1 Members shall be designed for the factored axial load, P_u, and the moment magnified for the effects of member curvature, M_u. The magnified moment shall be determined either by Section 11.3.5.5.2 or Section 11.3.5.5.3.

11.3.5.5.2 Moment and deflection calculations in this Section are based on simple support conditions top and bottom. For other support and fixity conditions, moments, and deflections shall be calculated using established principles of mechanics.

The procedures set forth in this section shall be used when the factored axial load stress at the location of maximum moment satisfies the requirement calculated by Equation 11-17.

$$\left(\frac{P_u}{A_g} \right) \leq 0.20 f'_{AAC} \qquad \text{(Equation 11-17)}$$

When the ratio of effective height to nominal thickness, h/t, exceeds 30, the factored axial stress shall not exceed $0.05 f'_{AAC}$

Factored moment and axial force shall be determined at the midheight of the wall and shall be used for design. The factored moment, M_u, at the midheight of the wall shall be calculated using Equation 11-18.

COMMENTARY

11.3.5.5.2 This section only includes design equations based on walls having simple support conditions at the top and bottom of the walls. In actual design and construction, there may be varying support conditions, thus changing the curvature of the wall under lateral loading. Through proper calculation and using the principles of mechanics, the points of inflection can be determined and actual moments and deflection can be calculated under different support conditions. The designer should examine moment and deflection conditions to locate the critical section using the assumptions outlined in Section 11.3.5.

The required moment due to lateral loads, eccentricity of axial load, and lateral deformations is assumed maximum at mid-height of the wall. In certain design conditions, such as large eccentricities acting simultaneously with small lateral loads, the design maximum moment may occur elsewhere. When this occurs, the designer should use the maximum moment at the critical section rather than the moment determined from Equation 11-18.

CODE

$$M_u = \frac{w_u h^2}{8} + P_{uf}\frac{e_u}{2} + P_u\delta_u \qquad \text{(Equation 11-18)}$$

Where:

$$P_u = P_{uw} + P_{uf} \qquad \text{(Equation 11-19)}$$

The deflection due to factored loads (δ_u) shall be obtained using Equations (11-20) and (11-21).

a) Where $M_u < M_{cr}$

$$\delta_u = \frac{5M_u h^2}{48 E_{AAC} I_n} \qquad \text{(Equation 11-20)}$$

(b) Where $M_{cr} \le M_u \le M_n$

$$\delta_u = \frac{5M_{cr} h^2}{48 E_{AAC} I_n} + \frac{5\left(M_u - M_{cr}\right) h^2}{48 E_{AAC} I_{cr}}$$

$$\text{(Equation 11-21)}$$

11.3.5.5.3   The factored moment, M_u, shall be determined either by a second-order analysis, or by a first-order analysis and Equations 11-22 through 11-24.

$$M_u = \psi M_{u,0} \qquad \text{(Equation 11-22)}$$

Where $M_{u,0}$ is the factored moment from first-order analysis.

$$\psi = \frac{1}{1 - \dfrac{P_u}{P_e}} \qquad \text{(Equation 11-23)}$$

Where:

$$P_e = \frac{\pi^2 E_{AAC} I_{eff}}{h^2} \qquad \text{(Equation 11-24)}$$

For $M_u < M_{cr}$, I_{eff} shall be taken as $0.75 I_n$. For $M_u \ge M_{cr}$, I_{eff} shall be taken as I_{cr}. P_u/P_e cannot exceed 1.0.

11.3.5.5.4 The cracking moment of the wall shall be calculated using Equation 11-25, where f_{rAAC} is given by Section 11.1.8.3:

$$M_{cr} = S_n\left(f_{rAAC} + \frac{P}{A_n}\right) \qquad \text{(Equation 11-25)}$$

If the section of AAC masonry contains a horizontal leveling bed, the value of f_{rAAC} shall not exceed 50 psi (345 kPa).

11.3.5.5.5 The neutral axis for determining the cracked moment of inertia, I_{cr}, shall be determined in accordance with the design assumptions of Section 11.3.2. The effects of axial load shall be permitted to be included when calculating I_{cr}.

COMMENTARY

11.3.5.5.3 The moment magnifier provisions in this section were developed to provide an alternative to the traditional P-delta methods of Section 11.3.5.5.2. These provisions also allow other second-order analyses to be used.

The proposed moment magnification equation is very similar to that used for slender wall design for reinforced concrete. Concrete design provisions use a factor of 0.75 in the denominator of the moment magnifier to account for uncertainties in the wall stiffness. This factor is retained for uncracked walls. It is not used for cracked walls. Instead, the cracked moment of inertia is conservatively used for the entire wall height. Trial designs indicated that using this approach matches design using Section 11.3.5.5.2. If a 0.75 factor were included along with using the cracked moment of inertia for the entire height would result in design moments approximately 7% greater than using Section 11.3.5.5.2. The committee did not see any reason for the additional conservatism.

CODE

Unless stiffness values are obtained by a more comprehensive analysis, the cracked moment of inertia for a solidly grouted wall or a partially grouted wall with the neutral axis in the face shell shall be obtained from Equation 11-26 and Equation 11-27.

$$I_{cr} = n\left(A_s + \frac{P_u}{f_y}\frac{t_{sp}}{2d}\right)(d-c)^2 + \frac{b(c)^3}{3}$$

(Equation 11-26)

$$c = \frac{A_s f_y + P_u}{0.57 f'_{AAC}\, b}$$

(Equation 11-27)

11.3.5.5.6 The design strength for out-of-plane wall loading shall be in accordance with Equation 11-28.

$$M_u \le \phi M_n$$

(Equation 11-28)

The nominal moment shall be calculated using Equations 11-29 and 11-30 if the reinforcing steel is placed in the center of the wall.

$$M_n = \left(A_s f_y + P_u\right)\left(d - \frac{a}{2}\right)$$

(Equation 11-29)

$$a = \frac{\left(P_u + A_s f_y\right)}{0.85 f'_{AAC}\, b}$$

(Equation 11-30)

11.3.5.6 *Deflections* — The horizontal midheight deflection, δ_s, under allowable stress design load combinations shall be limited by the relation:

$$\delta_s \le 0.007\, h$$

(Equation 11-31)

P-delta effects shall be included in deflection calculation using either Section 11.3.5.6.1 or Section 11.3.5.6.2.

11.3.5.6.1 For simple support condition top and bottom, the midheight deflection, δ_s, shall be calculated using either Equation 11-20 or Equation 11-21, as applicable, and replacing M_u with M_{ser} and δ_u with δ_s.

11.3.5.6.2 The deflection, δ_s, shall be determined by a second-order analysis that includes the effects of cracking, or by a first-order analysis with the calculated deflections magnified by a factor of $1/(1-P/P_e)$, where P_e is determined from Equation 11-24.

COMMENTARY

CODE

11.3.6 *Wall design for in-plane loads*

    11.3.6.1 *Scope* — The requirements of Section 11.3.6 shall apply to the design of walls to resist in-plane loads.

    11.3.6.2 *Reinforcement* — Reinforcement shall be in accordance with the following:

(a) Reinforcement shall be provided perpendicular to the shear reinforcement and shall be at least equal to one-third A_v. The reinforcement shall be uniformly distributed and shall not exceed a spacing of 8 ft (2.44 m).

(b) The maximum reinforcement ratio shall be determined in accordance with Section 11.3.3.5.

    11.3.6.3 *Flexural and axial strength* — The nominal flexural and axial strength shall be determined in accordance with Section 11.3.4.1.1.

    11.3.6.4 *Shear strength* — The nominal shear strength shall be calculated in accordance with Section 11.3.4.1.2.

    11.3.6.5 *Flexural cracking strength* — The flexural cracking strength shall be calculated in accordance with Equation 11-32, where f_{rAAC} is given by Section 11.1.8.3:

$$V_{cr} = \frac{S_n}{h}\left(f_{rAAC} + \frac{P}{A_n} \right)$$

                   (Equation 11-32)

    If the section of AAC masonry contains a horizontal leveling bed, the value of f_{rAAC} shall not exceed 50 psi (345 kPa).

    11.3.6.6 The maximum reinforcement requirements of Section 11.3.3.5 shall not apply if a shear wall is designed to satisfy the requirements of Sections 11.3.6.6.1 through 11.3.6.6.4.

        11.3.6.6.1 The need for special boundary elements at the edges of shear walls shall be evaluated in accordance with Section 11.3.6.6.2 or 11.3.6.6.3. The requirements of Section 11.3.6.6.4 shall also be satisfied.

        11.3.6.6.2 This Section applies to walls bending in single curvature in which the flexural limit state response is governed by yielding at the base of the wall. Walls not satisfying those requirements shall be designed in accordance with Section 11.3.6.6.3.

(a) Special boundary elements shall be provided over portions of compression zones where:

$$c \geq \frac{l_w}{600\left(C_d \delta_{ne}/h_w\right)}$$

COMMENTARY

    11.3.6.6 While requirements for confined boundary elements have not been developed for AAC shear walls, they have not been developed for conventional masonry shear walls either, and the monolithic nature of AAC shear walls favors possible applications involving boundary elements. Also see Commentary Section 9.3.6.5.

    11.3.6.6.1 See Commentary Section 9.3.6.5.2.

    11.3.6.6.2 See Commentary Section 9.3.6.5.3.

CODE

and c is calculated for the P_u given by ASCE 7 Load Combination 5 $(1.2D + 1.0E + L + 0.2S)$ or the corresponding strength design load combination of the legally adopted building code, and the corresponding nominal moment strength, M_n, at the base critical section. The load factor on L in Load Combination 5 is reducible to 0.5, as per exceptions to Section 2.3.2 of ASCE 7.

(b) Where special boundary elements are required by Section 11.3.6.6.2 (a), the special boundary element reinforcement shall extend vertically from the critical section a distance not less than the larger of l_w or $M_u/4V_u$.

11.3.6.6.3   Shear walls not designed to the provisions of Section 11.3.6.6.2 shall have special boundary elements at boundaries and edges around openings in shear walls where the maximum extreme fiber compressive stress, corresponding to factored forces including earthquake effect, exceeds $0.2 f'_{AAC}$. The special boundary element shall be permitted to be discontinued where the calculated compressive stress is less than $0.15 f'_{AAC}$. Stresses shall be calculated for the factored forces using a linearly elastic model and gross section properties. For walls with flanges, an effective flange width as defined in Section 5.1.1.2.3 shall be used.

11.3.6.6.4   Where special boundary elements are required by Section 11.3.6.6.2 or 11.3.6.6.3, (a) through (d) shall be satisfied and tests shall be performed to verify the strain capacity of the element:

(a) The special boundary element shall extend horizontally from the extreme compression fiber a distance not less than the larger of $(c - 0.1l_w)$ and $c/2$.

(b) In flanged sections, the special boundary element shall include the effective flange width in compression and shall extend at least 12 in. (305 mm) into the web.

(c) Special boundary element transverse reinforcement at the wall base shall extend into the support at least the development length of the largest longitudinal reinforcement in the boundary element unless the special boundary element terminates on a footing or mat, where special boundary element transverse reinforcement shall extend at least 12 in. (305 mm) into the footing or mat.

(d) Horizontal shear reinforcement in the wall web shall be anchored to develop the specified yield strength, f_y, within the confined core of the boundary element.

COMMENTARY

11.3.6.6.3 See Commentary Section 9.3.6.5.4.

11.3.6.6.4 See Commentary Section 9.3.6.5.5.

This page intentionally left blank

PART 4: PRESCRIPTIVE DESIGN METHODS

CHAPTER 12
VENEER

CODE

12.1 — General

12.1.1 *Scope*

This chapter provides requirements for design and detailing of anchored masonry veneer and adhered masonry veneer.

COMMENTARY

12.1 — General

12.1.1 *Scope*

Adhered and anchored veneer definitions given in Section 2.2 are variations of those used in model building codes. Modifications have been made to the definitions to clearly state how the veneer is handled in design. Veneer is an element that is not considered to add strength or stiffness to the wall. The design of the veneer backing should be in compliance with the appropriate standard for the material. See Figures CC-12.1-1 and CC-12.1-2 for typical examples of anchored and adhered veneer, respectively.

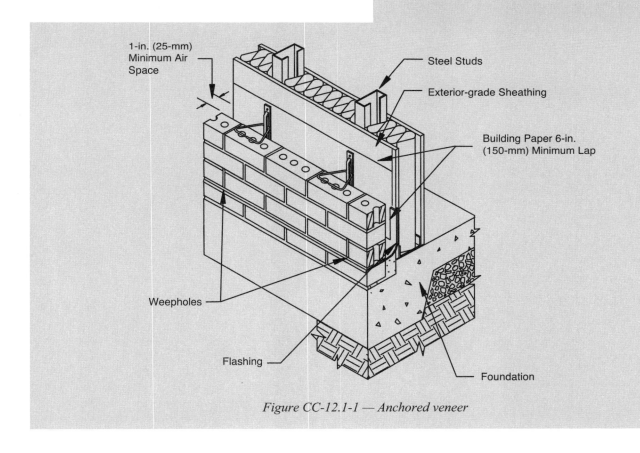

1-in. (25-mm) Minimum Air Space

Steel Studs

Exterior-grade Sheathing

Building Paper 6-in. (150-mm) Minimum Lap

Weepholes

Flashing

Foundation

Figure CC-12.1-1 — Anchored veneer

COMMENTARY

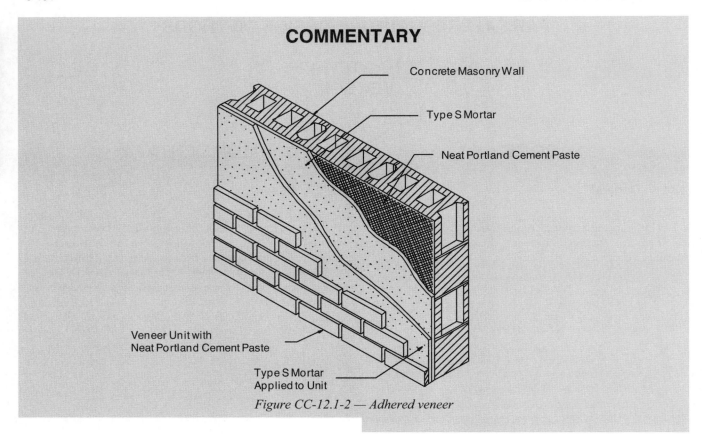

Figure CC-12.1-2 — Adhered veneer

CODE

12.1.1.1 The provisions of Part 1, excluding Sections 1.2.1(c) and 1.2.2; Chapter 4, excluding Sections 4.1 and 4.3; and Chapter 6 shall apply to design of anchored and adhered veneer except as specifically stated in this Chapter.

12.1.1.2 Section 4.5 shall not apply to adhered veneer.

12.1.1.3 Articles 1.4 A and B and 3.4 C of TMS 602/ACI 530.1/ASCE 6 shall not apply to any veneer. Articles 3.4 B and F shall not apply to anchored veneer. Articles 3.3 B and 3.4 A, B, E and F shall not apply to adhered veneer.

12.1.2 *Design of anchored veneer*

Anchored veneer shall meet the requirements of Section 12.1.6 and shall be designed rationally by Section 12.2.1 or detailed by the prescriptive requirements of Section 12.2.2.

COMMENTARY

12.1.1.1 Because there is no consideration of stress in the veneer, there is no need to specify the compressive strength of masonry.

12.1.1.3 The Specification was written for construction of masonry subjected to design stresses in accordance with the other chapters of this Code. Masonry veneer, as defined by this Code, is not subject to those design provisions. The Specification articles that are excluded address materials and requirements that are not applicable to veneer construction or are items addressed by specific requirements in this Chapter and are put here to be inclusive.

12.1.2 *Design of anchored veneer*

Implicit within these requirements is the knowledge that the veneer transfers out-of-plane loads through the veneer anchors to the backing. The backing accepts and resists the anchor loads and is designed to resist the out-of-plane loads.

When utilizing anchored masonry veneer, the designer should consider the following conditions and assumptions:

a) The veneer may crack in flexure under service load.

b) Deflection of the backing should be limited to control crack width in the veneer and to provide veneer stability.

c) Connections of the anchor to the veneer and to the backing should be sufficient to transfer applied loads.

d) Differential movement should be considered in the design, detailing, and construction.

e) Water will penetrate the veneer, and the wall system should be designed, detailed, and constructed to prevent water penetration into the building.

f) Requirements for corrosion protection and fire resistance must be included.

If the backing is masonry and the exterior masonry wythe is not considered to add to the strength of the wall in resisting out-of-plane load, the exterior wythe is masonry veneer. However, if the exterior wythe is considered to add to the strength of the wall in resisting out-of-plane load, the wall is properly termed either a multiwythe, non-composite or composite wall rather than a veneer wall.

CODE

COMMENTARY

Manufacturers of steel studs and sheathing materials have published literature on the design of steel stud backing for anchored masonry veneer. Some recommendations have included composite action between the stud and the sheathing and load carrying participation by the veneer. The Metal Lath/Steel Framing Association has promoted a deflection limit of stud span length divided by 360 (Brown and Arumula, 1982). The Brick Industry Association has held that an appropriate deflection limit should be in the range of stud span length divided by 600 to 720. The deflection is calculated assuming that all of the load is resisted by the studs (BIA TN 28B, 2005). Neither set of assumptions will necessarily ensure that the veneer remains uncracked at service load. In fact, the probability of cracking may be high (Grimm and Klingner, 1990). However, post-cracking performance is satisfactory if the wall is properly designed, constructed and maintained with appropriate materials (Kelly et al, 1990). Plane frame computer programs are available for the rational structural design of anchored masonry veneer (Grimm and Klingner, 1990).

A deflection limit of stud span length divided by 200 multiplied by the specified veneer thickness provides a maximum uniform crack width for various heights and various veneer thicknesses. Deflection limits do not reflect the actual distribution of load. They are simply a means of obtaining a minimum backing stiffness. The National Concrete Masonry Association provides a design methodology by which the stiffness properties of the masonry veneer and its backing are proportioned to achieve compatibility (NCMA TEK 16-3A, 1995).

Masonry veneer with wood frame backing has been used successfully on one- and two-family residential construction for many years. Most of these applications are installed without a deflection analysis.

CODE

12.1.3 *Design of adhered veneer*

Adhered veneer shall meet the requirements of Section 12.1.6, and shall be designed rationally by Section 12.3.1 or detailed by the prescriptive requirements of Section 12.3.2.

12.1.4 *Dimension stone*

The provisions of Sections 12.1.1, 12.1.3 and 12.3 shall apply to design of adhered dimension stone veneer. Anchored dimension stone veneer is not addressed by this Code. Such a veneer system shall be considered a Special System, and consideration for approval of its use shall be submitted to the Building Official.

12.1.5 *Autoclaved aerated concrete masonry veneer*

Autoclaved aerated concrete masonry as a veneer wythe is not addressed by this Chapter. Such a veneer system shall be considered a Special System, and consideration for approval of its use shall be submitted to the Building Official.

12.1.6 *General design requirements*

12.1.6.1 Design and detail the backing system of exterior veneer to resist water penetration. Exterior sheathing shall be covered with a water-resistant membrane, unless the sheathing is water resistant and the joints are sealed.

12.1.6.2 Design and detail flashing and weep holes in exterior veneer wall systems to resist water penetration into the building interior. Weepholes shall be at least $^3/_{16}$ in. (4.8 mm) in diameter and spaced less than 33 in. (838 mm) on center.

12.1.6.3 Design and detail the veneer to accommodate differential movement.

COMMENTARY

12.1.3 *Design of adhered veneer*

Adhered veneer differs from anchored veneer in its means of attachment. The designer should consider conditions and assumptions given in Code Section 12.3.1 when designing adhered veneer.

12.1.4 *Dimension stone*

Anchored dimension stone veneer should be considered as a Special System of Construction, under Code Section 1.3.

12.1.5 *Autoclaved aerated concrete masonry veneer*

Veneer anchors described in Chapter 12 are not suitable for use in AAC masonry because of the narrow joints. No testing of such anchors has been performed for AAC masonry. Therefore AAC masonry anchored veneer must be considered a Special System. The method of adhering veneer, as described in Specification Article 3.3 C, has not been evaluated with AAC masonry and shear strength requirements for adhesion of AAC masonry veneer have not been established. Therefore, AAC masonry adhered veneer must be considered a Special System.

12.1.6 *General design requirements*

Water penetration through the exterior veneer is expected. The wall system must be designed and constructed to prevent water from entering the building.

The requirements given here and the minimum air space dimensions of Sections 12.2.2.6.3, 12.2.2.7.4, and 12.2.2.8.2 are those required for a drainage wall system. Proper drainage requires weep holes and a clear air space. It may be difficult to keep a 1-in. (25-mm) air space free from mortar bridging. Other options are to provide a wider air space, a vented air space, or to use the rain screen principle.

Masonry veneer can be designed with horizontal and vertical bands of different materials. The dissimilar physical properties of the materials should be considered when deciding how to accommodate differential movement.

Industry recommendations are available regarding horizontal bands of clay and concrete masonry, and address such items as joint reinforcement, slip joints, and sealant joints (NCMA TEK 5-2A, 2002; BIA, 2000; BIA TN 18A, 2006). Vertical movement joints can be used to accommodate differential movement between vertical bands of dissimilar materials.

CODE

12.2 — Anchored veneer

12.2.1 *Alternative design of anchored masonry veneer*
The alternative design of anchored veneer, which is permitted under Section 1.3, shall satisfy the following conditions:

(a) Loads shall be distributed through the veneer to the anchors and the backing using principles of mechanics.

(b) Out-of-plane deflection of the backing shall be limited to maintain veneer stability.

(c) The veneer is not subject to the flexural tensile stress provisions of Section 8.2 or the nominal flexural tensile strength provisions of Section 9.1.9.2.

(d) The provisions of Section 12.1, Section 12.2.2.9, and Section 12.2.2.10 shall apply.

12.2.2 *Prescriptive requirements for anchored masonry veneer*

12.2.2.1 Except as provided in Section 12.2.2.11, prescriptive requirements for anchored masonry veneer shall not be used in areas where the velocity pressure, q_z, exceeds 40 psf (1.92 kPa) as given in ASCE 7.

12.2.2.2 Connect anchored veneer to the backing with anchors that comply with Section 12.2.2.5 and Article 2.4 of TMS 602/ACI 530.1/ASCE 6.

12.2.2.3 *Vertical support of anchored masonry veneer*

12.2.2.3.1 The weight of anchored veneer shall be supported vertically on concrete or masonry foundations or other noncombustible structural construction, except as permitted in Sections 12.2.2.3.1.1, 12.2.2.3.1.4, and 12.2.2.3.1.5.

COMMENTARY

12.2 — Anchored veneer

12.2.1 *Alternative design of anchored masonry veneer*
There are no rational design provisions for anchored veneer in any code or standard. The intent of Section 12.2.1 is to permit the designer to use alternative means of supporting and anchoring masonry veneer. See Commentary Section 12.1.1 for conditions and assumptions to consider. The designer may choose to not consider stresses in the veneer or may limit them to a selected value, such as the allowable stresses of Section 8.2, the anticipated cracking stress, or some other limiting condition. The rational analysis used to distribute the loads must be consistent with the assumptions made. See Commentary Section 12.2.2.5 for information on anchors.

The designer should provide support of the veneer; control deflection of the backing; consider anchor loads, stiffness, strength and corrosion; water penetration; and air and vapor transmission.

12.2.2 *Prescriptive requirements for anchored masonry veneer*
The provisions are based on the successful performance of anchored masonry veneer. These have been collected from a variety of sources and reflect current industry practices. Changes result from logical conclusions based on engineering consideration of the backing, anchor, and veneer performance.

12.2.2.1 The wind speed triggers used in the 2008 MSJC were replaced with strength level velocity pressures in the 2011 edition. These velocity pressure triggers were based on the 25 psf (1.20 kPa) working stress velocity pressure that had been used in previous editions of this Code multiplied by 1.6 to convert to strength levels.

12.2.2.3 *Vertical support of anchored masonry veneer* — These requirements are based on current industry practice and current model building codes. Support does not need to occur at the floor level; it can occur at a window head or other convenient location.

12.2.2.3.1 There are no restrictions on the height limit of veneer backed by masonry or concrete, nor are there any requirements that the veneer weight be carried by intermediate supports. The designer should consider the effects of differential movement on the anchors and connection of the veneer to other building components.

CODE

12.2.2.3.1.1 Anchored veneer shall be permitted to be supported vertically by preservative-treated wood foundations. The height of veneer supported by wood foundations shall not exceed 18 ft (5.49 m) above the support.

12.2.2.3.1.2 Anchored veneer with a backing of wood framing shall not exceed 30 ft (9.14 m), or 38 ft (11.58 m) at a gable, in height above the location where the veneer is supported.

12.2.2.3.1.3 If anchored veneer with a backing of cold-formed steel framing exceeds 30 ft (9.14 m), or 38 ft (11.58 m) at a gable, in height above the location where the veneer is supported, the weight of the veneer shall be supported by noncombustible construction at each story above 30 ft (9.14 m) in height.

12.2.2.3.1.4 When anchored veneer is used as an interior finish on wood framing, it shall have a weight of 40 psf (195 kg/m^2) or less and be installed in conformance with the provisions of this Chapter.

12.2.2.3.1.5 Exterior masonry veneer having an installed weight of 40 psf (195 kg/m^2) or less and height of no more than 12 ft (3.7 m) shall be permitted to be supported on wood construction. A vertical movement joint in the masonry veneer shall be used to isolate the veneer supported by wood construction from that supported by the foundation. Masonry shall be designed and constructed so that masonry is not in direct contact with wood. The horizontally spanning element supporting the masonry veneer shall be designed so that deflection due to dead plus live loads does not exceed l/600 or 0.3 in. (7.6 mm).

12.2.2.3.2 When anchored veneer is supported by floor construction, the floor shall be designed to limit deflection as required in Section 5.2.1.4.1.

12.2.2.3.3 Provide noncombustible lintels or supports attached to noncombustible framing over openings where the anchored veneer is not self-supporting. Lintels shall have a length of bearing not less than 4 in. (102 mm). The deflection of such lintels or supports shall conform to the requirements of Section 5.2.1.4.1.

12.2.2.4 *Masonry units* — Masonry units shall be at least $2^5/_8$ in. (66.7 mm) in actual thickness.

12.2.2.5 *Anchor requirements*
12.2.2.5.1 *Corrugated sheet-metal anchors*
12.2.2.5.1.1 Corrugated sheet-metal anchors shall be at least $^7/_8$ in. (22.2 mm) wide, have a base metal thickness of at least 0.03 in. (0.8 mm), and shall have corrugations with a wavelength of 0.3 to 0.5 in. (7.6 to 12.7 mm) and an amplitude of 0.06 to 0.10 in. (1.5 to 2.5 mm).

COMMENTARY

12.2.2.3.1.1 The full provisions for preservative-treated wood foundations are given in the National Forest Products Association Technical Report 7 (NFPA TR No. 7, 1987).

12.2.2.3.1.5 Support of anchored veneer on wood is permitted in previous model building codes. The vertical movement joint between the veneer on different supports reduces the possibility of cracking due to differential settlement. The height limit of 12 ft (3.7 m) was considered to be the maximum single story height and is considered to be a reasonable fire safety risk.

12.2.2.5 *Anchor requirements* — It could be argued that the device between the veneer and its backing is not an anchor as defined in the Code. That device is often referred to as a tie. However, the term anchor is used because of the widespread use of anchored veneer in model building codes and industry publications, and the desire to differentiate from tie as used in other chapters.

CODE

12.2.2.5.1.2 Corrugated sheet-metal anchors shall be placed as follows:

(a) With solid units, embed anchors in the mortar joint and extend into the veneer a minimum of $1\frac{1}{2}$ in. (38.1 mm), with at least $\frac{5}{8}$-in. (15.9-mm) mortar cover to the outside face.

(b) With hollow units, embed anchors in mortar or grout and extend into the veneer a minimum of $1\frac{1}{2}$ in. (38.1 mm), with at least $\frac{5}{8}$-in. (15.9-mm) mortar or grout cover to the outside face.

12.2.2.5.2 *Sheet-metal anchors*
12.2.2.5.2.1 Sheet-metal anchors shall be at least $\frac{7}{8}$ in. (22.2 mm) wide, shall have a base metal thickness of at least 0.06 in. (1.5 mm), and shall:

(a) have corrugations as given in Section 12.2.2.5.1.1, or

(b) be bent, notched, or punched to provide equivalent performance in pull-out or push-through.

12.2.2.5.2.2 Sheet-metal anchors shall be placed as follows:

(a) With solid units, embed anchors in the mortar joint and extend into the veneer a minimum of $1\frac{1}{2}$ in. (38.1 mm), with at least $\frac{5}{8}$-in. (15.9-mm) mortar cover to the outside face.

(b) With hollow units, embed anchors in mortar or grout and extend into the veneer a minimum of $1\frac{1}{2}$ in. (38.1 mm), with at least $\frac{5}{8}$-in. (15.9-mm) mortar or grout cover to the outside face.

12.2.2.5.3 *Wire anchors*
12.2.2.5.3.1 Wire anchors shall be at least wire size W1.7 (MW11) and have ends bent to form an extension from the bend at least 2 in. (50.8 mm) long. Wire anchors shall be without drips.

12.2.2.5.3.2 Wire anchors shall be placed as follows:

(a) With solid units, embed anchors in the mortar joint and extend into the veneer a minimum of $1\frac{1}{2}$ in. (38.1 mm), with at least $\frac{5}{8}$-in. (15.9-mm) mortar cover to the outside face.

(b) With hollow units, embed anchors in mortar or grout and extend into the veneer a minimum of $1\frac{1}{2}$ in. (38.1 mm), with at least $\frac{5}{8}$-in. (15.9-mm) mortar or grout cover to the outside face.

12.2.2.5.4 *Joint reinforcement*
12.2.2.5.4.1 Ladder-type or tab-type joint reinforcement is permitted. Cross wires used to anchor masonry veneer shall be at least wire size W1.7 (MW11) and shall be spaced at a maximum of 16 in. (406 mm) on center. Cross wires shall be welded to longitudinal wires, which shall be at least wire size W1.7 (MW11). Cross wires

COMMENTARY

When first introduced in 1995, U.S. industry practice was combined with the requirements of the Canadian Standards Association (CSA, 1984) to produce the requirements given at that time. Each anchor type has physical requirements that must be met. Minimum embedment requirements have been set for each of the anchor types to ensure load resistance against push-through or pull-out of the mortar joint. Maximum air space dimensions are set in Sections 12.2.2.6 through 12.2.2.8.

There are no performance requirements for veneer anchors in previous codes. Indeed, there are none in the industry. Tests on anchors have been reported (Brown and Arumula, 1982; BIA TN 28, 1966). Many anchor manufacturers have strength and stiffness data for their proprietary anchors.

Veneer anchors typically allow for movement in the plane of the wall but resist movement perpendicular to the veneer. The mechanical play in adjustable anchors and the stiffness of the anchor influence load transfer between the veneer and the backing. Stiff anchors with minimal mechanical play provide more uniform transfer of load, increase the stress in the veneer, and reduce veneer deflection.

Veneer anchors of wire with drips are not permitted because of their reduced load capacity. The anchors listed in Section 12.2.2.5.6.1 are thought to have lower strength or stiffness than the more rigid plate-type anchors. Thus fewer plate-type anchors are required. The number of anchors required by this Code is based on the requirements of the 1991 UBC. The number of required anchors is increased in the higher Seismic Design Categories. Anchor spacing is independent of backing type.

Anchor frequency should be calculated independently for the wall surface in each plane. That is, horizontal spacing of veneer anchors should not be continued from one plane of the veneer to another.

In the 1995 edition of the Code, when anchored veneer provisions were first introduced, the use of adjustable single-pintle anchors was not permitted. Based on testing of tie capacity (Klingner and Torrealva, 2005) and Committee consideration, the use of the adjustable single pintle anchor was permitted in the 2011 edition of the Code.

The term "offset" in Code Section 12.2.2.5.5.4 refers to the vertical distance between a wire eye and the horizontal leg of a bent wire tie inserted into that eye, or the vertical distance between functionally similar components of a pintle anchor.

CODE

and tabs shall be without drips.

12.2.2.5.4.2 Embed longitudinal wires of joint reinforcement in the mortar joint with at least $^5/_8$-in. (15.9-mm) mortar cover on each side.

12.2.2.5.5 *Adjustable anchors*

12.2.2.5.5.1 Sheet-metal and wire components of adjustable anchors shall conform to the requirements of Section 12.2.2.5.2 or 12.2.2.5.3. Adjustable anchors with joint reinforcement shall also meet the requirements of Section 12.2.2.5.4.

12.2.2.5.5.2 Maximum clearance between connecting parts of the tie shall be $^1/_{16}$ in. (1.6 mm).

12.2.2.5.5.3 Adjustable anchors shall be detailed to prevent disengagement.

12.2.2.5.5.4 Pintle anchors shall have one or more pintle legs of wire size W2.8 (MW18) and shall have an offset not exceeding $1^1/_4$ in. (31.8 mm).

12.2.2.5.5.5 Adjustable anchors of equivalent strength and stiffness to those specified in Sections 12.2.2.5.5.1 through 12.2.2.5.5.4 are permitted.

12.2.2.5.6 *Anchor spacing*

12.2.2.5.6.1 For adjustable two-piece anchors, anchors of wire size W1.7 (MW11), and 22 gage (0.8 mm) corrugated sheet-metal anchors, provide at least one anchor for each 2.67 ft^2 (0.25 m^2) of wall area.

12.2.2.5.6.2 For other anchors, provide at least one anchor for each 3.5 ft^2 (0.33 m^2) of wall area.

12.2.2.5.6.3 Space anchors at a maximum of 32 in. (813 mm) horizontally and 25 in. (635 mm) vertically, but not to exceed the applicable requirements of Section 12.2.2.5.6.1 or 12.2.2.5.6.2.

12.2.2.5.6.4 Provide additional anchors around openings larger than 16 in. (406 mm) in either dimension. Space anchors around perimeter of opening at a maximum of 3 ft (0.91 m) on center. Place anchors within 12 in. (305 mm) of openings.

12.2.2.5.7 *Joint thickness for anchors* — Mortar bed joint thickness shall be at least twice the thickness of the embedded anchor.

COMMENTARY

CODE

12.2.2.6 *Masonry veneer anchored to wood backing*

12.2.2.6.1 Veneer shall be attached with any anchor permitted in Section 12.2.2.5.

12.2.2.6.2 Attach each anchor to wood studs or wood framing with a corrosion-resistant 8d common nail, or with a fastener having equivalent or greater pullout strength. For corrugated sheet-metal anchors, locate the nail or fastener within $1/2$ in. (12.7 mm) of the 90-degree bend in the anchor.

12.2.2.6.3 When corrugated sheet metal anchors are used, a maximum distance between the inside face of the veneer and outside face of the solid sheathing of 1 in. (25.4 mm) shall be specified. When other anchors are used, a maximum distance between the inside face of the veneer and the wood stud or wood framing of 4½ in. (114 mm) shall be specified. A 1-in. (25.4-mm) minimum air space shall be specified.

12.2.2.7 *Masonry veneer anchored to steel backing*

12.2.2.7.1 Attach veneer with adjustable anchors.

12.2.2.7.2 Attach each anchor to steel framing with at least a No. 10 corrosion-resistant screw (nominal shank diameter of 0.190 in. (4.8 mm)), or with a fastener having equivalent or greater pullout strength.

12.2.2.7.3 Cold-formed steel framing shall be corrosion resistant and have a minimum base metal thickness of 0.043 in. (1.1 mm).

12.2.2.7.4 A 4½ in. (114-mm) maximum distance between the inside face of the veneer and the steel framing shall be specified. A 1 in. (25.4 mm) minimum air space shall be specified.

12.2.2.8 *Masonry veneer anchored to masonry or concrete backing*

12.2.2.8.1 Attach veneer to masonry backing with wire anchors, adjustable anchors, or joint reinforcement. Attach veneer to concrete backing with adjustable anchors.

12.2.2.8.2 A 4½ in. (114-mm) maximum distance between the inside face of the veneer and the outside face of the masonry or concrete backing shall be specified. A 1 in. (25.4 mm) minimum air space shall be specified.

12.2.2.9 *Veneer not laid in running bond* — Anchored veneer not laid in running bond shall have joint reinforcement of at least one wire, of size W1.7 (MW11), spaced at a maximum of 18 in. (457 mm) on center vertically.

COMMENTARY

12.2.2.6 *Masonry veneer anchored to wood backing* — These requirements are similar to those used by industry and given in model building codes for years. The limitation on fastening corrugated anchors at a maximum distance from the bend is to achieve better performance. The maximum distances between the veneer and the sheathing or wood stud is provided in order to obtain minimum compression capacity of anchors.

12.2.2.7 *Masonry veneer anchored to steel backing* — These requirements generally follow recommendations in current use (BIA TN 28B, 2005; Drysdale and Suter, 1991). The minimum base metal thickness is given to provide sufficient pull-out resistance of screws.

Increasingly energy efficiency building envelopes may require more than 3.5 in. (89 mm) of insulation in the wall cavity. With a code requirement for a minimum specified air gap of 1 in. (25 mm), the system would need to be designed using the alternative procedures.

12.2.2.8 *Masonry veneer anchored to masonry or concrete backing* — These requirements are similar to those used by industry and have been given in model building codes for many years.

Increasingly energy efficiency building envelopes may require more than 3.5 in. (89 mm) of insulation in the wall cavity. With a code requirement for a minimum specified air gap of 1 in. (25 mm), the system would need to be designed using the alternative procedures.

12.2.2.9 *Veneer not laid in running bond* — Masonry not laid in running bond has similar requirements in Section 4.5. The area of joint reinforcement required in Section 12.2.2.9 is equivalent to that in Section 4.5 for a nominal 4-in. (102-mm) wythe.

CODE

12.2.2.10   *Requirements in seismic areas*
12.2.2.10.1   *Seismic Design Category C*
12.2.2.10.1.1   The requirements of this section apply to anchored veneer for buildings in Seismic Design Category C.

12.2.2.10.1.2   Isolate the sides and top of anchored veneer from the structure so that vertical and lateral seismic forces resisted by the structure are not imparted to the veneer.

12.2.2.10.2   *Seismic Design Category D*
12.2.2.10.2.1   The requirements for Seismic Design Category C and the requirements of this section apply to anchored veneer for buildings in Seismic Design Category D.

12.2.2.10.2.2   Reduce the maximum wall area supported by each anchor to 75 percent of that required in Sections 12.2.2.5.6.1 and 12.2.2.5.6.2. Maximum horizontal and vertical spacings are unchanged.

12.2.2.10.2.3   For masonry veneer anchored to wood backing, attach each veneer anchor to wood studs or wood framing with a corrosion-resistant 8d ring-shank nail, a No. 10 corrosion-resistant screw with a minimum nominal shank diameter of 0.190 in. (4.8 mm) or with a fastener having equivalent or greater pullout strength.

12.2.2.10.3   *Seismic Design Categories E and F*
12.2.2.10.3.1   The requirements for Seismic Design Category D and the requirements of this section apply to anchored veneer for buildings in Seismic Design Categories E and F.

12.2.2.10.3.2   Support the weight of anchored veneer for each story independent of other stories.

12.2.2.11   *Requirements in areas of high winds* — The following requirements apply in areas where the velocity pressure, q_z, exceeds 40 psf (1.92 kPa) but does not exceed 55 psf (2.63 kPa) and the building's mean roof height is less than or equal to 60 ft (18.3 m):

(a) Reduce the maximum wall area supported by each anchor to 70 percent of that required in Sections 12.2.2.5.6.1 and 12.2.2.5.6.2.

(b) Space anchors at a maximum 18 in. (457 mm) horizontally and vertically.

(c) Provide additional anchors around openings larger than 16 in. (406 mm) in either direction. Space anchors around perimeter of opening at a maximum of 24 in. (610 mm) on center. Place anchors within 12 in. (305 mm) of openings.

COMMENTARY

12.2.2.10   *Requirements in seismic areas* — These requirements provide several cumulative effects to improve veneer performance under seismic load. Many of them are based on similar requirements given in earlier model building codes (UBC, 1991). The isolation from the structure reduces accidental loading and permits larger building deflections to occur without veneer damage. Support at each floor articulates the veneer and reduces the size of potentially damaged areas. An increased number of anchors increases veneer stability and reduces the possibility of falling debris. Added expansion joints further articulate the veneer, permit greater building deflection without veneer damage and limit stress development in the veneer.

Shake table tests of panel (Klingner et al, 2010(a)) and full-scale wood frame/brick veneer buildings (Reneckis and LaFave, 2009) have demonstrated that 8d common nails are not sufficient to resist seismic loading under certain conditions. 8d ring-shank nails or #10 screws were recommended by the researchers for use in areas of significant seismic loading.

12.2.2.10.3 *Seismic Design Categories E and F* — The 1995 through 2011 editions of the MSJC Code required that masonry veneer in Seismic Design Categories E and F be provided with joint reinforcement, mechanically attached to anchors with clips or hooks. Shaking-table research (Klingner et al, 2010(b)) has shown that the requirement is not necessary or useful so the requirement was removed in the 2013 edition of the MSJC Code.

12.2.2.11   *Requirements in areas of high winds* — The provisions in this section are based on a reduction in tributary area by 30%. The velocity pressure trigger was therefore raised by 1/0.7, and rounded to 55 psf (2.63 kPa).

CODE

12.3 — Adhered veneer

12.3.1 *Alternative design of adhered masonry veneer*
The alternative design of adhered veneer, which is permitted under Section 1.3, shall satisfy the following conditions:

(a) Loads shall be distributed through the veneer to the backing using principles of mechanics.

(b) Out-of-plane curvature shall be limited to prevent veneer unit separation from the backing.

(c) The veneer is not subject to the flexural tensile stress provisions of Section 8.2 or the nominal flexural tensile strength provisions of Section 9.1.9.2.

(d) The provisions of Section 12.1 shall apply.

12.3.2 *Prescriptive requirements for adhered masonry veneer*

12.3.2.1 *Unit sizes* — Adhered veneer units shall not exceed $2^5/_8$ in. (66.7 mm) in specified thickness, 36 in. (914 mm) in any face dimension, nor more than 5 ft^2 (0.46 m^2) in total face area, and shall not weigh more than 15 psf (73 kg/m^2).

12.3.2.2 *Wall area limitations* — The height, length, and area of adhered veneer shall not be limited except as required to control restrained differential movement stresses between veneer and backing.

12.3.2.3 *Backing* — Backing shall provide a continuous, moisture-resistant surface to receive the adhered veneer. Backing is permitted to be masonry, concrete, or metal lath and portland cement plaster applied to masonry, concrete, steel framing, or wood framing.

COMMENTARY

12.3 — Adhered veneer

12.3.1 *Alternative design of adhered masonry veneer*
There are no rational design provisions for adhered veneer in any code or standard. The intent of Section 12.3.1 is to permit the designer to use alternative unit thicknesses and areas for adhered veneer. The designer should provide for adhesion of the units, control curvature of the backing, and consider freeze-thaw cycling, water penetration, and air and vapor transmission. The Tile Council of America limits the deflection of the backing supporting ceramic tiles to span length divided by 360 (TCA, 1996).

12.3.2 *Prescriptive requirements for adhered masonry veneer*
Similar requirements for adhered veneer first appeared in the 1967 Uniform Building Code. The construction requirements for adhered veneer in the Specification have a history of successful performance (Dickey, 1982).

12.3.2.1 *Unit sizes* — The dimension, area, and weight limits are imposed to reduce the difficulties of handling and installing large units and to assure good bond.

12.3.2.2 *Wall area limitations* — Selecting proper location for movement joints involves many variables. These include: changes in moisture content, inherent movement of materials, temperature exposure, temperature differentials, strength of units, and stiffness of the backing.

12.3.2.3 *Backing* — These surfaces have demonstrated the ability to provide the necessary adhesion when using the construction method described in the Specification. Model building codes contain provisions for metal lath and portland cement plaster. For masonry or concrete backing, it may be desirable to apply metal lath and plaster. Also, refer to ACI 524R, "Guide to Portland Cement Plastering" (1993) for metal lath, accessories, and their installation. These publications also contain recommendations for control of cracking.

CODE

12.3.2.4 Adhesion developed between adhered veneer units and backing shall have a shear strength of at least 50 psi (345 kPa) based on gross unit surface area when tested in accordance with ASTM C482, or shall be adhered in compliance with Article 3.3 C of TMS 602/ACI 530.1/ASCE 6.

COMMENTARY

12.3.2.4 The required shear strength of 50 psi (345 kPa) is an empirical value based on judgment derived from historical use of adhered veneer systems similar to those permitted by Article 3.3 C of TMS 602/ACI 530.1/ASCE 6. This value is easily obtained with workmanship complying with the Specification. It is anticipated that the 50 psi (345 kPa) will account for differential shear stress between the veneer and its backing in adhered veneer systems permitted by this Code and Specification.

The test method is used to verify shear strength of adhered veneer systems that do not comply with the construction requirements of the Specification or as a quality assurance test for systems that do comply.

This page intentionally left blank

CHAPTER 13
GLASS UNIT MASONRY

CODE

13.1 — General

13.1.1 *Scope*

This chapter provides requirements for empirical design of glass unit masonry as non-load-bearing elements in exterior or interior walls.

13.1.1.1 The provisions of Part 1 and Part 2, excluding Sections 1.2.1(c), 1.2.2, 4.1, 4.2, and 4.3, shall apply to design of glass unit masonry, except as stated in this Chapter.

13.1.1.2 Article 1.4 of TMS 602/ACI 530.1/ASCE 6 shall not apply to glass unit masonry.

13.1.2 *General design requirements*

Design and detail glass unit masonry to accommodate differential movement.

13.1.3 *Units*

13.1.3.1 Hollow or solid glass block units shall be standard or thin units.

13.1.3.2 The specified thickness of standard units shall be at least $3^{7}/_{8}$ in. (98.4 mm).

13.1.3.3 The specified thickness of thin units shall be $3^{1}/_{8}$ in. (79.4 mm) for hollow units or 3 in. (76.2 mm) for solid units.

13.2 — Panel size

COMMENTARY

13.1 — General

13.1.1 *Scope*

Glass unit masonry is used as a non-load-bearing element in interior and exterior walls, partitions, window openings, and as an architectural feature. Design provisions in the Code are empirical. These provisions are cited in previous codes, are based on successful performance, and are recommended by manufacturers.

13.1.1.1 Because there is no consideration of stress in glass unit masonry, there is no need to specify the compressive strength of masonry.

13.2 — Panel size

The Code limitations on panel size are based on structural and performance considerations. Height limits are more restrictive than length limits based on historical requirements rather than actual field experience or engineering principles. Fire resistance rating tests of assemblies may also establish limitations on panel size. Glass block manufacturers can be contacted for technical data on the fire resistance ratings of panels and local building code should be consulted for required fire resistance ratings for glass unit masonry panels. In addition, fire resistance ratings for glass unit masonry panels may be listed with Underwriters Laboratories, Inc. at www.ul.com.

CODE

13.2.1 *Exterior standard-unit panels*

The maximum area of each individual standard-unit panel shall be based on the design wind pressure, in accordance with Figure 13.2-1. The maximum dimension between structural supports shall be 25 ft (7.62 m) horizontally or 20 ft (6.10 m) vertically.

COMMENTARY

13.2.1 *Exterior standard-unit panels*

The wind load resistance curve (Pittsburgh Corning, 1992; Glashaus, 1992, NCMA, 1992) (Figure CC-13.2-1) is representative of the ultimate load limits for a variety of panel conditions. Historically, a 144-ft^2 (13.37-m^2) area limit has been referenced in building codes as the maximum area permitted in exterior applications, without reference to any safety factor or design wind pressure. The 144-ft^2 (13.37-m^2) area also reflects the size of panels tested by the National Concrete Masonry Association (NCMA, 1992). The 144-ft^2 (13.37-m^2) area limitation provides a safety factor of 2.7 when the design wind pressure is 20 psf (958 Pa) (Smolenski, 1992).

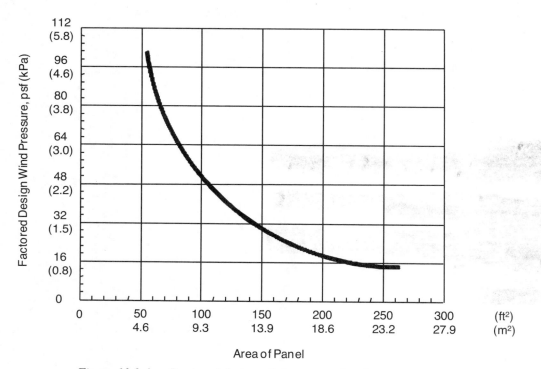

Figure 13.2-1 — *Factored design wind pressure for glass unit masonry*

COMMENTARY

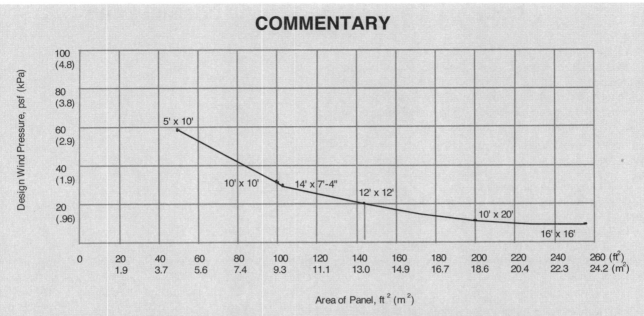

Note: The above historical glass masonry design chart reflects different sizes of glass unit masonry panels tested to ultimate pressures, resulting in a design curve that reflects a 2.7 safety factor of ultimate loading. As an example, the recommended design pressure of 20 psf (958 Pa) for a 144 ft^2 (13.37-m^2) panel, reflects a safety factor of 2.7 of its ultimate strength of 54 psf (2,586 Pa).

Figure CC-13.2-1 — Historical glass masonry design chart

CODE

13.2.2 *Exterior thin-unit panels*

The maximum area of each individual thin-unit panel shall be 100 ft^2 (9.29 m^2). The maximum dimension between structural supports shall be 15 ft (4.57 m) wide or 10 ft (3.05 m) high. Thin units shall not be used in applications where the factored design wind pressure per ASCE 7 exceeds 32 psf (1,532 Pa).

13.2.3 *Interior panels*

13.2.3.1 When the factored wind pressure does not exceed 16 psf (768 Pa), the maximum area of each individual standard-unit panel shall be 250 ft^2 (23.22 m^2) and the maximum area of each thin-unit panel shall be 150 ft^2 (13.94 m^2). The maximum dimension between structural supports shall be 25 ft (7.62 m) wide or 20 ft (6.10 m) high.

13.2.3.2 When the factored wind pressure exceeds 16 psf (768 Pa), standard-unit panels shall be designed in accordance with Section 13.2.1 and thin-unit panels shall be designed in accordance with Section 13.2.2.

COMMENTARY

13.2.2 *Exterior thin-unit panels*

There is limited historical data for developing a curve for thin units. The Committee recommends limiting the exterior use of thin units to areas where the factored design wind pressure does not exceed 32 psf (1,532 Pa).

CODE

13.2.4 *Curved panels*

The width of curved panels shall conform to the requirements of Sections 13.2.1, 13.2.2, and 13.2.3, except additional structural supports shall be provided at locations where a curved section joins a straight section and at inflection points in multi-curved walls.

13.3 — Support

13.3.1 *General requirements*

Glass unit masonry panels shall be isolated so that in-plane loads are not imparted to the panel.

13.3.2 *Vertical*

13.3.2.1 Maximum total deflection of structural members supporting glass unit masonry shall not exceed $l/600$.

13.3.2.2 Glass unit masonry having an installed weight of 40 psf (195 kg/m^2) or less and a maximum height of 12 ft (3.7 m) shall be permitted to be supported on wood construction.

13.3.2.3 A vertical expansion joint in the glass unit masonry shall be used to isolate the glass unit masonry supported by wood construction from that supported by other types of construction.

13.3.3 *Lateral*

13.3.3.1 Glass unit masonry panels, more than one unit wide or one unit high, shall be laterally supported along the top and sides of the panel. Lateral support shall be provided by panel anchors along the top and sides spaced not more than 16 in. (406 mm) on center or by channel-type restraints. Glass unit masonry panels shall be recessed at least 1 in. (25.4 mm) within channels and chases. Channel-type restraints must be oversized to accommodate expansion material in the opening, and packing and sealant between the framing restraints and the glass unit masonry perimeter units. Lateral supports for glass unit masonry panels shall be designed to resist applied loads, or a minimum of 200 lb per linear ft (2919 N/m) of panel, whichever is greater.

13.3.3.2 Glass unit masonry panels that are no more than one unit wide shall conform to the requirements of Section 13.3.3.1, except that lateral support at the top of the panel is not required.

13.3.3.3 Glass unit masonry panels that are no more than one unit high shall conform to the requirements of Section 13.3.3.1, except that lateral support at the sides of the panels is not required.

13.3.3.4 Glass unit masonry panels that are a single glass masonry unit shall conform to the requirements of Section 13.3.3.1, except that lateral support shall not be provided by panel anchors.

COMMENTARY

13.3 — Support

13.3.1 *General requirements*

13.3.2 *Vertical*

Support of glass unit masonry on wood has historically been permitted in model building codes. The Code requirements for expansion joints and for asphalt emulsion at the sill isolate the glass unit masonry within the wood framing. These requirements also reduce the possibility of contact of the glass units and mortar with the wood framing. The height limit of 12 ft. (3.7 m) was considered to be the maximum single story height.

13.3.3 *Lateral*

The Code requires glass unit masonry panels to be laterally supported by panel anchors or channel-type restraints. See Figures CC-13.3-1 and CC-13.3-2 for panel anchor construction and channel-type restraint construction, respectively. Glass unit masonry panels may be laterally supported by either construction type or by a combination of construction types. The channel-type restraint construction can be made of any channel-shaped concrete, masonry, metal, or wood elements so long as they provide the required lateral support.

COMMENTARY

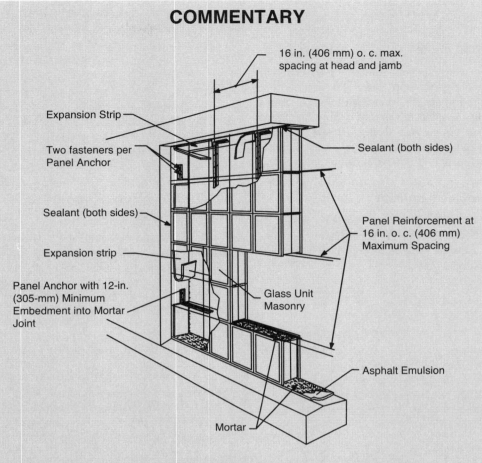

Figure CC-13.3-1 — Panel anchor construction

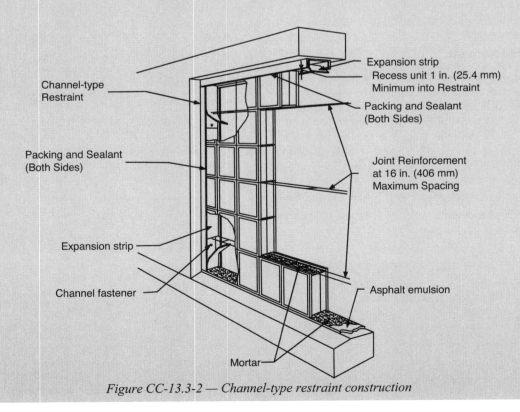

Figure CC-13.3-2 — Channel-type restraint construction

CODE

13.4 — Expansion joints

Glass unit masonry panels shall be provided with expansion joints along the top and sides at structural supports. Expansion joints shall have sufficient thickness to accommodate displacements of the supporting structure, but shall not be less than $^3/_8$ in. (9.5 mm) in thickness. Expansion joints shall be entirely free of mortar or other debris and shall be filled with resilient material.

13.5 — Base surface treatment

The surface on which glass unit masonry panels are placed shall be coated with a water-based asphaltic emulsion or other elastic waterproofing material prior to laying the first course.

13.6 — Mortar

Glass unit masonry shall be laid with Type S or N mortar.

13.7 — Reinforcement

Glass unit masonry panels shall have horizontal joint reinforcement spaced not more than 16 in. (406 mm) on center, located in the mortar bed joint, and extending the entire length of the panel but not across expansion joints. Longitudinal wires shall be lapped a minimum of 6 in. (152 mm) at splices. Joint reinforcement shall be placed in the bed joint immediately below and above openings in the panel. The reinforcement shall have at least two parallel longitudinal wires of size W1.7 (MW11) and have welded cross wires of size W1.7 (MW11).

COMMENTARY

13.5 — Base surface treatment

Current industry practice and recommendations by glass block manufacturers state that surfaces on which glass unit masonry is placed be coated with an asphalt emulsion Pittsburgh Corning, 1992; Glashau, 1992). The asphalt emulsion provides a slip plane at the panel base. This is in addition to the expansion provisions at head and jamb locations. The asphalt emulsion also waterproofs porous panel bases.

Glass unit masonry panels subjected to structural investigation tests by the National Concrete Masonry Association (1992) to confirm the validity and use of the Glass Unit Masonry Design Wind Load Resistance chart (Figure CC-13.2-1), were constructed on bases coated with asphalt emulsion. Asphalt emulsion on glass unit masonry panel bases is needed to be consistent with these tests.

CHAPTER 14
MASONRY PARTITION WALLS

CODE

14.1 — General

14.1.1 *Scope*
This chapter provides requirements for the design of masonry partition walls.

14.1.2 *Design of partition walls*
Partition walls shall be designed by one of the following:

(a) the requirements of Part 1, Part 2 and the requirements of Chapter 8, Chapter 9, Chapter 10, Chapter 11, or Chapter 13; or

(b) the prescriptive design requirements of Section 14.2 through 14.5.

14.2 — Prescriptive design of partition walls

14.2.1 *General*
   14.2.1.1 The provisions of Part 1 and Part 2, excluding Sections 1.2.1(c), 1.2.2, 4.1, 4.2, and 4.3, shall apply to prescriptive design of masonry partition walls

   14.2.1.2 Article 1.4 of TMS 602/ACI 530.1/ASCE 6 shall not apply to prescriptively designed masonry partition walls.

14.2.2 *Thickness Limitations*
   14.2.2.1 *Minimum thickness* — The minimum nominal thickness of partition walls shall be 4 in. (102 mm).
   14.2.2.2 *Maximum thickness* — The maximum nominal thickness of partition walls shall be 12 in. (305 mm).

COMMENTARY

14.2 — Prescriptive design of partition walls

The prescriptive design requirements of this Chapter were originally based on empirical rules and formulas for the design of masonry structures that were developed by experience. Design is based on the condition that vertical loads are reasonably centered on the walls and lateral loads are limited. Walls have minimum and maximum thicknesses and additional limitations as noted in Section 14.2.3. The masonry is laid in running bond for horizontally spanning walls. Specific limitations on building height, seismic, wind, and horizontal loads exist. Buildings are of limited height. Members not participating in the lateral-force-resisting system of a building may be designed by the prescriptive provisions of this Chapter even though the lateral-force-resisting system is designed under another Chapter.

14.2.2 *Thickness Limitations* — The minimum and maximum thicknesses set practical limits on walls to be designed with this simplified prescriptive method. The permitted l/t or h/t values in Table 14.3.1(5) and Table 14.3.1(10) are based on analyses of partition walls ranging from 4 in. (102 mm) to 12 in. (305 mm) in nominal thickness.

CODE

14.2.3 *Limitations*

14.2.3.1 *Vertical loads* — The prescriptive design requirements of Chapter 14 shall not apply to the design of partition walls that support vertical compressive, service loads of more than 200 lb/linear ft (2919 N/m) in addition to their own weight. The resultant of vertical loads shall be placed within the center third of the wall thickness. The prescriptive design requirements of Chapter 14 shall not apply to the design of partition walls that resist net axial tension.

14.2.3.2 *Lateral loads* — The prescriptive design requirements of Chapter 14 shall not apply to partition walls resisting service level unfactored lateral loads that exceed 5 psf (0.239 kPa) when using Table 14.3.1(5) or 10 psf (0.479 kPa) when using Table 14.3.1(10).

14.2.3.3 *Seismic Design Category* — The prescriptive design requirements of Chapter 14 shall not apply to the design of masonry partition walls in Seismic Design Categories D, E, or F.

COMMENTARY

14.2.3 *Limitations*

14.2.3.1 *Vertical loads* — This provision allows miscellaneous light loads, such as pictures, emergency lighting, etc., to be applied to interior partition walls, while limiting the load to less than what the Code defines as a load-bearing wall, which is a wall supporting vertical loads greater than 200 lb/linear ft (2919 N/m) in addition to its own weight. The allowable stress analyses performed to establish the permitted span to thickness ratios included a 200 lb/linear ft (2919 N/m) compressive, unfactored load applied at the top of the wall with an eccentricity of $t/6$.

Net axial tension is not permitted in partition walls designed in accordance with this chapter.

14.2.3.2 *Lateral loads* — Out-of-plane loads on the partition walls must not exceed 5 psf (0.239 kPa) service load levels to use Table 14.3.1(5) and must not exceed 10 psf (0.479 kPa) service load levels to use Table 14.3.1(10).

Section 1607.14 "Interior walls and partitions" in the Live Loads section of the 2012 International Building Code (IBC) states, "Interior walls and partitions that exceed 6 feet (1829 mm) in height, including their finish materials, shall have adequate strength to resist the loads to which they are subjected but not less than a horizontal load of 5 psf (0.240 kN/m2)."

Two tables are provided for the use of the designer, one for the code prescribed minimum lateral load of 5 psf (0.239 kPa) as noted above and, one that may be used at the designer's discretion for conditions where the 5 psf (0.239 kPa) minimum is exceeded (but no more than 10 psf (0.479 kPa) maximum) – one example: seismic loading includes out-of-plane lateral loading as a factor of self-weight even on nonparticipating elements such as partition walls and those lateral loads may exceed 5 psf (0.239kPa) in certain conditions especially in Seismic Design Category C.

CODE

14.2.3.4 *Nonparticipating Elements* — Partition walls designed using the prescriptive requirements of Chapter 14 shall be designed as 'nonparticipating elements' in accordance with the requirements of Section 7.3.1.

14.2.3.5 *Enclosed Buildings* — The prescriptive design requirements of Chapter 14 shall only be permitted to be applied to the design of masonry partition walls in Enclosed Buildings as defined by ASCE 7.

14.2.3.6 *Risk Category IV* — The prescriptive design requirements of Chapter 14 shall not apply to the design of masonry partition walls in Risk Category IV as defined in ASCE 7.

14.2.3.7 *Masonry not laid in running bond* — The prescriptive design requirements of Chapter 14 shall not apply to the design of masonry not laid in running bond in horizontally spanning walls.

14.2.3.8 *Glass unit masonry* — The prescriptive design requirements of Chapter 14 shall not apply to the design of glass unit masonry.

14.2.3.9 *AAC masonry* — The prescriptive design requirements of Chapter 14 shall not apply to the design of AAC masonry.

14.2.3.10 *Concrete masonry* — Concrete masonry, designed in accordance with Chapter 14, shall comply with one of the following:

(a) The minimum normalized web area of concrete masonry units, determined in accordance with ASTM C140, shall not be less than 27 in.^{2}/ft^2 (187,500 mm^2/m^2), or

(b) the member shall be grouted solid.

14.2.3.11 *Support* — The provisions of Chapter 14 shall not apply to masonry vertically supported on wood construction.

COMMENTARY

14.2.3.5 *Enclosed Buildings* — Partition walls, as defined by this Code, are interior walls without structural function. Therefore, the requirement that the provisions of this Chapter be limited to Enclosed Buildings as defined by ASCE 7 is appropriate.

14.2.3.7 *Masonry not laid in running bond* — The analyses performed in establishing the permitted span to thickness ratios for the prescriptive design of partition walls were based on the allowable flexural tensile stresses for clay masonry and concrete masonry. This Code does not permit flexural tensile stress parallel to bed joints in unreinforced masonry not laid in running bond unless the masonry has a continuous grout section parallel to the span. Therefore, the prescriptive requirements of Chapter 14 limit the use of masonry that is not laid in running bond to vertically spanning walls that are solidly grouted.

14.2.3.10 *Concrete masonry* — Concrete masonry units are required to have a normalized web area of 27 in.^{2}/ft^2 (187,500 mm^2/m^2) to allow designers to avoid checking shear stress by providing sufficient web area such that web shear stresses do not control a design. This approach is consistent with the goal of keeping the provisions of the Chapter 14 more prescriptive and simplified. If the normalized web area is less than 27 in.^{2}/ft^2 (187,500 mm^2/m^2), solid grouting is required to provide additional shear area.

CODE

14.3 — Lateral support

14.3.1 *Maximum l/t and h/t*

Masonry partition walls without openings shall be laterally supported in either the horizontal or the vertical direction so that l/t or h/t does not exceed the values given in Table 14.3.1(5) or Table 14.3.1(10). It shall not be permitted to decrease the cross-section of the partition wall between supports unless permitted by Section 14.3.2.

14.3.2 *Openings*

Masonry partition walls with single or multiple openings shall be laterally supported in either the horizontal or vertical direction so that l/t or h/t does not exceed the values given in Table 14.3.1(5) or Table 14.3.1(10) divided by $\sqrt{W_T / W_S}$.

W_S is the dimension of the structural wall strip measured perpendicular to the span of the wall strip and perpendicular to the thickness as shown in Figure 14.3.1-1. W_S is measured from the edge of the opening. W_S shall be no less than $3t$ on each side of each opening. Therefore, at walls with multiple openings, jambs shall be no less than $6t$ between openings. For design purposes, the effective W_S shall not be assumed to be greater than $6t$. At non-masonry lintels, the edge of the opening shall be considered the edge of the non-masonry lintel. W_S shall occur uninterrupted over the full span of the wall.

W_T is the dimension, parallel to W_S, from the center of the opening to the opposite end of W_S as shown in Figure 14.3.1-1. Where there are multiple openings perpendicular to W_S, W_T shall be measured from the center of a virtual opening that encompasses such openings. Masonry elements within the virtual opening must be designed in accordance with Chapter 8 or 9.

For walls with openings that span no more than 4 feet, parallel to W_S, if W_S is no less than 4 feet, then it shall be permitted to ignore the effect of those openings.

The span of openings, parallel to W_S, shall be limited so that the span divided by t does not exceed the values given in Table 14.3.1(5) or Table 14.3.1(10).

COMMENTARY

14.3 — Lateral support

14.3.1 *Maximum l/t and h/t*

Lateral support requirements are included to limit the flexural tensile stress due to out-of-plane loads. The requirements provide relative out-of-plane resistance that limit the maximum width of opening and provide sufficient masonry sections between the openings.

The permitted span to thickness ratios for prescriptively designed partition walls were established based on Allowable Stress Design and service level (unfactored) loads of no more than 200 lb/ft (2919 N/m) (vertical) and 5 psf (0.239 kPa) (lateral out-of-plane) or 10 psf (0.479 kPa) (lateral out-of-plane), and a conservative wall self-weight. Critical sections were assumed to be at mid-span and the walls were conservatively assumed to be pinned at both supports.

Table 14.3.1(5) and Table 14.3.1(10) provide maximum l/t and h/t ratios that are a function of mortar type, mortar cementitous materials, unit solidity, and extent of grouting. Second order effects of axial forces combined with progressively larger deflections were not calculated explicitly. However, the combined effects of axial and flexure loads were analyzed using Allowable Stress Design provisions. Secondary bending effects resulting from the axial loads are ignored since axial forces are limited.

Decreases in partition wall cross-section must be accounted for by treating any such decrease as an opening. As one example, a vertical movement joint would need to be accounted for in a horizontal spanning wall.

Table 14.3.1(5) — Maximum l/t^1 or h/t^1 for 5 psf (0.239 kPa) lateral load[2]

Unit and Masonry Type	Mortar types			
	Portland cement/lime or mortar cement		Masonry cement or air entrained portland cement/lime	
	M or S	N	M or S	N
Ungrouted and partially grouted hollow units[3]	26	24	22	18
Solid units and fully grouted hollow units[3]	40	36	33	26

[1] t by definition is the nominal thickness of member

[2]   See Section 14.2.3.2.

[3]   For non-cantilevered walls laterally supported at both ends. See Section 14.3.3 for cantilevered walls.

Table 14.3.1(10) — Maximum l/t^1 or h/t^1 for 10 psf (0.479 kPa) lateral load[2]

Unit and Masonry Type	Mortar types			
	Portland cement/lime or mortar cement		Masonry cement or air entrained portland cement/lime	
	M or S	N	M or S	N
Ungrouted and partially grouted hollow units[3]	18	16	14	12
Solid units and fully grouted hollow units[3]	28	24	22	18

[1] t by definition is the nominal thickness of member

[2]   See Section 14.2.3.2.

[3]   For non-cantilevered walls laterally supported at both ends. See Section 14.3.3 for cantilevered walls.

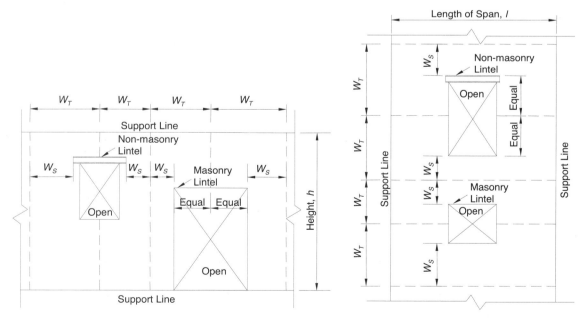

W_S and W_T for Walls Spanning Vertically W_S and W_T for Walls Spanning Horizontally

Figure 14.3.1-1 — Graphical representation of W_S and W_T

CODE

14.3.3 *Cantilever walls*

The ratio of height-to-nominal-thickness for cantilevered partition walls shall not exceed 6 for solid masonry or 4 for hollow masonry.

14.3.4 *Support elements*

Lateral support shall be provided by cross walls, pilasters, or structural frame members when the limiting distance is taken horizontally; or by floors, roofs acting as diaphragms, or structural frame members when the limiting distance is taken vertically.

14.4 — Anchorage

14.4.1 *General*

Masonry partition walls shall be anchored in accordance with this section.

14.4.2 *Intersecting walls*

Masonry partition walls depending upon one another for lateral support shall be anchored or bonded at locations where they meet or intersect by one of the following methods:

14.4.2.1 Fifty percent of the units at the intersection shall be laid in an overlapping masonry bonding pattern, with alternate units having a bearing of at least 3 in. (76.2 mm) on the unit below.

14.4.2.2 Walls shall be anchored at their intersection at vertical intervals of not more than 16 in. (406 mm) with joint reinforcement or $^{1}/_{4}$ in. (6.4 mm) mesh galvanized hardware cloth.

14.4.2.3 Other metal ties, joint reinforcement or anchors, if used, shall be spaced to provide equivalent area of anchorage to that required by Section 14.4.2.2.

14.5 — Miscellaneous requirements

14.5.1 *Chases and recesses*

Masonry directly above chases or recesses wider than 12 in. (305 mm) shall be supported on lintels.

14.5.2 *Lintels*

The design of masonry lintels shall be in accordance with the provisions of Section 5.2.

14.5.3 *Lap splices*

Lap splices for bar reinforcement or joint reinforcement, required by Section 7.4.3.1 and located in masonry partition walls designed in accordance with this Chapter, shall be a minimum of $48d_b$.

COMMENTARY

14.3.3 *Cantilever walls*

The span to thickness ratios permitted for cantilevered walls are based on historical use and confirming analyses using design assumptions similar to those used to develop Table 14.3.1(5) and Table 14.3.1(10).

14.5.3 *Lap splices*

Because Chapter 14 does not have f'_m requirements, designing lap splice requirements in accordance with Chapters 8 or 9 can be problematic when using Chapter 14. The reinforcement required in Chapter 14 is prescriptive. The minimum lap splice length of 48 d_b for reinforcement is based on historical use and the use of a No. 4 (M13) bar or W1.7 (MW1.1) joint reinforcement.

PART 5: APPENDICES

APPENDIX A
EMPIRICAL DESIGN OF MASONRY

CODE

A.1 — General

A.1.1 *Scope*

This appendix provides requirements for empirical design of masonry.

A.1.1.1 The provisions of Part 1 and Part 2, excluding Part 1 Sections 1.2.1(c), 1.2.2, 4.1, 4.2, and 4.3, shall apply to empirical design, except as specifically stated in this Chapter.

A.1.1.2 Article 1.4 of TMS 602/ACI 530.1/ASCE 6 shall not apply to empirically designed masonry.

A.1.2 *Limitations*

A.1.2.1 *Gravity Loads* — The resultant of gravity loads shall be placed within the center third of the wall thickness and within the central area bounded by lines at one-third of each cross-sectional dimension of foundation piers.

A.1.2.2 *Seismic* — Empirical requirements shall not apply to the design of masonry for buildings, parts of buildings or other structures in Seismic Design Categories D, E, or F as defined in ASCE 7, and shall not apply to the design of the seismic-force-resisting system for structures in Seismic Design Categories B or C.

COMMENTARY

A.1 — General

Empirical design procedures of Appendix A are permitted in certain instances. Empirical design is permitted for buildings of limited height and low seismic risk.

Empirical rules and formulas for the design of masonry structures were developed by experience. These are part of the legacy of masonry's long use, predating engineering analysis. Design is based on the condition that gravity loads are reasonably centered on the load-bearing walls and foundation piers. Figure CC-A.1-1 illustrates the location of the resultant of gravity loads on foundation piers. The effect of any steel reinforcement, if used, is neglected. The masonry should be laid in running bond. Specific limitations on building height, seismic, wind, and horizontal loads exist. Buildings are of limited height. Members not participating in the lateral-force-resisting system of a building, other than partition walls, may be empirically designed even though the lateral-force-resisting system is designed under other chapters of this Code.

These procedures have been compiled through the years (Baker, 1909; NBS, 1924; NBS, 1931; ASA, 1944; ANSI, 1953). The most recent of these documents (ANSI, 1953) is the basis for this chapter.

Empirical design is a procedure of sizing and proportioning masonry elements. It is not design analysis. This procedure is conservative for most masonry construction. Empirical design of masonry was developed for buildings of smaller scale, with more masonry interior walls and stiffer floor systems than built today. Thus, the limits imposed are valid.

Because empirically designed masonry is based on the gross compressive strength of the units, there is no need to specify the compressive strength of masonry.

Table CC-A.1.1 is a checklist to assist the Architect/Engineer in designing masonry structures using the empirical design provisions. The checklist identifies the applicable Sections of the Code that need to be considered. There may be additional specific Code requirements that have to be met, depending on the project. The checklist simply serves as a guide.

CODE

A.1.2.3 *Wind* — Empirical requirements shall be permitted to be applied to the design of masonry elements defined by Table A.1.1, based on building height and basic wind speed that are applicable to the building.

A.1.2.4 *Buildings and other structures in Risk Category IV* — Empirical requirements shall not apply to the design of masonry for buildings, parts of buildings or other structures in Risk Category IV as defined in ASCE 7.

A.1.2.5 *Other horizontal loads* — Empirical requirements shall not apply to structures resisting horizontal loads other than permitted wind or seismic loads or foundation walls as provided in Section A.6.3.

A.1.2.6 *Glass unit masonry* — The provisions of Appendix A shall not apply to glass unit masonry.

A.1.2.7 *AAC masonry* — The provisions of Appendix A shall not apply to AAC masonry.

A.1.2.8 *Concrete masonry* — Concrete masonry, designed in accordance with Appendix A, shall comply with one of the following:

(a) The minimum normalized web area of concrete masonry units, determined in accordance with ASTM C140, shall not be less than 27 in.^{2}/ft^2 (187,500 mm^2/m^2), or

(b) the member shall be grouted solid.

A.1.2.9 *Support* — The provisions of Appendix A shall not apply to masonry vertically supported on wood construction.

A.1.2.10 *Partition walls* — The provisions of Appendix A shall not apply to partition walls.

COMMENTARY

A.1.2.3 *Wind* — There is a change in the wind speed values listed in the table from previous versions of the Code. The values listed were adjusted to strength levels for use with ASCE 7-10 wind speed maps and are designed to maintain the strength level velocity pressures below approximately 40 psf (1.92 kPa) for a wide range of building configurations.

A.1.2.8 *Concrete masonry* — When the empirical design provisions for masonry were initially standardized in the early 20th century, only a limited number of concrete masonry unit configurations were available. In contrast, there is a near limitless array of unit shapes and sizes commercially available today. The requirements of this section establish a minimum web area that is consistent with the configuration of concrete masonry units prevalent when the empirical design provisions first began to take shape, thereby maintaining assumptions inherent in the empirical design provisions. Alternatively, the assembly can be solidly grouted, in which case the configuration of the web is structurally irrelevant.

A.1.2.10 *Partition walls* — Partition wall design is not included in this Appendix. Partition wall design is permitted by Chapter 14 of this code.

Table A.1.1 Limitations based on building height and basic wind speed

Element Description	Building Height, ft (m)	Basic Wind Speed, mph (mps)[1]			
		Less than or equal to 115 (51)	Over 115 (51) and less than or equal to-120 (54)	Over 120 (54) and less than or equal to 125 (56)	Over 125 (56)
Masonry elements that are part of the lateral-force-resisting system	35 (11) and less	Permitted			Not Permitted
Interior masonry loadbearing elements that are not part of the lateral-force-resisting system in buildings other than enclosed as defined by ASCE 7	Over 180 (55)	Not Permitted			
	Over 60 (18) and less than or equal to 180 (55)	Permitted	Not Permitted		
	Over 35 (11) and less than or equal to 60 (18)	Permitted		Not Permitted	
	35 (11) and less	Permitted			Not Permitted
Exterior masonry elements that are not part of the lateral-force-resisting system	Over 180 (55)	Not Permitted			
	Over 60 (18) and less than or equal to 180 (55)	Permitted	Not Permitted		
	Over 35 (11) and less than or equal to 60 (18)	Permitted		Not Permitted	
Exterior masonry elements	35 (11) and less	Permitted			Not Permitted

[1] Basic wind speed as given in ASCE 7

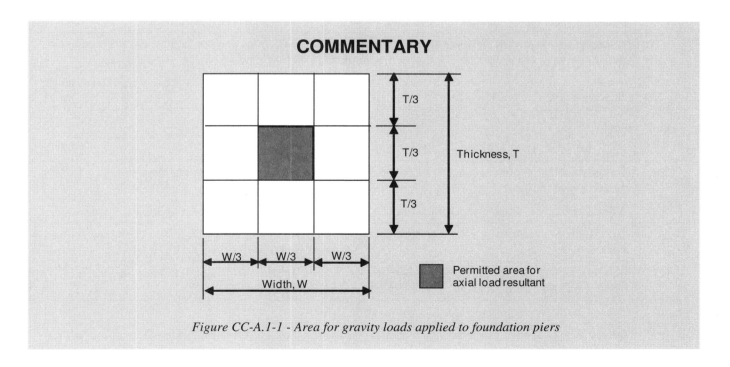

Figure CC-A.1-1 - Area for gravity loads applied to foundation piers

COMMENTARY

Table CC-A.1.1 — Checklist for use of Appendix A – Empirical Design of Masonry

1.	Risk Category IV structures are not permitted to be designed using Appendix A.
2.	Partitions are not permitted to be designed using Appendix A.
3.	Use of empirical design is limited based on Seismic Design Category, as described in the following table.

Seismic Design Category	Participating Walls	Non-Participating Walls, except partition walls
A	Allowed by Appendix A	Allowed by Appendix A
B	Not Allowed	Allowed by Appendix A
C	Not Allowed	With prescriptive reinforcement per 7.4.3.1[1]
D, E, and F	Not Allowed	Not Allowed

[1] Lap splices are required to be designed and detailed in accordance with the requirements of Chapters 8 or 9.

4.	Use of empirical design is limited based on wind speed at the project site, as described in Code A.1.2.3 and Code Table A.1.1.
5.	If wind uplift on roofs result in net tension, empirical design is not permitted (A.8.3.1).
6.	Loads used in the design of masonry must be listed on the design drawings (1.2.1b).
7.	Details of anchorage to structural frames must be included in the design drawings (1.2.1e).
8.	The design is required to include provisions for volume change (1.2.1h). The design drawings are required to include the locations and sizing of expansion, control, and isolation joints.
9.	If walls are connected to structural frames, the connections and walls are required to be designed to resist the interconnecting forces and to accommodate deflections (4.4). This provision requires a lateral load and uplift analysis for exterior walls that receive wind load and are supported by or are supporting a frame or roofing system.
10.	Masonry not laid in running bond (for example, stack bond masonry) is required to have horizontal reinforcement (4.5).
11.	A project quality assurance plan is required (3.1) with minimum requirements given in Table 3.1.1.
12.	The resultant of gravity loads must be determined and assured to be located within certain limitations for walls and piers (A.1.2.1).
13.	Ensure compliance of the design with prescriptive floor, roof, and wall-to-structural framing anchorage requirements, as well as other anchorage requirements (A.8.3 and A.8.4).
14.	Type N mortar is not permitted for foundation walls (A.6.3.1(g)).
15.	Design shear wall lengths, spacings, and orientations to meet the requirements of Code A.3.1.

CODE

A.2 — Height

Buildings relying on masonry walls as part of their lateral-force-resisting system shall not exceed 35 ft (10.67 m) in height.

A.3 — Lateral stability

A.3.1 *Shear walls*

Where the structure depends upon masonry walls for lateral stability, shear walls shall be provided parallel to the direction of the lateral forces resisted.

A.3.1.1 In each direction in which shear walls are required for lateral stability, shear walls shall be positioned in at least two separate planes parallel with the direction of the lateral force. The minimum cumulative length of shear walls provided along each plane shall be 0.2 multiplied by the long dimension of the building. Cumulative length of shear walls shall not include openings or any element whose length is less than one-half its height.

A.3.1.2 Shear walls shall be spaced so that the length-to-width ratio of each diaphragm transferring lateral forces to the shear walls does not exceed values given in Table A.3.1.

A.3.2 *Roofs*

The roof construction shall be designed so as not to impart out-of-plane lateral thrust to the walls under roof gravity load.

COMMENTARY

A.3 — Lateral stability

Lateral stability requirements are a key provision of empirical design. Obviously, shear walls must be in two directions to provide stability. Load-bearing walls can serve as shear walls. The height of a wall refers to the shortest unsupported height in the plane of the wall such as the shorter of a window jamb on one side and a door jamb on the other. See Figure CC-A.3-1 for cumulative length of shear walls. See Figure CC-A.3-2 for diaphragm panel length to width ratio determination.

Table A.3.1 — Diaphragm length-to-width ratios

Floor or roof diaphragm construction	Maximum length-to-width ratio of diaphragm panel
Cast-in-place concrete	5:1
Precast concrete	4:1
Metal deck with concrete fill	3:1
Metal deck with no fill	2:1
Wood	2:1

COMMENTARY

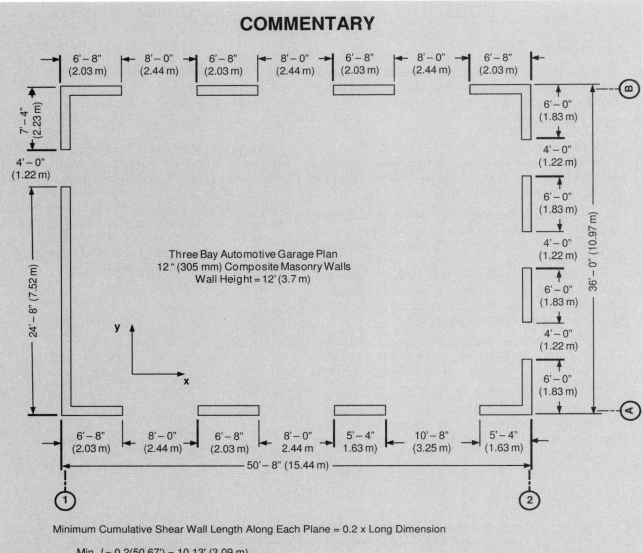

Minimum Cumulative Shear Wall Length Along Each Plane = 0.2 x Long Dimension

Min. l = 0.2(50.67') = 10.13' (3.09 m)

Wall line 1: l = (24.67 + 7.33) = 32.0′ > 10.13′ OK
l = (7.52 m + 2.23 m) = 9.75 m > 3.09 m OK

Wall line 2: l = (6.0′ + 6.0′ + 6.0′ + 6.0') = 24.0′ > 10.13′ OK
l = (1.83 m + 1.83 m + 1.83 m + 1.83 m) = 7.32 m > 3.09 m OK

Wall line A: Note, 5'-4"(1.62 m) wall segments not included as they are less than ½ of 12' (3.66 m) wall height
l = (6.67′ + 6.67′) = 13.33′ > 10.13′ OK
l = (2.03 m + 2.03 m) = 4.06 m > 3.09 m OK

Wall line B: l = (6.67′ + 6.67′ + 6.67′ + 6.67') = 26.67′ > 10.13′ OK
l = (2.03 m + 2.03 m + 2.03 m + 2.03 m) = 8.13 m > 3.09 m OK

Figure CC-A.3-1 — Cumulative length of shear walls

COMMENTARY

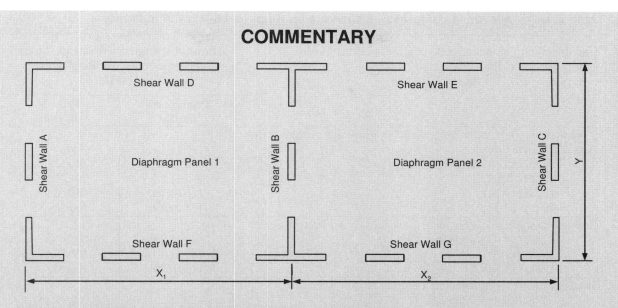

Diaphragm Panel Length = Dimension perpendicular to the resisting shear wall

Diaphragm Panel Width = Dimension parallel to the resisting shear wall

For example:

       For Shear Walls A and B, the diaphragm panel length to width ratio is X_1/Y

       For Shear Walls D and F, the diaphragm panel length to width ratio is Y/X_1

Note: Shear walls should be placed on all four sides of the diaphragm panel or the resulting torsion should be accounted for.

Figure CC-A.3-2 — Diaphragm panel length to width ratio determination for shear wall spacing

---

CODE

A.4 — Compressive stress requirements

A.4.1 *Calculations*

Dead loads and live loads shall be in accordance with the legally adopted building code of which this Code forms a part, with such live load reductions as are permitted in the legally adopted building code. Compressive stresses in masonry due to vertical dead plus live loads (excluding wind or seismic loads) shall be determined in accordance with the following:

(a) Stresses shall be calculated based on specified dimensions.

(b) Calculated compressive stresses for single wythe walls and for multiwythe composite masonry walls shall be determined by dividing the design load by the gross cross-sectional area of the member. The area of openings, chases, or recesses in walls shall not be included in the gross cross-sectional area of the wall.

A.4.2 *Allowable compressive stresses*

The compressive stresses in masonry shall not exceed the values given in Table A.4.2. In multiwythe walls, the allowable stresses shall be based on the weakest combination of the units and mortar used in each wythe.

COMMENTARY

A.4 — Compressive stress requirements

These are average compressive stresses based on gross area using specified dimensions. The course immediately under the point of bearing should be a solid unit or fully filled with mortar or grout.

Table A.4.2 — Allowable compressive stresses for empirical design of masonry

Construction; compressive strength of masonry unit, gross area, psi (MPa)	Allowable compressive stresses[1] based on gross cross-sectional area, psi (MPa)	
	Type M or S mortar	Type N mortar
Solid masonry of brick and other solid units of clay or shale; sand-lime or concrete brick:		
8,000 (55.16) or greater	350 (2.41)	300 (2.07)
4,500 (31.03)	225 (1.55)	200 (1.38)
2,500 (17.23)	160 (1.10)	140 (0.97)
1,500 (10.34)	115 (0.79)	100 (0.69)
Grouted masonry of clay or shale; sand-lime or concrete:		
4,500 (31.03) or greater	225 (1.55)	200 (1.38)
2,500 (17.23)	160 (1.10)	140 (0.97)
1,500 (10.34)	115 (0.79)	100 (0.69)
Solid masonry of solid concrete masonry units:		
3,000 (20.69) or greater	225 (1.55)	200 (1.38)
2,000 (13.79)	160 (1.10)	140 (0.97)
1,200 (8.27)	115 (0.79)	100 (0.69)
Masonry of hollow load-bearing units of clay or shale[2]:		
2,000 (13.79) or greater	140 (0.97)	120 (0.83)
1,500 (10.34)	115 (0.79)	100 (0.69)
1,000 (6.90)	75 (0.52)	70 (0.48)
700 (4.83)	60 (0.41)	55 (0.38)
Masonry of hollow load-bearing concrete masonry units, up to and including 8 in. (203 mm) nominal thickness:		
2,000 (13.79) or greater	140 (0.97)	120 (0.83)
1,500 (10.34)	115 (0.79)	100 (0.69)
1,000 (6.90)	75 (0.52)	70 (0.48)
700 (4.83)	60 (0.41)	55 (0.38)
Masonry of hollow load-bearing concrete masonry units, greater than 8 and up to 12 in. (203 to 305 mm) nominal thickness:		
2,000 (13.79) or greater	125 (0.86)	110 (0.76)
1,500 (10.34)	105 (0.72)	90 (0.62)
1,000 (6.90)	65 (0.45)	60 (0.41)
700 (4.83)	55 (0.38)	50 (0.35)

Table A.4.2 (continued) — Allowable compressive stresses for empirical design of masonry

Construction; compressive strength of masonry unit, gross area, psi (MPa)	Allowable compressive stresses[1] based on gross cross-sectional area, psi (MPa)	
	Type M or S mortar	Type N mortar
Masonry of hollow load-bearing concrete masonry units, 12 in. (305 mm) nominal thickness and greater:		
2,000 (13.79) or greater	115 (0.79)	100 (0,69)
1,500 (10.34)	95 (0.66)	85 (0.59)
1,000 (6.90)	60 (0.41)	55 (0.38)
700 (4.83)	50 (0.35)	45 (0.31))
Multiwythe non-composite walls[2]:		
Solid units:		
2500 (17.23) or greater	160 (1.10)	140 (0.97)
1500 (10.34)	115 (0.79)	100 (0.69)
Hollow units of clay or shale	75 (0.52)	70 (0.48)
Hollow units of concrete masonry of nominal thickness,		
up to and including 8 in. (203 mm):	75 (0.52)	70 (0.48)
greater than 8 and up to 12 in. (203-305 mm):	70 (0.48)	65 (0.45)
12 in. (305 mm) and greater:	60 (0.41)	55(0.38)
Stone ashlar masonry:		
Granite	720 (4.96)	640 (4.41)
Limestone or marble	450 (3.10)	400 (2.76)
Sandstone or cast stone	360 (2.48)	320 (2.21)
Rubble stone masonry:		
Coursed, rough, or random	120 (0.83)	100 (0.69)

1 Linear interpolation shall be permitted for determining allowable stresses for masonry units having compressive strengths which are intermediate between those given in the table.

2 In non-composite walls, where floor and roof loads are carried upon one wythe, the gross cross-sectional area is that of the wythe under load; if both wythes are loaded, the gross cross-sectional area is that of the wall minus the area of the cavity between the wythes.

CODE

A.5 — Lateral support

A.5.1 *Maximum l/t and h/t*

Masonry walls without openings shall be laterally supported in either the horizontal or the vertical direction so that l/t or h/t does not exceed the values given in Table A.5.1.

Masonry walls with single or multiple openings shall be laterally supported in either the horizontal or vertical direction so that l/t or h/t does not exceed the values given in Table A.5.1 divided by $\sqrt{W_T/W_S}$.

W_S is the dimension of the structural wall strip measured perpendicular to the span of the wall strip and perpendicular to the thickness as shown in Figure A.5.1-1. W_S is measured from the edge of the opening. W_S shall be no less than $3t$ on each side of each opening. Therefore, at walls with multiple openings, jambs shall be no less than $6t$ between openings. For design purposes, the effective W_S shall not be assumed to be greater than $6t$. At non-masonry lintels, the edge of the opening shall be considered the edge of the non-masonry lintel. W_S shall occur uninterrupted over the full span of the wall.

W_T is the dimension, parallel to W_S, from the center of the opening to the opposite end of W_S as shown in Figure A.5.1-1. Where there are multiple openings perpendicular to W_S, W_T shall be measured from the center of a virtual opening that encompasses such openings. Masonry elements within the virtual opening must be designed in accordance with Chapter 8 or 9.

For walls with openings that span no more than 4 feet, parallel to W_S, if W_S is no less than 4 feet, then it shall be permitted to ignore the effect of those openings.

The span of openings, parallel to W_S, shall be limited so that the span divided by t does not exceed the values given in Table A.5.1.

In addition to these limitations, lintels shall be designed for gravity loads in accordance with Section A.9.2.

COMMENTARY

A.5 — Lateral support

Lateral support requirements are included to limit the flexural tensile stress due to out-of-plane loads. Masonry headers resist shear stress and permit the entire cross-section to perform as a single element. This is not the case for non-composite walls connected with wall ties. For such non-composite walls, the use of the sum of the thicknesses of the wythes has been used successfully for a long time and is a traditional approach that is acceptable within the limits imposed by Code Table A.5.1. Requirements were added in the 2008 edition to provide relative out-of-plane resistance that limit the maximum width of opening and provide sufficient masonry sections between the openings.

Table A.5.1 — Wall lateral support requirements

Construction	Maximum *l/t* or *h/t*
Load-bearing walls	
Solid units or fully grouted	20
Other than solid units or fully grouted	18
Non-load-bearing walls	
Exterior	18

In calculating the ratio for multiwythe walls, use the following thickness:
1. The nominal wall thicknesses for solid walls and for hollow walls bonded with masonry headers (Section A.7.2).
2. The sum of the nominal thicknesses of the wythes for non-composite walls connected with wall ties (Section A.7.3).

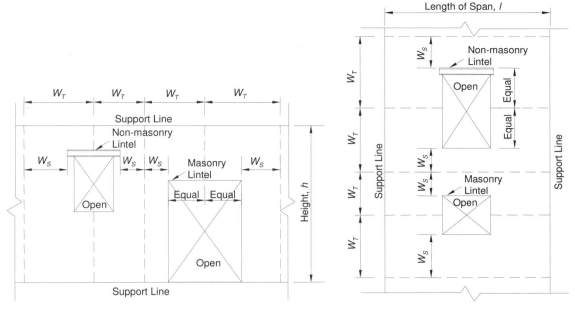

W_S and W_T for Walls Spanning Vertically W_S and W_T for Walls Spanning Horizontally

Figure A.5.1-1 — Graphical representation of W_S and W_T

CODE

A.5.2 *Cantilever walls*

Except for parapets, the ratio of height-to-nominal-thickness for cantilever walls shall not exceed 6 for solid masonry or 4 for hollow masonry. For parapets see Section A.6.4.

A.5.3 *Support elements*

Lateral support shall be provided by cross walls, pilasters, or structural frame members when the limiting distance is taken horizontally; or by floors, roofs acting as diaphragms, or structural frame members when the limiting distance is taken vertically.

A.6 — Thickness of masonry

A.6.1 *General*

Minimum thickness requirements shall be based on nominal dimensions of masonry.

A.6.2 *Minimum thickness*

A.6.2.1 *Load-bearing walls* — The minimum thickness of load-bearing walls of one story buildings shall be 6 in. (152 mm). The minimum thickness of load-bearing walls of buildings more than one story high shall be 8 in. (203 mm).

A.6.2.2 *Rubble stone walls* — The minimum thickness of rough, random, or coursed rubble stone walls shall be 16 in. (406 mm).

COMMENTARY

A.6 — Thickness of masonry

A.6.1 *General*

Experience of the committee has shown that the present ANSI A 41.1 (1953) thickness ratios are not always conservative. These requirements represent the consensus of the committee for more conservative design.

CODE

A.6.2.3 *Shear walls* — The minimum thickness of masonry shear walls shall be 8 in. (203 mm).

A.6.2.4 *Foundation walls* — The minimum thickness of foundation walls shall be 8 in. (203 mm).

A.6.2.5 *Foundation piers* — The minimum thickness of foundation piers shall be 8 in. (203 mm).

A.6.2.6 *Parapet walls* — The minimum thickness of parapet walls shall be 8 in. (203 mm).

A.6.2.7 *Partition walls* — The minimum thickness of partition walls shall be 4 in. (102 mm).

A.6.2.8 *Change in thickness* — Where walls of masonry of hollow units or masonry bonded hollow walls are decreased in thickness, a course or courses of solid masonry units or fully grouted hollow masonry units shall be interposed between the wall below and the thinner wall above, or special units or construction shall be used to transmit the loads from face shells or wythes above to those below.

A.6.3 *Foundation walls*

A.6.3.1 Foundation walls shall comply with the requirements of Table A.6.3.1, which are applicable when:

(a) the foundation wall does not exceed 8 ft (2.44 m) in height between lateral supports,

(b) the terrain surrounding foundation walls is graded to drain surface water away from foundation walls,

(c) backfill is drained to remove ground water away from foundation walls,

(d) lateral support is provided at the top of foundation walls prior to backfilling,

(e) the length of foundation walls between perpendicular masonry walls or pilasters is a maximum of 3 multiplied by the basement wall height,

(f) the backfill is granular and soil conditions in the area are non-expansive, and

(g) masonry is laid in running bond using Type M or S mortar.

A.6.3.2 Where the requirements of Section A.6.3.1 are not met, foundation walls shall be designed in accordance with Part 1, Part 2, and Chapter 8, 9, or 10.

A.6.4 *Foundation piers*

Design of foundation piers shall comply with Appendix A and the following:

(a) Length, measured perpendicular to its thickness, shall not exceed 3 times its thickness.

(b) Height shall be equal to or less than 4 times its thickness

COMMENTARY

A.6.3 *Foundation walls*

Empirical criteria for masonry foundation wall thickness related to the depth of unbalanced fill have been contained in building codes and federal government standards for many years. The use of Code Table A.6.3.1, which lists the traditional allowable backfill depths, is limited by a number of requirements that were not specified in previous codes and standards. These restrictions are enumerated in Section A.6.3.1. Further precautions are recommended to guard against allowing heavy earth-moving or other equipment close enough to the foundation wall to develop high earth pressures. Experience with local conditions should be used to modify the values in Table A.6.3.1 when appropriate.

A.6.4 *Foundation piers*

Foundation piers are masonry members that are unique to the Empirical Design method. Use of empirically designed foundation piers has been common practice in many areas of the country for many years. ANSI A 41.1 (1953) provisions for empirically designed piers (Section A.3) include a requirement for a maximum h/t ratio of 4. The length and height requirements provide the basis on which the design requirements were developed and differentiate a foundation pier from other members such as columns or piers.

Table A.6.3.1 — Foundation wall construction

Wall construction	Nominal wall thickness, in. (mm)	Maximum depth of unbalanced backfill, ft (m)
Masonry of hollow units	8 (203)	5 (1.52)
	10 (254)	6 (1.83)
	12 (305)	7 (2.13)
Masonry of solid units	8 (203)	5 (1.52)
	10 (254)	7 (2.13)
	12 (305)	7 (2.13)
Fully grouted masonry	8 (203)	7 (2.13)
	10 (254)	8 (2.44)
	12 (305)	8 (2.44)

CODE

A.7 — Bond

A.7.1 *General*
Wythes of multiple wythe masonry walls shall be bonded in accordance with the requirements of Section A.7.2, Section A.7.3, or Section A.7.4.

A.7.2 *Bonding with masonry headers*
A.7.2.1 *Solid units* — Where adjacent wythes of solid masonry walls are bonded by means of masonry headers, no less than 4 percent of the wall surface area of each face shall be composed of headers extending not less than 3 in. (76.2 mm) into each wythe. The distance between adjacent full-length headers shall not exceed 24 in. (610 mm) either vertically or horizontally. In multi-wythe walls that are thicker than the length of a header, each wythe shall be connected to the adjacent wythe by adjacent headers that overlap a minimum of 3 in. (76.2 mm).

A.7.2.2 *Hollow units* — Where two or more wythes are constructed using hollow units, the stretcher courses shall be bonded at vertical intervals not exceeding 34 in. (864 mm) by lapping at least 3 in. (76.2 mm) over the unit below, or by lapping at vertical intervals not exceeding 17 in. (432 mm) with units which are at least 50 percent greater in thickness than the units below.

A.7.3 *Bonding with wall ties or joint reinforcement*
A.7.3.1 Where adjacent wythes of masonry walls are bonded with wire size W2.8 (MW18) wall ties or metal wire of equivalent stiffness embedded in the horizontal mortar joints, there shall be at least one metal tie for each $4^{1}/_{2}$ ft^2 (0.42 m^2) of wall area. The maximum vertical distance between ties shall not exceed 24 in. (610 mm), and the maximum horizontal distance shall not exceed 36 in. (914 mm). Rods or ties bent to rectangular shape shall be used with hollow masonry units laid with the cells vertical. In other walls, the ends of ties shall be bent to 90-degree angles to provide hooks no less than 2 in. (50.8 mm) long. Wall ties shall be without drips and shall be non-adjustable. Additional bonding ties shall be provided at openings, spaced not more than 3 ft (0.91 m) apart around the perimeter and within 12 in. (305 mm) of the opening.

CODE

COMMENTARY

A.7 — Bond
Figure CC-A.7-1 depicts the requirements listed. Wall ties with drips are not permitted because of their reduced load capacity.

COMMENTARY

A.7.3.2 Where adjacent wythes of masonry are bonded with prefabricated joint reinforcement, there shall be at least one cross wire serving as a tie for each $2^2/_3$ ft^2 (0.25 m^2) of wall area. The vertical spacing of the joint reinforcement shall not exceed 24 in. (610 mm). Cross wires on prefabricated joint reinforcement shall be not smaller than wire size W1.7 (MW11) and shall be without drips. The longitudinal wires shall be embedded in the mortar.

A.7.4 *Natural or cast stone*

A.7.4.1 *Ashlar masonry* — In ashlar masonry, uniformly distributed bonder units shall be provided to the extent of not less than 10 percent of the wall area. Such bonder units shall extend not less than 4 in. (102 mm) into the backing wall.

A.7.4.2 *Rubble stone masonry* — Rubble stone masonry 24 in. (610 mm) or less in thickness shall have bonder units with a maximum spacing of 3 ft (0.91 m) vertically and 3 ft (0.91 m) horizontally, and if the masonry is of greater thickness than 24 in. (610 mm), shall have one bonder unit for each 6 ft^2 (0.56 m^2) of wall surface on both sides.

A.8 — Anchorage

A.8.1 *General*

Masonry elements shall be anchored in accordance with this section.

A.8.2 *Intersecting walls*

Masonry walls depending upon one another for lateral support shall be anchored or bonded at locations where they meet or intersect by one of the following methods:

A.8.2.1 Fifty percent of the units at the intersection shall be laid in an overlapping masonry bonding pattern, with alternate units having a bearing of not less than 3 in. (76.2 mm) on the unit below.

A.8.2.2 Walls shall be anchored by steel connectors having a minimum section of $^1/_4$ in. (6.4 mm) by $1^1/_2$ in. (38.1 mm) with ends bent up at least 2 in. (50.8 mm), or with cross pins to form anchorage. Such anchors shall be at least 24 in. (610 mm) long and the maximum spacing shall be 4 ft (1.22 m).

A.8.2.3 Walls shall be anchored by joint reinforcement spaced at a maximum distance of 8 in. (203 mm). Longitudinal wires of such reinforcement shall be at least wire size W1.7 (MW11) and shall extend at least 30 in. (762 mm) in each direction at the intersection.

A.8.2.4 Other metal ties, joint reinforcement or anchors, if used, shall be spaced to provide equivalent area of anchorage to that required by Sections A.8.2.2 through A.8.2.4.

A.8 — Anchorage

The requirements of Sections A.8.2.2 through A.8.2.4 are less stringent than those of Section 5.1.1.2.5. Anchorage requirements in Section A.8.3.3 are intended to comply with the Steel Joist Institute's Standard Specification (SJI, 2002) for end anchorage of steel joists.

COMMENTARY

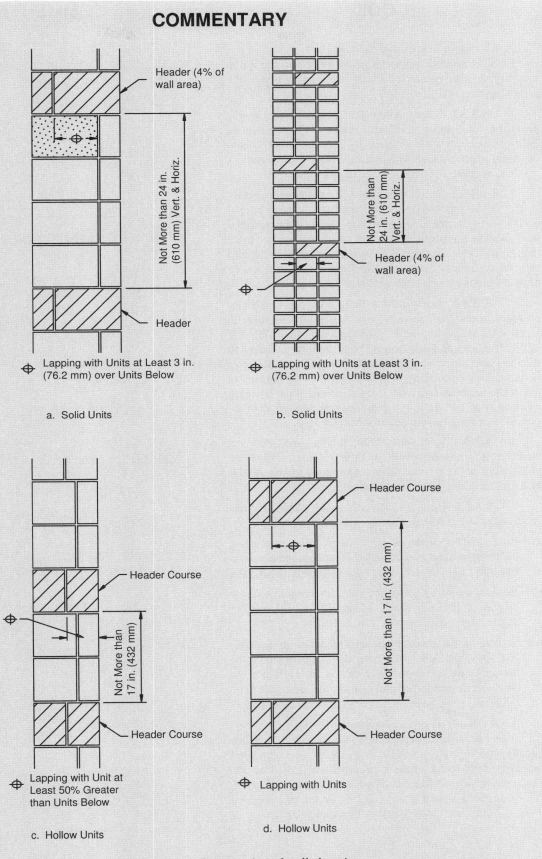

Figure CC-A.7-1 — Cross section of wall elevations

CODE

A.8.3 *Floor and roof anchorage*

Floor and roof diaphragms providing lateral support to masonry shall be connected to the masonry by one of the following methods:

A.8.3.1 Roof loading shall be determined by the provisions of Section 4.1.2 and, where net uplift occurs, uplift shall be resisted entirely by an anchorage system designed in accordance with the provisions of Sections 8.1 and 8.3, Sections 9.1 and 9.3, or Chapter 10.

A.8.3.2 Wood floor joists bearing on masonry walls shall be anchored to the wall at intervals not to exceed 6 ft (1.83 m) by metal strap anchors. Joists parallel to the wall shall be anchored with metal straps spaced not more than 6 ft (1.83 m) on centers extending over or under and secured to at least 3 joists. Blocking shall be provided between joists at each strap anchor.

A.8.3.3 Steel joists that are supported by masonry walls shall bear on and be connected to steel bearing plates. Maximum joist spacing shall be 6 ft (1.83 m) on center. Each bearing plate shall be anchored to the wall with a minimum of two ½ in. (12.7 mm) diameter bolts, or their equivalent. Where steel joists are parallel to the wall, anchors shall be located where joist bridging terminates at the wall and additional anchorage shall be provided to comply with Section A.8.3.4.

A.8.3.4 Roof and floor diaphragms shall be anchored to masonry walls with a minimum of ½ in. (12.7 mm) diameter bolts at a maximum spacing of 6 ft (1.83 m) on center or their equivalent.

A.8.3.5 Bolts and anchors required by Sections A.8.3.3 and A.8.3.4 shall comply with the following:

(a) Bolts and anchors at steel floor joists and floor diaphragms shall be embedded in the masonry at least 6 in. (152 mm) or shall comply with Section A.8.3.5 (c).

(b) Bolts at steel roof joists and roof diaphragms shall be embedded in the masonry at least 15 in. (381 mm) or shall comply with Section A.8.3.5(c).

(c) In lieu of the embedment lengths listed in Sections A.8.3.5(a) and A.8.3.5(b), bolts shall be permitted to be hooked or welded to not less than 0.20 in.^{2} (129 mm^2) of bond beam reinforcement placed not less than 6 in. (152 mm) below joist bearing or bottom of diaphragm.

A.8.4 *Walls adjoining structural framing*

Where walls are dependent upon the structural frame for lateral support, they shall be anchored to the structural members with metal anchors or otherwise keyed to the structural members. Metal anchors shall consist of $^1/_2$-in. (12.7-mm) bolts spaced at 4 ft (1.22 m) on center embedded 4 in. (102 mm) into the masonry, or their equivalent area.

COMMENTARY

CODE

COMMENTARY

A.9 — Miscellaneous requirements

A.9.1 *Chases and recesses*
Masonry directly above chases or recesses wider than 12 in. (305 mm) shall be supported on lintels.

A.9.2 *Lintels*
The design of masonry lintels shall be in accordance with the provisions of Section 5.2.

This page intentionally left blank

APPENDIX B
DESIGN OF MASONRY INFILL

CODE

B.1 — General

B.1.1 *Scope*

This chapter provides minimum requirements for the structural design of concrete masonry, clay masonry, and AAC masonry infills, either non-participating or participating. Infills shall comply with the requirements of Part 1, Part 2, excluding Sections 5.2, 5.3, 5.4, and 5.5, Section B.1, and either Section B.2 or B.3.

COMMENTARY

B.1 — General

B.1.1 *Scope*

The provisions of Appendix B outline a basic set of design provisions for masonry infill based upon experimental research and anecdotal performance of these masonry assemblies. The provisions address both non-participating infills, which are structurally isolated from the lateral force-resisting system, as well as participating infills, which are used to resist in-plane forces due to wind and earthquake. While masonry infills have been a part of contemporary construction for nearly a century, research investigations into their performance, particularly during seismic events, is still ongoing. A comprehensive review of available research data on the performance of masonry infills is provided by Tucker (2007).

As with masonry systems designed by other chapters of the Code, masonry infill must also be designed per the applicable requirements of Part 1 and Part 2. By reference to Part 1, masonry infill must comply with the prescriptive requirements of Chapter 7 for seismic design and detailing. This includes the prescriptive detailing requirements of Section 7.3.1 for non-participating infills and Section 7.3.2 for participating infills. Properly detailed masonry infills have shown considerable system ductility (Henderson et al, 2006). When participating infills are used to resist in-plane loads as part of a concrete or steel frame structure, a hybrid system is effectively created that may not otherwise be defined in Table 12.2-1 of ASCE 7 for seismic force-resistance. Until further research is completed, the Committee recommends using the smallest R and C_d value for the combination of the frame and masonry infill be used to design the system.

Over time, masonry materials expand and contract due to fluctuations in temperature and moisture content as discussed in Code Commentary Sections 4.2.3, 4.2.4, and 4.2.5. Volumetric changes in the masonry infill will open and close the gap between the infill and the bounding frame, which can have a significant impact on the strength and performance of the infill assembly. Such volumetric changes must be considered as required by Section 4.1.5.

When Appendix B (Design of Masonry Infill) was originally developed, information was not available regarding the performance of infills made of AAC masonry and designed according to the provisions of that Appendix. Information has subsequently become available regarding that performance (Ravichandran, 2009; Ravichandran and Klingner, 2011a; Ravichandran and Klingner, 2011b; Ravichandran and Klingner, 2011c).

CODE

COMMENTARY

Infills of AAC masonry can safely be designed using the provisions of Appendix B, and using f'_{AAC} instead of f'_m.

While Ravichandran's investigation illustrated that the provisions of Appendix B are accurate for stiffness and give conservative (low) values for strength, the user should be aware that underestimating the strength of AAC masonry infill may in turn underestimate the forces that can be transmitted from the infill to the bounding frame. Ravichandran (2009) suggests that this can be addressed by designing the frame for an upper fractile of the calculated infill capacity.

B.1.2 *Required strength*

Required strength shall be determined in accordance with the strength design load combinations of the legally adopted building code. When the legally adopted building code does not provide load combinations, structures and members shall be designed to resist the combination of loads specified in ASCE 7 for strength design.

B.1.3 *Design strength*

Infills shall be proportioned so that the design strength equals or exceeds the required strength. Design strength is the nominal strength multiplied by the strength-reduction factor, ϕ, as specified in Section B.1.4.

B.1.4 *Strength-reduction factors*

The value of ϕ shall be taken as 0.60, and applied to the shear, flexure, and axial strength of a masonry infill panel.

B.1.4 *Strength-reduction factors*

See Code Commentary Section 9.1.4 for additional discussion on strength reduction factors applicable to concrete and clay masonry. See Code Commentary Section 11.1.5 for additional discussion on strength reduction factors applicable to AAC masonry. The strength reduction factor applies only to the design of the masonry infill. The strength reduction factors for the anchorage (Section 9.1.4.1 or 11.1.5.1, as appropriate) and bearing (Section 9.1.4.2 or 11.1.5.2, as appropriate) remain unchanged.

B.1.5 *Limitations*

Partial infills and infills with openings shall not be considered as part of the lateral force-resisting system. Their effect on the bounding frame, however, shall be considered.

B.1.5 *Limitations*

Structures with partial-height infills have generally performed very poorly during seismic events. Partial-height infills create short columns, which attract additional load due to their increased stiffness. This has led to premature column failure. Concrete columns bounding partial-height infills are particularly vulnerable to shear failure (Chiou et al, 1999).

CODE

B.2 — Non-participating infills

Non-participating infills shall comply with the requirements of Sections B.2.1 and B.2.2.

B.2.1 *In-plane isolation joints for non-participating infills*

B.2.1.1   In-plane isolation joints shall be designed between the infill and the sides and top of the bounding frame.

B.2.1.2   In-plane isolation joints shall be specified to be at least 3/8 in. (9.5 mm) wide in the plane of the infill, and shall be sized to accommodate the design displacements of the bounding frame.

B.2.1.3   In-plane isolation joints shall be free of mortar, debris, and other rigid materials, and shall be permitted to contain resilient material, provided that the compressibility of that material is considered in establishing the required size of the joint.

B.2.2 *Design of non-participating infills for out-of-plane loads*

Connectors supporting non-participating infills against out-of-plane loads shall be designed to meet the requirements of Sections B.2.2.1 through B.2.2.4. The infill shall be designed to meet the requirements of Section B.2.2.5.

B.2.2.1   The connectors shall be attached to the bounding frame.

B.2.2.2   The connectors shall not transfer in-plane forces.

B.2.2.3   The connectors shall be designed to satisfy the requirements of ASCE 7.

B.2.2.4   The connectors shall be spaced at a maximum of 4 ft (1.22 m) along the supported perimeter of the infill.

B.2.2.5   The infill shall be designed to resist out-of-plane bending between connectors in accordance with Section 9.2 for unreinforced concrete masonry or clay masonry infill, Section 11.2 for unreinforced AAC masonry infill, Section 9.3 for reinforced concrete masonry or clay masonry infill, or Section 11.3 for reinforced AAC masonry infill.

COMMENTARY

B.2.1 *In-plane isolation joints for non-participating infills*

To preclude the unintentional transfer of in-plane loads from the bounding frame to the non-participating infill, gaps are required between the top and sides of the masonry infill assembly. These gaps must be free of materials that could transfer loads between the infill and bounding frame and must be capable of accommodating frame displacements, including inelastic deformation during seismic events.

B.2.2 *Design of non-participating infills for out-of-plane loads*

Mechanical connection between the infill and bounding frame is required for out-of-plane support of the masonry. Masonry infill can be modeled as spanning vertically, horizontally, or both. Connectors between the infill and the bounding frame must be sized and located to maintain load path continuity.

CODE

B.3 — Participating infills

Participating infills shall comply with the requirements of Sections B.3.1 through B.3.6.

B.3.1　General

Infills with in-plane isolation joints not meeting the requirements of Section B.2.1 shall be considered as participating infills. For such infills the displacement shall be taken as the bounding frame displacement minus the specified width of the gap between the bounding column and infill.

B.3.1.1 The maximum ratio of the nominal vertical dimension to nominal thickness of participating infills shall not exceed 30.

B.3.1.2 Participating infills that are not constructed in contact with the bounding beam or slab adjacent to their upper edge shall be designed in accordance with Section B.3.1.2.1 or B.3.1.2.2.

B.3.1.2.1 Where the specified gap between the bounding beam or slab at the top of the infill is less than 3/8 in. (9.5 mm) or the gap is not sized to accommodate design displacements, the infill shall be designed in accordance with Sections B.3.4 and B.3.5, except that the calculated stiffness and strength of the infill shall be multiplied by a factor of 0.5.

B.3.1.2.2 If the gap between the infill and the overlying bounding beam or slab is sized such that in-plane forces cannot be transferred between the bounding beam or slab and the infill, the infill shall be considered a partial infill and shall comply with Section B.1.5.

B.3.2　*In-plane connection requirements for participating infills*

Mechanical connections between the infill and the bounding frame shall be permitted provided that they do not transfer in-plane forces between the infill and the bounding frame.

COMMENTARY

B.3.1　*General*

Flanagan and Bennett (1999a) tested an infilled frame with a 1.0 in. gap between the infill and bounding column. Once the gap was closed, the specimen performed like an infilled frame with no gap.

B.3.1.1 The maximum permitted ratio of height to thickness is based on practical conditions for stability.

B.3.1.2.1 Dawe and Seah (1989a) noted a slight decrease in stiffness and strength when a bond breaker (a polyethylene sheet) was used at the top interface. Riddington (1984) showed an approximate 50% decrease in stiffness but little reduction in peak load with a top gap that was 0.1% of the height of the infill. Dawe and Seah (1989a) showed an approximate 50% reduction in stiffness and a 60% reduction in strength with a top gap that was 0.8% of the height of the infill. A top gap that is in compliance with Section B.2.1.2 is generally less than 0.5% of the infill height. Thus, a 50% reduction in strength and stiffness seems appropriate.

B.3.1.2.2 In cases where the gap at the top of the infill is sufficiently large so that forces cannot be transferred between the bounding frame or beam and the masonry infill, the infill is considered to be partial infill and not permitted to considered part of the lateral force-resisting system.

B.3.2　*In-plane connection requirements for participating infills*

The modeling provisions of Appendix B for participating infills assume that in-plane loads are resisted by the infill by a diagonal compression strut, which does not rely upon mechanical connectors to transfer in-plane load. While mechanical connections, including the use of reinforcement, are permitted, they must be detailed to preclude load transfer between the infill and bounding frame. This is because mechanical connectors between the infill and bounding frame can cause premature damage along the boundaries of the infill under in-plane loading (Dawe and Seah, 1989a). This damage actually reduces the out-of-plane capacity of the infill, as the ability of the infill to have arching action is reduced.

CODE

COMMENTARY

B.3.3 *Out-of-plane connection requirements for participating infills*

    B.3.3.1   Participating infills shall be supported out-of-plane by connectors attached to the bounding frame.

    B.3.3.2   Connectors providing out-of-plane support shall be designed to satisfy the requirements of ASCE 7.

    B.3.3.3 Connectors providing out-of-plane support shall be spaced at a maximum of 4 ft (1.22 m) along the supported perimeter of the infill.

B.3.4 *Design of participating infills for in-plane forces*

    B.3.4.1   Unless the stiffness of the infill is obtained by a more comprehensive analysis, a participating infill shall be analyzed as an equivalent strut, capable of resisting compression only; whose width is calculated using Equation B-1; whose thickness is the specified thickness of the infill; and whose elastic modulus is the elastic modulus of the infill.

$$w_{inf} = \frac{0.3}{\lambda_{strut} \, \cos\theta_{strut}} \qquad \text{(Equation B-1)}$$

where

$$\lambda_{strut} = \sqrt[4]{\frac{E_m \, t_{net\,inf} \, \sin 2\theta_{strut}}{4 \, E_{bc} \, I_{bc} \, h_{inf}}} \qquad \text{(Equation B-2a)}$$

for the design of concrete masonry and clay masonry infill; and

$$\lambda_{strut} = \sqrt[4]{\frac{E_{AAC} \, t_{net\,inf} \, \sin 2\theta_{strut}}{4 \, E_{bc} \, I_{bc} \, h_{inf}}} \qquad \text{(Equation B-2b)}$$

for the design of AAC masonry infill.

    B.3.4.2   Design forces in equivalent struts, as defined in Section B.3.4.1, shall be determined from an elastic analysis of a braced frame including such equivalent struts.

CODE

B.3.4.3 $V_{n\,inf}$ shall be the smallest of (a), (b), and (c) for concrete masonry and clay masonry infill and (b), (d), and (e) for AAC masonry infill:

(a) $(6.0\ in.) t_{net\,inf}\, f'_m$ (Equation B-3)

(b)   the calculated horizontal component of the force in the equivalent strut at a horizontal racking displacement of 1.0 in. (25 mm)

(c) $\dfrac{V_n}{1.5}$ (Equation B-4)

where V_n is the smallest nominal shear strength from Section 9.2.6, calculated along a bed joint.

(d) $(6.0\ in.)\, t_{net\,inf}\, f'_{AAC}$ (Equation B-5)

(e) $\dfrac{V_{nAAC}}{1.5}$ (Equation B-6)

where V_{nAAC} is the smallest nominal shear strength from Section 11.2.5, calculated along a bed joint.

B.3.5   *Design of frame elements with participating infills for in-plane loads*

B.3.5.1   Design each frame member not in contact with an infill for shear, moment, and axial force not less than the results from the equivalent strut frame analysis.

B.3.5.2   Design each bounding column in contact with an infill for shear and moment equal to not less than 1.1 multiplied by the results from the equivalent strut frame analysis, and for axial force not less than the results from that analysis. In addition, increase the design shear at each end of the column by the horizontal component of the equivalent strut force acting on that end under design loads.

B.3.5.3   Design each beam or slab in contact with an infill for shear and moment equal to at least 1.1 multiplied by the results from the equivalent strut frame analysis, and for an axial force not less than the results from that analysis. In addition, increase the design shear at each end of the beam or slab by the vertical component of the equivalent strut force acting on that end under design loads.

COMMENTARY

B.3.4.3 The capacity of the infill material is often referred to as corner crushing, although the failure may occur elsewhere as well. Flanagan and Bennett (1999a) compared six methods for determining the strength of the infill material to experimental results of structural clay tile infills in steel frames. The method given in the Code is the simplest method, and also quite accurate, with a coefficient of variation of the ratio of the measured strength to the predicted strength of the infill of 24%. Flanagan and Bennett (2001) examined the performance of this method for predicting the strength of 58 infill tests reported in the literature. Clay tile, clay brick, and concrete masonry infills in both steel and concrete bounding frames were examined. For the 58 tests considered, the coefficient of variation of the ratio of measured to predicted strength of the infill was 21%.

Flanagan and Bennett (1999a) determined that in-plane displacement is a better indicator of infill performance than in-plane drift (displacement divided by height). This was based on comparing the results of approximately 8-ft high (2.4 m) infill tests to 24-ft (7.3 m) high infill tests on similar material. Thus, a displacement limit rather than a drift limit is given in the Code. As a general rule, the strength of the infill is reached at smaller displacements for stiffer bounding columns. For more flexible bounding columns, the strength of the infill is controlled by the displacement limit of 1.0 in. (25 mm).

Equation B-4 is intended to address shear failure along a bed joint. The use of a formula from Section 9.2 is not intended to imply that concrete masonry and clay masonry infills are necessarily unreinforced. Shear resistance along a bed joint is similar for the equations of Section 9.2 and Section 9.3, and the former are more clearly related to failure along a bed joint. The same reasoning applies to Equation B-6 for AAC masonry infill.

CODE

B.3.6 *Design of participating infills for out-of-plane forces*

The nominal out-of-plane flexural capacity to resist out-of-plane forces of the infill per unit area shall be determined in accordance with Equation B-7a for concrete masonry and clay masonry and Equation B-7b for AAC masonry:

$$q_{n\,\text{inf}} = 105\left(f'_m\right)^{0.75} t_{\text{inf}}^2 \left(\frac{\alpha_{arch}}{l_{\text{inf}}^{2.5}} + \frac{\beta_{arch}}{h_{\text{inf}}^{2.5}}\right)$$

(Equation B-7a)

$$q_{n\,\text{inf}} = 105\left(f'_{AAC}\right)^{0.75} t_{\text{inf}}^2 \left(\frac{\alpha_{arch}}{l_{\text{inf}}^{2.5}} + \frac{\beta_{arch}}{h_{\text{inf}}^{2.5}}\right)$$

(Equation B-7b)

where:

$$\alpha_{arch} = \frac{1}{h_{\text{inf}}}\left(E_{bc}\, I_{bc}\, h_{\text{inf}}^2\right)^{0.25} < 35$$

(Equation B-8)

$$\beta_{arch} = \frac{1}{l_{\text{inf}}}\left(E_{bb}\, I_{bb}\, l_{\text{inf}}^2\right)^{0.25} < 35$$

(Equation B-9)

In Equation B-7, t_{inf} shall not be taken greater than 1/8 h_{inf}. When bounding columns of different cross-sectional properties are used on either side of the infill, average properties shall be used to calculate this capacity. When bounding beams of different cross-sectional properties are used above and below the infill, average properties shall be used to calculate this capacity. In the case of a single story frame, the cross-sectional properties of the bounding beam above the infill shall be used to calculate this capacity. When a side gap is present, α_{arch} shall be taken as zero. When a top gap is present, β_{arch} shall be taken as zero.

COMMENTARY

B.3.6 *Design of participating infills for out-of-plane forces*

It is not appropriate to calculate the out-of-plane flexural capacity of unreinforced masonry infills using values for flexural tensile capacity. The predominant out-of-plane resisting mechanism for masonry infills is arching. Even infills with dry-stacked block have been shown to have significant out-of-plane strength (Dawe and Seah, 1989b).

The out-of-plane resistance of masonry infill as calculated by Equation B-7 is based upon an arching model of the infill in the bounding frame and therefore neglects the contribution of any reinforcement that may be present in the infill in determining the out-of-plane flexural strength of participating infill. Masonry infill may require reinforcement, however, to resist out-of-plane flexure between points of connection with the bounding frame, or to meet the prescriptive seismic detailing requirements of Chapter 7.

The thickness used in calculations of out-of-plane flexural resistance is limited because infills with low height-to-thickness ratios are less influenced by membrane compression and more influenced by plate bending.

The out-of-plane flexural capacity of the masonry infill is determined based on the work of Dawe and Seah (1989b). They first developed a computer program based on a modified yield line analysis that included the flexibility of the bounding frame. The program coincided quite well with their experimental results, with an average ratio of observed to predicted capacity of 0.98 and a coefficient of variation of 6%. Dawe and Seah (1989b) then used the program for an extensive parametric study that resulted in the empirical equation given here.

Two other equations are available. The first, proposed by Abrams et al. (1993), is used in ASCE 41 (2006). The second was proposed by Klingner et al. (1997). In Flanagan and Bennett (1999b), each of these three proposed equations is checked against the results of 31 experimental tests from seven different test programs including clay brick infills in concrete frames, clay tile infills in steel frames, clay brick infills in steel frames, and concrete masonry infills in steel frames. Flanagan and Bennett (1999b) determined that Dawe and Seah's (1989b) equation is the best predictor of out-of-plane strength, with an average ratio of observed to predicted strength of 0.92, and a coefficient of variation of 0.28. The coefficient of variation of observed to predicted capacity was 28%. Results are summarized in Figure CC-B.3-1. The experimental tests involved infills with height-to-thickness ratios ranging from 6.8 to 35.3. Some infills had joint reinforcement, but this did not affect the results. Two of the specimens had a top gap. Arching still occurred, but was one-way arching. The code equation is thus quite robust.

COMMENTARY

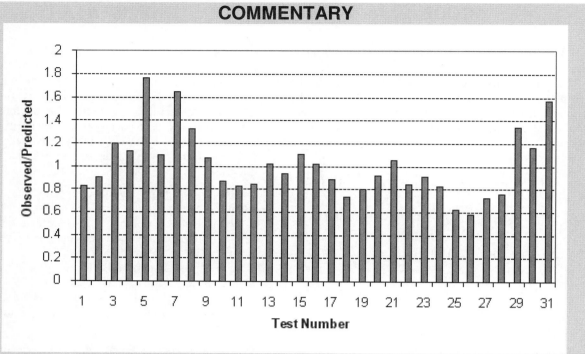

Figure CC-B.3-1: Ratios of observed to predicted strengths for infills loaded out-of-plane
(Flanagan and Bennett 1999b)

APPENDIX C
LIMIT DESIGN METHOD

CODE

C. *General* — The limit design method shall be permitted to be applied to a line of lateral load resistance consisting of special reinforced masonry shear walls that are designed per the strength design provisions of Chapter 9, except that the provisions of Section 9.3.3.5 and Section 9.3.6.5 shall not apply.

C.1 *Yield mechanism* — It shall be permitted to use limit analysis to determine the controlling yield mechanism and its corresponding base-shear strength, V_{lim}, for a line of lateral load resistance, provided that (a) through (e) are satisfied:

(a) The relative magnitude of lateral seismic forces applied at each floor level shall correspond to the loading condition producing the maximum base shear at the line of resistance in accordance with analytical procedures permitted in Section 12.6 of ASCE 7.

(b) In the investigation of potential yield mechanisms induced by seismic loading, plastic hinges shall be considered to form at the faces of joints and at the interfaces between masonry components and the foundation.

(c) The axial forces associated with Load Combination 7 of Section 2.3.2 of ASCE 7 shall be used when determining the strength of plastic hinges, except that axial loads due to horizontal seismic forces shall be permitted to be neglected.

(d) The strength assigned to plastic hinges shall be based on the nominal flexural strength, M_n, but shall not exceed the moment associated with one-half of the nominal shear strength, V_n, calculated using MSJC Section 9.3.4.1.2.

(e) At locations other than the plastic hinges identified in C.1(b), moments shall not exceed the strengths assigned in C.1(d) using the assumptions of C.1(c).

COMMENTARY

C. *General* — This section provides alternative design provisions for special reinforced masonry shear walls subjected to in-plane seismic loading. The limit design method is presented as an alternative to the requirements of 9.3.3.5 and 9.3.6.5. All other sections in Chapter 9 are applicable. Limit design is considered to be particularly useful for perforated wall configurations for which a representative yield mechanism can be determined (Lepage et al, 2011).

C.1 *Yield mechanism* — This section defines the basic conditions for allowing the use of limit analysis to determine the base shear strength of a line of resistance subjected to seismic loading.

Item (a) allows the use of conventional methods of analysis permitted in ASCE 7 to determine the distribution of lateral loads. The designer should use the seismic loading condition that produces the maximum base shear demand at the line of resistance.

Item (b) allows the location of yielding regions at the interfaces between wall segments and their supporting members.

Item (c) prescribes the use of the loading condition that induces the lowest axial force due to gravity loads. For wall segments loaded with axial forces below the balanced point, this loading condition gives the lowest flexural strength and therefore leads to lower mechanism strengths. Axial loads from seismic overturning are permitted to be neglected only in the initial process of establishing the plastic capacity of the selected mechanism. Axial loads from seismic overturning are required to be considered subsequently, in determining the deformation capacity of plastic hinges.

Item (d) limits the flexural strength that is assigned to a plastic hinge so that the maximum shear that can be developed does not exceed one-half the shear strength of the wall segment. This stratagem effectively reduces the strength of the controlling yield mechanism involving wall segments vulnerable to shear failure. In addition to a reduction in strength there is a reduction in deformation capacity as indicated in C.3.2.

Item (e) requires the designer to verify that the selected mechanism is the critical one. If yielding is detected away from the selected plastic hinge locations, the designer has the choice of changing the selected plastic hinge location to recognize that yielding, or of placing additional reinforcement at the section where yielding is detected.

CODE

C.2 *Mechanism strength* — The yield mechanism associated with the limiting base-shear strength, V_{lim}, shall satisfy the following:

$$\phi V_{lim} \geq V_{ub} \qquad \text{(Equation C-1)}$$

The value of ϕ assigned to the mechanism strength shall be taken as 0.8. The base-shear demand, V_{ub}, shall be determined from analytical procedures permitted in Section 12.6 of ASCE 7.

C.3 *Mechanism deformation* — The rotational deformation demand on plastic hinges shall be determined by imposing the design displacement, δ_u, at the roof level of the yield mechanism. The rotational deformation capacity of plastic hinges shall satisfy C.3.1 to C.3.3.

C.3.1 The rotational deformation capacity of plastic hinges shall be taken as 0.5 $l_w \, \varepsilon_{mu} / c$. The value of c shall be calculated for the P_u corresponding to Load Combination 5 of Section 2.3.2 of ASCE 7.

C.3.2 The angular deformation capacity of masonry components whose plastic hinge strengths are limited by shear as specified in C.1(d), shall be taken as 1 / 400. The angular deformation capacity shall be permitted to be taken as 1 / 200 for masonry components satisfying the following requirements:

(a) The areas of transverse and longitudinal reinforcement shall each not be less than 0.001 multiplied by the gross cross-sectional area of the component, using specified dimensions;

(b) Spacing of transverse and longitudinal reinforcement shall not exceed the smallest of 24 in. (610 mm), $l_w / 2$, and $h_w / 2$.

(c) Reinforcement ending at a free edge of masonry shall be anchored around perpendicular reinforcing bars with a standard hook.

C.3.3 The P_u corresponding to load combination 5 of Section 2.3.2 of ASCE 7 shall not exceed a compressive stress of 0.3 $f_m' A_g$ at plastic hinges in the controlling mechanism.

COMMENTARY

C.2 *Mechanism strength* — Because the controlling yield mechanism is investigated using nominal strengths, an overall strength reduction factor of $\phi = 0.8$ is applied to the limiting base shear strength. For simplicity, a single value of ϕ is adopted.

C.3 *Mechanism deformation* — This section defines the ductility checks required by the limit design method. The deformation demands at locations of plastic hinges are determined by imposing the calculated design roof displacement to the controlling yield mechanism.

C.3.1 The rotational deformation capacity is calculated assuming an ultimate curvature of ε_{mu} / c over a plastic hinge length of 0.5 l_w. The resulting expression is similar to that used in 9.3.6.5.3(a) to determine the need for special boundary elements. In the latter case, it is multiplied by wall height. The value of P_u includes earthquake effects, and may be calculated using a linearly elastic model.

C.3.2 In shear-dominated elements (elements whose hinge strength is assigned a value lower than their nominal flexural strength due to limitations in C.1(d)), the angular deformation capacity is limited to 1 / 400 or 1 / 200, depending on the percentage and maximum spacing of transverse and longitudinal reinforcement.

C.3.3 The limit of 30% of f_m' is intended to ensure that all yielding components respond below the balanced point of the *P-M* interaction diagram.

EQUATION CONVERSIONS

The equations in this Code are for use with the specified inch-pound units only. The equivalent equations for use with SI units follow.

Code Equation No. or Section No.	SI Unit Equivalent Equation	Units
4.2.2.2.1	$E_m = 700 f'_m$ for clay masonry $E_m = 900 f'_m$ for concrete masonry	E_m in MPa f'_m in MPa
4.2.2.3.1	$E_{AAC} = 888 (f'_{AAC})^{0.6}$	E_{AAC} in MPa f'_{AAC} in MPa
4.2.2.4	$500 f'_g$	f'_g in MPa
(5-1)	$I_{eff} = I_n \left(\dfrac{M_{cr}}{M_a} \right)^3 + I_{cr} \left[1 - \left(\dfrac{M_{cr}}{M_a} \right)^3 \right] \leq I_n$	I_{eff} in mm^4 I_n in mm^4 I_{cr} in mm^4 M_{cr} in N-mm M_a in N-mm
(5-2a)	(1) When $1 \leq \dfrac{l_{eff}}{d_v} < 2$, $z = 0.2(l_{eff} + 2d_v)$	l_{eff} in mm d_v in mm z in mm
(5-2b)	(2) When $\dfrac{l_{eff}}{d_v} < 1$, $z = 0.6 l_{eff}$	l_{eff} in mm d_v in mm z in mm
(5-3a)	(1) When $1 \leq \dfrac{l_{eff}}{d_v} < 3$, $z = 0.2(l_{eff} + 1.5d_v)$	l_{eff} in mm d_v in mm z in mm
(5-3b)	(2) When $\dfrac{l_{eff}}{d_v} < 1$, $z = 0.5 l_{eff}$	l_{eff} in mm d_v in mm z in mm
(6-1)	$A_{pt} = \pi l_b^2$	A_{pt} in mm^2 l_b in mm
(6-2)	$A_{pv} = \dfrac{\pi l_{be}^2}{2}$	A_{pv} in mm^2 l_{be} in mm
(8-1)	$B_{ab} = 0.104 A_{pt} \sqrt{f'_m}$	A_{pt} in mm^2 B_{ab} in N f'_m in MPa $\sqrt{f'_m}$ result in MPa
(8-2)	$B_{as} = 0.6 A_b f_y$	A_b in mm^2 B_{as} in N f_y in MPa
(8-3)	$B_{ab} = 0.104 A_{pt} \sqrt{f'_m}$	A_{pt} in mm^2 B_{ab} in N f'_m in MPa $\sqrt{f'_m}$ result in MPa
(8-4)	$B_{ap} = 0.6 f'_m e_b d_b + 0.83\pi(l_b + e_b + d_b)d_b$	f'_m in MPa e_b in mm d_b in mm l_b in mm B_{ap} in N
(8-5)	$B_{as} = 0.6 A_b f_y$	A_b in mm^2 B_{as} in N f_y in MPa

Code Equation No. or Section No.	SI Unit Equivalent Equation	Units
(8-6)	$$B_{vb} = 0.104 A_{pv} \sqrt{f'_m}$$	A_{pv} in mm^2 B_{vb} in N f'_m in MPa $\sqrt{f'_m}$ result in MPa
(8-7)	$$B_{vc} = 1072 \sqrt[4]{f'_m A_b}$$	A_b in mm^2 B_{vc} in N f'_m in MPa $\sqrt[4]{f'_m A_b}$ result in N
(8-8)	$$B_{vpry} = 2.0 B_{ab} = 0.208 A_{pt} \sqrt{f'_m}$$	A_{pt} in mm^2 B_{ab} in N B_{vpry} in N f'_m in MPa $\sqrt{f'_m}$ result in MPa
(8-9)	$$B_{vs} = 0.36 A_b f_y$$	A_b in mm^2 B_{vs} in N f_y in MPa
(8-10)	$$\frac{b_a}{B_a} + \frac{b_v}{B_v} \le 1$$	b_a in N b_v in N B_a in N B_v in N
8.1.4.2(c)	$$0.108 \sqrt{\text{specified unit compressive strength of header}}$$	in MPa
(8-11)	$$l_d = 0.22 d_b F_s$$	d_b in mm F_s in MPa l_d in mm
(8-12)	$$l_d = \frac{1.57 d_b^2 f_y \gamma}{K \sqrt{f'_m}}$$	d_b in mm f'_m in MPa $\sqrt{f'_m}$ result in MPa f_y in MPa K in mm l_d in mm
8.1.6.4.1.5(b)	$$A_v \ge 0.41 \left(\frac{b_w s}{f_y} \right)$$ $$s \le \left(\frac{d}{8 \beta_b} \right)$$	A_v in mm^2 b_w in mm s in mm f_y in MPa d in mm β_b is dimensionless
(8-13)	$$\xi = 1.0 - \frac{11.6 A_{sc}}{d_b^{2.5}} \text{ where } \frac{11.6 A_{sc}}{d_b^{2.5}} \le 1.0$$	A_{sc} in mm^2 d_b in mm
(8-14)	$$\frac{f_a}{F_a} + \frac{f_b}{F_b} \le 1$$	F_a in MPa F_b in MPa f_a in MPa f_b in Mpa
(8-15)	$$P \le \left(\frac{1}{4} \right) P_e$$	P in N P_e in N
(8-16)	$$F_a = \left(\frac{1}{4} \right) f'_m \left[1 - \left(\frac{h}{140r} \right)^2 \right]$$	F_a in MPa f'_m in MPa h in mm r in mm

Code and
Commentary, C-239

Code Equation No. or Section No.	SI Unit Equivalent Equation	Units
(8-17)	$F_a = \left(\dfrac{1}{4}\right)f'_m\left(\dfrac{70r}{h}\right)^2$	F_a in MPa f'_m in MPa h in mm r in mm
(8-18)	$F_b = \left(\dfrac{1}{3}\right)f'_m$	F_b in MPa f'_m in MPa
(8-19)	$P_e = \dfrac{\pi^2 E_m I_n}{h^2}\left(1 - 0.577\dfrac{e}{r}\right)^3$	E_m in MPa e in mm h in mm I_n in mm^4 P_e in N r in mm
(8-20)	$f_v = \dfrac{VQ}{I_n b}$	b in mm f_v in MPa I_n in mm^4 Q in mm^3 V in N
8.2.6.2(a)	$0.125\sqrt{f'_m}$	f'_m in MPa $\sqrt{f'_m}$ result in MPa
8.2.6.2(c)	$0.255 + 0.45\,N_v/A_n$	A_n in mm^2 N_v in N Answer in MPa
8.2.6.2(d)	$0.255 + 0.45\,N_v/A_n$	A_n in mm^2 N_v in N Answer in MPa
8.2.6.2(e)	$0.414 + 0.45\,N_v/A_n$	A_n in mm^2 N_v in N Answer in MPa
(8-21)	$P_a = (0.25f'_m A_n + 0.65 A_{st}F_s)\left[1 - \left(\dfrac{h}{140r}\right)^2\right]$	A_n in mm^2 A_{st} in mm^2 F_s in MPa f'_m in MPa h in mm P_a in N r in mm
(8-22)	$P_a = (0.25f'_m A_n + 0.65 A_{st}F_s)\left(\dfrac{70r}{h}\right)^2$	A_n in mm^2 A_{st} in mm^2 F_s in MPa f'_m in MPa h in mm P_a in N r in mm
(8-23)	$\rho_{max} = \dfrac{nf'_m}{2f_y\left(n + \dfrac{f_y}{f'_m}\right)}$	f_y in MPa f'_m in MPa
(8-24)	$f_v = \dfrac{V}{A_{nv}}$	A_{nv} in mm^2 f_v in MPa V in N
(8-25)	$F_v = (F_{vm} + F_{vs})\gamma_g$	F_v in MPa F_{vm} in MPa F_{vs} in MPa

Code and Commentarv. C-240

Code Equation No. or Section No.	SI Unit Equivalent Equation	Units
(8-26)	$F_v \le \left(0.249\sqrt{f'_m}\right)\gamma_g$ For $M/(Vd_v) \le 0.25$	d_v in mm f'_m in MPa $\sqrt{f'_m}$ result in MPa F_v in MPa M in N-mm V in N
(8-27)	$F_v \le \left(0.167\sqrt{f'_m}\right)\gamma_g$ For $M/(Vd_v) \ge 1.0$	d_v in mm f'_m in MPa $\sqrt{f'_m}$ result in MPa F_v in MPa M in N-mm V in N
(8-28)	$F_{vm} = 0.021\left[\left(4.0 - 1.75\left(\dfrac{M}{Vd_v}\right)\right)\sqrt{f'_m}\right] + 0.25\dfrac{P}{A_n}$	A_n in mm^2 d_v in mm f'_m in MPa $\sqrt{f'_m}$ result in MPa F_{vm} in MPa M in N-mm P in N V in N
(8-29)	$F_{vm} = 0.042\left[\left(4.0 - 1.75\left(\dfrac{M}{Vd_v}\right)\right)\sqrt{f'_m}\right] + 0.25\dfrac{P}{A_n}$	A_n in mm^2 d_v in mm f'_m in MPa $\sqrt{f'_m}$ result in MPa F_{vm} in MPa M in N-mm P in N V in N
(8-30)	$F_{vs} = 0.5\left(\dfrac{A_v F_s d_v}{A_{nv}s}\right)$	A_{nv} in mm^2 A_v in mm^2 d_v in mm F_s in MPa F_{vs} in MPa s in mm
(9-1)	$B_{anb} = 0.332A_{pt}\sqrt{f'_m}$	A_{pt} in mm^2 B_{anb} in N f'_m in MPa $\sqrt{f'_m}$ result in MPa
(9-2)	$B_{ans} = A_b f_y$	A_b in mm^2 f_y in MPa B_{ans} in N
(9-3)	$B_{anb} = 0.332A_{pt}\sqrt{f'_m}$	A_{pt} in mm^2 B_{anb} in N f'_m in MPa $\sqrt{f'_m}$ result in MPa

Code Equation No. or Section No.	SI Unit Equivalent Equation	Units
(9-4)	$B_{anp} = 1.5 f'_m e_b d_b + 2.07\pi(l_b + e_b + d_b)d_b$	f'_m in MPa e_b in mm d_b in mm l_b in mm B_{anp} in N
(9-5)	$B_{ans} = A_b f_y$	A_b in mm^2 f_y in MPa B_{ans} in N
(9-6)	$B_{vnb} = 0.332 A_{pv}\sqrt{f'_m}$	A_{pv} in mm^2 B_{vnb} in N f'_m in MPa $\sqrt{f'_m}$ result in MPa
(9-7)	$B_{vnc} = 3216\sqrt[4]{f'_m\ A_b}$	A_b in mm^2 B_{vnc} in N f'_m in MPa $\sqrt[4]{f'_m A_b}$ result in N
(9-8)	$B_{vnpry} = 2.0 B_{anb} = 0.664 A_{pt}\sqrt{f'_m}$	A_{pt} in mm^2 B_{anb} in N B_{vnpry} in N f'_m in MPa $\sqrt{f'_m}$ result in MPa
(9-9)	$B_{vns} = 0.6 A_b f_y$	A_b in mm^2 f_y in MPa B_{vns} in N
(9-10)	$\dfrac{b_{af}}{\phi\, B_{an}} + \dfrac{b_{vf}}{\phi\, B_{vn}} \le 1$	b_{af} in N b_{vf} in N B_{an} in N B_{vn} in N
9.1.7.2(c)	$0.216\sqrt{\text{specified unit compressive strength of header}}$	in MPa
(9-11)	$P_n = 0.80\left\{ 0.80 A_n\, f'_m\left[1 - \left(\dfrac{h}{140r}\right)^2\right]\right\}$ For $\dfrac{h}{r} \le 99$	P_n in N A_n in mm^2 f'_m in MPa h in mm r in mm
(9-12)	$P_n = 0.80\left(0.80 A_n\, f'_m\left(\dfrac{70r}{h}\right)^2\right)$ For $\dfrac{h}{r} > 99$	P_n in N A_n in mm^2 f'_m in MPa h in mm r in mm
(9-13)	$M_u = \psi M_{u,0}$	M_u in N-mm $M_{u,0}$ in N-mm
(9-14)	$\psi = \dfrac{1}{1 - \dfrac{P_u}{A_n f'_m\left(\dfrac{70r}{h}\right)^2}}$	A_n in mm^2 f'_m in MPa P_u in N h in mm r in mm
9.2.6.1(a)	$0.316 A_{nv}\sqrt{f'_m}$ in N	A_{nv} in mm^2 f'_m in MPa
9.2.6.1(b)	$2.07 A_{nv}$ in N	A_{nv} in mm^2
9.2.6.1(c)	$0.386 A_{nv} + 0.45 N_u$ in N	A_{nv} in mm^2 N_u in N

Code Equation No. or Section No.	SI Unit Equivalent Equation	Units
9.2.6.1(d)	$0.386 A_{nv} + 0.45 N_u$ in N	A_{nv} in mm^2 N_u in N
9.2.6.1(e)	$0.620 A_{nv} + 0.45 N_u$ in N	A_{nv} in mm^2 N_u in N
9.2.6.1(f)	$0.159 A_{nv}$ in N	A_{nv} in mm^2
(9-15)	$l_e = 13 d_b$	l_e in mm d_b in mm
(9-16)	$l_d = \dfrac{1.57 d_b{}^2 f_y \gamma}{K \sqrt{f'_m}}$	d_b in mm f'_m in MPa $\sqrt{f'_m}$ result in MPa f_y in MPa K in mm l_d in mm
(9-17)	$l_d = 48 d_b$	l_d in mm d_b in mm
(9-18)	$\xi = 1.0 - \dfrac{11.6 A_{sc}}{d_b^{2.5}}$ where $\dfrac{11.6 A_{sc}}{d_b^{2.5}} \le 1.0$	A_{sc} in mm^2 d_b in mm
(9-19)	$P_n = 0.80 \left[0.80 f'_m (A_n - A_{st}) + f_y A_{st} \right] \left[1 - \left(\dfrac{h}{140 r} \right)^2 \right]$	A_n in mm^2 A_{st} in mm^2 f'_m in MPa f_y in MPa P_n in N h in mm r in mm
(9-20)	$P_n = 0.80 \left[0.80 f'_m (A_n - A_{st}) + f_y A_{st} \right] \left(\dfrac{70 r}{h} \right)^2$	A_n in mm^2 A_{st} in mm^2 f'_m in MPa f_y in MPa P_n in N h in mm r in mm
(9-21)	$V_n = (V_{nm} + V_{ns}) \gamma_g$	V_{nm} in N V_{ns} in N V_n in N
(9-22)	$V_n \le \left(0.498 A_{nv} \sqrt{f'_m} \right) \gamma_g$ For $\dfrac{M_u}{V_u d_v} \le 0.25_v$	A_{nv} in mm^2 M_u in N-mm V_u in N d_v in mm f'_m in MPa $\sqrt{f'_m}$ result in MPa V_n in N
(9-23)	$V_n \le \left(0.332 A_{nv} \sqrt{f'_m} \right) \gamma_g$ For $\dfrac{M_u}{V_u d_v} \ge 1.0$	A_{nv} in mm^2 M_u in N-mm V_u in N f'_m in MPa $\sqrt{f'_m}$ result in MPa d_v in mm V_n in N

Code Equation No. or Section No.	SI Unit Equivalent Equation	Units
(9-24)	$$V_{nm} = 0.083\left[4.0 - 1.75\left(\dfrac{M_u}{V_u d_v}\right)\right]A_{nv}\sqrt{f'_m} + 0.25P_u$$	A_{nv} in mm^2 M_u in N-mm V_u in N f'_m in MPa $\sqrt{f'_m}$ result in MPa d_v in mm P_u in N V_{nm} in N
(9-25)	$$V_{ns} = 0.5\left(\dfrac{A_v}{s}\right)f_y\, d_v$$	A_v in mm^2 f_y in MPa d_v in mm s in mm V_{ns} in N
(9-26)	$$\left(\dfrac{P_u}{A_g}\right) \le 0.20 f'_m$$	P_u in N A_g in mm^2 f'_m in MPa
(9-27)	$$M_u = \dfrac{w_u h^2}{8} + P_{uf}\dfrac{e_u}{2} + P_u\delta_u$$	h in mm w_u in N/mm P_{uf} in N e_u in mm P_u in N δ_u in mm M_u in N-mm
(9-28)	$$P_u = P_{uw} + P_{uf}$$	P_u in N P_{uf} in N P_{uw} in N
(9-29)	$$\delta_u = \dfrac{5M_u h^2}{48 E_m I_n} \quad \text{For} \quad M_u < M_{cr}$$	δ_u in mm h in mm E_m in MPa I_n in mm^4 M_u in N-mm M_{cr} in N-mm
(9-30)	$$\delta_u = \dfrac{5M_{cr} h^2}{48 E_m I_n} + \dfrac{5(M_u - M_{cr})h^2}{48 E_m I_{cr}}$$ $$\text{For } M_{cr} \le M_u \le M_n$$	δ_u in mm h in mm E_m in Mpa I_{cr} in mm^4 I_n in mm^4 M_{cr} in N-mm M_n in N-mm M_u in N-mm
(9-31)	$$M_u = \psi M_{u,0}$$	
(9-32)	$$\psi = \dfrac{1}{1 - \dfrac{P_u}{P_e}}$$	
(9-33)	$$P_e = \dfrac{\pi^2 E_m I_{eff}}{h^2}$$	

Code Equation No. or Section No.	SI Unit Equivalent Equation	Units
(9-34)	$I_{cr} = n\left(A_s + \dfrac{P_u}{f_y}\dfrac{t_{sp}}{2d}\right)(d-c)^2 + \dfrac{bc^3}{3}$	I_{cr} in mm^4 A_s in mm^2 P_u in N t_{sp} in mm f_y in MPa d in mm c in mm b in mm
(9-35)	$c = \dfrac{A_s f_y + P_u}{0.64 f'_m b}$	c in mm A_s in mm^2 f_y in MPa P_u in N f'_m in MPa b in mm
(9-36)	$\delta_s \le 0.007 h$	δ_s in mm h in mm
9.3.6.5.1	$P_u \le 0.10 A_g f'_m$ $P_u \le 0.05 A_g f'_m$	P_u in N A_g in mm^2 f'_m in MPa
9.3.6.5.1	$\dfrac{M_u}{V_u d_v} \le 1.0$	M_u in N-mm V_u in N l_w in mm
9.3.6.5.1	$V_u \le 0.25 A_{nv}\sqrt{f'_m}$ and $\dfrac{M_u}{V_u d_v} \le 3.0$	A_n in mm^2 f'_m in MPa l_w in mm M_u in N-mm V_u in N
9.3.6.5.3 (a)	$c \ge \dfrac{l_w}{600\left(C_d \delta_{ne}/h_w\right)}$	c in mm h_w in mm l_w in mm δ_{ne} in mm
(10-1)	$a = \dfrac{f_{ps}A_{ps} + f_y A_s + P_u/\phi}{0.80 f'_m b}$	a in mm f_{ps} in MPa A_{ps} in mm^2 f_y in MPa A_s in mm^2 P_u in N f'_m in MPa b in mm
(10-2)	$M_n = \left(f_{ps}A_{ps} + f_y A_s + P_u/\phi\right)\left(d - \dfrac{a}{2}\right)$	M_n in N-mm f_{ps} in MPa A_{ps} in mm^2 f_y in MPa A_s in mm^2 P_u in N d in mm a in mm
(10-3)	$f_{ps} = f_{se} + 0.03\left(\dfrac{E_{ps}d}{l_p}\right)\left(1 - 1.56\dfrac{A_{ps}f_{ps}+P}{f'_m bd}\right)$	f_{ps} in MPa f_{se} in MPa d in mm l_p in mm E_{ps} in MPa A_{ps} in mm^2 b in mm f'_m in MPa P in N

Code Equation No. or Section No.	SI Unit Equivalent Equation	Units
(11-1)	$$f_{t\,AAC} = 0.199\sqrt{f'_{AAC}}$$	$f_{t\,AAC}$ in MPa $\sqrt{f'_{AAC}}$ result in MPa
(11-2)	$$f_v = 0.15 f'_{AAC}$$	f_v in MPa f'_{AAC} in MPa
(11-3)	$$P_n = 0.80\left\{0.85 A_n\, f'_{AAC}\left[1-\left(\frac{h}{140r}\right)^2\right]\right\}$$	h in mm r in mm A_n in mm^2 f'_{AAC} in MPa P_n in N
(11-4)	$$P_n = 0.80\left[0.85 A_n\, f'_{AAC}\left(\frac{70r}{h}\right)^2\right]$$	h in mm r in mm A_n in mm^2 f'_{AAC} in MPa P_n in N
(11-5)	$$l_e = 13 d_b$$	l_e in mm d_b in mm
(11-6)	$$l_d = \frac{1.57 d_b^{\,2} f_y \gamma}{K_{AAC}\sqrt{f'_g}}$$	l_d, in mm d_b in mm f'_g in MPa $\sqrt{f'_g}$ result in MPa f_y in MPa K_{AAC} in mm
(11-7)	$$P_n = 0.80\left[0.85 f'_{AAC}(A_n - A_{st}) + f_y A_{st}\left[1-\left(\frac{h}{140r}\right)^2\right]\right]$$	h in mm r in mm A_n in mm^2 A_{st} in mm^2 f_y in MPa f'_{AAC} in MPa P_n in N
(11-8)	$$P_n = 0.80\left[0.85 f'_{AAC}(A_n - A_{st}) + f_y A_{st}\left(\frac{70r}{h}\right)^2\right]$$	h in mm r in mm A_n in mm^2 A_{st} in mm^2 f_y in MPa f'_{AAC} in MPa P_n in N
(11-9)	$$V_n = V_{nAAC} + V_{ns}$$	V_n in N V_{nAAC} in N V_{ns} in N
(11-10)	$$V_n = \mu_{AAC} P_u$$	V_n in N P_u in N
(11-11)	$$V_n \le 0.498 A_{nv}\sqrt{f'_{AAC}}$$	V_n in N f'_{AAC} in MPa $\sqrt{f'_{AAC}}$ result in MPa A_{nv} in mm^2
(11-12)	$$V_n \le 0.332 A_{nv}\sqrt{f'_{AAC}}$$	V_n in N f'_{AAC} in MPa $\sqrt{f'_{AAC}}$ result in MPa A_{nv} in mm^2

Code Equation No. or Section No.	SI Unit Equivalent Equation	Units
(11-13a)	$$V_{nAAC} = 0.0789\, l_w\, t\, \sqrt{f'_{AAC}}\, \sqrt{1 + \dfrac{P_u}{0.199\sqrt{f'_{AAC}}\, l_w\, t}}$$	V_{nAAC} in N P_u in N f'_{AAC} in MPa $\sqrt{f'_{AAC}}$ result in MPa l_w in mm t in mm
(11-13b)	$$V_{nAAC} = 0.0548\, l_w\, t\, \sqrt{f'_{AAC}}\, \sqrt{1 + \dfrac{P_u}{0.199\sqrt{f'_{AAC}}\, l_w\, t}}$$	V_{nAAC} in N P_u in N f'_{AAC} in MPa $\sqrt{f'_{AAC}}$ result in MPa l_w in mm t in mm
(11-13c)	$$V_{nAAC} = 0.0747\, \sqrt{f'_{AAC}}\, A_{nv} + 0.05 P_u$$	V_{nAAC} in N P_u in N f'_{AAC} in MPa $\sqrt{f'_{AAC}}$ result in MPa A_{nv} in mm^2
(11-14)	$$V_{nAAC} = 0.17 f'_{AAC} t\, \dfrac{h \cdot l_w^{\,2}}{h^2 + (\frac{3}{4} l_w)^2}$$	V_{nAAC} in N f'_{AAC} in MPa t in mm h in mm l_w in mm
(11-15)	$$V_{ns} = 0.5 \left(\dfrac{A_v}{s} \right) f_y d_v$$	V_{ns} in N f_y in MPa s in mm d_v in mm A_v in mm^2
(11-16)	$$V_{nAAC} = 0.0664\, \sqrt{f'_{AAC}}\, bd$$	V_{nAAC} in N f'_{AAC} in MPa $\sqrt{f'_{AAC}}$ result in MPa b in mm d in mm
(11-17)	$$\dfrac{P_u}{A_g} \le 0.2 f'_{AAC}$$	P_u in N f'_{AAC} in MPa A_g in mm^2
(11-18)	$$M_u = \dfrac{w_u h^2}{8} + P_{uf}\, \dfrac{e_u}{2} + P_u \delta_u$$	P_u in N P_{uf} in N h in mm e_u in mm δ_u in mm w_u in N/mm M_u in N-mm
(11-19)	$$P_u = P_{uw} + P_{uf}$$	P_u in N P_{uw} in N P_{uf} in N
(11-20)	$$\delta_u = \dfrac{5 M_u h^2}{48 E_{AAC} I_n}$$	δ_u in mm I_n in mm^4 h in mm E_{AAC} in MPa M_u in N-mm

Code Equation No. or Section No.	SI Unit Equivalent Equation	Units
(11-21)	$\delta_u = \dfrac{5M_{cr}h^2}{48E_{AAC}I_n} + \dfrac{5(M_u - M_{cr})h^2}{48E_{AAC}I_{cr}}$	δ_u in mm I_n in mm^4 I_{cr} in mm^4 h in mm E_{AAC} in MPa M_{cr} in N-mm M_u in N-mm
(11-22)	$M_u = \psi M_{u,0}$	M_u in N-mm $M_{u.0}$ in N-mm
(11-23)	$\psi = \dfrac{1}{1 - \dfrac{P_u}{P_e}}$	P_e in N P_u in N
(11-24)	$P_e = \dfrac{\pi^2 E_{AAC} I_{eff}}{h^2}$	P_e in N E_{AAC} in MPa I_{eff} in mm^4 h in mm
(11-25)	$M_{cr} = S_n\left(f_{rAAC} + \dfrac{P}{A_n}\right)$	S_n in mm^3 A_n in mm^2 f_{rAAC} in MPa P in N M_{cr} in N-mm.
(11-26)	$I_{cr} = n\left(A_s + \dfrac{P_u}{f_y}\dfrac{t_{sp}}{2d}\right)(d-c)^2 + \dfrac{b(c)^3}{3}$	I_{cr} in mm^4 A_s in mm^2 P_u in N t_{sp} in mm f_y in MPa d in mm c in mm b in mm
(11-27)	$c = \dfrac{A_s f_y + P_u}{0.57 f'_{AAC} b}$	c in mm A_s in mm^2 f_y in MPa P_u in N f'_{AAC} in MPa b in mm
(11-28)	$M_u \le \phi M_n$	M_u in N-mm M_n in N-mm
(11-29)	$M_n = (A_s f_y + P_u)\left(d - \dfrac{a}{2}\right)$	P_u in N a in mm d in mm A_s in mm^2 f_y in MPa M_n in N-mm
(11-30)	$a = \dfrac{(P_u + A_s f_y)}{0.85 f'_{AAC} b}$	a in mm P_u in N b in mm A_s in mm^2 f'_{AAC} in MPa f_y in MPa
(11-31)	$\delta_s \le 0.007 h$	δ_s in mm h in mm

Code Equation No. or Section No.	SI Unit Equivalent Equation	Units
(11-32)	$V_{cr} = \dfrac{S_n}{h}\left(f_{rAAC} + \dfrac{P}{A_n}\right)$	S_n in mm^3 A_n in mm^2 h in mm f_{rAAC} in MPa P in N V_{cr} in N
11.3.6.6.2 (a)	$c \geq \dfrac{l_w}{600\left(C_d \delta_{ne}/h_w\right)}$	c in mm h_w in mm l_w in mm δ_{ne} in mm
(B-1)	$w_{\inf} = \dfrac{0.3}{\lambda_{strut}\cos\theta_{strut}}$	w_{inf} in. mm θ_{strut} in degrees $\lambda_{strut} =$ mm^{-1}
(B-2a)	$\lambda_{strut} = \sqrt[4]{\dfrac{E_m\, t_{net\,inf}\,\sin 2\theta_{strut}}{4\,E_{bc}\,I_{bc}\,h_{\inf}}}$	$\lambda_{strut} =$ mm^{-1} E_{bc} in MPa E_m in MPa h_{inf} in mm I_{bc} in mm^4 $t_{net\,inf}$ in mm θ_{strut} in degrees
(B-2b)	$\lambda_{strut} = \sqrt[4]{\dfrac{E_{AAC}\, t_{net\,inf}\,\sin 2\theta_{strut}}{4\,E_{bc}\,I_{bc}\,h_{\inf}}}$	$\lambda_{strut} =$ mm^{-1} E_{AAC} in MPa E_{bc} in MPa h_{inf} in mm I_{bc} in mm^4 $t_{net\,inf}$ in mm θ_{strut} in degrees
(B-3)	$(150\text{mm})\,t_{net\,inf}\,f'_m$	f'_m in MPa $t_{net\,inf}$ in mm
(B-4)	$\dfrac{V_n}{1.5}$	V_n in N
(B-5)	$(150\text{mm})\,t_{net\,inf}\,f'_{AAC}$	f'_{AAC} in MPa $t_{net\,inf}$ in mm
(B-6)	$\dfrac{V_{nAAC}}{1.5}$	V_{nAAC} in N
(B-7a)	$q_{n\,inf} = 729000\left(f'_m\right)^{0.75} t_{\inf}^2 \left(\dfrac{\alpha_{arch}}{l_{\inf}^{2.5}} + \dfrac{\beta_{arch}}{h_{\inf}^{2.5}}\right)$	$q_{n\,inf}$ in Pa f'_m in MPa h_{inf} in mm l_{inf} in mm t_{inf} in mm α_{arch} in N$^{0.25}$ β_{arch} in N$^{0.25}$
(B-7b)	$q_{n\,inf} = 729000\left(f'_{AAC}\right)^{0.75} t_{\inf}^2 \left(\dfrac{\alpha_{arch}}{l_{\inf}^{2.5}} + \dfrac{\beta_{arch}}{h_{\inf}^{2.5}}\right)$	$q_{n\,inf}$ in Pa f'_{AAC} in MPa h_{inf} in mm l_{inf} in mm t_{inf} in mm α_{arch} in N$^{0.25}$ β_{arch} in N$^{0.25}$
(B-8)	$\alpha_{arch} = \dfrac{1}{h_{\inf}}(E_{bc}\,I_{bc}\,h_{\inf}^2)^{0.25} < 50$	α_{arch} in N$^{0.25}$ E_{bc} in MPa h_{inf} in mm I_{bc} in mm^4

Code Equation No. or Section No.	SI Unit Equivalent Equation	Units
(B-9)	$$\beta_{arch} = \frac{1}{l_{inf}} (E_{bb}\, I_{bb}\, l_{inf}^2)^{0.25} < 50$$	β_{arch} in $N^{0.25}$ E_{bb} in MPa l_{inf} in mm I_{bb} in mm^4
(C-1)	$$\phi V_{lim} \geq V_{ub}$$	V_{lim} in N V_{ub} in N

CONVERSION OF INCH-POUND UNITS TO SI UNITS

TO CONVERT FROM	TO	MULTIPLY BY
inches (in.)	millimeters (mm)	25.4
square inches (in.^{2})	square millimeters (mm^2)	645.2
cubic inches (in.^{3})	cubic millimeters (mm^3)	16,390
inches to the fourth power (in.^{4})	millimeters to the fourth power (mm^4)	416,200
pound-force (lb)	newton (N)	4.448
pounds per linear foot (plf)	newtons per millimeter (N/mm)	0.01459
pounds per square inch (psi)	megapascal (MPa)	0.006895
pounds per square foot (psf)	kilo pascal (kPa)	0.04788
inch-pounds (in-lb)	newton-millimeters (N-mm)	113.0
$\sqrt{psi}$, result in psi	$\sqrt{MPa}$, result in MPa	0.08304

PREFIXES

POWER	PREFIX	ABBREVIATION
$1,000,000 = 10^6$	mega	M
$1,000 = 10^3$	kilo	k
$0.001 = 10^{-3}$	milli	m

This page is intentionally left blank.

REFERENCES FOR THE CODE COMMENTARY

References, Chapter 1

Argudo, 2003. Argudo, Jaime, "Evaluation and Synthesis of Experimental Data for Autoclaved Aerated Concrete," MS Thesis, Department of Civil Engineering, The University of Texas at Austin, August 2003.

Tanner et al, 2005(a). Tanner, J.E., Varela, J.L., Klingner, R.E., "Design and Seismic Testing of a Two-story Full-scale Autoclaved Aerated Concrete (AAC) Assemblage Specimen," *Structures Journal*, American Concrete Institute, Farmington Hills, Michigan, Vol. 102, No. 1, January - February 2005, pp. 114-119.

References, Chapter 2

BIA TN 2, 1999. "Glossary of Terms Relating to Brick Masonry," Technical Notes on Brick Construction, No. 2 (Revised), Brick Industry Association, Reston, VA, 1999, 4 pp.

IMI, 1981. "The Masonry Glossary," International Masonry Institute, Washington, DC, 1981, 144 pp.

NCMA TEK 1-4, 2004. "Glossary of Concrete Masonry Terms," NCMA TEK Bulletin No. 1-4, National Concrete Masonry Association, Herndon, VA, 2004, 6 pp.

References, Chapter 4

ASCE, 1978. *Structural Design of Tall Concrete and Masonry Buildings*, Monograph on Planning and Design of Tall Buildings, V. CB, Council on Tall Buildings and Urban Habitat/American Society of Civil Engineers, New York, NY, 1978, 960 pp.

Colville et al, 1993. Colville, J., Miltenberger, M.A., and Wolde-Tinsae (Amde), A.M. "Hollow Concrete Masonry Modulus of Elasticity," 6th North American Masonry Conference, Philadelphia, PA, June 1993, pp. 1195-1208, The Masonry Society, Longmont, CO.

Copeland, 1957. Copeland, R.E., "Shrinkage and Temperature Stresses in Masonry," ACI Journal, *Proceedings* Vol. 53, No. 8, American Concrete Institute, Detroit MI, Feb. 1957, pp. 769-780.

Grimm, 1986. Grimm, C.T., "Probabilistic Design of Expansion Joints in Brick Cladding," *Proceedings*, Vol. 1, 4th Canadian Masonry Symposium, University of Fredericton, 1986, pp. 553-568.

Kalouseb, 1954. Kalouseb, L., "Relation of Shrinkage to Moisture Content in Concrete Masonry Units," *Paper* No. 25, Housing and Home Finance Agency, Washington, DC, 1954.

Lenczner and Salahuddin, 1976. Lenczner, D., and Salahuddin, J., "Creep and Moisture Movements in Masonry Piers and Walls," *Proceedings*, 1st Canadian Masonry Symposium, University of Calgary, June 1976, pp. 72-86.

NCMA TEK 3-1C, 2002. "All Weather Concrete Masonry Construction," NCMA TEK 3-1C, National Concrete Masonry Association, Herndon, VA, 2002, 4 pp.

NCMA TEK 10-1A, 2005. "Crack Control in Concrete Masonry Walls," NCMA TEK 10-1A, National Concrete Masonry Association, Herndon, VA, 2005, 4 pp.

NCMA TEK 10-2C, 2010. "Control Joints for Concrete Masonry Walls – Empirical Method," NCMA TEK 10-2C, National Concrete Masonry Association, Herndon, VA, 2010, 8 pp.

NCMA TEK 10-3, 2003. "Control Joints for Concrete Masonry Walls – Alternative Engineered Method," NCMA TEK 10-3, National Concrete Masonry Association, Herndon, VA, 2003, 4 pp.

NCMA TEK 14-1B, 2007. "Section Properties of Concrete Masonry Walls," *NCMA-TEK* 14-01B, National Concrete Masonry Association, Herndon, VA, 2007, 8 pp.

NCMA TEK 18-2B, 2012. "Sampling and Testing Concrete Masonry Units," NCMA TEK 18-2B, National Concrete Masonry Association, Herndon, VA, 2012, 4 pp.

Plummer, 1962. Plummer, H.C., *Brick and Tile Engineering*, Brick Institute of America (now Brick Industry Association), Reston, VA, 1962, 736 pp.

PTI, 2006. Post-Tensioning Institute. "Chapter 4-Specifying Post-Tensioning," *Post-Tensioning Manual*, 6th Edition, Phoenix, AZ, 2006, pp. 73-79.

RILEM, 1993. *"Autoclaved Aerated Concrete Properties, Testing and Design,"* RILEM Recommended Practice, RILEM Technical Committees 78-MCA and 51-ALC. Edited by: S. Aroni, G.J. de Grood, M.F. Robinson, G. Svanholm and F.H. Wittman, E & FN SPON, London, 1993.

Smith, 1973. Smith, R.G., "Moisture Expansion of Structural Ceramics – Long Term Unrestrained Expansion of Test Bricks," Journal of the British Ceramic Society, Stoke-on-Trent, England, Jan. 1973, pp. 1-5.

Wolde-Tinsae et al, 1993. Wolde-Tinsae, A.M., Atkinson, R.H. and Hamid, A.A., "State-of-the-Art: Modulus of Elasticity," 6th North American Masonry Conference. Philadelphia, PA, June 1993, pp. 1209-1220, The Masonry Society, Longmont, CO.

References, Chapter 5

Arora, 1988. Arora, S.K., "Performance of masonry walls under concentrated load." Proceedings of the British Masonry Society, 1988, Vol. 2, pp. 50-55.

Bennett et al, 2007. Bennett, R.M., McGinley, W.M., and Bryja, J., "Deflection Criteria for Masonry Beams." *Journal of ASTM International*, 2007, Vol. 4, No. 1, Paper ID: JAI100442.

Branson, 1965. Branson, D.E., "Instantaneous and Time-Dependent Deflections on Simple and Continuous Reinforced Concrete Beams." HPR Report No. 7, Part 1, Alabama Highway Department, Bureau of Public Roads, August, 1965, pp. 1-78.

CEB-FIP, 1990. *CEB-FIP Model Code 1990: Design Code.* Comité Euro-International du Béton (Euro-International Committee for Concrete, CEB) and the Fédération International de la Précontrainte (International Federation for Prestressing, FIP), Thomas Telford Ltd, 1993.

CSA, 2004. *Design of Masonry Structures*, CSA S304.1-04, Canadian Standards Association, 2004.

Dickey and MacIntosh, 1971. Dickey, W. and MacIntosh, A., "Results of Variation of b' or Effective Width in Flexure in Concrete Block Panels," Masonry Institute of America, Los Angeles, CA, 1971.

Fonseca et al, 2011. Fonseca, F.S., Mathew, S., and Bennett, R.M., "MSJC Deep Beam Requirements," *TMS Journal*, Vol. 29, No. 1, pp. 49-61, The Masonry Society, Longmont, CO, 2011.

Galambos and Ellingwood, 1986. Galambos, T.V., and Ellingwood, B., "Serviceability limit states: deflection." *Journal of Structural Engineering*, ASCE, 1986, Vol. 112, No. 1, pp. 67-84.

Hansell and Winter ,1959 Hansell, W. and Winter, G., "Lateral Stability of Reinforced Concrete Beams." *ACI Journal*, Proceedings, 1959, Vol. 56, No. 5, pp. 193-214.

He and Priestley, 1992. He, L., and Priestley, M.J.N., Seismic Behavior of Flanged Masonry Shear Walls - Final Report, TCCMAR Report No. 4.1-2, November 1992, 279 pp.

Horton and Tadros, 1990. Horton, R.T., and Tadros, M.K., "Deflection of reinforced masonry members." *ACI Structural Journal*, 1990, Vol. 87, No. 4, pp. 453-463.

Longworth and Warwaruk, 1983. Lee, R., Longworth, J. and Warwaruk, J. (1983). "Behavior of restrained masonry beams." 3rd Canadian Masonry Symposium, Edmonton, Alberta, 37/1-16.

Page and Shrive, 1987 Page, A.W., and Shrive, N.G., "Concentrated loads on hollow masonry – load dispersion through bond beams," *TMS Journal*, Vol. 6, No. 2, T45-T51 pp, The Masonry Society, Longmont, CO, 1987.

Park et al, 1975. Park, Robert and Paulay, Thomas. *Reinforced Concrete Structures*, John Wiley & Sons, 1975.

Pfister, 1964. Pfister, J.F., "Influence of Ties on the Behavior of Reinforced Concrete Columns," ACI Journal, *Proceedings* Vol. 61, No. 5, American Concrete Institute, Detroit, MI, May 1964, pp. 521-537.

Revanthi and Menon, 2006. Revanthi, P. and Menon, D., "Estimation of Critical Buckling Moments in Slender Reinforced Concrete Beams." *ACI Structural Journal*, 2006, Vol. 103, No. 2, pp. 296-303.

References, Chapter 6

ACI 318, 1983. ACI Committee 318, "Building Code Requirements for Reinforced Concrete (ACI 318-83)," American Concrete Institute, Detroit, MI 1983, 111 pp.

Allen et al, 2000. Allen, R., Borchelt, J. G., Klingner, R. E. and Zobel, R., "Proposed Provisions for Design of Anchorage to Masonry," *TMS Journal*, Vol. 18, No. 2, pp. 35-59, The Masonry Society, Longmont, CO, 2000.

Brown and Whitlock, 1983. Brown, R.H. and Whitlock, A.R., "Strength of Anchor Bolts in Concrete Masonry," *Journal of the Structural Division*, Vol. 109, No. 6, pp. 1362-1374, American Society of Civil Engineers, New York, NY, 1983.

Dickey, 1982. Dickey, W.L., "Joint Reinforcement and Masonry," *Proceedings*, 2nd North American Masonry Conference, College Park, MD, Aug. 1982, The Masonry Society, Longmont, CO, pp. 15-1 through 15-15.

Priestley and Bridgeman , 1974. Priestley, M.J.N., and Bridgeman, D.O., "Seismic Resistance of Brick Masonry Walls," *Bulletin*, New Zealand National Society for Earthquake Engineering (Wellington), Vol. 7, No. 4, Dec. 1974, pp. 167-187.

Rad and Mueller, 1998. Rad, F. N, Winnen, J., M., and Mueller, W. H., "An Experimental Study on the Strength of Grouted Anchors in Masonry Walls," Report submitted to the Masonry & Ceramic Tile Institute of Oregon, Portland State University, Portland, OR, 1998.

Tubbs et al, 2000. Tubbs, J. B., Pollock, D. G. and McLean, D. I., "Testing of Anchor Bolts in Concrete Block Masonry," *TMS Journal*, Vol. 18, No. 2, pp. 75-88, The Masonry Society, Longmont, CO, 2000.

References, Chapter 7

ASTM C1093-95. ASTM C1093-95 (reapproved 2001), "Standard Practice for Accreditation of Testing Agencies for Unit Masonry," ASTM International, West Conshohocken, Pennsylvania.

BIA 1988. "Technical Notes 39B, *Testing for Engineered Brick Masonry—Quality Control*", Brick Industry Association, Reston, VA, Mar. 1988.

BIA 2001. "Technical Notes 39, *Testing for Engineered Brick Masonry—Brick and Mortar*", Brick Industry Association, Reston, VA, Nov. 2001.

Brown and Melander, 1999. Brown, R. and Melander, J. "Flexural Bond Strength of Unreinforced Grouted Masonry Using PCL and MC Mortars", Proceedings of the Eighth North American Masonry Conference, Austin, TX, June, 1999, The Masonry Society, Longmont, CO.

Chrysler 2010. Chrysler, J., "Reinforced Concrete Masonry Construction Inspector's Handbook", 7th Edition, Masonry Institute of America and International Code Council, Torrance, CA, 2010.

Gulkan et al, 1979. Gulkan, P., Mayes, R.L., and Clough, R.W., "Shaking Table Study of Single-Story Masonry Houses Volumes 1 and 2," *Report* No. UCB/EERC-79/23 and 24, Earthquake Engineering Research Center, University of California, Berkeley, CA, Sept. 1979.

Hamid et al, 1979. Hamid, A., Drysdale, R., and Heidebrecht, A. "Shear Strength of Concrete Masonry Joints," Journal of Structural Engineering, ASCE Vol. 105, ST7, American Society of Civil Engineers, Reston, Virginia, pp. 1227-1240, 1979.

Klingner et al, 2010. Klingner, R. E., P. Benson Shing, W. Mark McGinley , David I. McLean, Hussein Okail , and Seongwoo Jo, "Seismic Performance Tests of Masonry and Masonry Veneer," Journal of ASTM International, Vol. 7, No. 3, ASTM International, West Conshohocken, PA January 2010.

Minaie et al (2009). Minaie, Ehsan; Hamid, Ahmad; and Moon, Franklin, Summary of the Research on Behavior of Fully Grouted Reinforced Concrete and Clay Masonry Shear Walls, SN2902b, Portland Cement Association, Skokie, Illinois, USA, 2009, 8 pages.

NCMA 2008. "Inspection and Testing of Concrete Masonry Construction", National Concrete Masonry Association and International Code Council, Herndon, VA, 2008.

References, Chapter 8

ACI 318 (1983). ACI Committee 318, "Commentary on Building Code Requirements for Reinforced Concrete (ACI 318-83)," American Concrete Institute, Detroit, MI, 1983, 155 pp.

ACI 531, 1983. ACI Committee 531, "Building Code Requirements for Concrete Masonry Structures (ACI 531-79) (Revised 1983)," American Concrete Institute, Detroit, MI, 1983, 20 pp.

Ahmed et al, 1983(a). Ahmed, M.H., Porter, M.L., and Wolde-Tinsae, A.M., "Behavior of Reinforced Brick-to-Block Walls," Ph.D. dissertation, M. H. Ahmed, Iowa State University, Ames, IA, 1983, Part 2A.

Ahmed et al, 1983(b). Ahmed, M.H., Porter, M.L., and Wolde-Tinsae, A.M., "Behavior of Reinforced Brick-to-Block Walls," Ph.D. dissertation, M. H. Ahmed, Iowa State University, Ames, IA, 1983, Part 2B.

Anand, 1985. Anand, S.C., "Shear Stresses in Composite Masonry Walls," *New Analysis Techniques for Structural Masonry*, American Society of Civil Engineers, New York, NY, Sept. 1985, pp. 106-127.

Anand and Rahman, 1986. Anand, S.C. and Rahman, M.A., "Temperature and Creep Stresses in Composite Masonry Walls," *Advances in Analysis of Structural Masonry*, American Society of Civil Engineers, New York, NY, 1986, pp. 111-133.

Anand and Young, 1982. Anand, S.C. and Young, D.T., "A Finite Element Model for Composite Masonry," *Proceedings*, American Society of Civil Engineers, Vol. 108, ST12, New York, NY, Dec. 1982, pp. 2637-2651.

ASTM A185/A185M, 2007. ASTM A185/A185M – 07, Standard Specification for Steel Welded Wire Reinforcement, Plain, for Concrete, ASTM International, West Conshohocken, PA.

ASTM A497/A497M, 2007. ASTM A497/A497M – 07, Standard Specification for Steel Welded Wire Reinforcement, Deformed, for Concrete, ASTM International, West Conshohocken, PA.

ASTM A951/A951M, 2011. ASTM A951/A951M – 11, Standard Specification for Steel Wire for Masonry Joint Reinforcement, ASTM International, West Conshohocken, PA.

BIA, 1969. "Recommended Practices for Engineered Brick Masonry," Brick Institute of America (now Brick Industry Association), Reston, VA, pp. 337, 1969.

Borchelt and Tann, 1996. Borchelt, J.G. and J.A. Tann. "Bond Strength and Water Penetration of Low IRA Brick and Mortar," Proceedings of the Seventh North American Masonry Conference, South Bend, IN, 1996, The Masonry Society, Longmont, CO, pp. 206-216.

Brown and Melander, 1999. Brown, R.H. and Melander, J.M., "Flexural Bond Strength of Unreinforced Grouted Masonry using PCL and MC Mortars," *Proceedings,* 8th North American Masonry Conference, Austin, TX, 1999, The Masonry Society, Longmont, CO, pp. 694-705.

Brown and Palm, 1982. Brown, R. and Palm, B., "Flexural Strength of Brick Masonry Using the Bond Wrench," *Proceedings*, 2nd North American Masonry Conference, The Masonry Society, Longmont, CO, 1982, pp. 1-1 through 1-15.

Colville, 1978. Colville, J., "Simplified Design of Load Bearing Masonry Walls," *Proceedings*, 5th International Symposium on Loadbearing Brickwork, *Publication* No. 27, British Ceramic Society, London, Dec. 1978, pp. 2171-2234.

Colville, 1979. Colville, J., "Stress Reduction Design Factors for Masonry Walls," *Proceedings*, American Society of Civil Engineers, Vol. 105, ST10, New York, NY, Oct. 1979, pp. 2035-2051.

Colville et al, 1987. Colville, J., Matty, S.A., and Wolde-Tinsae, A.M., "Shear Capacity of Mortared Collar Joints," *Proceedings*, 4th North American Masonry Conference, Los Angeles, CA, Aug. 1987, Vol. 2 pp. 60-1 through 60-15, The Masonry Society, Longmont, CO.

Colville, 1992). Colville, J., "Service Load Design Equations for Unreinforced Masonry Construction." *TMS Journal*, Vol. 11, No. 1, pp. 9-20, The Masonry Society, Longmont, CO, 1992.

CSA, 1984. "Connectors for Masonry," (CAN 3-A370-M84), Canadian Standards Association, Rexdale, Ontario, 1984.

Davis at al, 2010. Davis, C.L., McLean, D.I., and Ingham, J.M., "Evaluation of Design Provisions for In-Plane Shear in Masonry Walls," The Masonry Society Journal, Vol. 28, No.2, Dec, 2010, pp. 41-59.

Drysdale and Hamid, 1984. Drysdale, R.G. and Hamid, A.A., "Effect of Grouting on the Flexural Tensile Strength of Concrete Block Masonry," *TMS Journal*, Vol. 3, No. 2, pp. T-1,T-9, The Masonry Society, Longmont, CO, 1984.

Ellifritt, 1977. Ellifritt, D.S., "The Mysterious $^1/_3$ Stress Increase," *Engineering Journal*, ASIC, 4th Quarter, 1977, Vol. 14, No. 4, pp. 138-140.

Ellingwood et al, 1980. Ellingwood, B., Galambos, T.V., MacGregor, J.G., and Cornell, C.A., "Development of a Probability Based Load Criteria for American National Standard A58," NBS Special Publication 577, National Bureau of Standards, 1980.

Fattal and Cattaneo, 1976. Fattal, S.G. and Cattaneo, L.E., "Structural Performance of Masonry Walls Under Compression and Flexure," *Building Science Series* No. 73, National Bureau of Standards, Washington, DC, 1976, 57 pp.

Ferguson and Matloob, 1959. Ferguson, P. M., and Matloob, F. N., "Effect of Bar Cutoff on Bond and Shear Strength of Reinforced Concrete Beams," ACI Journal, *Proceedings,* Vol. 56, No. 1, American Concrete Institute, Detroit, MI, July 1959, pp. 5-24.

Gallagher, 1935. Gallagher, E.F., "Bond Between Reinforcing Steel and Brick Masonry," *Brick and Clay Record*, Vol. 5, Cahners Publishing Co., Chicago, IL, Mar. 1935, pp. 86-87.

Gustafson and Felder, 1991. Gustafson, D. P., and Felder, A. L., "Questions and Answers on ASTM A 706 Reinforcing Bars," Concrete International, Vol. 13, No. 7, July 1991, pp. 54-57.

Hamid et al, 1979). Hamid, A.A., Drysdale, R.G., and Heidebrecht, A.C., "Shear Strength of Concrete Masonry Joints," *Proceedings*, American Society of Civil Engineers, Vol. 105, ST7, New York, NY, July 1979, pp. 1227-1240.

Hamid, 1981. Hamid, A.A., "Effect of Aspect Ratio of the Unit on the Flexural Tensile Strength of Brick Masonry," *TMS Journal*, The Masonry Society, Longmont, CO, 1981, Vol. 1, No. 1, pp. T-11 through T-16.

Hamid, 1985. Hamid, A.A., "Bond Characteristics of Sand-Molded Brick Masonry," *TMS Journal*, Vol. 4, No. 1, pp. T-18,T-22, The Masonry Society, Longmont, CO, 1985.

Hatzinikolas et al, 1978. Hatzinikolas, M., Longworth, J., and Warwaruk, J., "Concrete Masonry Walls," *Structural Engineering Report* No. 70, Department of Civil Engineering, University of Alberta, Canada, Sept. 1978.

Hedstrom et al, 1991. Hedstrom, E.G., Tarhini, K.M., Thomas, R.D., Dubovoy, V.S., Klingner, R.E., and Cook, R.A., "Flexural Bond Strength of Concrete Masonry Prisms using Portland Cement and Hydrated Lime Mortars." *TMS Journal*, Vol. 9 No. 2, pp. 8-23, The Masonry Society, Longmont, CO, 1991.

Hogan, et al, 1997. Hogan, M.B., Samblanet, P.J., and Thomas, R.D., "Research Evaluation of Reinforcing Bar Splices in Concrete Masonry," Proceedings of the 11th International Brick/Block Masonry Conference, Tongji University, Shanghai, China, October 1997, pp. 227-238

IIT, 1963. "Development of Adjustable Wall Ties," *ARF Project* No. B869, Illinois Institute of Technology, Chicago, IL, Mar. 1963.

Kim and Bennett, 2002. Kim, Y.S. and Bennett, R.M., "Flexural Tension in Unreinforced Masonry: Evaluation of Current Specifications." *TMS Journal*, Vol. 20, No. 1, pp. 23-30, The Masonry Society, Longmont, CO, 2002.

McCarthy et al, 1985. McCarthy, J.A., Brown, R.H., and Cousins, T.E., "An Experimental Study of the Shear Strength of Collar Joints in Grouted and Slushed Composite Masonry Walls," *Proceedings*, 3rd North American Masonry Conference, Arlington, TX, June 1985, pp. 39-1 through 39-16, The Masonry Society, Longmont, CO.

Melander and Ghosh, 1996. Melander, J.M. and Ghosh, S.K., "Development of Specifications for Mortar Cement," Masonry: Esthetics, Engineering and Economy, STP 1246, D. H. Taubert and J.T. Conway, Ed., American Society for Testing and Materials, Philadelphia, 1996.

Minaie et al, 2010. Minaie, M. Mota,; F. L. Moon, M.ASCE; and A. A. Hamid, "In-Plane Behavior of Partially Grouted Reinforced Concrete Masonry Shear Walls, ASCE Journal of Structural Engineering. September 2010, Vol. 136, No. 9, pp. 1089-1097.

Mjelde et al, 2009. Mjelde, Z., McLean, D.I., Thompson, J. J. and McGinley, W. M., "Performance of Lap Splices in Concrete Masonry Shear Walls," *TMS Journal*, The Masonry Society. Longmont, CO, 2009, Vol. 27, No. 1, pp. 35-54.

NCMA TEK 12-1B, 2011. "Anchors and Ties for Masonry," NCMA TEK 12-1B, National Concrete Masonry Association, Herndon, VA, 2011, 4 pp.

NCMA, 2009. National Concrete Masonry Association, "Effects of Confinement Reinforcement on Bar Splice Performance – Summary of Research and Design Recommendations", MR33, Research Report, Herndon VA, July, 2009.

Nolph and ElGawady, 2011. Nolph, S.M. and ElGawady M.A.,"In-Plane Shear Strength of Partially Grouted Masonry Shear Walls", Proceedings of the 11th North American Masonry Conference. Minneapolis, MN, June 2011, The Masonry Society, Longmont, CO.

Nuss et al, 1978. Nuss, L.K., Noland, J.L., and Chinn, J., "The Parameters Influencing Shear Strength Between Clay Masonry Units and Mortar," *Proceedings*, North American Masonry Conference, University of Colorado, Longmont, CO, Aug. 1978, pp. 13-1 through 13-27.

PCI, 1980. Joint PCI/WRI Ad Hoc Committee on Welded Wire Fabric for Shear Reinforcement, "Welded Wire Fabric for Shear Reinforcement," *Journal*, Prestressed Concrete Institute, Vol. 25, No. 4, Chicago, IL, July-Aug. 1980, pp. 32-36.

Pook, 1986. Pook, L.L., Stylianou, M.A., and Dawe, J.L., "Experimental Investigation of the Influence of Compression on the Shear Strength of Masonry Joints," *Proceedings*, 4th Canadian Masonry Symposium, Fredericton, New Brunswick, June 1986, pp. 1053-1062.

Porter et al, 1986. Porter, M.L., Wolde-Tinsae, A.M., and Ahmed, M.H., "Strength Analysis of Composite Walls," *Advances in Analysis of Structural Masonry*, Proceedings of Structures Congress '86, American Society of Civil Engineers, New York, NY, 1986.

Porter et al, 1987. Porter, M.L., Wolde-Tinsae, A.M., and Ahmed, M.H., "Strength Design Method for Brick Composite Walls," *Proceedings*, 4th International Masonry Conference, London, Aug. 1987.

Ribar, 1982. Ribar, J., "Water Permeance of Masonry: A Laboratory Study," *Masonry: Properties and Performance*, STP-778, ASTM International, Philadelphia, PA, 1982, pp. 200-221.

Richart, 1949. Richart, F.E., "Bond Tests Between Steel and Mortar," Structural Clay Products Institute (now Brick Industry Association), Reston, VA, 1949.

Schultz, 1996a. Schultz, A. E., "Seismic Resistance of Partially-Grouted Masonry Shear Walls," Paper No. 1221, Proceedings, 11th World Conference on Earthquake Engineering (WCEE), Acapulco, Mexico, Elsevier Science Ltd, 1996.

Schultz, 1996b. Schultz, A. E., "Seismic Resistance of Partially-Grouted Masonry Shear Walls," Worldwide Advances in Structural Concrete and Masonry, A. E. Schultz and S. L. McCabe, ed., Proceedings of CCMS Symposium (ASCE Structures Congress XIV), pp. 211-222, 1996.

Schultz and Hutchison, 2001. Schultz, A. E. and Hutchinson, R. S. (2001). "Seismic Behavior of Partially-Grouted Masonry Shear Walls, Phase 2: Effectiveness of Bed-Joint Reinforcement," NIST GCR 01-808, National Institute of Standards and Technology, Gaithersburg, MD, February, 2001, 442 pp.

Stevens and Anand, 1985. Stevens, D.J. and Anand, S.C., "Shear Stresses in Composite Masonry Walls Using a 2-D Modes," *Proceedings*, 3rd North American Masonry Conference, Arlington, TX, June 1985, p. 41-1 through 40-15, The Masonry Society, Longmont, CO.

Stewart and Lawrence, 2000. Stewart, M. G. and Lawrence, S., "Bond Strength Variability and Structural Reliability of Masonry Walls in Flexure," Proc. 12th International Brick/Block Masonry Conf., Madrid, Spain, 2000.

Treece and Jirsa, 1989. Treece, R.A. and Jirsa, J.O., "Bond Strength of Epoxy-Coated Reinforcing Bars," ACI Materials Journal, Vol. 86, No. 2, 1989, pp 167-174.

Williams and Geschwinder, 1982. Williams, R. and Geschwinder, L., "Shear Stress Across Collar Joints in Composite Masonry," presented at *Proceedings*, 2nd North American Masonry Conference, College Park, MD, 1982, *Paper* No. 8, The Masonry Society, Longmont, CO.

Wolde-Tinsae et al, 1985(a). Wolde-Tinsae, A.M., Porter, M.L., and Ahmed, M.H., "Behavior of Composite Brick Walls," *Proceedings*, 7th International Brick Masonry Conference, Melbourne, New South Wales, Feb. 1985, Vol. 2, pp. 877-888.

Wolde-Tinsae et al, 1985(b). Wolde-Tinsae, A.M., Porter, M.L., and Ahmed, M.H., "Shear Strength of Composite Brick-to-Brick Panels," *Proceedings*, 3rd North American Masonry Conference, Arlington, TX, June 1985, pp. 40-1 through 40-13, The Masonry Society, Longmont, CO.

Woodward and Ranking, 1984. Woodward, K. and Ranking, F., "Influence of Vertical Compressive Stress on Shear Resistance of Concrete Block Masonry Walls," U.S. Department of Commerce, National Bureau of Standards, Washington, D.C., Oct. 1984, 62 pp.

Yokel, 1971. Yokel, F.Y., "Stability and Load Capacity of Members with no Tensile Strength," *Proceedings*, American Society of Civil Engineers, Vol. 97, ST7, New York, NY, July 1971, pp. 1913-1926.

Yokel and Dikkers, 1971. Yokel, F.Y., and Dikkers, R.D., "Strength of Load-Bearing Masonry Walls," *Proceedings*, American Society of Engineers, Vol. 97, ST5, New York, NY, `May 1971, pp. 1593-1609.

Yokel and Dikkers, 1973. Yokel, F.Y., and Dikkers, R.D., Closure to "Strength of Load-Be3ring Masonry Walls," *Proceedings*, American Society of Engineers, Vol. 99, ST5, New York, NY, May 1973, pp. 948-950.

References, Chapter 9

Abboud et al, 1993. Abboud, B., Hamid, A. and Harris, H.," Flexural Behavior and Strength of Reinforced Masonry Walls Built with Masonry Cement Mortar," TMS Journal Longmont, CO. Vol.12, No. 1, August 1993.

Allen et al, 2000. Allen, R., Borchelt, J.G., Klingner, R.E. and Zobel, R., "Proposed Provisions for Design of Anchorage to Masonry," *TMS Journal*, Vol. 18, No. 2, pp. 35-59, The Masonry Society, Longmont, CO, 2000.

Amrhein and Lee, 1984. Amrhein, J.E., and Lee, D.E., "Design of Reinforced Masonry Tall Slender Walls", 1984, Western States Clay Products Association, 46 pp.

Assis and Hamid, 1990. Assis, G.F. and Hamid, A.A., "Compression Behavior of Concrete Masonry Prisms Under Strain Gradient", *Proceedings*, 5th North American Masonry Conference, The Masonry Society, Longmont, CO, 1990, pp. 615-626.

Baenziger and Porter, 2011. Baenziger, G. P., Porter, M. L., "Joint Reinforcement for Masonry Shear Walls," 11th North American Masonry Conference, Paper No. 51, Minneapolis, MN, May, 2011.

Brown and Whitlock, 1983. Brown, R.H. and Whitlock, A.R., "Strength of Anchor Bolts in Concrete Masonry," Journal of the Structural Division, American Society of Civil Engineers, New York, NY, Vol. 109, No. 6, June, 1983, pp. 1362-1374.

Brown, 1987. Brown, R.H., "Compressive Stress Distribution of Grouted Hollow Clay Masonry Under Strain Gradient", *Proceedings*, 4th North American Masonry Conference,, The Masonry Society, Longmont, CO, 1987, pp. 45-1 through 45-12.

Brown et al, 2001. Brown, R. H., Borchelt, J. G., and Burgess, R. E., "Strength of Anchor Bolts in the Top of Clay Masonry Walls," Proceedings of the 9th Canadian Masonry Symposium, Fredericton, New Brunswick, Canada, June 2001.

Davis et al, 2010. Davis, C.L., McLean, D.I., and Ingham, J.M., "Evaluation of Design Provisions for In-Plane Shear in Masonry Walls," The Masonry Society Journal, Vol. 28, No.2, Dec, 2010, pp. 41-59.

Fuchs et al, 1995. Fuchs, W., Eligenhausen, R. and Breen, J. "Concrete Capacity Design (CCD) Approach for Fastening to Concrete," ACI Structural Journal, Vol. 92, No. a, 1995, pp. 73-93.

Hamid et al, 1990. Hamid, A., Hatem, M., Harris, H. and Abboud, B.," Hysteretic Response and Ductility of Reinforced Concrete Masonry Walls under Out-of-Plane Loading," Proc. 5th North American Masonry Conference, University of Illinois, Urbana-Champaign, June 1990, pp. 397-410.

Hatzinikolos et al, 1980. Hatzinikolos, M., Longworth, J., and Warwaruk, J., "Strength and Behavior of Anchor Bolts Embedded in Concrete Masonry," Proceedings, 2nd Canadian Masonry Conference, Carleton University, Ottawa, Ontario, June, 1980. pp. 549-563.

MacGregor et al 1970. MacGregor, J.G., Breen, J.E., and Pfrang, E.O., "Design of slender concrete columns." ACI Journal, 1970, Vol. 67, No. 1, pp. 6-28.

Malik et al, 1982. Malik, J.B., Mendonca, J.A., and Klingner, R.E., "Effect of Reinforcing Details on the Shear Resistance of Short Anchor Bolts under Reversed Cyclic Loading," Journal of the American Concrete Institute, Proceedings, Vol. 79, No. 1, January-February 1982, pp. 3-11.

Minaie et al, 2010. Minaie, M. Mota,; F. L. Moon, M.ASCE; and A. A. Hamid, "In-Plane Behavior of Partially Grouted Reinforced Concrete Masonry Shear Walls, ASCE Journal of Structural Engineering. September 2010, Vol. 136, No. 9, pp. 1089-1097.

Mirza, 1987. Mirza, S.A., Lee, P.M., and Morgan, D.L.. "ACI stability resistance factor for RC columns." Journal of Structural Engineering, ASCE, 1987, Vol. 113, No. 9, pp. 1963-1976.

Mjelde et al, 2009. Mjelde, Z., McLean, D.I., Thompson, J. J. and McGinley, W. M., "Performance of Lap Splices in Concrete Masonry Shear Walls," *TMS Journal*, The Masonry Society. Longmont, CO, 2009, Vol. 27, No. 1, pp. 35-54.

NCMA, 2008. National Concrete Masonry Association, "Effects of Confinement Reinforcement on Bar Splice Performance – Summary of Research and Design Recommendations", Research Report, Herndon VA, February, 2009.

NCMA, 2009. National Concrete Masonry Association, "Effects of Confinement Reinforcement on Bar Splice Performance – Summary of Research and Design Recommendations", MR33, Research Report, Herndon VA, July, 2009.

Noland and Kingsley, 1995. Noland, J., and Kingsley, G., "U.S. Coordinated Program for Masonry Building Research: Technology Transfer, Research Transformed into Practice", Implementation of NSF Research, Proceedings from the Conference, Arlington, Virginia, June 14-16, 1995, pp. 360-371.

Nolph and ElGawady, 2011. Nolph, S.M. and ElGawady M.A.,"In-Plane Shear Strength of Partially Grouted Masonry Shear Walls", Proceedings of the 11th North American Masonry Conference. Minneapolis, MN, June 2011, The Masonry Society, Longmont, CO.

Porter and Baenziger, 2007. Porter, M. L., and Baenziger, G. P., "Joint Reinforcement as Shear Reinforcement for Masonry Shear Walls", Proceedings, Tenth North American Masonry Conference, St. Louis, MO, June 3-6, 2007, 860-871.

Porter and Braun, 1998. Porter, M. L., Braun, R. A., "Horizontal Reinforcement Elongation in Masonry Mortar Joints", Proceedings, Eighth Canadian Masonry Symposium, Jasper, Canada, May 31-June 3, 1998, 599-609.

Porter and Braun, 1999. Porter, M. L. and Braun, R. L., "An Effective Gage Length for Joint Reinforcement in Masonry", Proceedings, Paper 1A.2, Eighth North American Masonry Conference, Austin, Texas, June 6-9, 1999.

Rad et al, 1998. Rad, F.N., Muller, W.H. and Winnen, J.M., "An Experimental Study on the Strength of Grouted Anchors in Masonry Walls," Report to the Masonry & Ceramic Tile Institute of Oregon, Portland State University, Portland, Oregon, October 1998.

Schultz, 1996a. Schultz, A.E., "Minimum Horizontal Reinforcement Requirements for Seismic Design of Masonry Walls," The Masonry Society Journal, 14(1), August, 1996, 49-64.

Schultz, 1996b. Schultz, A. E., "Seismic Resistance of Partially-Grouted Masonry Shear Walls," Paper No. 1221, Proceedings, 11th World Conference on Earthquake Engineering (WCEE), Acapulco, Mexico, Elsevier Science Ltd, 1996.

Schultz, 1996c. Schultz, A. E., "Seismic Resistance of Partially-Grouted Masonry Shear Walls," Worldwide Advances in Structural Concrete and Masonry, A. E. Schultz and S. L. McCabe, ed., Proceedings of CCMS Symposium (ASCE Structures Congress XIV), pp. 211-222, 1996.

Schultz, 2004. Schultz, A. E. (2004). "A Reevaluation of Reinforcing Bar Splice Requirements for Masonry Structures according to the 2002 MSJC Strength Design Provisions," International Masonry Institute, Annapolis, MD, May, 2004, 37 pp.

Schultz, 2005. Schultz, A. E., "An Evaluation of Reinforcing Bar Splice Requirements for Strength Design of Masonry Structures," Council for Masonry Research, Herndon, VA, December, 2005, 94 pp.

Schultz and Hutchinson, 2001a. Schultz, A. E., Hutchinson, R. S. "Seismic Behavior of Partially-Grouted Masonry Shear Walls: Phase 2 - Effectiveness of Bed-Joint Reinforcement" Minneapolis, MN : Building and Fire Research Laboratory, National Institute of Standards and Technology, Department of Civil Engineering, Universtiy of Minnesota, 2001. NIST GCR 01-808.

Schultz and Hutchison, 2001b. Schultz, A. E. and Hutchinson, R. S. (2001). "Seismic Behavior of Partially-Grouted Masonry Shear Walls, Phase 2: Effectiveness of Bed-Joint Reinforcement," NIST GCR 01-808, National Institute of Standards and Technology, Gaithersburg, MD, February, 2001, 442 pp.

Shing et al, 1990a. Shing, P.B., Schuller, M.P., Hoskere, V.S., and Carter, E., "Flexural and Shear Response of Reinforced MasonryWalls", American Concrete Institute Structural Journal, Farmington Hills, MI, Vol. 87, No. 6, November-December 1990a, pp. 646-656.

Shing et al, 1990b. Shing, P.B., Schuller, M.P., and Hoskere, V.S., "In-Plane Resistance of Reinforced Masonry Shear Walls", American Society of Civil Engineers Structural Journal, Reston, VA, Vol. 116, No. 3, March 1990b, pp. 619-640.

Sveinsson et al, 1985. Sveinsson, B. I., McNiven, H. D., Sucuoglu, H., "Cyclic Loading Tests of Masonry Single Piers – Volume 4; Additional Tests with Height to Width Ratio of 1," UCB/EERC-85/15, Earthquake Engineering Research Center, University of California, Berkeley, December, 1985.

Tubbs et al, 1999. Tubbs, J.B., Pollock, D.G., Jr., McLean, D.I. and Young, T.C., "Performance of Anchor Bolts in Concrete Block Masonry", Proceedings, 8th North American Masonry Conference, Austin, TX, 1999, The Masonry Society, Longmont, CO, pp. 866-877.

UBC, 1997. Uniform Building Code (UBC), International Conference of Building Officials, Whittier, CA, 1997.

Wallace and Moehle, 1992. Wallace, J.W. and Moehle, J.P., "Ductility and Detailing Requirements of Bearing Wall Buildings," Journal of Structural Engineering, ASCE, V. 118, No. 6, 1992, pp. 1625-1644.

Wallace and Orakcal, 2002. Wallace, J.W. and Orakcal, K., "ACI 318-99 Provisions for Seismic Design of Structural Walls," ACI Structural Journal, American Concrete Institute, 2002, Vol. 99, No. 4, pp. 499-508.

Weigel et al, 2002. Weigel, T.A., Mohsen, J.P., Burke, A., Erdmann, K. and Schad, A., "Tensile Strength of Headed Anchor Bolts in Tops of CMU Walls," TMS Journal, Vol. 20, No. 1, pp 61-70, The Masonry Society, Longmont, CO, 2002.

References, Chapter 10

ASTM A416, 2006. ASTM A416-06, *Standard Specification for Steel Strand, Uncoated Seven-Wire for Prestressed Concrete*, ASTM International, West Conshohocken, PA.

ASTM A421, 2005. ASTM A421-05, *Standard Specification for Uncoated Stress-Relieved Steel Wire for Prestressed Concrete*, ASTM International, West Conshohocken, PA.

ASTM A722, 2007. ASTM A722-07, *Standard Specification for Uncoated High-Strength Steel Bars for Prestressing Concrete*, ASTM International, West Conshohocken, PA.

Bean and Schultz, 2003. Bean, J.R. and Schultz A.E., "Flexural Capacity of Post-Tensioned Masonry Walls: Code Review and Recommended Procedure", *PTI Journal*, Vol. 1, No. 1, January 2003, pp. 28-44.

Bean Popehn, 2007. Bean Popehn, Jennifer R. "Mechanics and Behavior of Slender, Post-Tensioned Masonry Walls to Transverse Loading", Ph.D. dissertation, University of Minnesota, 2007.

Bean Popehn and Schultz, 2010. Bean Popehn, J. R. and Schultz, A.E., "Design Provisions for Post-Tensioned Masonry Walls Loaded Out-of-Plane", *TMS Journal*, Vol. 28, No. 2, December 2010, pp. 9 – 26, The Masonry Society, Longmont, CO.

Biggs and Ganz, 1998. Biggs, D.T. and Ganz, H.R., "The Codification of Prestressed Masonry in the United States", *Proceedings,* Fifth International Masonry Conference, London, UK, October 1998, pp. 363-366.

BSI, 1985. *Code of Practice for the Use of Masonry, Part 2: Reinforced and Prestressed Masonry*, BS 5628, British Standards Institution, London, England, 1985.

Curtin et al, 1988. Curtin, W.G., Shaw, G., and Beck, J.K., *Design of Reinforced and Prestressed Masonry*, Thomas Telford Ltd., London, England, 1988, 244 pp.

Hamilton and Badger, 2000. Hamilton III, H.R. and Badger, C.C.R., "Creep Losses in Post-Tensioned Concrete Masonry," *TMS Journal*, Vol. 18, No. 1, pp. 19-30, The Masonry Society, Longmont, CO, 2000.

Lenczner, 1985. Lenczner, D., "Creep and Stress Relaxation in Stack-Bonded Brick Masonry Prisms, A Pilot Study," Department of Civil Engineering, Clemson University, Clemson, SC, May 1985, 28 pp.

Lenczner, 1987. Lenczner, D., "Creep and Loss of Prestress in Stack Bonded Brick Masonry Prisms, Pilot Study - Stage II," Department of Civil Engineering, University of Illinois, Urbana-Champaign, IL, August 1987, 29 pp.

NCMA TEK 14-20A, 2002. NCMA TEK-14-20A, "Post-tensioned Concrete Masonry Wall Design", National Concrete Masonry Association, Herndon, VA, 2002, 6 pp.

PCI, 1975. "Recommendations for Estimating Prestress Losses," Report of PCI Committee on Prestress Losses, *Journal of the Prestressed Concrete Institute*, Vol. 20, No. 4, Chicago, IL, July-August 1975, pp. 43-75.

Phipps and Montague, 1976. Phipps, M.E. and Montague, T.I., "The Design of Prestressed Concrete Blockwork Diaphragm Walls," *Aggregate Concrete Block Association*, England, 1976, 18 pp.

Phipps, 1992. Phipps, M.E., "The Codification of Prestressed Masonry Design," *Proceedings*, Sixth Canadian Masonry Symposium, Saskatoon, Saskatchewan, Canada, June 1992, pp. 561-572.

PTI, 1990. "Guide Specifications for Post-Tensioning Materials," *Post-Tensioning Manual*, 5th Edition, Post-Tensioning Institute, Phoenix, AZ, 1990, pp. 208-216.

Sanders et al, 1987. Sanders, D.H., Breen, J.E., and Duncan, R.R. III, "Strength and Behavior of Closely Spaced Post-Tensioned Monostrand Anchorages," Post-Tensioning Institute, Phoenix, AZ, 1987, 49 pp.

Schultz and Scolforo, 1991. Schultz, A.E. and Scolforo, M.J., "An Overview of Prestressed Masonry," *TMS Journal*, Vol. 10, No. 1, pp. 6-21, The Masonry Society, Longmont, CO, 1991.

Schultz and Scolforo, 1992(a). Schultz, A.E. and Scolforo, M.J., "Engineering Design Provisions for Prestressed Masonry, Part 1: Masonry Stresses," *TMS Journal*, Vol. 10, No. 2, pp. 29-47, The Masonry Society, Longmont, CO, 1992.

Schultz and Scolforo, 1992. Schultz, A.E., and Scolforo, M.J., "Engineering Design Provisions for Prestressed Masonry, Part 2: Steel Stresses and Other Considerations," *TMS Journal*, Vol. 10, No. 2, pp. 48-64, The Masonry Society, Longmont, CO, 1992.

Schultz et al, 2003. Schultz, A.E., Bean, J.R., and Stolarski, H. K., "Resistance of Slender Post-Tensioned Masonry Walls with Unbonded Tendons to Transverse Loading", *Proceedings*, 9th North American Masonry Conference, Clemson, SC, June 2003, The Masonry Society, Longmont, CO, pp. 463-474.

Scolforo and Borchelt, 1992. Scolforo, M.J. and Borchelt, J.G., "Design of Reinforced and Prestressed Slender Masonry Walls," *Proceedings*, Innovative Large Span Structures, The Canadian Society of Civil Engineers, Montreal, Canada, July 1992, pp. 709-720.

Shrive, 1988. Shrive, N.G., "Effects of Time Dependent Movements in Composite and Post-Tensioned Masonry," *Masonry International*, Vol. 2, No. 1, British Masonry Society, London, England, Spring 1988, pp. 1-34.

Stierwalt and Hamilton, 2000. Stierwalt, D.D. and Hamilton III, H.R., "Restraint Effectiveness in Unbonded Tendons for Post-tensioned Masonry," *ACI Structural Journal*, Nov/Dec 2000, Vol. 97, No. 6, pp. 840-848.

VSL, 1990. *Post-Tensioned Masonry Structures*, VSL International Ltd., VSL Report Series, Berne, Switzerland, 1990, 35 pp.

Woodham and Hamilton, 2003. Woodham, D.B. and Hamilton III, H.R., "Monitoring Prestress Losses in Post-Tensioned Concrete Masonry," *Proceedings*, 9th North American Masonry Conference, Clemson, SC, June 2003, The Masonry Society, Longmont, CO, pp. 488-498.

References, Chapter 11

Argudo, 2003. Argudo, Jaime, "Evaluation and Synthesis of Experimental Data for Autoclaved Aerated Concrete," MS Thesis, Department of Civil Engineering, The University of Texas at Austin, August 2003.

ASTM C 78, 2002. ASTM C78-02 *Test Method for Flexural Strength of Concrete (Using Simple Beam with Third-Point Loading)*, ASTM International, West Conshohocken, PA.

Cancino, 2003. Cancino, Ulises, "Behavior of Autoclaved Aerated Concrete Shear Walls with Low-Strength AAC," MS Thesis, Department of Civil Engineering, The University of Texas at Austin, December, 2003.

Costa et al, 2011. Costa A., Penna A., Maganes G. "Seismic Performance of Autoclaved Aerated Concrete (AAC) Masonry: From Experimental Testing of the In-plane Capacity of Walls to Building Response Simulation." The Journal of Earthquake Engineering, V 15, No. 1, January 2011, pp. 1-31.

Forero and Klingner, 2011. Forero M.H. and Klingner R.E., "Interface Shear Transfer between Grout and AAC Masonry." Proceedings Eleventh North American Masonry Conference, Minneapolis, MN, June 2011, The Masonry Society, Longmont, CO.

Fouad, 2002. Fouad, Fouad; Dembowski, Joel; Newman, David, "Material Properties and Structural Behavior of Plain and Reinforced Components," Department of Civil and Environmental Engineering at The University of Alabama at Birmingham, February 28, 2002.

Kingsley et al, 1985. Kingsley, G.R., Tulin, L. G. and Noland, J.L., "The Influence of Water Content and Unit Absorption Properties on Grout Compressive Strength and Bond Strength in Hollow Clay Unit Masonry," *Proceedings*, 3rd North American Masonry Conference, The Masonry Society, Longmont, CO, 1985, pp. 7-1 through 7-12.

Tanner et al, 2005(a). Tanner, J.E., Varela, J.L., Klingner, R.E., "Design and Seismic Testing of a Two-story Full-scale Autoclaved Aerated Concrete (AAC) Assemblage Specimen," *Structures Journal*, American Concrete Institute, Farmington Hills, Michigan, Vol. 102, No. 1, January - February 2005, pp. 114-119.

Tanner et al, 2005(b). Tanner, J.E., Varela, J.L., Klingner, R.E., Brightman M. J. and Cancino, U., "Seismic Testing of Autoclaved Aerated Concrete (AAC) Shear Walls: A Comprehensive Review," *Structures Journal*, American Concrete Institute, Farmington Hills, Michigan, Vol. 102, No. 3, May - June 2005, pp. 374-382.

Tanner et al, 2011. Tanner J.E., Varela, J.L., Klingner R.E., "Validation of Material Properties and Masonry Standards Joint Committee Code Provisions for Autoclaved Aerated Concrete Masonry." Proceedings Eleventh North American Minneapolis, MN, June 2011, The Masonry Society, Longmont, CO.

Varela et al, 2006. Varela, J.L., Tanner, J.E. and Klingner, R.E., "Development of Seismic Force-Reduction and Displacement Amplification Factors for AAC Structures," *EERI Spectra*, Vol. 22, No. 1, February 2006, pp. 267-286.

Vratsanou and Langer, 2001. Vratsanou, V. and Langer, P., "Untersuchung des Schubtragverhaltens von Wänden aus Porenbeton-Plansteinmauerwerk" (Research on Shear Behavior of Aerated Concrete Masonry Walls), Mauerwerk, Vol. 5, No. 6, 2001, pp. 210-215.

References, Chapter 12

ACI 524R, 1993. Guide to Portland Cement Plastering, ACI 524R-93, American Concrete Institute, Farmington Hills, MI, 1993.

BIA, 2000. BIA E&R Digest on Accent Bands in Brick Construction, Brick Industry Association, Reston, VA, August 2000.

BIA TN 18A, 2006. BIA Technical Notes 18A Accommodating Brickwork Expansion, Brick Industry Association, Reston, VA, November 2006.

BIA TN 28, 1966. "Brick Veneer - New Frame Construction, Existing Frame Construction," Technical Notes on Brick and Tile Construction No. 28, Structural Clay Products Institute (now Brick Industry Association), Reston, VA, August 1966.

BIA TN 28B, 2005. "Brick Veneer / Steel Stud Walls," Technical Note on Brick Construction No. 28B, Brick Industry Association, Reston, VA, December 2005.

Brown and Arumula, 1982. Brown, R.H. and Arumula, J.O., "Brick Veneer with Metal Stud Backup - An Experimental and Analytical Study," Proceedings Second North American Masonry Conference, The Masonry Society, Longmont, CO, August 1982, pp. 13-1 to 13-20.

CSA, 1984. "Connectors for Masonry," CAN3-A370-M84, Canadian Standards Association, Rexdale, Ontario, Canada, 1984.

Dickey, 1982. Dickey, W.L., "Adhered Veneer in Earthquake, Storm, and Prefabrication," *Proceedings*, 2nd North American Masonry Conference, The Masonry Society, Longmont, CO, 1982, pp. 21-1 through 21-16.

Drysdale and Suter, 1991. Drysdale, R.G. and Suter, G.T., "Exterior Wall Construction in High-Rise Buildings: Brick Veneer on Concrete, Masonry or Steel Stud Wall System," Canada Mortgage and Housing Corporation, Ottawa, Ontario, Canada, 1991.

Grimm and Klingner, 1990. Grimm, C.T. and Klingner, R.E., "Crack Probability in Brick Veneer over Steel Studs," Proceedings Fifth North American Masonry Conference, The Masonry Society, Longmont, CO, June 1990, pp. 1323-1334.

Kelly et al, 1990. Kelly, T., Goodson, M., Mayes, R., and Asher, J., "Analysis of the Behavior of Anchored Brick Veneer on Metal Stud Systems Subjected to Wind and Earthquake Forces," Proceedings Fifth North American Masonry Conference, The Masonry Society, Longmont, CO, June 1990, pp. 1359-1370.

Klingner and Torrealva , 2005. Testing of Masonry Ties, A Report to Heckmann Building Products, Inc. by Richard E. Klingner and Fernando Torrealva (The University of Texas at Austin), dated June 17, 2005

Klingner et al, 2010(a). Klingner, R. E., Shing, P. B., McGinley, W, M., McLean, D. M., Okail, H. and Jo, S., "Seismic Performance Tests of Masonry and Masonry Veneer", ASTM Masonry Symposium, June 2010.

Klingner et al, 2010(b). Klingner, R. E., P. Benson Shing, W. Mark McGinley, David I. McLean, Hussein Okail, and Seongwoo Jo, "Seismic Performance Tests of Masonry and Masonry Veneer," *Journal of ASTM International*, Vol. 7, No. 3, ASTM International, West Conshohocken, PA, January 2010.

NCMA TEK 5-2A, 2002. NCMA TEK 5-2A: Clay and Concrete Masonry Banding Details, National Concrete Masonry Association, Herndon, VA, 2002.

NCMA TEK 16-3A, 1995. "Structural Backup Systems for Concrete Masonry Veneers," NCMA TEK 16-3A, National Concrete Masonry Association, Herndon, VA, 1995.

NFPA TR No. 7, 1987. "The Permanent Wood Foundation System," Technical Report No. 7, National Forest Products Association (now the American Forest and Paper Association), Washington, DC, January 1987.

Reneckis and LaFave, 2009. Reneckis, D., and LaFave, J. M., "Seismic Performance of Anchored Brick Veneer," Newmark Structural Laboratory Report Series No. NSEL-016, University of Illinois, Urbana, IL, August 2009.

TCA, 1996. "Handbook for Ceramic Tile Installation," Tile Council of America, Anderson, SC, January 1996.

UBC, 1991. Uniform Building Code, International Conference of Building Officials, Whittier, CA, 1991.

References, Chapter 13

Glashaus, 1992. "WECK Glass Blocks," Glashaus Inc., Arlington Heights, IL, 1992.

NCMA, 1992. Structural Investigation of Pittsburgh Corning Glass Block Masonry, National Concrete Masonry Association Research and Development Laboratory, Herndon, VA, August 1992.

Pittsburgh Corning, 1992. "PC Glass Block Products," Installation Brochure (GB-185), Pittsburgh Corning Corp., Pittsburgh, PA, 1992.

Smolenski, 1992. Smolenski, Chester P., "A Study of Mortared PCC Glass Block Panel Lateral Load Resistance (Historical Perspective and Design Implications)," Pittsburgh Corning Corporation, Pittsburgh, PA, 1992.

UL R2556, 1995. "Fire Resistance Directory – Volume 3," File No. R2556, Underwriters Laboratories, Inc., Northbrook, IL, 1995.

References, Appendix A

ANSI, 1953. "American Standard Building Code Requirements for Masonry," (ANSI A 41.1), American National Standards Institute, New York, NY, 1953 (1970).

ASA, 1944. "American Standard Building Code Requirements for Masonry," (ASA A 41.1), American Standards Association, New York, NY, 1944.

Baker, 1909. Baker, I.O., *A Treatise on Masonry Construction*, University of Illinois, Champaign, IL, 1889, 1899, 1903. Also, 10th Edition, John Wiley & Sons, New York, NY, 1909, 745 pp.

NBS, 1924. "Recommended Minimum Requirements for Masonry Wall Construction," *Publication* No. BH6, National Bureau of Standards, Washington, DC, 1924.

NBS, 1931. "Modifications in Recommended Minimum Requirements for Masonry Wall Construction," National Bureau of Standards, Washington, DC, 1931.

SJI, 2002. "Standard Specifications and Load Tables for Steel Joists and Joist Girders", Steel Joist Institute, Myrtle Beach, SC, 2002.

References, Appendix B

Abrams et al, 1993. Abrams, D. P., Angel, R., and Uzarski, J, Transverse Strength of Damaged URM Infills," *Proceedings*, 6th North American Masonry Conference, The Masonry Society, Longmont, CO, 1993, pp. 347-358.

ASCE 41, 2006. ASCE 41-06, Seismic Rehabilitation of Existing Buildings, Structural Engineering Institute of the American Society of Civil Engineers, Reston, VA, 2006.

Chiou et al, 1999. Chiou, Y., Tzeng, J., and Liou, Y., "Experimental and Analytical Study of Masonry Infilled Frames." Journal of Structural Engineering, 1999, Vol. 125, No. 10, pp. 1109-1117.

Dawe and Seah, 1989a. Dawe, J.L, and Seah, C.K., "Behavior of masonry infilled steel frames." Canadian Journal of Civil Engineering, Ottawa, 1989, Vol. 16, pp. 865-876.

Dawe and Seah, 1989b. Dawe, J.L., and Seah, C.K., "Out-of-plane resistance of concrete masonry infilled panels." Canadian Journal of Civil Engineering, Ottawa, 1989, Vol. 16, pp. 854-864.

Flanagan and Bennett, 1999a. Flanagan, R.D., and Bennett, R.M. "In-plane behavior of structural clay tile infilled frames." Journal of Structural Engineering, ASCE, 1999, Vol. 125, No. 6, pp. 590-599.

Flanagan and Bennett, 1999b. Flanagan, R.D., and Bennett, R.M., "Arching of masonry infilled frames: comparison of analytical methods." Practice Periodical on Structural Design and Construction, ASCE, 1999, Vol. 4, No. 3, pp. 105-110.

Flanagan and Bennett, 2001. Flanagan, R.D., and Bennett, R.M., "In-plane analysis of masonry infill materials." Practice Periodical on Structural Design and Construction, ASCE, 2001, Vol. 6, No. 4, pp. 176-182.

Henderson et al, 2006. Henderson, R. C., Porter, M.L., Jones, W.D., Burdette, E.G. (2006). "Prior Out-of-plane Damage on the In-plane Behavior of Masonry Infilled Frames" *TMS Journal*, Vol. 24, No. 1, pp. 71-82, The Masonry Society, Longmont, CO, 2006.

Klingner et al, 1997. Klingner, R. E., Rubiano, N. R., Bashandy, T. and Sweeney, S., "Evaluation and Analytical Verification of Infilled Frame Test Data," *TMS Journal*, The Masonry Society, Longmont, CO, 1997, Vol. 15, No. 2, pp. 33-41.

Ravichandran, 2009. Ravichandran, S. S., "Behavior and Design of AAC Infills," Ph.D. Dissertation, The University of Texas at Austin, December 2009.

Ravichandran and Klingner, 2011a. Ravichandran, S. S. and Klingner, R. E., "Behavior of Steel Moment Frames with AAC Infills," *Proceedings*, 11th North American Masonry Conference, Minneapolis, Minnesota, June 2011, The Masonry Society, Longmont, CO.

Ravichandran and Klingner, 2011b. Ravichandran, S. S. and Klingner, R. E.,, "Seismic Design Factors for Steel Moment Frames with Masonry Infills: Part 1," *Proceedings*, 11th North American Masonry Conference, Minneapolis, Minnesota, June 2011, The Masonry Society, Longmont, CO.

Ravichandran and Klingner, 2011c. Ravichandran, S. S. and Klingner, R. E., "Seismic Design Factors for Steel Moment Frames with Masonry Infills: Part 2," *Proceedings*, 11th North American Masonry Conference, Minneapolis, Minnesota, June 2011, The Masonry Society, Longmont, CO.

Riddington, 1984. Riddington, J.R., "The influence of initial gaps on infilled frame behavior." Proceedings Insitution of Civil Engineers, 1984, Vol. 77, pp. 295-310.

Tucker, 2007. Tucker, C. (2007). "Predicting the In-plane Capacity of Masonry Infilled Frames." Ph.D. Dissertation, Tennessee Technological University, December 2007.

References, Appendix C

Lepage et al, 2011. Andres Lepage, Steve Dill, Matthew Haapala, and Reynaldo Sanchez, "Seismic Design of Reinforced Masonry Walls: Current Methods and Proposed Limit-Design Alternative," *Proceedings*, 11th North American Masonry Conference, Minneapolis, Minnesota, June 2011, The Masonry Society, Longmont, CO.

This page is intentionally left blank.

Specification for Masonry Structures
(TMS 602-13/ACI 530.1-13/ASCE 6-13)

TABLE OF CONTENTS

This page is intentionally left blank.

Specification for Masonry Structures
(TMS 602-13/ACI 530.1-13/ASCE 6-13)

SYNOPSIS

This Specification for Masonry Structures (TMS 602-13/ACI 530.1-13/ASCE 6-13) is written as a master specification and is required by Building Code Requirements for Masonry Structures (TMS 402-13/ACI 530-13/ASCE 5-13) to control materials, labor, and construction. Thus, this Specification covers minimum construction requirements for masonry in structures. Included are quality assurance requirements for materials; the placing, bonding, and anchoring of masonry; and the placement of grout and of reinforcement. This Specification may be referenced in the Project Manual. Individual project requirements may supplement the provisions of this Specification.

Keywords: AAC masonry, anchors; autoclaved aerated concrete (AAC) masonry, clay brick; clay tile; concrete block; concrete brick; construction; construction materials; curing; grout; grouting; inspection; joints; masonry; materials handling; mortars (material and placement); quality assurance and quality control; reinforcing steel; specifications; ties; tests; tolerances.

Specification and Commentary, S-iii

This page is intentionally left blank.

SPECIFICATION

PREFACE

P1. This Preface is included for explanatory purposes only; it does not form a part of Specification TMS 602-13/ACI 530.1-13/ASCE 6-13.

P2. TMS 602-13/ACI 530.1-13/ASCE 6-13 is written in the three-part section format of the Construction Specifications Institute. The language is generally imperative and terse.

P3. TMS 602-13/ACI 530.1-13/ASCE 6-13 establishes minimum construction requirements for the materials and workmanship used to construct masonry structures. It is the means by which the designer conveys to the contractor the performance expectations upon which the design is based, in accordance with Code TMS 402-13/ACI 530-13/ASCE 5-13.

P4. The Checklists and the Forward to Specification Checklists are non-mandatory and do not form part of Specification TMS 602-13/ACI 530.1/ASCE 6-13.

.

COMMENTARY

COMMENTARY

Part 1 of the *Building Code Requirements for Masonry Structures* (TMS 402-13/ACI 530-13/ASCE 5-13) makes the *Specification for Masonry Structures* (TMS 602-13/ACI 530.1-13/ASCE 6-13) an integral part of the Code. TMS 602-13/ACI 530.1-13/ASCE 6-13 Specification sets minimum construction requirements regarding the materials used in and the erection of masonry structures. Specifications are written to set minimum acceptable levels of performance for the contractor. This commentary is directed to the Architect/Engineer writing the project specifications.

This Commentary explains some of the topics that the Masonry Standards Joint Committee (MSJC) considered in developing the provisions of this Specification. Comments on specific provisions are made under the corresponding article numbers of this Specification.

Specification TMS 602-13/ACI 530.1-13/ASCE 6-13 is a reference standard that the Architect/Engineer may cite in the contract documents for any project. It establishes the minimum construction requirements to assure compliance of the construction with the Code-based design. Owners, through their representatives (Architect/Engineer), may write requirements into contract documents that are more stringent than those of TMS 602-13/ACI 530.1-13/ASCE 6-13. As an example, requirements to satisfy visual aesthetics may be added in a project specification. This can be accomplished with supplemental specifications to this Specification.

The contractor should not be required through contract documents to comply with the Code or to assume responsibility regarding design (Code) requirements. The Code is not intended to be made a part of the contract documents.

The Preface and the Foreword to Specification Checklists contain information that explains the scope of this Specification. The Checklists are a summary of the Articles that require a decision by the Architect/Engineer preparing the contract documents. Project specifications should include the information that relates to those Checklist items that are pertinent to the project. Each project requires response to the mandatory requirements.

This page is intentionally left blank.

PART 1 — GENERAL

SPECIFICATION

1.1 — Summary

1.1 A. This Specification addresses requirements for materials and construction of masonry structures. SI values shown in parentheses are provided for information only and are not part of this Specification.

1.1 B. The Specification supplements the legally adopted building code and governs the construction of masonry elements designed in accordance with the Code. In areas without a legally adopted building code, this Specification defines the minimum acceptable standards of construction practice.

1.1 C. This article addresses the furnishing and construction of masonry including the following:

1. Furnishing and placing masonry units, grout, mortar, masonry lintels, sills, copings, through-wall flashing, and connectors.

2. Furnishing, erecting and maintaining of bracing, forming, scaffolding, rigging, and shoring.

3. Furnishing and installing other equipment for constructing masonry.

4. Cleaning masonry and removing surplus material and waste.

5. Installing lintels, nailing blocks, inserts, window and door frames, connectors, and construction items to be built into the masonry, and building in vent pipes, conduits and other items furnished and located by other trades.

1.2 — Definitions

A. *Acceptable, accepted* — Acceptable to or accepted by the Architect/Engineer.

B. *Architect/Engineer* — The architect, engineer, architectural firm, engineering firm, or architectural and engineering firm, issuing drawings and specifications, or administering the work under project specifications and project drawings, or both.

C. *Area, gross cross-sectional* — The area delineated by the out-to-out dimensions of masonry in the plane under consideration.

D. *Area, net cross-sectional* — The area of masonry units, grout, and mortar crossed by the plane under consideration based on out-to-out dimensions.

E. *Autoclaved aerated concrete* — low-density cementitious product of calcium silicate hydrates.

COMMENTARY

1.1 — Summary

1.1 C. The scope of the work is outlined in this article. All of these tasks and materials will not appear in every project.

1.2 — Definitions

For consistent application of this Specification, it is necessary to define terms that have particular meaning in this Specification. The definitions given are for use in application of this Specification only and do not always correspond to ordinary usage. Other terms are defined in referenced documents and those definitions are applicable. If any term is defined in both this Specification and in a referenced document, the definition in this Specification applies. Referenced documents include ASTM standards. Terminology standards include ASTM C1232 Standard Terminology of Masonry and ASTM C1180 Standard Terminology of Mortar and Grout for Unit Masonry. Definitions have been coordinated between the Code and Specification.

SPECIFICATION

1.2 — Definitions (Continued)

F. *Autoclaved aerated concrete (AAC) masonry —* Autoclaved aerated concrete units, manufactured without reinforcement, set on a mortar leveling bed, bonded with thin-bed mortar, placed with or without grout, and placed with or without reinforcement.

G. *Bond beam —* A horizontal, sloped, or stepped element that is fully grouted, has longitudinal bar reinforcement, and is constructed within a masonry wall.

COMMENTARY

G. *Bond beam —* This reinforced member is usually constructed horizontally, but may be sloped or stepped to match an adjacent roof, for example, as shown in Figure CC-2.2-2.

Notes:

(1) Masonry wall
(2) Fully grouted bond beam with reinforcement
(3) Sloped top of wall
(4) Length of noncontact lap splice
(5) Spacing between bars in noncontact lap splice

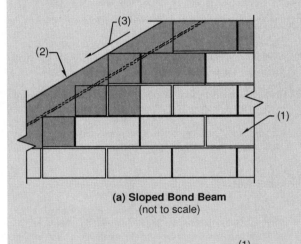

(a) Sloped Bond Beam
(not to scale)

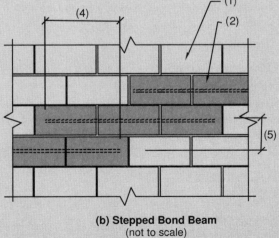

(b) Stepped Bond Beam
(not to scale)

Figure SC-1— Sloped and stepped bond beams

SPECIFICATION

1.2 — Definitions (Continued)

H. *Bonded prestressing tendon* — Prestressing tendon that is encapsulated by prestressing grout in a corrugated duct that is bonded to the surrounding masonry through grouting.

I. *Cleanouts* — Openings that are sized and spaced to allow removal of debris from the bottom of the grout space.

J. *Collar joint* — Vertical longitudinal space between wythes of masonry or between masonry and back up construction, which is permitted to be filled with mortar or grout.

K. *Compressive strength of masonry* — Maximum compressive force resisted per unit of net cross-sectional area of masonry, determined by testing masonry prisms; or a function of individual masonry units, mortar and grout in accordance with the provisions of this Specification.

L. *Contract Documents* — Documents establishing the required Work, and including in particular, the Project Drawings and Project Specifications.

M. *Contractor* — The person, firm, or corporation with whom the Owner enters into an agreement for construction of the Work.

N. *Cover, grout* — thickness of grout surrounding the outer surface of embedded reinforcement, anchor, or tie.

O. *Cover, masonry* — thickness of masonry units, mortar, and grout surrounding the outer surface of embedded reinforcement, anchor, or tie.

P. *Cover, mortar* — thickness of mortar surrounding the outer surface of embedded reinforcement, anchor, or tie.

Q. *Dimension, nominal* — The specified dimension plus an allowance for the joints with which the units are to be laid. Nominal dimensions are usually stated in whole numbers. Thickness is given first, followed by height and then length.

R. *Dimensions, specified* — Dimensions specified for the manufacture or construction of a unit, joint, or element.

S. *Glass unit masonry* — Non-load-bearing masonry composed of glass units bonded by mortar.

T. *Grout* — (1) A plastic mixture of cementitious materials, aggregates, and water, with or without admixtures, initially produced to pouring consistency without segregation of the constituents during placement. (2) The hardened equivalent of such mixtures.

U. *Grout, self-consolidating* — A highly fluid and stable grout typically with admixtures, that remains homogeneous when placed and does not require puddling or vibration for consolidation.

COMMENTARY

Q & R. The permitted tolerances for units are given in the appropriate materials standards. Permitted tolerances for joints and masonry construction are given in this Specification. Nominal dimensions are usually used to identify the size of a masonry unit. The thickness or width is given first, followed by height and length. Nominal dimensions are normally given in whole numbers nearest to the specified dimensions. Specified dimensions are most often used for design calculations.

SPECIFICATION

1.2 — Definitions (Continued)

V. *Grout lift* — An increment of grout height within a total grout pour. A grout pour consists of one or more grout lifts.

W. *Grout pour* — The total height of masonry to be grouted prior to erection of additional masonry. A grout pour consists of one or more grout lifts.

X. *Inspection, continuous* — The Inspection Agency's full-time observation of work by being present in the area where the work is being performed.

Y. *Inspection, periodic* — The Inspection Agency's part-time or intermittent observation of work during construction by being present in the area where the work has been or is being performed, and observation upon completion of the work.

Z. *Masonry, partially grouted* — Construction in which designated cells or spaces are filled with grout, while other cells or spaces are ungrouted.

AA. *Masonry unit, hollow* — A masonry unit with net cross-sectional area of less than 75 percent of its gross cross-sectional area when measured in any plane parallel to the surface containing voids.

AB. *Masonry unit, solid* — A masonry unit with net cross-sectional area of 75 percent or more of its gross cross-sectional area when measured in every plane parallel to the surface containing voids.

AC. *Mean daily temperature* — The average daily temperature of temperature extremes predicted by a local weather bureau for the next 24 hours.

AD. *Minimum daily temperature* — The low temperature forecast by a local weather bureau to occur within the next 24 hours.

AE. *Minimum/maximum (not less than . . . not more than)* — Minimum or maximum values given in this Specification are absolute. Do not construe that tolerances allow lowering a minimum or increasing a maximum.

AF. *Otherwise required* — Specified differently in requirements supplemental to this Specification.

AG. *Owner* — The public body or authority, corporation, association, partnership, or individual for whom the Work is provided.

AH. *Partition wall* — An interior wall without structural function.

COMMENTARY

X & Y. The Inspection Agency is required to be on the project site whenever masonry tasks requiring continuous inspection are in progress. During construction requiring periodic inspection, the Inspection Agency is only required to be on the project site intermittently, and is required to observe completed work. The frequency of periodic inspections should be defined by the Architect/Engineer as part of the quality assurance plan, and should be consistent with the complexity and size of the project.

SPECIFICATION

1.2 — Definitions (Continued)

AI. *Post-tensioning* — Method of prestressing in which prestressing tendons are tensioned after the masonry has been placed.

AJ. *Prestressed masonry* — Masonry in which internal compressive stresses have been introduced by prestressed tendons to counteract potential tensile stresses resulting from applied loads.

AK. *Prestressing grout* — A cementitious mixture used to encapsulate bonded prestressing tendons.

AL. *Prestressing tendon* — Steel element such as wire, bar, or strand, or a bundle of such elements, used to impart prestress to masonry.

AM. *Pretensioning* — Method of prestressing in which prestressing tendons are tensioned before the transfer of stress into the masonry.

AN. *Prism* — An assemblage of masonry units and mortar, with or without grout, used as a test specimen for determining properties of the masonry.

AO. *Project Drawings* — The Drawings that, along with the Project Specifications, complete the descriptive information for constructing the Work required or referred to in the Contract Documents.

AP. *Project Specifications* — The written documents that specify requirements for a project in accordance with the service parameters and other specific criteria established by the Owner or his agent.

AQ. *Quality assurance* — The administrative and procedural requirements established by the Contract Documents to assure that constructed masonry is in compliance with the Contract Documents.

AR. *Reinforcement* — Nonprestressed steel reinforcement.

AS. *Running bond* — The placement of masonry units such that head joints in successive courses are horizontally offset at least one-quarter the unit length.

AT. *Slump flow* — The circular spread of plastic self-consolidating grout, which is evaluated in accordance with ASTM C1611/C1611M.

AU. *Specified compressive strength of masonry, f'_m* — Minimum compressive strength, expressed as force per unit of net cross-sectional area, required of the masonry used in construction by the Project Specifications or Project Drawings, and upon which the project design is based.

COMMENTARY

AS. *Running bond* — The Code requires horizontal reinforcement in masonry that is not laid in running bond. Stack bond, which is commonly interpreted as a pattern with aligned head joints, is one bond pattern that is required to be reinforced horizontally

SPECIFICATION

1.2 — Definitions (Continued)

AV. *Stone masonry* — Masonry composed of field, quarried, or cast stone units bonded by mortar.

    1. *Stone masonry, ashlar* — Stone masonry composed of rectangular units having sawed, dressed, or squared bed surfaces and bonded by mortar.

    2. *Stone masonry, rubble* — Stone masonry composed of irregular shaped units bonded by mortar.

AW. *Submit, submitted* — Submit, submitted to the Architect/Engineer for review.

AX. *Tendon anchorage* — In post-tensioning, a device used to anchor the prestressing tendon to the masonry or concrete member; in pretensioning, a device used to anchor the prestressing tendon during hardening of masonry mortar, grout, prestressing grout, or concrete.

AY. *Tendon coupler* — A device for connecting two tendon ends, thereby transferring the prestressing force from end to end.

AZ. *Tendon jacking force* — Temporary force exerted by a device that introduces tension into prestressing tendons.

BA. *Unbonded prestressing tendon* — Prestressing tendon that is not bonded to masonry.

BB. *Veneer, adhered* — Masonry veneer secured to and supported by the backing through adhesion.

BC. *Visual stability index (VSI)* — An index, defined in ASTM C1611/C1611M, that qualitatively indicates the stability of self-consolidating grout

BD. *Wall* — A vertical element with a horizontal length to thickness ratio greater than 3, used to enclose space.

BE. *Wall, load-bearing* — A wall supporting vertical loads greater than 200 lb per linear foot (2919 N/m) in addition to its own weight.

BF. *Wall, masonry bonded hollow* — A multiwythe wall built with masonry units arranged to provide an air space between the wythes and with the wythes bonded together with masonry units.

BG. *When required* — Specified in requirements supplemental to this Specification.

BH. *Work* — The furnishing and performance of equipment, services, labor, and materials required by the Contract Documents for the construction of masonry for the project or part of project under consideration.

BI. *Wythe* — Each continuous vertical section of a wall, one masonry unit in thickness.

SPECIFICATION

1.3 — Reference standards

Standards referred to in this Specification are listed below with their serial designations, including year of adoption or revision, and are declared to be part of this Specification as if fully set forth in this document except as modified here.

American Concrete Institute

A. ACI 117-10 Standard Specifications for Tolerances for Concrete Construction and Materials

American National Standards Institute

B. ANSI A 137.1-08 Standard Specification for Ceramic Tile

ASTM International

C. ASTM A36/A36M-08 Standard Specification for Carbon Structural Steel

D. ASTM A82/A82M-07 Standard Specification for Steel Wire, Plain, for Concrete Reinforcement

E. ASTM A123/A123M-12 Standard Specification for Zinc (Hot-Dip Galvanized) Coatings on Iron and Steel Products

F. ASTM A153/A153M-09 Standard Specification for Zinc Coating (Hot-Dip) on Iron and Steel Hardware

G. ASTM A185/A185M-07 Standard Specification for Steel Welded Wire Reinforcement, Plain, for Concrete

H. ASTM A240/A240M-12a Standard Specification for Chromium and Chromium-Nickel Stainless Steel Plate, Sheet, and Strip for Pressure Vessels and for General Applications

I. ASTM A307-12 Standard Specification for Carbon Steel Bolts, Studs, and Threaded Rod, 60,000 PSI Tensile Strength

J. ASTM A416/A416M-12a Standard Specification for Steel Strand, Uncoated Seven-Wire for Prestressed Concrete

K. ASTM A421/A421M-10 Standard Specification for Uncoated Stress-Relieved Steel Wire for Prestressed Concrete

L. ASTM A480/A480M-12 Standard Specification for General Requirements for Flat-Rolled Stainless and Heat-Resisting Steel Plate, Sheet, and Strip

M. ASTM A496/A496M-07 Standard Specification for Steel Wire, Deformed, for Concrete Reinforcement

COMMENTARY

1.3 — Reference standards

This list of standards includes material specifications, sampling, test methods, detailing requirements, design procedures, and classifications. Standards produced by ASTM International (ASTM) are referenced whenever possible. Material manufacturers and testing laboratories are familiar with ASTM standards that are the result of a consensus process. In the few cases where standards do not exist for materials or methods, the committee developed requirements. Specific dates are given because changes to the standards alter this Specification. Many of these standards require compliance with additional standards.

Contact information for these organizations is given below:

American Concrete Institute
38800 Country Club Drive
Farmington Hills, MI 48331
www.aci-int.org

American National Standards Institute
25 West 43rd Street,
New York, NY 10036
www.ansi.org

ASTM International
100 Barr Harbor Drive
West Conshohocken, PA 19428-2959
www.astm.org

American Welding Society
8669 NW 36th Street, Suite 130
Miami, Florida 33166-6672
www.aws.org

Federal Test Method Standard from:
U.S. Army General Material and Parts Center
Petroleum Field Office (East)
New Cumberland Army Depot
New Cumberland, PA 17070

SPECIFICATION

1.3 — Reference standards (Continued)

N.   ASTM A497/A497M-07   Standard Specification for Steel Welded Wire Reinforcement, Deformed, for Concrete

O.   ASTM A510/A510M-11 Standard Specification for General Requirements for Wire Rods and Coarse Round Wire, Carbon Steel

P.   ASTM A580/A580M-12a Standard Specification for Stainless Steel Wire

Q.   ASTM A615/A615M-12 Standard Specification for Deformed and Plain Carbon-Steel Bars for Concrete Reinforcement

R.   ASTM A641/A641M-09a Standard Specification for Zinc-Coated (Galvanized) Carbon Steel Wire

S.   ASTM A653/A653M-11 Standard Specification for Steel Sheet, Zinc-Coated (Galvanized) or Zinc-Iron Alloy-Coated (Galvannealed) by the Hot-Dip Process

T.   ASTM A666-10 Standard Specification for Annealed or Cold-Worked Austenitic Stainless Steel Sheet, Strip, Plate, and Flat Bar

U.   ASTM A706/A706M-09b Standard Specification for Low-Alloy Steel Deformed and Plain Bars for Concrete Reinforcement

V.   ASTM A722/A722M-12 Standard Specification for Uncoated High-Strength Steel Bars for Prestressing Concrete

W.   ASTM A767/A767M-09   Standard Specification for Zinc-Coated (Galvanized) Steel Bars for Concrete Reinforcement

X.   ASTM A775/A775M-07b Standard Specification for Epoxy-Coated Steel Reinforcing Bars

Y.   ASTM A884/A884M-12 Standard Specification for Epoxy-Coated Steel Wire and Welded Wire Reinforcement

Z.   ASTM A899-91(2007) Standard Specification for Steel Wire, Epoxy-Coated

AA.   ASTM A951/A951M-11 Standard Specification for Steel Wire for Masonry Joint Reinforcement

AB.   ASTM A996/A996M-09b Standard Specification for Rail-Steel and Axle-Steel Deformed Bars for Concrete Reinforcement

AC.   ASTM A1008/A1008M-12a Standard Specification for Steel, Sheet, Cold-Rolled, Carbon, Structural, High-Strength Low-Alloy, High-Strength Low-Alloy with Improved Formability, Solution Hardened, and Bake Hardenable

AD.   ASTM B117-11   Standard Practice for Operating Salt Spray (Fog) Apparatus

COMMENTARY

SPECIFICATION

1.3 — Reference standards (Continued)

AE. ASTM C34-12 Standard Specification for Structural Clay Load-Bearing Wall Tile

AF. ASTM C55-11 Standard Specification for Concrete Building Brick

AG. ASTM C56-12 Standard Specification for Structural Clay Nonloadbearing Tile

AH. ASTM C62-12 Standard Specification for Building Brick (Solid Masonry Units Made from Clay or Shale)

AI. ASTM C67-12 Standard Test Methods for Sampling and Testing Brick and Structural Clay Tile

AJ. ASTM C73-10 Standard Specification for Calcium Silicate Brick (Sand-Lime Brick)

AK. ASTM C90-12 Standard Specification for Loadbearing Concrete Masonry Units

AL. ASTM C109/C109M-12 Standard Test Method for Compressive Strength of Hydraulic Cement Mortars (Using 2-in. or [50-mm] Cube Specimens)

AM. ASTM C126-12a Standard Specification for Ceramic Glazed Structural Clay Facing Tile, Facing Brick, and Solid Masonry Units

AN. ASTM C129-11 Standard Specification for Nonloadbearing Concrete Masonry Units

AO. ASTM C143/C143M-12 Standard Test Method for Slump of Hydraulic-Cement Concrete

AP. ASTM C144-11 Standard Specification for Aggregate for Masonry Mortar

AQ. ASTM C150/C150M-12 Standard Specification for Portland Cement

AR. ASTM C212-10 Standard Specification for Structural Clay Facing Tile

AS. ASTM C216-12a Standard Specification for Facing Brick (Solid Masonry Units Made from Clay or Shale)

AT. ASTM C270-12a Standard Specification for Mortar for Unit Masonry

AU. ASTM C476-10 Standard Specification for Grout for Masonry

AV. ASTM C482-02 (2009) Standard Test Method for Bond Strength of Ceramic Tile to Portland Cement Paste

AW. ASTM C503/C503M-10 Standard Specification for Marble Dimension Stone

AX. ASTM C568/C568M-10 Standard Specification for Limestone Dimension Stone

COMMENTARY

SPECIFICATION

COMMENTARY

1.3 — Reference standards (Continued)

AY. ASTM C615/C615M-11 Standard Specification for Granite Dimension Stone

AZ. ASTM C616/C616M-10 Standard Specification for Quartz-Based Dimension Stone

BA. ASTM C629/C629-10 Standard Specification for Slate Dimension Stone

BB. ASTM C652-12a Standard Specification for Hollow Brick (Hollow Masonry Units Made from Clay or Shale)

BC. ASTM C744-11 Standard Specification for Prefaced Concrete and Calcium Silicate Masonry Units

BD. ASTM C901-10 Standard Specification for Prefabricated Masonry Panels

BE. ASTM C920-11 Standard Specification for Elastomeric Joint Sealants

BF. ASTM C1006-07 Standard Test Method for Splitting Tensile Strength of Masonry Units

BG. ASTM C1019-11 Standard Test Method for Sampling and Testing Grout

BH. ASTM C1072-12 Standard Tests Method for Measurement of Masonry Flexural Bond Strength

BI. ASTM C1088-12 Standard Specification for Thin Veneer Brick Units Made from Clay or Shale

BJ. ASTM C1314-12 Standard Test Method for Compressive Strength of Masonry Prisms

BK. ASTM C1405-12 Standard Specification for Glazed Brick (Single Fired, Brick Units)

BL. ASTM C1532/C1532M-12 Standard Practice for Selection, Removal and Shipment of Manufactured Masonry Units and Masonry Specimens from Existing Construction

BM. ASTM C1611/C1611M-09b[e1] Standard Test Method for Slump Flow of Self-Consolidating Concrete

BN. ASTM C1634-11 Standard Specification for Concrete Facing Brick

BO. ASTM C 1660-10 Standard Specification for Thin-bed Mortar for Autoclaved Aerated Concrete (AAC) Masonry

BP. ASTM C1691-11 Standard Specification for Unreinforced Autoclaved Aerated Concrete (AAC) Masonry Units

BQ. ASTM C 1692-11 Standard Practice for Construction and Testing of Autoclaved Aerated Concrete (AAC) Masonry.

SPECIFICATION

COMMENTARY

1.3 — Reference standards (Continued)

BR. ASTM D92-12a Standard Test Method for Flash and Fire Points by Cleveland Open Cup Tester

BS. ASTM D95-05(2010) Standard Test Method for Water in Petroleum Products and Bituminous Materials by Distillation

BT. ASTM D512-12 Standard Test Methods for Chloride Ion in Water

BU. ASTM D566-02(2009) Standard Test Method for Dropping Point of Lubricating Grease

BV. ASTM D610-08(2012) Standard Practice for Evaluating Degree of Rusting on Painted Steel Surfaces

BW. ASTM D638-10 Standard Test Method for Tensile Properties of Plastics

BX. ASTM D994/D994M-11 Standard Specification for Preformed Expansion Joint Filler for Concrete (Bituminous Type)

BY. ASTM D1056-07 Standard Specification for Flexible Cellular Materials — Sponge or Expanded Rubber

BZ. ASTM D1187/D1187M-97 (2011)$^{\varepsilon 1}$ Standard Specification for Asphalt-Base Emulsions for Use as Protective Coatings for Metal

CA. ASTM D1227-95 (2007) Standard Specification for Emulsified Asphalt Used as a Protective Coating for Roofing

CB. ASTM D2000-12 Standard Classification System for Rubber Products in Automotive Applications

CC. ASTM D2265-06 Standard Test Method for Dropping Point of Lubricating Grease Over Wide Temperature Range

CD. ASTM D2287-12 Standard Specification for Nonrigid Vinyl Chloride Polymer and Copolymer Molding and Extrusion Compounds

CE. ASTM D4289-03 (2008) Standard Test Method for Elastomer Compatibility of Lubricating Greases and Fluids

CF. ASTM E72-10 Standard Test Methods of Conducting Strength Tests of Panels for Building Construction

CG. ASTM E328-02 (2008) Standard Test Methods for Stress Relaxation Tests for Materials and Structures

CH. ASTM E518/E518M-10 Standard Test Methods for Flexural Bond Strength of Masonry

CI. ASTM E519/E519M-10 Standard Test Method for Diagonal Tension (Shear) in Masonry Assemblages

SPECIFICATION

1.3 — Reference standards (Continued)

CJ. ASTM F959-09 Standard Specification for Compressible-Washer-Type Direct Tension Indicators for Use with Structural Fasteners

CK. ASTM F959M-07 Standard Specification for Compressible-Washer-Type Direct Tension Indicators for Use with Structural Fasteners [Metric]

American Welding Society

CL. AWS D 1.4/D1.4M:2011 Structural Welding Code – Reinforcing Steel

Federal Test Method Standard

CM. FTMS 791B (1974) Oil Separation from Lubricating Grease (Static Technique). Federal Test Method Standard from the U.S. Army General Material and Parts Center, Petroleum Field Office (East), New Cumberland Army Depot, New Cumberland, PA 17070

1.4 — System description

1.4 A. *Compressive strength requirements* — Compressive strength of masonry in each masonry wythe and grouted collar joint shall equal or exceed the applicable f'_m or f'_{AAC}. For partially grouted masonry, the compressive strength of both the grouted and ungrouted masonry shall equal or exceed the applicable f'_m. At the transfer of prestress, the compressive strength of the masonry shall equal or exceed f'_{mi}.

1.4 B. *Compressive strength determination*

1. *Methods for determination of compressive strength* — Determine the compressive strength for each wythe by the unit strength method or by the prism test method as specified here.

COMMENTARY

1.4 — System description

1.4 A. *Compressive strength requirements* — Design is based on a certain f'_m or f'_{AAC} and this compressive strength value must be achieved or exceeded. In a multiwythe wall designed as a composite wall, the compressive strength of masonry for each wythe or grouted collar joint must equal or exceed f'_m or f'_{AAC}.

1.4 B. *Compressive strength determination*

1. *Methods for determination of compressive strength* — Two methods are permitted to verify compliance with the specified compressive strength of masonry during construction: the unit strength method and the prism test method. The unit strength method has several advantages. It is less expensive than the prism test method, and it eliminates the possibility of unrepresentative low values due to errors in the construction, transport and testing of prisms. The prism test method also has advantages. Although it often requires specialized testing equipment that may not be readily available in all areas, it generally provides higher values than the unit strength method, when properly executed. Local practices and jobsite conditions may favor one method over the other.

The Specification permits the contractor to select the method of verifying compliance with the specified compressive strength of masonry, unless a method is stipulated in the Project Specifications or Project Drawings.

SPECIFICATION

2. *Unit strength method*

a. *Clay masonry* — Use Table 1 to determine the compressive strength of clay masonry based on the strength of the units and the type of mortar specified. The following requirements apply to masonry:

1) Units are sampled and tested to verify conformance with ASTM C62, ASTM C216, or ASTM C652.

2) Thickness of bed joints does not exceed $^5/_8$ in. (15.9 mm).

3) For grouted masonry, the grout conforms to Article 2.2:

COMMENTARY

2. *Unit strength method* — Compliance with the requirement for f'_m, based on the compressive strength of masonry units, grout, and mortar type, is permitted instead of prism testing.

The influence of mortar joint thickness is noted by the maximum joint thickness. Grout strength greater than or equal to f'_m fulfills the requirements of Specification Article 1.4 A and Code Section 3.1.6.1.

a. *Clay masonry* — The original values of net area compressive strength of clay masonry in Table 1 were derived from research conducted by the Structural Clay Products Institute (SCPI, 1969).

The original values were based on testing of solid clay masonry units (SCPI, 1969) and portland cement-lime mortar. Further testing (Brown and Borchelt, 1990) has shown that the values are applicable for hollow and solid clay masonry units with all mortar types. A plot of the data is shown in Figure SC-2.

SCPI (1969) uses a height-to-thickness ratio of five as a basis to establish prism compressive strength. The Code uses a different method to design for axial stress so it was necessary to change the basic prism *h/t* ratio to two. This corresponds to the *h/t* ratio used for concrete masonry in the Code and for all masonry in other codes. The net effect is to increase the net area compressive strength of brick masonry as shown in Table 1 by 22 percent over that in Figure SC-2.

Table 1 — Compressive strength of masonry based on the compressive strength of clay masonry units and type of mortar used in construction

Net area compressive strength of clay masonry, psi (MPa)	Net area compressive strength of clay masonry units, psi (MPa)	
	Type M or S mortar	**Type N mortar**
1,000 (6.90)	1,700 (11.72)	2,100 (14.48)
1,500 (10.34)	3,350 (23.10)	4,150 (28.61)
2,000 (13.79)	4,950 (34.13)	6,200 (42.75)
2,500 (17.24)	6,600 (45.51)	8,250 (56.88)
3,000 (20.69)	8,250 (56.88)	10,300 (71.02)
3,500 (24.13)	9,900 (68.26)	—
4,000 (27.58)	11,500 (79.29)	—

COMMENTARY

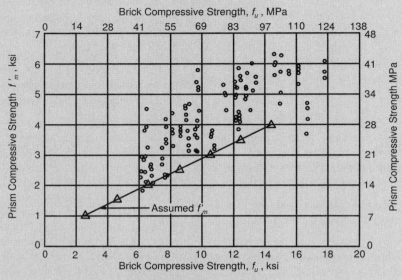

(a) Prism Strength vs. Brick Strength
(Type S Mortar, Commercial Laboratories)

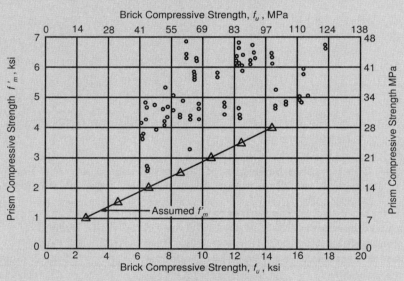

(b) Prism Strength vs. Brick Strength
(Type S Mortar, SCPI Laboratory)

*Figure SC-2 — Compressive strength of masonry versus clay masonry unit strength
(See Commentary Article 1.4 B.2.a)*

SPECIFICATION

1.4 B.2. *Unit strength method* (Continued)

b. *Concrete masonry* — Use Table 2 to determine the compressive strength of concrete masonry based on the strength of the unit and type of mortar specified. The following Articles must be met:

1) Units are sampled and tested to verify conformance with, ASTM C90.

2) Thickness of bed joints does not exceed $^5/_8$ in. (15.9 mm).

3) For grouted masonry, the grout conforms to Article 2.2.

COMMENTARY

b. *Concrete masonry* — Prior to the 2013 Specification, the standardized correlations between unit compressive strength, mortar type, and resulting assembly compressive strength of concrete masonry were established using prism test results collected from the 1950s through the 1980s. The result was a database of prism compressive strengths with statistically high variability, which when introduced into the Specification, drove the lower bound design values between unit, mortar, and prism to very conservative values. The reasons for the inherent historical conservatism in the unit strength table are twofold: 1) When originally introduced, the testing procedures and equipment used to develop the prism test data were considerably less refined than they are today. Changes introduced into ASTM C1314, particularly requirements for stiffer/thicker bearing platens on testing equipment, produce more consistent, repeatable compressive strength results. 2) Previous testing procedures either did not control the construction, curing, and testing of masonry prisms, or permitted many procedures for doing so. As a result, a single set of materials could produce prism test results that varied significantly depending upon how the prisms were constructed, cured, and tested. Often, a field-constructed and field-cured prism would test to a lower value than a laboratory-constructed and laboratory-cured prism. Consequently, the compressive-strength values for concrete masonry prisms used to develop historical versions of the unit strength tables are not directly comparable to the compressive-strength values that would be obtained today.

Table 2 — Compressive strength of masonry based on the compressive strength of concrete masonry units and type of mortar used in construction

Net area compressive strength of concrete masonry, psi (MPa)[1]	Net area compressive strength of ASTM C90 concrete masonry units, psi (MPa)	
	Type M or S mortar	Type N mortar
1,700 (11.72)	---	1,900 (13.10)
1,900 (13.10)	1,900 (13.10)	2,350 (16.20)
2,000 (13.79)	2,000 (13.79)	2,650 (18.27)
2,250 (15.51)	2,600 (17.93)	3,400 (23.44)
2,500 (17.24)	3,250 (22.41)	4,350 (28.96)
2,750 (18.96)	3,900 (26.89)	-----
3,000 (20.69)	4,500 (31.03)	-----

[1]For units of less than 4 in. (102 mm) nominal height, use 85 percent of the values listed.

SPECIFICATION

1.4 B.2.b *Unit strength method* (Continued)

COMMENTARY

In 2010, the National Concrete Masonry Association (NCMA, 2012) began compiling prism test data to create a new database that would permit the development of a new unit strength table for concrete masonry that would better represent results from current prism tests. Concrete brick (ASTM C55 and ASTM C1634) are not included in Table 2 because the NCMA research program did not include these units. Most concrete brick are used in applications not requiring that f'_m be specified (such as veneer). Where f'_m is required for concrete brick applications, prism testing is required to verify the compressive strength.

The unit strength method was generated using prism test data as shown in Figures SC-3 and SC-4. The values in Table 2 are based on a consistent statistical criterion, with slight modifications based on engineering judgment.

For each specified unit strength and mortar type, the resulting masonry assembly compressive strengths were assumed to be normally distributed. Using the NCMA data for each specified unit strength and mortar type, and including the effects of sample size, the 75th percent confidence level on the 10-percentile value was calculated. That is, the value that would be expected to exceed the lower 10% fractile of the entire population 75% of the time. The criterion gives results that are reasonably consistent with other codes and standards (Bennett, 2010). Choosing the 10-percentile value results in an approximately 1% probability that the average of three prism test specimens will be less than the tabulated value.

For a given unit strength and mortar type, the resulting masonry assembly compressive strength also depends on the height of the units. The lateral expansion of the unit due to unit and mortar incompatibility increases with reduced unit height (Drysdale et al, 1999). A reduction factor in the compressive strength of masonry is required for masonry constructed of units less than 4 in. (102 mm) in nominal height, but need not be applied to masonry in which occasional units are cut to fit.

COMMENTARY

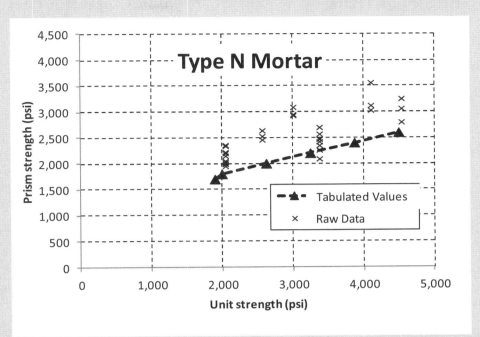

Figure SC-3 — Compressive strength of concrete masonry versus compressive strength of concrete masonry units – Type N Mortar

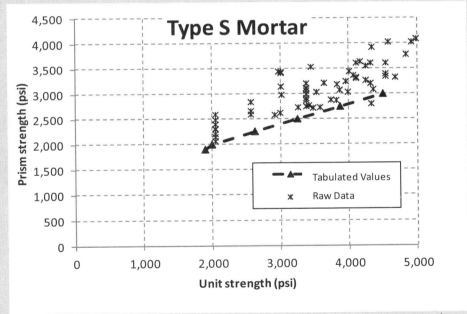

Figure SC-4 — Compressive strength of concrete masonry versus compressive strength of concrete masonry units – Type S Mortar

SPECIFICATION

1.4 B.2.   *Unit strength method* (Continued)

c. *AAC masonry* — Determine the compressive strength of masonry based on the strength of the AAC masonry unit only. The following requirements apply to the masonry:

1) Units conform to Article 2.3 E.

2) Thickness of bed joints does not exceed 1/8 in. (3.2 mm).

3) For grouted masonry, the grout conforms to Article 2.2.

3. *Prism test method* — Determine the compressive strength of clay masonry and concrete masonry by the prism test method in accordance with ASTM C1314.

COMMENTARY

c. *AAC masonry* — The strength of AAC masonry, f'_{AAC}, is controlled by the strength class of the AAC unit as defined by ASTM C1693. The strength of the thin-bed mortar and its bond in compression and shear will exceed the strength of the unit.

3. *Prism test method* — The prism test method described in ASTM C1314 was selected as a uniform method of testing clay masonry and concrete masonry to determine their compressive strengths. Masonry design is based on the compressive strength established at 28 days. The prism test method is used as an alternative to the unit strength method.

ASTM C1314 provides for testing masonry prisms at 28 days or at any designated test age. Therefore, a shorter time period, such as a 7-day test, could be used to estimate the 28-day strength based on a previously established relationship between the results of tests conducted at the shorter time period and results of the 28 day tests. Materials and workmanship of the previously established relationship must be representative of the prisms being tested.

Compliance with the specified compressive strength of masonry can be determined by the prism method instead of the unit strength method. ASTM C1314 uses the same materials and workmanship to construct the prisms as those to be used in the structure. Atkinson and Kingsley (1985), Priestley and Elder (1983), Miller et al (1979), Noland (1982) and Hegemier et al (1978) discuss prism testing. Many more references on the prism test method parameters and results could be added. The adoption of ASTM C1314 alleviates most of the concerns stated in the above references. ASTM C1314 replaced ASTM E447 (1997), which was referenced in editions of the Specification prior to 1999.

SPECIFICATION

1.4 B. *Compressive strength determination* (Continued)

4. *Testing prisms from constructed masonry* — When approved by the building official, acceptance of masonry that does not meet the requirements of Article 1.4 B.2 or 1.4 B.3 is permitted to be based on tests of prisms cut from the masonry construction.

a. *Prism sampling and removal* — For each 5,000 square feet (465 m²) of wall area in question, saw-cut a minimum of three prisms from completed masonry. Select, remove and transport prisms in accordance with ASTM C1532/C1532M. Determine the length, width and height dimensions of the prism and test prisms when at least 28 days old in accordance with ASTM C1314.

b. *Compressive strength calculations* — Calculate the compressive strength of prisms in accordance with ASTM C1314.

c. *Compliance* — Strengths determined from saw-cut prisms shall equal or exceed the specified compressive strength of masonry. Additional testing of specimens cut from construction in question is permitted.

1.4 C. *Adhered veneer requirements* — When adhered veneer is not placed in accordance with Article 3.3 C, determine the adhesion of adhered veneer unit to backing in accordance with ASTM C482.

COMMENTARY

4. *Testing prisms from constructed masonry* — While uncommon, there are times when the compressive strength of masonry determined by the unit strength method or prism test method may be questioned or may be lower than the specified strength. Because low strengths could be a result of inappropriate testing procedures or unintentional damage to the test specimens, prisms may be saw-cut from the completed masonry wall and tested. This section prescribes procedures for such tests.

Such testing is difficult, is performed on masonry walls constructed at least 28 days before the test, and requires replacement of the sampled wall area. Therefore, concerted efforts should be taken so that strengths determined by the unit strength method or prism test method are adequate.

a. *Prism sampling and removal* — Removal of prisms from a constructed wall requires care so that the prism is not damaged and that damage to the wall is minimal. Prisms must be representative of the wall, yet not contain any reinforcing steel, which would bias the results. As with a prism test taken during construction, a prism test from existing masonry requires three prism specimens.

b. *Compressive strength calculations* — Compressive strength calculations from saw-cut specimens must be based on the net mortar bedded area, or the net mortar bedded area plus the grouted area for grouted prisms. The net area must be determined by the testing agency before the prism is tested.

1.4 C. *Adhered veneer requirements* — Adhesion should be verified if a form release agent, an applied coating, or a smooth surface is present on the backing.

SPECIFICATION

1.5 — Submittals

1.5 A. Obtain written acceptance of submittals prior to the use of the materials or methods requiring acceptance.

1.5 B. Submit the following:

1. Mix designs and test results

   a. One of the following for each mortar mix, excluding thin-bed mortar for AAC:

   1) Mix designs indicating type and proportions of ingredients in compliance with the proportion specification of ASTM C270, or

   2) Mix designs and mortar tests performed in accordance with the property specification of ASTM C270.

   b. One of the following for each grout mix:

   1) Mix designs indicating type and proportions of the ingredients according to the proportion requirements of ASTM C476, or

   2) Mix designs and grout strength test performed in accordance with ASTM C476, or

   3) Compressive strength tests performed in accordance with ASTM C1019, and slump flow and Visual Stability Index (VSI) as determined by ASTM C1611/C1611M.

2. Material certificates — Material certificates for the following, certifying that each material is in compliance.

   a. Reinforcement

   b. Anchors, ties, fasteners, and metal accessories

   c. Masonry units

   d. Mortar, thin-bed mortar for AAC, and grout materials

   e. Self-consolidating grout

3. Construction procedures

   a. Cold weather construction procedures

   b. Hot weather construction procedures

COMMENTARY

1.5 — Submittals

Submittals and their subsequent acceptance or rejection on a timely basis will keep the project moving smoothly. If the specifier wishes to require a higher level of quality assurance than the minimum required by this Specification, submittals may be required for one or more of the following: shop drawings for reinforced masonry and lintels; sample specimens of masonry units, colored mortar, each type of movement joint accessory, anchor, tie, fastener, and metal accessory; and test results for masonry units, mortar, and grout.

SPECIFICATION

1.6 — Quality assurance

1.6 A. *Testing Agency's services and duties*

1. Sample and test in accordance with Table 3, 4, or 5, as specified for the project.

2. Unless otherwise required, report test results to the Architect/Engineer, Inspection Agency, and Contractor promptly after they are performed. Include in test reports a summary of conditions under which test specimens were stored prior to testing and state what portion of the construction is represented by each test.

3. When there is reason to believe that any material furnished or work performed by the Contractor fails to fulfill the requirements of the Contract Documents, report such discrepancy to the Architect/Engineer, Inspection Agency, and Contractor.

4. Unless otherwise required, the Owner will retain the Testing Agency.

COMMENTARY

1.6 — Quality assurance

Quality assurance consists of the actions taken by an owner or owner's representative, including establishing the quality assurance requirements, to provide assurance that materials and workmanship are in accordance with the contract documents. Quality assurance includes quality control measures as well as testing and inspection to verify compliance. The term quality control was not used in the Specification because its meaning varies with the perspective of the parties involved in the project.

The owner and Architect/Engineer may require a testing laboratory to provide some or all of the tests mentioned in Specification Tables 3, 4, and 5.

The quality objectives are met when the building is properly designed, completed using materials complying with product specifications using adequate construction practices, and is adequately maintained. Special Inspection and testing are important components of the quality assurance program, which is used to meet the objective of quality in construction.

Laboratories that comply with the requirements of ASTM C1093 are more likely to be familiar with masonry materials and testing. Specifying that the testing agencies comply with the requirements of ASTM C1093 is suggested.

1.6 A. *Testing Agency's services and duties* — Implementation of testing and inspection requirements contained in the Quality Assurance Tables requires detailed knowledge of the appropriate procedures. Comprehensive (Chrysler, 2010; NCMA, 2008; BIA TN 39, 2001; BIA TN 39B, 1988) and summary (SCI and MIA, 2006(a) SCI and MIA, 2006(a)) testing and inspection procedures are available from recognized industry sources which may be referenced for assistance in complying with the specified Quality Assurance program.

Table 3 — Level A Quality Assurance

MINIMUM VERIFICATION
Prior to construction, verify certificates of compliance used in masonry construction

Table 4 — Level B Quality Assurance

MINIMUM TESTS
Verification of Slump flow and Visual Stability Index (VSI) as delivered to the project site in accordance with Article 1.5 B.1.b.3 for self-consolidating grout
Verification of f'_m and f'_{AAC} in accordance with Article 1.4 B prior to construction, except where specifically exempted by the Code.

MINIMUM SPECIAL INSPECTION				
Inspection Task	**Frequency** [a]		**Reference for Criteria**	
	Continuous	Periodic	TMS 402/ ACI 530/ ASCE 5	TMS 602/ ACI 530.1/ ASCE 6
1. Verify compliance with the approved submittals		X		Art. 1.5
2. As masonry construction begins, verify that the following are in compliance:				
a. Proportions of site-prepared mortar		X		Art. 2.1, 2.6 A
b. Construction of mortar joints		X		Art. 3.3 B
c. Grade and size of prestressing tendons and anchorages		X		Art. 2.4 B, 2.4 H
d. Location of reinforcement, connectors, and prestressing tendons and anchorages		X		Art. 3.4, 3.6 A
e. Prestressing technique		X		Art. 3.6 B
f. Properties of thin-bed mortar for AAC masonry	X [b]	X [c]		Art. 2.1 C
3. Prior to grouting, verify that the following are in compliance:				
a. Grout space		X		Art. 3.2 D, 3.2 F
b. Grade, type, and size of reinforcement and anchor bolts, and prestressing tendons and anchorages		X	Sec. 6.1	Art. 2.4, 3.4
c. Placement of reinforcement, connectors, and prestressing tendons and anchorages		X	Sec. 6.1, 6.2.1, 6.2.6, 6.2.7	Art. 3.2 E, 3.4, 3.6 A
d. Proportions of site-prepared grout and prestressing grout for bonded tendons		X		Art. 2.6 B, 2.4 G.1.b
e. Construction of mortar joints		X		Art. 3.3 B

Table 4 — Level B Quality Assurance (Continued)

MINIMUM SPECIAL INSPECTION				
Inspection Task	Frequency [a]		Reference for Criteria	
	Continuous	Periodic	TMS 402/ ACI 530/ ASCE 5	TMS 602/ ACI 530.1/ ASCE 6
4. Verify during construction:				
a. Size and location of structural elements		X		Art. 3.3 F
b. Type, size, and location of anchors, including other details of anchorage of masonry to structural members, frames, or other construction		X	Sec. 1.2.1(e), 6.1.4.3, 6.2.1	
c. Welding of reinforcement	X		Sec.8.1.6.7.2, 9.3.3.4 (c), 11.3.3.4(b)	
d. Preparation, construction, and protection of masonry during cold weather (temperature below 40°F (4.4°C)) or hot weather (temperature above 90°F (32.2°C))		X		Art. 1.8 C, 1.8 D
e. Application and measurement of prestressing force	X			Art. 3.6 B
f. Placement of grout and prestressing grout for bonded tendons is in compliance	X			Art. 3.5, 3.6 C
g. Placement of AAC masonry units and construction of thin-bed mortar joints	X [b]	X [c]		Art. 3.3 B.9, 3.3 F.1.b
5. Observe preparation of grout specimens, mortar specimens, and/or prisms		X		Art. 1.4 B.2.a.3, 1.4 B.2.b.3, 1.4 B.2.c.3, 1.4 B.3, 1.4 B.4

(a) Frequency refers to the frequency of Special Inspection, which may be continuous during the task listed or periodic during the listed task, as defined in the table.

(b) Required for the first 5000 square feet (465 square meters) of AAC masonry.

(c) Required after the first 5000 square feet (465 square meters) of AAC masonry.

Table 5 — Level C Quality Assurance

MINIMUM TESTS
Verification of f'_m and f'_{AAC} in accordance with Article 1.4 B prior to construction and for every 5,000 sq. ft (465 sq. m) during construction
Verification of proportions of materials in premixed or preblended mortar, prestressing grout, and grout other than self-consolidating grout as delivered to the project site
Verification of Slump flow and Visual Stability Index (VSI) as delivered to the project site in accordance with Article 1.5 B.1.b.3 for self-consolidating grout

MINIMUM SPECIAL INSPECTION				
Inspection Task	Frequency [a]		Reference for Criteria	
	Continuous	Periodic	TMS 402/ ACI 530/ ASCE 5	TMS 602/ ACI 530.1/ ASCE 6
1. Verify compliance with the approved submittals		X		Art. 1.5
2. Verify that the following are in compliance:				
a. Proportions of site-mixed mortar, grout, and prestressing grout for bonded tendons		X		Art. 2.1, 2.6 A, 2.6 B, 2.6 C, 2.4 G.1.b
b. Grade, type, and size of reinforcement and anchor bolts, and prestressing tendons and anchorages		X	Sec. 6.1	Art. 2.4, 3.4
c. Placement of masonry units and construction of mortar joints		X		Art. 3.3 B
d. Placement of reinforcement, connectors, and prestressing tendons and anchorages	X		Sec. 6.1, 6.2.1, 6.2.6, 6.2.7	Art. 3.2 E, 3.4, 3.6 A
e. Grout space prior to grouting	X			Art. 3.2 D, 3.2 F
f. Placement of grout and prestressing grout for bonded tendons	X			Art. 3.5, 3.6 C
g. Size and location of structural elements		X		Art. 3.3 F
h. Type, size, and location of anchors including other details of anchorage of masonry to structural members, frames, or other construction	X		Sec. 1.2.1(e), 6.1.4.3, 6.2.1	
i. Welding of reinforcement	X		Sec. 8.1.6.7.2, 9.3.3.4 (c), 11.3.3.4(b)	
j. Preparation, construction, and protection of masonry during cold weather (temperature below 40°F (4.4°C)) or hot weather (temperature above 90°F (32.2°C))		X		Art. 1.8 C, 1.8 D
k. Application and measurement of prestressing force	X			Art. 3.6 B
l. Placement of AAC masonry units and construction of thin-bed mortar joints	X			Art. 3.3 B.9, 3.3 F.1.b
m. Properties of thin-bed mortar for AAC masonry	X			Art. 2.1 C.1
3. Observe preparation of grout specimens, mortar specimens, and/or prisms	X			Art. 1.4 B.2.a.3, 1.4 B.2.b.3, 1.4 B.2.c.3, 1.4 B.3, 1.4 B.4

(a)   Frequency refers to the frequency of Special Inspection, which may be continuous during the task listed or periodic during the listed task, as defined in the table.

SPECIFICATION

1.6 B. *Inspection Agency's services and duties*

1. Inspect and evaluate in accordance with Table 3, 4, or 5, as specified for the project.

2. Unless otherwise required, report inspection results to the Architect/Engineer, and Contractor promptly after they are performed. Include in inspection reports a summary of conditions under which the inspections were made and state what portion of the construction is represented by each inspection.

3. Furnish inspection reports to the Architect/Engineer and Contractor.

4. When there is reason to believe that any material furnished or work performed by the Contractor fails to fulfill the requirements of the Contract Documents, report such discrepancy to the Architect/Engineer and to the Contractor.

5. Submit a final signed report stating whether the Work requiring Special Inspection was, to the best of the Inspection Agency's knowledge, in conformance. Submit the final report to the Architect/Engineer and Contractor.

6. Unless otherwise required, the Owner will retain the Inspection Agency.

1.6 C. *Contractor's services and duties*

1. Permit and facilitate access to the construction sites and the performance of activities for quality assurance by the Testing and Inspection Agencies.

2. The use of testing and inspection services does not relieve the Contractor of the responsibility to furnish materials and construction in full compliance.

3. To facilitate testing and inspection, comply with the following:

   a. Furnish necessary labor to assist the designated testing agency in obtaining and handling samples at the Project.

   b. Advise the designated Testing Agency and Inspection Agency sufficiently in advance of operations to allow for completion of quality assurance measures and for the assignment of personnel.

   c. Provide masonry materials required for preconstruction and construction testing.

4. Provide and maintain adequate facilities for the sole use of the testing agency for safe storage and proper curing of test specimens on the Project Site.

5. In the submittals, include the results of testing performed to qualify the materials and to establish mix designs.

COMMENTARY

1.6 B. *Inspection Agency's services and duties* — The Code and this Specification require that masonry be inspected. The design provisions used in the Code are based on the premise that the work will be inspected, and that quality assurance measures will be implemented. Minimum testing and minimum Special Inspection requirements are given in Specification Tables 3, 4, and 5. The Architect/Engineer may increase the amount of testing and inspection required. Certain applications, such as Masonry Veneer (Chapter 12), Masonry Partition Walls (Chapter 14) and Empirical Design of Masonry (Appendix A), do not require compressive strength verification of masonry as indicated in Table 4. The method of payment for inspection services is usually addressed in general conditions or other contract documents and usually is not governed by this article.

1.6 C. *Contractor's services and duties* — The contractor establishes mix designs, the source for supply of materials, and suggests change orders.

The listing of duties of the inspection agency, testing agency, and contractor provide for a coordination of their tasks and a means of reporting results. The contractor is bound by contract to supply and place the materials required by the contract documents. Perfection is obviously the goal, but factors of safety included in the design method recognize that some deviation from perfection will exist. Engineering judgment must be used to evaluate reported discrepancies. Tolerances listed in Specification Article 3.3 F were established to assure structural performance and were not based on aesthetic criteria.

SPECIFICATION

1.6 D. *Sample panels*

    1. For masonry governed by Level B or C Quality Assurance (Table 4 or Table 5), construct sample panels of masonry walls.

        a. Use materials and procedures accepted for the Work.

        b. The minimum sample panel dimensions are 4 ft by 4 ft (1.22 m by 1.22 m).

    2. The acceptable standard for the Work is established by the accepted panel.

    3. Retain sample panels at the project site until Work has been accepted.

1.6 E. *Grout demonstration panel* — Prior to masonry construction, construct a grout demonstration panel if proposed grouting procedures, construction techniques, or grout space geometry do not conform to the applicable requirements of Articles 3.5 C, 3.5 D, and 3.5 E.

1.7 — Delivery, storage, and handling

1.7 A. Do not use damaged masonry units, damaged components of structure, or damaged packaged material.

1.7 B. Protect cementitious materials for mortar and grout from precipitation and groundwater.

1.7 C. Do not use masonry materials that are contaminated.

1.7 D. Store different aggregates separately.

1.7 E. Protect reinforcement, ties, and metal accessories from permanent distortions and store them off the ground.

COMMENTARY

1.6 D. *Sample panels* — Sample panels should contain the full range of unit and mortar color. Each procedure, including cleaning and application of coatings and sealants, should be demonstrated on the sample panel. The effect of these materials and procedures on the masonry can then be determined before large areas are treated. Because it serves as a comparison of the finished work, the sample panel should be maintained until the work has been accepted. Certain elements of sample panels, such as the type of mortar joint, can have structural implications with the performance of masonry. Construct sample panels within the tolerances of Article 3.3 F. The specifier has the option of permitting a segment of the masonry construction to serve as a sample panel or requiring a separate stand-alone panel.

1.7 — Delivery, storage, and handling

The performance of masonry materials can be reduced by contamination by dirt, water, and other materials during delivery or at the project site.

Reinforcement and metal accessories are less prone than masonry materials to damage from handling.

SPECIFICATION

1.8 — Project conditions

1.8 A. *Construction loads* — Do not apply construction loads that exceed the safe superimposed load capacity of the masonry and shores, if used.

1.8 B. *Masonry protection* — Cover top of unfinished masonry work to protect it from moisture intrusion.

1.8 C. *Cold weather construction* — When ambient air temperature is below 40°F (4.4°C), implement cold weather procedures and comply with the following:

1. Do not lay glass unit masonry.

2. *Preparation* — Comply with the following requirements prior to conducting masonry work:

   a. Do not lay masonry units having either a temperature below 20°F (-6.7°C) or containing frozen moisture, visible ice, or snow on their surface.

   b. Remove visible ice and snow from the top surface of existing foundations and masonry to receive new construction. Heat these surfaces above freezing, using methods that do not result in damage.

COMMENTARY

1.8 — Project conditions

1.8 B. *Masonry protection* — Many geographic areas are subject to unpredictable weather. Masonry under construction needs to be protected from detrimental moisture intrusion, particularly when there is a possibility of freezing temperatures. In areas where dry weather is consistent, covering walls to protect against moisture intrusion during the normal progress of construction may not be required.

1.8 C. *Cold weather construction* — The procedure described in this article represents the committee's consensus of current good construction practice and has been framed to generally agree with masonry industry recommendations (IMI, 1973).

The provisions of Article 1.8 C are mandatory, even if the procedures submitted under Article 1.5 B.3.a are not required. The contractor has several options to achieve the results required in Article 1.8 C. The options are available because of the climatic extremes and their duration. When the air temperature at the project site or unit temperatures fall below 40 F (4.4 C), the cold weather protection plan submitted becomes mandatory. Work stoppage may be justified if a short cold spell is anticipated. Enclosures and heaters can be used as necessary.

Temperature of the masonry mortar may be measured using a metal tip immersion thermometer inserted into a sample of the mortar. The mortar sample may be mortar as contained in the mixer, in hoppers for transfer to the working face of the masonry or as available on mortar boards currently being used. The critical mortar temperatures are the temperatures at the mixer and mortar board locations. The ideal mortar temperature is 60°F to 80°F (15.6°C to 26.7°C).

Temperature of the masonry unit may be measured using a metallic surface contact thermometer. Temperature of the units may be below the ambient temperature if the requirements of Article 1.8 C.2.a are met.

The contractor may choose to enclose the entire area rather than make the sequential materials conditioning and protection modifications. Ambient temperature conditions apply while work is in progress. Minimum daily temperatures apply to the time after grouted masonry is placed. Mean daily temperatures apply to the time after ungrouted masonry is placed.

Grout made with Type III portland cement gains strength more quickly than grout mixed with Type I portland cement. This faster strength gain eliminates the need to protect masonry for the additional 24 hr period.

SPECIFICATION

1.8 C. *Cold weather construction* (Continued)

3. *Construction* — These requirements apply to work in progress and are based on ambient air temperature. Do not heat water or aggregates used in mortar or grout above 140°F (60°C). Comply with the following requirements when the following ambient air temperatures exist:

a. 40°F to 32°F (4.4°C to 0°C):

   1) Heat sand or mixing water to produce mortar temperature between 40°F (4.4°C) and 120°F (48.9°C) at the time of mixing.

   2) Heat grout materials when the temperature of the materials is below 32°F (0°C).

b. Below 32°F to 25°F (0°C to -3.9°C):

   1) Heat sand and mixing water to produce mortar temperature between 40°F (4.4°C) and 120°F (48.9°C) at the time of mixing. Maintain mortar temperature above freezing until used in masonry.

   2) Heat grout aggregates and mixing water to produce grout temperature between 70°F (21.1°C) and 120°F (48.9°C) at the time of mixing. Maintain grout temperature above 70°F (21.1°C) at the time of grout placement.

   3) Heat AAC units to a minimum temperature of 40°F (4.4°C) before installing thin-bed mortar.

c. Below 25°F to 20°F (-3.9°C to –6.7°C): Comply with Article 1.8 C.3.b and the following:

   1) Heat masonry surfaces under construction to a minimum temperature of 40°F (4.4°C)

   2) Use wind breaks or enclosures when the wind velocity exceeds 15 mph (24 km/h).

   3) Heat masonry to a minimum temperature of 40°F (4.4°C) prior to grouting.

d. Below 20°F (-6.7°C): Comply with Article 1.8 C.3.c and the following: Provide an enclosure and auxiliary heat to maintain air temperature above 32°F (0°C) within the enclosure.

COMMENTARY

Construction experience, though not formally documented, suggests that AAC thin-bed mortar reaches full strength significantly faster than masonry mortar; however, it is more sensitive to cold weather applications. AAC masonry also holds heat considerably longer than concrete masonry. Cold weather requirements are therefore different for thin-bed mortar applications as compared to conventional mortar. Cold weather requirements for leveling course mortar and grout remain the same as for other masonry products.

SPECIFICATION

COMMENTARY

1.8 C *Cold weather construction* (Continued)

4. *Protection* — These requirements apply after masonry is placed and are based on anticipated minimum daily temperature for grouted masonry and anticipated mean daily temperature for ungrouted masonry. Protect completed masonry in the following manner:

a. Maintain the temperature of glass unit masonry above 40°F (4.4°C) for the first 48 hr after construction.

b. Maintain the temperature of AAC masonry above 32°F (0°C) for the first 4 hr after thin-bed mortar application.

c. 40°F to 25°F (4.4°C to -3.9°C): Protect newly constructed masonry by covering with a weather-resistive membrane for 24 hr after being completed.

d. Below 25°F to 20°F (-3.9°C to -6.7°C): Cover newly constructed masonry completely with weather-resistive insulating blankets, or equal protection, for 24 hr after completion of work. Extend time period to 48 hr for grouted masonry, unless the only cement in the grout is Type III portland cement.

e. Below 20°F (-6.7°C): Maintain newly constructed masonry temperature above 32°F (0°C) for at least 24 hr after being completed by using heated enclosures, electric heating blankets, infared lamps, or other acceptable methods. Extend time period to 48 hr for grouted masonry, unless the only cement in the grout is Type III portland cement.

Specification and
Commentary, S-31

SPECIFICATION

1.8 D. *Hot weather construction* — Implement approved hot weather procedures and comply with the following provisions:

1. *Preparation* — Prior to conducting masonry work:

   a. When the ambient air temperature exceeds 100°F (37.8°C), or exceeds 90°F (32.2°C) with a wind velocity greater than 8 mph (12.9 km/hr):

      1) Maintain sand piles in a damp, loose condition.

      2) Provide necessary conditions and equipment to produce mortar having a temperature below 120°F (48.9°C).

   b. When the ambient temperature exceeds 115°F (46.1°C), or exceeds 105°F (40.6°C) with a wind velocity greater than 8 mph (12.9 km/hr), implement the requirements of Article 1.8 D.1.a and shade materials and mixing equipment from direct sunlight.

2. *Construction* — While masonry work is in progress:

   a. When the ambient air temperature exceeds 100°F (37.8°C), or exceeds 90°F (32.2°C) with a wind velocity greater than 8 mph (12.9 km/hr):

      1) Maintain temperature of mortar and grout below 120°F (48.9°C).

      2) Flush mixer, mortar transport container, and mortar boards with cool water before they come into contact with mortar ingredients or mortar.

      3) Maintain mortar consistency by retempering with cool water.

      4) Use mortar within 2 hr of initial mixing.

      5) Spread thin-bed mortar no more than four feet ahead of AAC masonry units.

      6) Set AAC masonry units within one minute after spreading thin-bed mortar.

   b. When the ambient temperature exceeds 115°F (46.1°C), or exceeds 105°F (40.6°C) with a wind velocity greater than 8 mph (12.9 km/hr), implement the requirements of Article 1.8 D.2.a and use cool mixing water for mortar and grout. Ice is permitted in the mixing water prior to use. Do not permit ice in the mixing water when added to the other mortar or grout materials.

3. *Protection* — When the mean daily temperature exceeds 100°F (37.8°C) or exceeds 90°F (32.2°C) with a wind velocity greater than 8 mph (12.9 km/hr), fog spray newly constructed masonry until damp, at least three times a day until the masonry is three days old.

COMMENTARY

1.8 D. *Hot weather construction* — High temperature and low relative humidity increase the rate of moisture evaporation. These conditions can lead to "dryout" (drying of the mortar or grout before sufficient hydration has taken place) of the mortar and grout (Tomasetti, 1990). Dryout adversely affects the properties of mortar and grout because dryout signals improper curing and associated reduction of masonry strength development. The preparation, construction, and protection requirements in the Specification are minimum requirements to avoid dryout of mortar and grout and to allow for proper curing. They are based on industry practice (BIA, 1992; PCA, 1993; Panarese et al, 1991). More stringent and extensive hot weather practices may be prudent where temperatures are high, winds are strong, and humidity is low.

During hot weather, shading masonry materials and equipment reduces mortar and grout temperatures. Scheduling construction to avoid hotter periods of the day should be considered.

See Specification Commentary Article 2.1 for considerations in selecting mortar materials. The most effective way of reducing mortar and grout batch temperatures is by using cool mixing water. Small batches of mortar are preferred over larger batches to minimize drying time on mortar boards. Mortar should not be used after a maximum of 2 hr after initial mixing in hot weather conditions. Use of cool water to retemper, when tempering is permitted, restores plasticity and reduces the mortar temperature (IMI, 1973; BIA, 1992; PCA, 1993).

Most mason's sand is delivered to the project in a damp, loose condition with a moisture content of about 4 to 6 percent. Sand piles should be kept cool and in a damp, loose condition by sprinkling and by covering with a plastic sheet to limit evaporation.

Research suggests that covering and moist curing of concrete masonry walls dramatically improves flexural bond strength compared to walls not covered or moist cured (NCMA, 1994).

SPECIFICATION

2.3 — Masonry unit materials

2.3 A. Provide concrete masonry units that conform to ASTM C55, C73, C90, C129, C744, or C1634 as specified.

COMMENTARY

2.3 — Masonry unit materials

2.3 A. Concrete masonry units are made from lightweight and normal weight aggregate, water, and cement. The units are available in a variety of shapes, sizes, colors, and strengths. Because the properties of the concrete vary with the aggregate type and mix proportions, there is a range of physical properties and weights available in concrete masonry units.

Masonry units are selected for the use and appearance desired, with minimum requirements addressed by each respective ASTM standard. When particular features are desired such as surface textures for appearance or bond, finish, color, or particular properties such as weight classification, higher compressive strength, fire resistance, thermal or acoustical performance, these features should be specified separately by the purchaser. Local suppliers should be consulted as to the availability of units having the desired features.

ASTM C73 designates sand-lime brick as either Grade SW or Grade MW. Grade SW brick are intended for use where they will be exposed to freezing temperatures in the presence of moisture. Grade MW brick are limited to applications in which they may be subjected to freezing temperature but in which they are unlikely to be saturated with water.

Table SC-3 summarizes the requirements for various concrete masonry units given in the referenced standards.

ASTM C744 addresses the properties of units with a resin facing. The units must meet the requirements of one of the other referenced standards.

Table SC-3 — Concrete masonry unit requirements

ASTM Specification	Unit	Strength	Weight	Type	Grade
C55	Concrete brick	yes	yes	no	no
C73	Sand-lime brick	yes	no	no	yes
C90	Load-bearing units	yes	yes	no	no
C129	Non-load-bearing units	yes	yes	no	no
C744	Prefaced units	—	—	—	—
C1634	Concrete facing brick	yes	yes	no	no

SPECIFICATION

2.3 B. Provide clay or shale masonry units that conform to ASTM C34, C56, C62, C126, C212, C216, C652, C1088, or C1405 or to ANSI A 137.1, as specified.

COMMENTARY

2.3 B. Clay or shale masonry units are formed from those materials and referred to as brick or tile. Clay masonry units may be molded, pressed, or extruded into the desired shape. Physical properties depend upon the raw materials, the method of forming, and the firing temperature. Incipient fusion, a melting and joining of the clay particles, is necessary to develop the strength and durability of clay masonry units. A wide variety of unit shapes, sizes, colors, and strengths is available.

The intended use determines which standard specification is applicable. Generally, brick units are smaller than tile, tile is always cored, and brick may be solid or cored. Clay brick is normally exposed in use, but clay tile is usually not exposed. Grade or class is determined by exposure condition and has requirements for durability, usually given by compressive strength and absorption. Dimensional variations and allowable chips and cracks are controlled by type.

Table SC-4 summarizes the requirements given in the referenced standards.

Table SC-4 — Clay brick and tile requirements

ASTM Specification	Unit	Minimum % solid	Grade Strength	Grade Weight	Grade Type
C34	Load-bearing wall tile	a	yes	yes	no
C56	Non-load-bearing wall tile	b	no	yes	no
C62	Building brick (solid)	75	yes	yes	no
C126	Ceramic glazed units	c	yes	no	yes
C212	Structural facing tile	b	yes	no	yes
C216	Facing brick (solid)	75	yes	yes	yes
C652	Hollow brick	a	yes	yes	yes

Notes:
a. A minimum percent is given in this specification. The percent solid is a function of the requirements for size and/or number of cells as well as the minimum shell and web thicknesses.
b. No minimum percent solid is given in this specification. The percent solid is a function of the requirements for the number of cells and weights per square foot.
c. Solid masonry units minimum percent solid is 75 percent. Hollow masonry units — no minimum percent solid is given in this specification. Their percent solid is a function of the requirements for number of cells and the minimum shell and web thicknesses.

SPECIFICATION

2.3 C. Provide stone masonry units that conform to ASTM C503, C568, C615, C616, or C629, as specified.

2.3 D. Provide hollow glass units that are partially evacuated and have a minimum average glass face thickness of $^3/_{16}$ in. (4.8 mm). Provide solid glass block units when required. Provide units in which the surfaces intended to be in contact with mortar are treated with polyvinyl butyral coating or latex-based paint. Do not use reclaimed units.

COMMENTARY

2.3 C. Stone masonry units are typically selected by color and appearance. The referenced standards classify building stones by the properties shown in Table SC-5. The values given in the standards serve as minimum requirements. Stone is often ordered by a particular quarry or color rather than the classification method in the standard.

2.3 D. Hollow glass masonry units are formed by fusing two molded halves of glass together to produce a partial vacuum in the resulting cavity. The resulting glass block units are available in a variety of shapes, sizes, and patterns.

The block edges are usually treated in the factory with a coating that can be clear or opaque. The primary purpose of the coating is to provide an expansion/contraction mechanism to reduce stress cracking and to improve the mortar bond.

Table SC-5 — Stone requirements

ASTM Specification	Stone	Absorption	Density	Compressive strength	Modulus of rupture	Abrasion resistance	Acid resistance
C503	Marble	minimum	range	minimum	minimum	minimum	none
C568	Limestone	range	range	range	range	range	none
C615	Granite	minimum	minimum	minimum	minimum	minimum	none
C616	Sandstone	range	range	range	range	range	none
C629	Slate	range	none	none	minimum	minimum	range

SPECIFICATION

2.3 E. Provide AAC masonry units that conform to ASTM C1691 and ASTM C1693 for the strength class specified in the Contract Documents.

2.4 — Reinforcement, prestressing tendons, and metal accessories

2.4 A. *Reinforcing bars* — Provide deformed reinforcing bars that conform to one of the following as specified:

1. ASTM A615/A615M

2. ASTM A706/A706M

3. ASTM A767/A767M

4. ASTM A775/A775M

5. ASTM A996/A996M

COMMENTARY

2.3 E. AAC masonry units are specified by both compressive strength and density. Various density ranges are given in ASTM C1693 for specific compressive strengths. Generally, the density is specified based on consideration of thermal, acoustical, and weight requirements. AAC masonry is structurally designed based on the minimum compressive strength of the AAC material as determined by ASTM C1691. ASTM C1386, the predecessor standard to ASTM C1693, specified average compressive strength values that corresponded to the minimum compressive strength of each grade of AAC specified. Average specified compressive strengths for AAC 2, AAC 4 and AAC 6 were 360 psi, 725 psi and 1090 psi, respectively. ASTM C1691 deletes the requirement for minimum average strength for each grade of AAC masonry and allows the AAC manufacturer to determine required target strengths in the manufacturing process in order to achieve the specified minimum strength.

2.4 — Reinforcement, prestressing tendons, and metal accessories

2.4 A. *Reinforcing bars* — Code Sections 9.1.9.3.1 and 9.1.9.3.2 limit the reinforcing bar's specified and actual yield strengths when the reinforcement is used to resist in-plane flexural tension, flexural tension perpendicular to bed joints, in-plane shear, or flexural tension parallel to bed joints in strength design. Test reports should be reviewed to verify conformance with the Code requirement.

See Table SC-6 for a summary of properties.

Table SC-6 — Reinforcement and metal accessories

ASTM specification	Material	Use	Yield strength, ksi (MPa)	Yield stress, MPa
A36/A36M	Structural steel	Connectors	36 (248.2)	250
A82/A82 M	Steel wire	Joint reinforcement, ties	70 (482.7)	485
A167	Stainless steel	Bolts, reinforcement, ties	30 (206.9)	205
A185/A185 M	Steel welded wire reinforcement	Welded wire reinforcement	75 (517.1)	485
A307	Carbon steel	Connectors	a	—
A366/A366M	Carbon steel	Connectors	—	—
A496/A496 M	Steel wire	Reinforcement	75 (517.1)	485
A497/A497 M	Steel welded wire reinforcement	Reinforcement, welded wire reinforcement	70 (482.7)	485
A615/A615M	Carbon-steel	Reinforcement	40, 60 (275.8, 413.7)	300, 420
A996/A996M	Rail and axle steel	Reinforcement	40, 50, 60 (275.8, 344.8, 413.7)	300, 350, 420
A706/A706M	Low-alloy steel	Reinforcement	60 (413.7)	—

a. ASTM does not define a yield strength value for ASTM A307, Grade A anchor bolts.

SPECIFICATION

2.4 B. *Prestressing tendons*

1. Provide prestressing tendons that conform to one of the following standards, except for those permitted in Articles 2.4 B.2 and 2.4 B.3:

   a. Wire ....ASTM A421/A421M

   b. Low-relaxation wire.............ASTM A421/A421M

   c. Strand..................................ASTM A416/A416M

   d. Low-relaxation strand ....ASTM A416/A416M

   e. Bar..ASTM A722/A722M

2. Wire, strands, and bars not specifically listed in ASTM A416/A416M, A421/A421M, or A722/A722M are permitted, provided that they conform to the minimum requirements in ASTM A416/A416M, A421/A421M, or A722/A722M and are approved by the Architect/Engineer.

3. Bars and wires of less than 150 ksi (1034 MPa) tensile strength and conforming to ASTM A82/A82M, A510/A510M, A615/A615M, A996/A996M, or A706/A706M are permitted to be used as prestressed tendons, provided that the stress relaxation properties have been assessed by tests according to ASTM E328 for the maximum permissible stress in the tendon.

2.4 C. *Joint reinforcement*

1. Provide joint reinforcement that conforms to ASTM A951. Maximum spacing of cross wires in ladder-type joint reinforcement and of points of connection of cross wires to longitudinal wires of truss-type joint reinforcement shall be 16 in. (400 mm).

2. *Deformed reinforcing wire* — Provide deformed reinforcing wire that conforms to ASTM A496/A496M.

3. *Welded wire reinforcement* — Provide welded wire reinforcement that conforms to one of the following specifications:

   a. Plain .... ASTM A185/A185M

   b. Deformed............................ ASTM A497/A497M

2.4 D. *Anchors, ties, and accessories* — Provide anchors, ties, and accessories that conform to the following specifications, except as otherwise specified:

1. Plate and bent-bar anchors........ ASTM A36/A 36M

2. Sheet-metal anchors and ties .... ASTM A1008/A1008M

3. Wire mesh ties .... ASTM A185/A185M

4. Wire ties and anchors .... ASTM A82/A82M

5. Headed anchor bolts .... ASTM A307, Grade A

COMMENTARY

2.4 B. *Prestressing tendons* — The constructibility aspects of prestressed masonry favor the use of rods or rigid strands with mechanical anchorage in ungrouted construction. Mild strength steel bars have been used in prestressed masonry installations in the United States (Schultz and Scolforo, 1991). The stress-relaxation characteristics of mild strength bars (of less than 150 ksi [1034 MPa]) should be determined by tests and those results should be documented.

2.4 C. *Joint reinforcement* — Code Section 9.1.9.3.2 limits the specified yield strength of joint reinforcement used to resist in-plane shear and flexural tension parallel to bed joints in strength design.

SPECIFICATION

2.4 D. *Anchors, ties, and accessories* (Continued)

6. Panel anchors (for glass unit masonry) — Provide 1 $^3/_4$-in. (44.5-mm) wide, 24-in. (610-mm) long, 20-gage steel strips, punched with three staggered rows of elongated holes, galvanized after fabrication.

2.4 E. *Stainless steel* — Stainless steel items shall be AISI Type 304 or Type 316, and shall conform to the following:

1. Joint reinforcement .... ASTM A580/A580M

2. Plate and bent-bar anchors.. .... ASTM A480/A480M and ASTM A666

3. Sheet-metal anchors and ties .... ASTM A480/A480M and ASTM A240/A240M

4. Wire ties and anchors .... ASTM A580/A580M

2.4 F. *Coatings for corrosion protection* — Unless otherwise required, protect carbon steel joint reinforcement, ties, anchors, and steel plates and bars from corrosion by galvanizing or epoxy coating in conformance with the following minimums:

1. Galvanized coatings:

   a. Mill galvanized coatings:

      1) Joint reinforcement.. ASTM A641/A641M (0.1 oz/ft^2) (0.031 kg/m^2)

      2) Sheet-metal ties and sheet-metal anchors ...... ASTM A653/A653M Coating Designation G60

   b. Hot-dip galvanized coatings:

      1) Joint reinforcement, wire ties, and wire anchors .... ASTM A153/A153M (1.50 oz/ft^2) (458 g/m^2)

      2) Sheet-metal ties and sheet-metal anchors .... ASTM A153/A153M Class B

      3) Steel plates and bars (as applicable to size and form indicated).............. ASTM A123/A123M .... or ASTM A153/A153M, Class B

2. Epoxy coatings:

   a. Joint reinforcement .... ASTM A884/A884M Class A .... Type 1 — 7 mils (175 μm)

   b. Wire ties and anchors.. ASTM A899/A899M Class C — 20 mils (508 μm)

   c. Sheet-metal ties and anchors................................. .... 20 mils (508 μm) per surface .... or manufacturer's specification

COMMENTARY

2.4 E. *Stainless steel* — Corrosion resistance of stainless steel is greater than that of the other steels listed. Thus, it does not have to be coated for corrosion resistance.

2.4 F. *Coatings for corrosion protection* — Amount of galvanizing required increases with severity of exposure (Grimm, 1985; Catani, 1985; NCMA TEK 12-4D, 2006). Project documents should specify the level of corrosion protection as required by Code Section 6.1.4.

SPECIFICATION

2.4 G. *Corrosion protection for tendons* — Protect tendons from corrosion when they are in exterior walls exposed to earth or weather or walls exposed to a mean relative humidity exceeding 75 percent). Select corrosion protection methods for bonded and unbonded tendons from one of the following:

1. *Bonded tendons* — Encapsulate bonded tendons in corrosion resistant and watertight corrugated ducts complying with Article 2.4 G.1.a. Fill ducts with prestressing grout complying with Article 2.4 G.1.b.

   a. Ducts — High-density polyethylene or polypropylene.

      1) Use ducts that are mortar-tight and non-reactive with masonry, tendons, and grout.

      2) Provide ducts with an inside diameter at least 1/4 in. (6.4 mm) larger than the tendon diameter.

      3) Maintain ducts free of water if members to be grouted are exposed to temperatures below freezing prior to grouting.

      4) Provide openings at both ends of ducts for grout injection.

COMMENTARY

2.4 G. *Corrosion protection for tendons* — The specified methods of corrosion protection for unbonded prestressing tendons are consistent with corrosion protection requirements developed for single-strand prestressing tendons in concrete (PTI, 2006). Masonry cover is not sufficient corrosion protection for bonded prestressing tendons in an environment with relative humidity over 75%. Therefore, complete encapsulation into plastic ducts is required. This requirement is consistent with corrosion protection for unbonded tendons. Alternative methods of corrosion protection, such as the use of stainless steel tendons or galvanized tendons, are permitted. Evidence should be provided that the galvanizing used on the tendons does not cause hydrogen embrittlement of the prestressing tendon.

Protection of prestressing tendons against corrosion is provided by a number of measures. Typically, a proprietary system is used that includes sheathing the prestressing tendon with a waterproof plastic tape or duct. Discussion of the various corrosion-protection systems used for prestressed masonry is available in the literature (Garrity, 1995). One example of a corrosion- protection system for the prestressing tendon is shown in Figure SC-5.

Chlorides, fluorides, sulfites, nitrates, or other chemicals in the prestressing grout may harm prestressing tendons and should not be used in harmful concentrations.

Historically, aggregates have not been used in grouts for bonded, post-tensioned concrete construction.

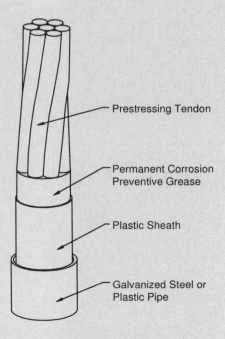

Figure SC-5 — An example of a corrosion-protection system for an unbonded tendon

SPECIFICATION

2.4 G. *Corrosion protection for tendons* (Continued)

b. Prestressing grout

    1) Select proportions of materials for prestressing grout using either of the following methods as accepted by the Architect/Engineer:

        a) Results of tests on fresh and hardened prestressing grout — prior to beginning grouting operations, or

        b) Prior documented experience with similar materials and equipment and under comparable field conditions.

    2) Use portland cement conforming to ASTM C150, Type I, II, or III, that corresponds to the type upon which selection of prestressing grout was based.

    3) Use the minimum water content necessary for proper pumping of prestressing grout; however, limit the water-cement ratio to a maximum of 0.45 by weight.

    4) Discard prestressing grout that has begun to set due to delayed use.

    5) Do not use admixtures, unless acceptable to the Architect/Engineer.

    6) Use water that is potable and free of materials known to be harmful to masonry materials and reinforcement.

COMMENTARY

b. Prestressing grout is a cementitious mixture, not conforming to ASTM C476, and is unique to bonded tendons.

SPECIFICATION

2.4 G. *Corrosion protection for tendons* (Continued)

2. *Unbonded tendons* — Coat unbonded tendons with a material complying with Article 2.4 G.2b and wrap with a sheathing complying with Article 2.4 G.2a. Acceptable materials include a corrosion-inhibiting coating material with a tendon sheathing.

   a. Provide continuous tendon sheathing over the entire tendon length to prevent loss of coating materials during tendon installation and stressing procedures. Provide a sheathing of medium-density or high-density polyethylene or polypropylene with the following properties:

   1) Sufficient strength to withstand damage during fabrication, transport, installation, and tensioning.

   2) Water-tightness over the entire sheathing length.

   3) Chemical stability without embrittlement or softening over the anticipated exposure temperature range and service life of the structure.

   4) Non-reactive with masonry and the tendon corrosion-inhibiting coating.

   5) In normal (non-corrosive) environments, a sheathing thickness of at least 0.025 in. (0.6 mm). In corrosive environments, a sheathing thickness of at least 0.040 in. (1.0 mm).

   6) An inside diameter at least 0.010 in. (0.3 mm) greater than the maximum diameter of the tendon.

   7) For applications in corrosive environments, connect the sheathing to intermediate and fixed anchorages in a watertight fashion, thus providing a complete encapsulation of the tendon.

   b. Provide a corrosion-inhibiting coating material with the following properties:

   1) Lubrication between the tendon and the sheathing.

   2) Resist flow from the sheathing within the anticipated temperature range of exposure.

   3) A continuous non-brittle film at the lowest anticipated temperature of exposure.

   4) Chemically stable and non-reactive with the tendon, sheathing material, and masonry.

   5) An organic coating with appropriate polar-moisture displacing and corrosion-preventive additives.

COMMENTARY

SPECIFICATION	COMMENTARY

SPECIFICATION

2.4 G.2.b. *Unbonded tendons* (Continued)

  6) A minimum weight not less than 2.5 lb of coating material per 100 ft (37.2 g of coating material per m) of 0.5-in. (12.7-mm) diameter tendon and 3.0 lb of coating material per 100 ft (44.6 g of coating material per m) of 0.6-in. (15.2-mm) diameter tendon. Use a sufficient amount of coating material to ensure filling of the annular space between tendon and sheathing.

  7) Extend the coating over the entire tendon length.

  8) Provide test results in accordance with Table 6 for the corrosion-inhibiting coating material.

  3. Alternative methods of corrosion protection that provide a protection level equivalent to Articles 2.4 G.1 and 2.4 G.2 are permitted. Stainless steel prestressing tendons or tendons galvanized according to ASTM A153/A153M, Class B, are acceptable alternative methods. If galvanized, further evidence must be provided that the coating will not produce hydrogen embrittlement of the steel.

2.4 H. *Prestressing anchorages, couplers, and end blocks*

  1. Provide anchorages and couplers that develop at least 95 percent of the specified breaking strength of the tendons or prestressing steel when tested in an unbonded condition, without exceeding anticipated set.

  2. Place couplers where accepted by Architect/Engineer. Enclose with housing that permits anticipated movements of the couplers during stressing.

  3. Protect anchorages, couplers, and end fittings against corrosion

  4. Protect exposed anchorages, couplers, and end fittings to achieve the fire-resistance rating required for the element by the legally adopted building code.

COMMENTARY

2.4 H. *Prestressing anchorages, couplers, and end blocks* — Typical anchorage and coupling devices are shown in Figure SC-6. Strength of anchorage and coupling devices should be provided by the manufacturer.

Protection of anchorage devices typically includes filling the opening of bearing pads with grease, grouting the recess in bearing pads, and providing drainage of cavities housing prestressing tendons with base flashing and weep holes.

When anchorages and end fittings are exposed, additional precautions to achieve the required fire ratings and mechanical protection for these elements must be taken.

Table 6 — Performance specification for corrosion-inhibiting coating

Test	Test Method	Acceptance Criteria
Dropping Point, °F (°C)	ASTM D566 or ASTM D2265	Minimum 300 (148.9)
Oil Separation @ 160°F (71.1°C) % by weight	FTMS 791B Method 321.2	Maximum 0.5
Water, % maximum	ASTM D95	0.1
Flash Point, °F (°C) (Refers to oil component)	ASTM D92	Minimum 300 (148.9)
Corrosion Test 5% Salt Fog @ 100°F (37.8°C) 5 mils (0.13 mm), minimum hours (Q Panel type S)	ASTM B117	For normal environments: Rust Grade 7 or better after 720 hr of exposure according to ASTM D610. For corrosive environments : Rust Grade 7 or better after 1000 hr of exposure according to ASTM D610.[1]
Water Soluble Ions[2] a. Chlorides, ppm maximum b. Nitrates, ppm maximum c. Sulfides, ppm maximum	ASTM D512	10 10 10
Soak Test 5% Salt Fog at 100°F (37.8°C) 5 mils (0.13 mm) coating, Q panels, type S. Immerse panels 50% in a 5% salt solution and expose to salt fog	ASTM B117 (Modified)	No emulsification of the coating after 720 hr of exposure
Compatibility with Sheathing a. Hardness and volume change of polymer after exposure to grease, 40 days @ 150°F (65.6°C). b. Tensile strength change of polymer after exposure to grease, 40 days @ 150°F (65.6°C).	ASTM D4289 ASTM D638	Permissible change in hardness 15% Permissible change in volume 10% Permissible change in tensile strength 30%

[1] Extension of exposure time to 1000 hours for greases used in corrosive environments requires use of more or better corrosion-inhibiting additives.

[2] Procedure: The inside (bottom and sides) of a 33.8 oz (1L) Pyrex beaker, approximate O.D. 4.1 in. (105 mm), height 5.7 in. (145 mm), is thoroughly coated with 35.3 ± 3.5 oz (1000 ± 100 g) corrosion-inhibiting coating material. The coated beaker is filled with approximately 30.4 oz (900 cc) of distilled water and heated in an oven at a controlled temperature of 100°F ± 2°F (37.8°C ± 1°C) for 4 hours. The water extraction is tested by the noted test procedures for the appropriate water soluble ions. Results are reported as ppm in the extracted water.

SPECIFICATION

2.5 — Accessories

2.5 A. Unless otherwise required, provide contraction (shrinkage) joint material that conforms to one of the following standards:

1. ASTM D2000, M2AA-805 Rubber shear keys with a minimum durometer hardness of 80.

2. ASTM D2287, Type PVC 654-4 PVC shear keys with a minimum durometer hardness of 85.

3. ASTM C920.

2.5 B. Unless otherwise required, provide expansion joint material that conforms to one of the following standards:

1. ASTM C920.

2. ASTM D994.

3. ASTM D1056, Class 2A

2.5 C. *Asphalt emulsion* — Provide asphalt emulsion as follows:

1. Metal surfaces.................... ASTM D1187, Type II

2. Porous surfaces... ASTM D1227, Type III, Class 1

2.5 D. *Masonry cleaner*

1. Use potable water and detergents to clean masonry unless otherwise acceptable.

2. Unless otherwise required, do not use acid or caustic solutions.

2.5 E. *Joint fillers* — Use the size and shape of joint fillers specified.

COMMENTARY

2.5 — Accessories

2.5 A. and B. Movement joints are used to allow dimensional changes in masonry, minimize random wall cracks, and other distress. Contraction joints (also called control joints or shrinkage joints) are used in concrete masonry to accommodate shrinkage. These joints are free to open as shrinkage occurs. Expansion joints permit clay brick masonry to expand. Material used in expansion joints must be compressible.

Placement of movement joints is recommended by several publications (Grimm, 1988; BIA TN 19, 2006; BIA TN 18A, 2006; NCMA TEK 10-2C, 2010). Typical movement joints are illustrated in Figure SC-7. Shear keys keep the wall sections on either side of the movement joint from moving out of plane. Proper configuration must be available to fit properly.

ASTM C920 addresses elastomeric joint sealants, either single or multi-component. Sealants that qualify as Grade NS, Class 50 (50% movement capability) or alternatively Class 25 (25% movement capability), Use M are applicable to masonry construction. Expansion joint fillers must be compressible so the anticipated expansion of the masonry can occur without imposing stress.

2.5 D. *Masonry cleaner* — Adverse reactions can occur between certain cleaning agents and masonry units. Hydrochloric acid has been observed to cause corrosion of metal ties. Care should be exercised in its use to minimize this potential problem. Manganese staining, efflorescence, "burning" of the units, white scum removal of the cement paste from the surface of the joints, and damage to metals can occur through improper cleaning. The manufacturers of the masonry units should be consulted for recommended cleaning agents.

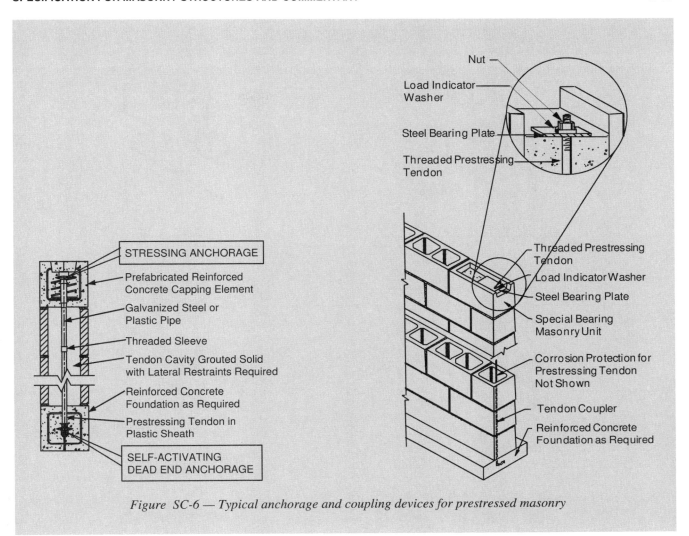

Figure SC-6 — Typical anchorage and coupling devices for prestressed masonry

COMMENTARY

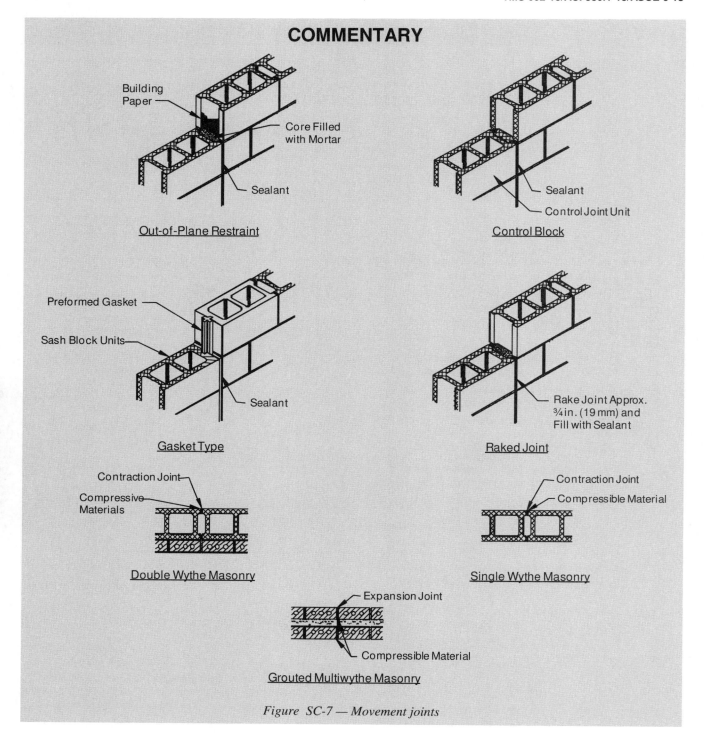

Figure SC-7 — Movement joints

SPECIFICATION

2.6 — Mixing

2.6 A. *Mortar*

1. Mix cementitious materials and aggregates between 3 and 5 minutes in a mechanical batch mixer with a sufficient amount of water to produce a workable consistency. Unless acceptable, do not hand mix mortar. Maintain workability of mortar by remixing or retempering. Discard mortar which has begun to stiffen or is not used within $2^1/_2$ hr after initial mixing.

2. Limit the weight of mineral oxide or carbon black pigments added to project-site prepared mortar to the following maximum percentages by weight of cement:

   a. Pigmented portland cement-lime mortar

      1) Mineral oxide pigment   10 percent

      2) Carbon black pigment   2 percent

   b. Pigmented mortar cement mortar

      1) Mineral oxide pigment   5 percent

      2) Carbon black pigment   1 percent

   c. Pigmented masonry cement mortar

      1) Mineral oxide pigment   5 percent

      2) Carbon black pigment   1 percent

   Do not add mineral oxide or carbon black pigment to preblended colored mortar or colored cement without the approval of the Architect/Engineer.

3. Do not use admixtures containing more than 0.2 percent chloride ions.

4. *Glass unit masonry* — Reduce the amount of water to account for the lack of absorption. Do not retemper mortar after initial set. Discard unused mortar within $1^1/_2$ hr after initial mixing.

COMMENTARY

2.6 — Mixing

2.6 A. *Mortar* — Caution must be exercised when adding color pigment in field-prepared mortar so that the proportions comply with the Specification requirements.

Preblended products are typically certified to the applicable ASTM Standard and the addition of color at the project site may impact mortar performance.

SPECIFICATION

2.6 B. *Grout*

1. Except for self-consolidating grout, mix grout in accordance with the requirements of ASTM C476.

2. Unless otherwise required, mix grout other than self-consolidating grout to a consistency that has a slump between 8 and 11 in. (203 and 279 mm).

3. Proportioning of self-consolidating grout at the project site is not permitted. Do not add water at the project site except in accordance with the self-consolidating grout manufacturer's recommendations.

COMMENTARY

2.6 B. *Grout* — The two types of grout are fine grout and coarse grout, which are defined by aggregate size. ASTM C476 requires the grout type to be specified by proportion or strength requirements, but not by both methods. ASTM proportion requirements are given in Table SC-7.

The permitted ranges in the required proportions of fine and coarse aggregates are intended to accommodate variations in aggregate type and gradation. As noted in Specification Table 7, the selection of the grout type depends on the size of the space to be grouted. Fine grout is selected for grout spaces with restricted openings. Coarse grout specified under ASTM C476 has a maximum aggregate size that will pass through a ½ in. (12.7 mm) and at least 85% that will pass through a 3/8 in. (9.5 mm) opening.

Grout meeting the proportion specifications of ASTM C476 typically has compressive strength ranges shown in Table SC-8 when measured by ASTM C1019. Grout compressive strength is influenced by the water cement ratio, aggregate content, and the type of units used.

Because grout is placed in an absorptive form made of masonry units, a high water content is required. A slump of at least 8 in. (203 mm) provides a mix fluid enough to be properly placed and supplies sufficient water to satisfy the water demand of the masonry units.

Small cavities or cells require grout with a higher slump than larger cavities or cells. As the surface area and unit shell thickness in contact with the grout decrease in relation to the volume of the grout, the slump of the grout should be reduced. Segregation of materials should not occur.

The grout in place will have a lower water-cement ratio than when mixed. This concept of high slump and absorptive forms is different from that of concrete.

Proportioning of self-consolidating grout at the project site is not permitted because the mixes can be sensitive to variations in proportions, and tighter quality control on the mix is required than can be achieved in the field. Typically, self-consolidating grout comes ready mixed from the manufacturer. Self-consolidating grout may also be available as a preblended dry mix requiring the addition of water at the project site. Manufacturers provide instructions on proper mixing techniques and amount of water to be added. Slump values for self-consolidating grout are expressed as a slump flow because they exceed the 8 in. to 11 in. (203 to 279 mm) slump range for non-self-consolidating grouts.

COMMENTARY

Table SC-7 — Grout proportions by volume

Grout type	Cement	Lime	Aggregate damp, loose[1]	
			Fine	Coarse
Fine	1	0 to 1/10	2¼ to 3	—
Coarse	1	0 to 1/10	2¼ to 3	1 to 2

[1] Times the sum of the volumes of the cementitious materials

Table SC-8 — Grout strengths

Grout type	Location	Compressive strength, psi (MPa)			Reference
		Low	Mean	High	
Coarse	Lab	1,965 (13.55)	3,106 (21.41)	4,000 (27.58)	ACI-SEASC, 1982
Coarse	Lab	3,611 (24.90)	4,145 (28.58)	4,510 (31.10)	Li and Neis, 1986
Coarse	Lab	5,060 (34.89)	5,455 (37.61)	5,940 (40.96)	ATL, 1982

SPECIFICATION

2.6 C. *Thin-bed mortar for AAC* – Mix thin-bed mortar for AAC masonry as specified by the thin-bed mortar manufacturer.

2.7 — Fabrication

2.7 A. *Reinforcement*

1. Fabricate reinforcing bars in accordance with the fabricating tolerances of ACI 117.

2. Unless otherwise required, bend bars cold and do not heat bars.

3. The minimum inside diameter of bend for stirrups shall be five bar diameters.

4. Do not bend Grade 40 bars in excess of 180 degrees. The minimum inside diameter of bend is five bar diameters.

5. The minimum inside bend diameter for other bars is as follows:

    a. No. 3 through No. 8 (M#10 through 25)....................
    ....6 bar diameters

    b. No. 9 through No. 11 (M#29 through 36)..................
    ....8 bar diameters

6. Provide standard hooks that conform to the following:

    a. A standard 180-degree hook: 180-degree bend plus a minimum extension of 4 bar diameters or $2^1/_2$ in. (64 mm), whichever is greater.

    b. A standard 90-degree hook: 90-degree bend plus a minimum extension of 12 bar diameters.

    c. For stirrups and tie hooks for a No. 5 (M#16) bar and smaller: a 90- or 135-degree bend plus a minimum of 6 bar diameters or $2^1/_2$ in. (64 mm), whichever is greater.

COMMENTARY

2.7 — Fabrication

2.7 A. *Reinforcement* — ACI 117 Specifications for Tolerances for Concrete Construction and Materials and Commentary contains fabrication tolerances for steel reinforcement. Recommended methods and standards for preparing design drawings, typical details, and drawings for the fabrications and placing of reinforcing steel in reinforced concrete structures are given in ACI 315 (1999) and may be used as a reference in masonry design and construction.

SPECIFICATION

2.7 B. *Prefabricated masonry*

1. Unless otherwise required, provide prefabricated masonry that conforms to the provisions of ASTM C901.

2. Unless otherwise required, provide prefabricated masonry lintels that have an appearance similar to the masonry units used in the wall surrounding each lintel.

3. Mark prefabricated masonry for proper location and orientation.

COMMENTARY

2.7 B. *Prefabricated masonry* — ASTM C901 addresses the requirements for prefabricated masonry panels, including materials, structural design, dimensions and variations, workmanship, quality control, identification, shop drawings, and handling.

PART 3 — EXECUTION

SPECIFICATION

3.1 — Inspection

3.1 A. Prior to the start of masonry construction, the Contractor shall verify:

1. That foundations are constructed within a level alignment tolerance of $\pm^1/_2$ in. (12.7 mm).

2. That reinforcing dowels are positioned in accordance with the Project Drawings.

3.1 B. If stated conditions are not met, notify the Architect/Engineer.

COMMENTARY

3.1 — Inspection

3.1 A. The tolerances in this Article are taken from ACI 117 (1990). The dimensional tolerances of the supporting concrete are important because they control such aspects as mortar joint thickness and bearing area dimensions, which influence the performance of the masonry. Tolerances for variation in grade or elevation are shown in Figure SC-8. The specified width of the foundation is obviously more critical than its specified length. A foundation wider than specified will not normally cause structural problems.

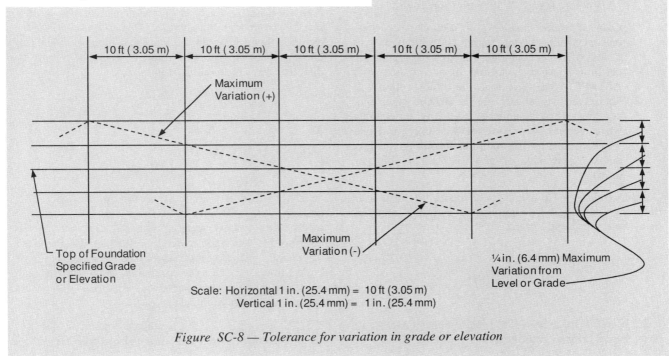

Figure SC-8 — Tolerance for variation in grade or elevation

SPECIFICATION

3.2 — Preparation

3.2 A. Clean reinforcement and shanks of anchor bolts by removing mud, oil, or other materials that will adversely affect or reduce bond at the time mortar or grout is placed. Reinforcement with rust, mill scale, or both are acceptable without cleaning or brushing provided that the dimensions and weights, including heights of deformations, of a cleaned sample are not less than required by the ASTM specification that governs this reinforcement.

3.2 B. Prior to placing masonry, remove laitance, loose aggregate, and anything else that would prevent mortar from bonding to the foundation.

3.2 C. *Wetting masonry units*

1. *Concrete masonry* — Unless otherwise required, do not wet concrete masonry or AAC masonry units before laying. Wet cutting is permitted.

2. *Clay or shale masonry* — Wet clay or shale masonry units having initial absorption rates in excess of 1 g per min. per in.^{2} (0.0016 g per min. per mm^2), when measured in accordance with ASTM C67, so the initial rate of absorption will not exceed 1 g per min. per in.^{2} (0.0016 g per min. per mm^2) when the units are used. Lay wetted units when surface dry. Do not wet clay or shale masonry units having an initial absorption rate less than 0.2 g per min. per in.^{2} (0.00031 g per min. per mm^2).

3.2 D. *Debris* — Construct grout spaces free of mortar dropping, debris, loose aggregates, and any material deleterious to masonry grout.

3.2 E. *Reinforcement* — Place reinforcement and ties in grout spaces prior to grouting.

3.2 F. *Cleanouts* — Provide cleanouts in the bottom course of masonry for each grout pour when the grout pour height exceeds 5 ft 4 in. (1.63 m).

1. Construct cleanouts so that the space to be grouted can be cleaned and inspected. In solid grouted masonry, space cleanouts horizontally a maximum of 32 in. (813 mm) on center.

2. Construct cleanouts with an opening of sufficient size to permit removal of debris. The minimum opening dimension shall be 3 in. (76.2 mm).

3. After cleaning, close cleanouts with closures braced to resist grout pressure.

COMMENTARY

3.2 C. *Wetting masonry units* — Concrete masonry units increase in volume when wetted and shrink upon subsequent drying. Water introduced during wet cutting is localized and does not significantly affect the shrinkage potential of concrete masonry. Clay masonry units with high absorption rates dry the mortar/unit interface. This may result in a lower extent of bond between the units and mortar, which may create paths for moisture intrusion. Selection of compatible units and mortar can mitigate this effect.

3.2 D. *Debris* — Continuity in the grout is critical for uniform stress distribution. A reasonably clean space to receive the grout is necessary for this continuity. Cells need not be vacuumed to achieve substantial cleanliness. Inspection of the bottom of the space prior to grouting is critical to ensure that it is substantially clean and does not have accumulations of deleterious materials that would prevent continuity of the grout.

3.2 E. *Reinforcement* — Loss of bond and misalignment of the reinforcement can occur if it is not placed prior to grouting.

3.2 F. *Cleanouts* — Cleanouts can be constructed by removing the exposed face shell of units in hollow unit grouted masonry or individual units when grouting between wythes. The purpose of cleanouts is to allow the grout space to be adequately cleaned prior to grouting. They can also be used to verify reinforcement placement and tying.

SPECIFICATION

3.3 — Masonry erection

3.3 A. *Bond pattern* — Unless otherwise required, lay masonry in running bond.

3.3 B. *Placing mortar and units*

1. *Bed joints at foundations* — In the starting course on foundations and other supporting members, construct bed joints so that the bed joint thickness is at least ¼ in. (6.4 mm) and not more than:

   a. ¾ in. (19.1 mm) when the masonry is ungrouted or partially grouted.

   b. 1¼ in. (31.8 mm) when the first course of masonry is solid grouted and supported by a concrete foundation.

COMMENTARY

3.3 B. *Placing mortar and units* — Article 3.3 B applies to masonry construction in which the units support their own weight.

1. *Bed joints at foundations* — The range of permitted mortar bed joint thickness at foundations for solid grouted masonry walls is compatible with the foundation tolerances of Article 3.1 A.1. Figure SC-9 shows the allowable foundation tolerance of ± ½ in. and the relationship of the mortar bed joint. The contractor should coordinate the mortar bed joint at foundations with the coursing requirements so that the intended masonry module is met at critical points, such as story height and top of wall, window and door openings. Either fine or coarse grout for the first course of masonry may be placed when normal masonry grouting is performed for fully grouted masonry, or may be placed after the first course is laid and prior to placement of additional courses when the masonry is not fully grouted.

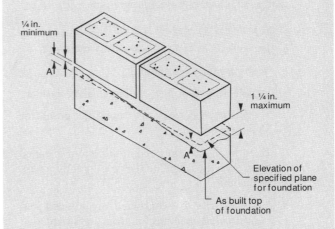

A—Foundation tolerance (±½ in.) is measured perpendicular to the specified plane to any point on the as–built surface

Figure SC-9 Mortar bed joint thickness for solid grouted walls on a foundation

SPECIFICATION

3.3 B. *Placing mortar and units* (Continued)

2. *Bed and head joints* — Unless otherwise required, construct $^3/_8$-in. (9.5-mm) thick bed and head joints, except at foundation or with glass unit masonry. Provide glass unit masonry bed and head joint thicknesses in accordance with Article 3.3 B.7.c. Provide AAC masonry bed and head joint thicknesses in accordance with Article 3.3 B.9.b. Construct joints that also conform to the following:

   a. Fill holes not specified in exposed and below grade masonry with mortar.

   b. Unless otherwise required, tool joint with a round jointer when the mortar is thumbprint hard.

   c. Remove masonry protrusions extending $^1/_2$ in. (12.7 mm) or more into cells or cavities to be grouted.

3. *Collar joints* — Unless otherwise required, solidly fill collar joints less than $^3/_4$ in. (19.1 mm) wide with mortar as the project progresses.

4. *Hollow units* — Place hollow units so:

   a. Face shells of bed joints are fully mortared.

   b. Webs are fully mortared in:

      1) all courses of piers, columns and pilasters;

      2) when necessary to confine grout or insulation.

   c. Head joints are mortared, a minimum distance from each face equal to the face shell thickness of the unit.

   d. Vertical cells to be grouted are aligned and unobstructed openings for grout are provided in accordance with the Project Drawings.

COMMENTARY

4. *Hollow units* — Face shell mortar bedding of hollow units is standard, except in locations detailed in Article 3.3 B.4.b. Figure SC-10 shows the typical placement of mortar for hollow-unit masonry walls. In partially grouted walls, however, cross webs next to cells that are to be grouted are usually mortared. If full mortar beds throughout are required for structural capacity, for example, the specifier must so stipulate in the Project Specifications or Project Drawings.

SPECIFICATION

3.3 B. *Placing mortar and units* (Continued)

5. *Solid units* — Unless otherwise required, place mortar so that bed and head joints are fully mortared and:

   a. Do not fill head joints by slushing with mortar.

   b. Construct head joints by shoving mortar tight against the adjoining unit.

   c. Do not deeply furrow bed joints.

6. *Open-end units with beveled ends* — Fully grout open-end units with beveled ends. Head joints of open-end units with beveled ends need not be mortared. At the beveled ends, form a grout key that permits grout within 5/8 in. (15.9 mm) of the face of the unit. Tightly butt the units to prevent leakage of grout.

7. *Glass units*

   a. Apply a complete coat of asphalt emulsion, not exceeding $1/8$ in. (3.2 mm) in thickness, to panel bases.

   b. Lay units so head and bed joints are filled solidly. Do not furrow mortar.

   c. Unless otherwise required, construct head and bed joints of glass unit masonry $1/4$ in. (6.4 mm) thick, except that vertical joint thickness of radial panels shall not be less than $1/8$ in. (3.2 mm). The bed-joint thickness tolerance shall be minus $1/16$ in. (1.6 mm) and plus $1/8$ in. (3.2 mm). The head-joint thickness tolerance shall be plus or minus $1/8$ in. (3.2 mm).

   d. Do not cut glass units.

COMMENTARY

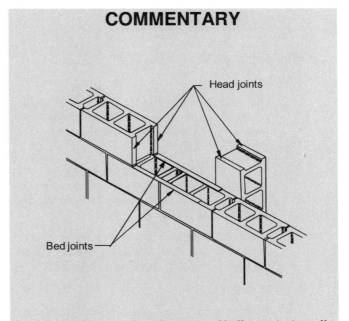

Figure SC-10 — Mortar placement of hollow units in walls

SPECIFICATION

3.3 B. *Placing mortar and units* (Continued)

8. *All units*

   a. Place clean units while the mortar is soft and plastic. Remove and re-lay in fresh mortar any unit disturbed to the extent that initial bond is broken after initial positioning.

   b. Except for glass units, cut exposed edges or faces of masonry units smooth, or position so that exposed faces or edges are unaltered manufactured surfaces.

   c. When the bearing of a masonry wythe on its support is less than two-thirds of the wythe thickness, notify the Architect/Engineer.

9. *AAC masonry*

   a. Place mortar for leveling bed joint in accordance with the requirements of Article 3.3 B.1.

   b. Lay subsequent courses using thin-bed mortar. Use special notched trowels manufactured for use with thin-bed mortar to spread thin-bed mortar so that it completely fills the bed joints. Unless otherwise specified in the Contract Documents, similarly fill the head joints. Spread mortar and place the next unit before the mortar dries. Place each AAC unit as close to head joint as possible before lowering the block onto the bed joint. Avoid excessive movement along bed joint. Make adjustments while thin-bed mortar is still soft and plastic by tapping to plumb and bring units into alignment. Set units into final position, in mortar joints at least 1/16-in. (1.5-mm) thick, by striking on the end and top with a rubber mallet.

   c. Lay units in alignment with the plane of the wall. Align vertically and plumb using the first course for reference. Make minor adjustments by sanding the exposed faces of the units and the bed joint surface with a sanding board manufactured for use with AAC masonry.

COMMENTARY

3.3 B.9 *AAC masonry* — AAC masonry can be cut, shaped and drilled with tools that are capable of cutting wood; however, saws, sanding boards, and rasps manufactured for use with AAC are recommended for field use. Because thin-bed mortar joints do not readily allow for plumbing of a wall, the ability of AAC masonry to be easily cut and shaped allows for field adjustment to attain required tolerances.

SPECIFICATION

3.3 C. *Placing adhered veneer*

1. Brush a paste of neat portland cement on the backing and on the back of the veneer unit.

2. Apply Type S mortar to the backing and to the veneer unit.

3. Tap the veneer unit into place, completely filling the space between the veneer unit and the backing. Sufficient mortar shall be used to create a slight excess to be forced out between the edges of the veneer units. The resulting thickness of the mortar in back of the veneer unit shall not be less than $^3/_8$ in. (9.5 mm) nor more than 1¼ in. (31.8 mm).

4. Tool the mortar joint with a round jointer when the mortar is thumbprint hard.

3.3 D. *Embedded items and accessories* — Install embedded items and accessories as follows:

1. Construct chases as masonry units are laid.

2. Install pipes and conduits passing horizontally through masonry partitions.

3. Place pipes and conduits passing horizontally through piers, pilasters, or columns.

4. Place horizontal pipes and conduits in and parallel to plane of walls.

5. Install and secure connectors, flashing, weep holes, weep vents, nailing blocks, and other accessories.

6. Install movement joints.

7. Aluminum — Do not embed aluminum conduits, pipes, and accessories in masonry, grout, or mortar, unless they are effectively coated or isolated to prevent chemical reaction between aluminum and cement or electrolytic action between aluminum and steel.

COMMENTARY

3.3 C *Placing adhered veneer* — Article 3.3 C applies to adhered veneer in which the backing supports the weight of the units. This basic method has served satisfactorily since the early 1950s. Properly filled and tooled joints (3.3 C.4) are essential for proper performance of adhered veneer.

SPECIFICATION

3.3 E. *Bracing of masonry* — Design, provide, and install bracing that will assure stability of masonry during construction.

3.3 F. *Site tolerances* — Erect masonry within the following tolerances from the specified dimensions.

1. Dimension of elements

   a. In cross section or elevation
       ....-$^1/_4$ in. (6.4 mm), +$^1/_2$ in. (12.7 mm)

   b. Mortar joint thickness

       bed joints between masonry courses

       ....±$^1/_8$ in. (3.2 mm)

       bed joint between flashing and masonry

       .... - ½ in. (12.7 mm), +$^1/_8$ in. (3.2 mm)

       head ....- $^1/_4$ in. (6.4 mm), + $^3/_8$ in. (9.5 mm)

       collar..........-$^1/_4$ in. (6.4 mm), + $^3/_8$ in. (9.5 mm)

       glass unit masonry............see Article 3.3 B.7.c

       AAC thin-bed mortar joint thickness...............

       .... -0, + 1/8 in. (3.2 mm)

   c. Grout space or cavity width, except for masonry walls passing framed construction

       ....-$^1/_4$ in. (6.4 mm), + $^3/_8$ in. (9.5 mm)

COMMENTARY

3.3 E. *Bracing of masonry* — For guidance on bracing of masonry walls for wind, consult Standard Practice for Bracing Masonry Walls Under Construction (MCAA, 2012).

3.3 F. *Site tolerances* — Tolerances are established to limit eccentricity of applied load. Because masonry is usually used as an exposed material, it is subjected to tighter dimensional tolerances than those for structural frames. The tolerances given are based on structural performance, not aesthetics.

The provisions for cavity width shown are for the space between wythes of non-composite masonry. The provisions do not apply to situations where masonry extends past floor slabs, spandrel beams, or other structural elements.

The remaining provisions set the standard for quality of workmanship and ensure that the structure is not overloaded during construction.

Mortar is required to bond masonry courses, but it is not required when masonry is laid on top of flashing.

SPECIFICATION

3.3 F. *Site tolerances* (Continued)

2. Elements

   a. Variation from level:

   bed joints
   .... ±$^1/_4$ in. (6.4 mm) in 10 ft (3.05 m)
   .... ±$^1/_2$ in. (12.7 mm) maximum

   top surface of load-bearing walls
   .... ±$^1/_4$ in. (6.4 mm) in 10 ft (3.05 m)
   .... ±$^1/_2$ in. (12.7 mm) maximum

   b. Variation from plumb
   .... ±$^1/_4$ in. (6.4 mm) in 10 ft (3.05 m)
   .... ±$^3/_8$ in. (9.5 mm) in 20 ft (6.10 m)
   .... ±$^1/_2$ in. (12.7 mm) maximum

   c. True to a line
   .... ±$^1/_4$ in. (6.4 mm) in 10 ft (3.05 m)
   .... ±$^3/_8$ in. (9.5 mm) in 20 ft (6.10 m)
   .... ±$^1/_2$ in. (12.7 mm) maximum

   d. Alignment of columns and walls
      (bottom versus top)
      ....±$^1/_2$ in. (12.7 mm) for
                        load-bearing walls and columns
      .±$^3/_4$ in. (19.1 mm) for non-load-bearing walls

3. Location of elements

   a. Indicated in plan
   .... ±$^1/_2$ in. (12.7 mm) in 20 ft (6.10 m)
   .... ±$^3/_4$ in. (19.1 mm) maximum

   b. Indicated in elevation
   .... ±$^1/_4$ in. (6.4 mm) in story height
   .... ±$^3/_4$ in. (19.1 mm) maximum

4. If the above conditions cannot be met due to previous construction, notify the Architect/ Engineer.

COMMENTARY

SPECIFICATION

3.4 — Reinforcement, tie, and anchor installation

3.4 A. *Basic requirements* — Place reinforcement, wall ties, and anchors in accordance with the sizes, types, and locations indicated on the Project Drawings and as specified. Do not place dissimilar metals in contact with each other.

3.4 B. *Reinforcement*

1. Support reinforcement to prevent displacement caused by construction loads or by placement of grout or mortar, beyond the allowable tolerances.

2. Completely embed reinforcing bars in grout in accordance with Article 3.5.

3. Maintain clear distance between reinforcing bars and the interior of masonry unit or formed surface of at least $1/4$ in. (6.4 mm) for fine grout and $1/2$ in. (12.7 mm) for coarse grout, except where cross webs of hollow units are used as supports for horizontal reinforcement.

4. Place reinforcing bars maintaining the following minimum cover:

   a. Masonry face exposed to earth or weather: 2 in. (50.8 mm) for bars larger than No. 5 (M #16); 1½ in. (38.1 mm) for No. 5 (M #16) bars or smaller.

   b. Masonry not exposed to earth or weather: 1½ in. (38.1 mm).

5. Maintain minimum clear distance between parallel bars of the nominal bar size or 1 in. (25.4 mm), whichever is greater.

6. In columns and pilasters, maintain minimum clear distance between vertical bars of one and one-half times the nominal bar size or 1½ in. (38.1 mm), whichever is greater.

7. Splice only where indicated on the Project Drawings, unless otherwise acceptable. When splicing by welding, provide welds in conformance with the provisions of AWS D 1.4.

8. Unless accepted by the Architect/Engineer, do not bend reinforcement after it is embedded in grout or mortar.

9. *Noncontact lap splices* — Position bars spliced by noncontact lap splice no farther apart transversely than one-fifth the specified length of lap nor more than 8 in. (203 mm)

COMMENTARY

3.4 — Reinforcement, tie, and anchor installation

The requirements given ensure that:

a. galvanic action is inhibited,

b. location is as assumed in the design,

c. there is sufficient clearance for grout and mortar to surround reinforcement, ties, and anchors so stresses are properly transferred,

d. corrosion is delayed, and

e. compatible lateral deflection of wythes is achieved.

Tolerances for placement of reinforcement in masonry first appeared in the 1985 Uniform Building Code (UBC, 1985). Reinforcement location obviously influences structural performance of the member. Figure SC-11 illustrates several devices used to secure reinforcement.

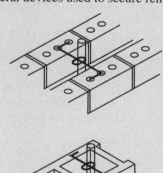

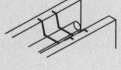

Figure SC-11 — Typical reinforcing bar positioners

9. *Noncontact lap splices* — Lap splices may be constructed with the bars in adjacent grouted cells if the requirements of this section are met.

SPECIFICATION

3.4 B. *Reinforcement* (Continued)

10. *Joint reinforcement*

   a. Place joint reinforcement so that longitudinal wires are embedded in mortar with a minimum cover of $1/2$ in. (12.7 mm) when not exposed to weather or earth; or $5/8$ in. (15.9 mm) when exposed to weather or earth.

   b. Provide minimum 6-in. (152-mm) lap splices for joint reinforcement.

   c. Ensure that all ends of longitudinal wires of joint reinforcement at laps are embedded in mortar or grout.

COMMENTARY

10. *Joint reinforcement* — There must be a minimum protective cover for the joint reinforcement as shown in Figure SC-12. Deeply tooled mortar joints, which provide inadequate protective cover for joint reinforcement, should be avoided.

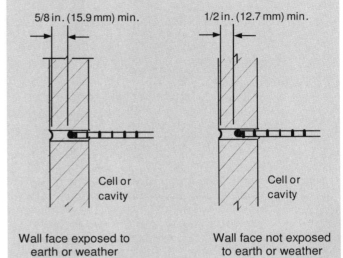

Figure SC-12 Joint Reinforcement Cover Requirements

   c. Where laps occur in longitudinal wires of joint reinforcement the minimum embedment provisions of Article 3.4 B.10.a apply. Figure SC-13 shows typical joint reinforcement lap splices in mortar or grout.

SPECIFICATION

COMMENTARY

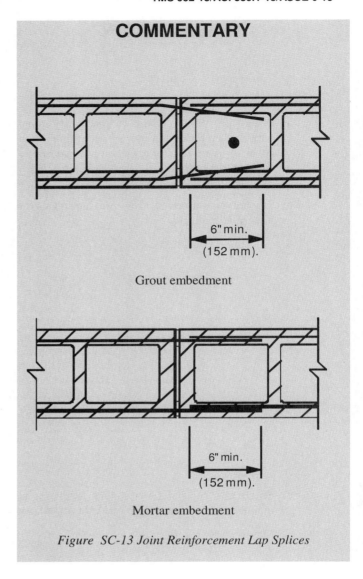

Figure SC-13 Joint Reinforcement Lap Splices

SPECIFICATION

3.4 B. *Reinforcement* (Continued)

11. *Placement tolerances*

a. Place reinforcing bars in walls and flexural elements within a tolerance of $\pm \frac{1}{2}$ in. (12.7 mm) when the distance from the centerline of reinforcing bars to the opposite face of masonry, *d*, is equal to 8 in. (203 mm) or less, $\pm$ 1 in. (25.4 mm) for *d* equal to 24 in. (610 mm) or less but greater than 8 in. (203 mm), and $\pm 1\frac{1}{4}$ in. (31.8 mm) for *d* greater than 24 in. (610 mm).

b. Place vertical bars within:

1) 2 in. (50.8 mm) of the required location along the length of the wall when the wall segment length exceeds 24 in. (610 mm).

2) 1 in. (25.4 mm) of the required location along the length of the wall when the wall segment length does not exceed 24 in. (610 mm)

c. If it is necessary to move bars more than one bar diameter or a distance exceeding the tolerance stated above to avoid interference with other reinforcing steel, conduits, or embedded items, notify the Architect/Engineer for acceptance of the resulting arrangement of bars.

COMMENTARY

11. *Placement tolerances*

a. Ways to measure *d* distance in various common masonry elements are shown in Figures SC-14 through SC-16 (Chrysler, 2010). The maximum permissible tolerance for placement of reinforcement in a wall, beam, and column is based on the *d* dimension of that element.

In masonry, the *d* dimension is measured perpendicular to the length of the element and is defined in the Specification as the distance from the center of the reinforcing bar to the compression face of masonry.

In a wall subject to out-of-plane loading, the distance, *d*, to the compression face is normally the larger distance when reinforcing bars are offset from the center of the wall, as shown in Figure SC-14.

The *d* dimension in masonry columns will establish the maximum allowable tolerance for placement of the vertical reinforcement. As shown in Figure SC-15, two dimensions for each vertical bar must be considered to establish the allowable tolerance for placement of the vertical reinforcement in each primary direction.

The *d* dimension in a masonry beam will establish the maximum allowable tolerance for placement of the horizontal reinforcement within the depth of the beam. As shown in Figure SC-16, the distance to the top of beam is used to establish the allowable tolerance for placement of the reinforcement.

b. The tolerance for placement of vertical reinforcing bars along the length of the wall is shown in Figure SC-14. As shown, the allowable tolerance is +/- 2 in. (50.8 mm), except for wall segments not exceeding 24 in. (610 mm) where the allowable tolerance is decreased to +/- 1 in. (25.4 mm). This tolerance applies to each reinforcing bar relative to the specified location in the wall. An accumulation of tolerances could result in bar placement that interferes with cross webs in hollow masonry units.

COMMENTARY

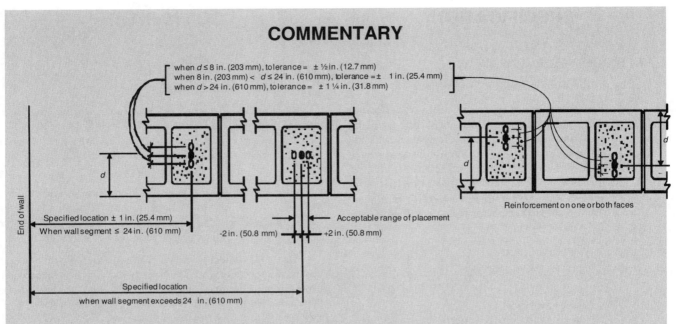

Figure SC-14 — Typical 'd' distance in a wall

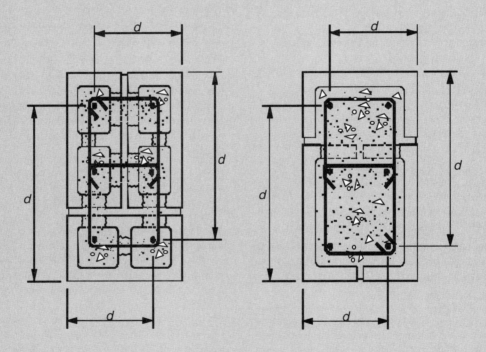

Figure SC-15 — Typical 'd' distance in a column

SPECIFICATION

3.4 B.11.   *Reinforcement, Placement tolerances*
(Continued)

d. Foundation dowels that interfere with unit webs are permitted to be bent to a maximum of 1 in. (25.4 mm) horizontally for every 6 in. (152 mm) of vertical height.

COMMENTARY

d. Misaligned foundation dowels may interfere with placement of the masonry units. Interfering dowels may be bent in accordance with this provision (see Figure SC-17) (Stecich et al, 1984; NCMA TEK 3-2A, 2005). Removing a portion of the web to better accommodate the dowel may also be acceptable as long as the dowel is fully encapsulated in grout and masonry cover is maintained.

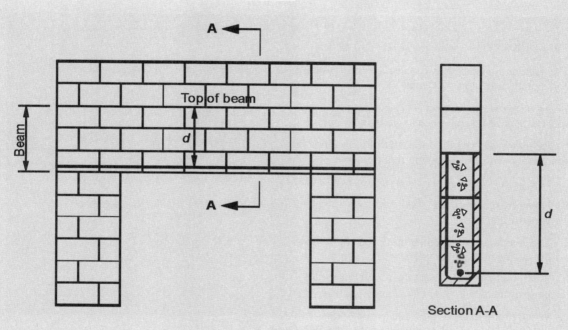

Figure SC-16 — Typical 'd' distance in a beam

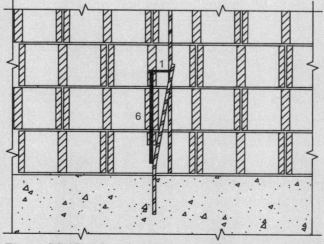

Figure SC-17 — Permitted Bending of Foundation Dowels

SPECIFICATION

3.4 C. *Wall ties*

1. Embed the ends of wall ties in mortar joints. Embed wall tie ends at least $1/2$ in. (12.7 mm) into the outer face shell of hollow units. Embed wire wall ties at least $1^1/2$ in. (38.1 mm) into the mortar bed of solid masonry units or solid grouted hollow units.

2. Unless otherwise required, bond wythes not bonded by headers with wall ties as follows:

Wire size	Minimum number of wall ties required
W1.7 (MW11)	One per 2.67 ft² (0.25 m²)
W2.8 (MW18)	One per 4.50 ft² (0.42 m²)

The maximum spacing between ties is 36 in. (914 mm) horizontally and 24 in. (610 mm) vertically.

3. Unless accepted by the Architect/Engineer, do not bend wall ties after being embedded in grout or mortar.

4. Unless otherwise required, install adjustable ties in accordance with the following requirements:

   a. One tie for each 1.77 ft² (0.16 m²) of wall area.

   b. Do not exceed 16 in. (406 mm) horizontal or vertical spacing.

   c. The maximum misalignment of bed joints from one wythe to the other is $1^1/4$ in. (31.8 mm).

   d. The maximum clearance between connecting parts of the ties is $1/16$ in. (1.6 mm)

   e. When pintle anchors are used, provide ties with one or more pintle leg made of wire size W2.8 (MW18).

COMMENTARY

3.4 C. *Wall ties* — The Code does not permit the use of cavity wall ties with drips, nor the use of Z-ties in ungrouted, hollow unit masonry. The requirements for adjustable ties are shown in Figure SC-18.

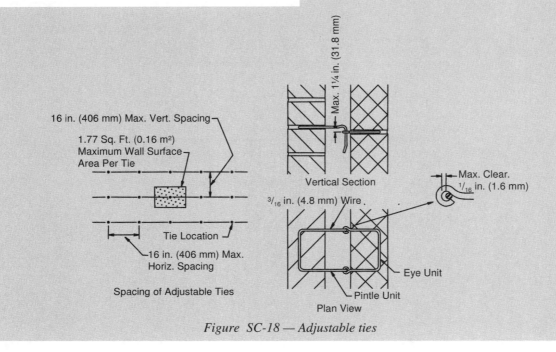

Figure SC-18 — Adjustable ties

SPECIFICATION

3.4 C. *Wall ties* (Continued)

5. Install wire ties perpendicular to a vertical line on the face of the wythe from which they protrude. Where one-piece ties or joint reinforcement are used, the bed joints of adjacent wythes shall align.

6. Unless otherwise required, provide additional unit ties around openings larger than 16 in. (406 mm) in either dimension. Space ties around perimeter of opening at a maximum of 3 ft (0.91 m) on center. Place ties within 12 in. (305 mm) of opening.

7. Unless otherwise required, provide unit ties within 12 in. (305 mm) of unsupported edges at horizontal or vertical spacing given in Article 3.4 C.2.

3.4 D. *Anchor bolts*

1. Embed headed and bent-bar anchor bolts larger than ¼ in. (6.4 mm) diameter in grout that is placed in accordance with Article 3.5 A and Article 3.5 B. Anchor bolts of ¼ in. (6.4 mm) diameter or less are permitted to be placed in grout or mortar bed joints that have a specified thickness of at least ½ in. (12.7 mm) thickness.

2. For anchor bolts placed in the top of grouted cells and bond beams, maintain a clear distance between the bolt and the face of masonry unit of at least ¼ in. (6.4 mm) when using fine grout and at least ½ in. (12.7 mm) when using coarse grout.

3. For anchor bolts placed through the face shell of a hollow masonry unit, drill a hole that is tight-fitting to the bolt or provide minimum clear distance that conforms to Article 3.4 D.2 around the bolt and through the face shell. For the portion of the bolt that is within the grouted cell, maintain a clear distance between the bolt and the face of masonry unit and between the head or bent leg of the bolt and the formed surface of grout of at least ¼ in. (6.4 mm) when using fine grout and at least ½ in. (12.7 mm) when using coarse grout.

4. Place anchor bolts with a clear distance between parallel anchor bolts not less than the nominal diameter of the anchor bolt, nor less than 1 in. (25.4 mm).

COMMENTARY

3. Quality assurance/control (QA/QC) procedures should assure that there is sufficient clearance around the bolts prior to grout placement. These procedures should also include observation during grout placement to assure that grout completely surrounds the bolts, as required by the QA Tables in Article 1.6.A

The clear distance requirement for grout to surround an anchor bolt does not apply where the bolt fits tightly in the hole of the face shell, but is required where the bolt is placed in an oversized hole in the face shell and where grout surrounds the anchor bolt in a grouted cell or cavity. See Figure SC-19.

COMMENTARY

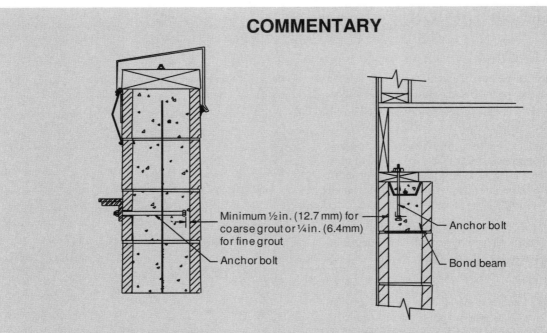

Figure SC-19 — Anchor bolt clearance requirements for headed anchor bolts – bent-bars are similar

SPECIFICATION

3.4 E. *Veneer anchors* — Place corrugated sheet-metal anchors, sheet-metal anchors, and wire anchors as follows:

1. With solid units, embed anchors in mortar joint and extend into the veneer a minimum of 1½ in. (38.1 mm), with at least $^5/_8$ in. (15.9 mm) mortar cover to the outside face.

2. With hollow units, embed anchors in mortar or grout and extend into the veneer a minimum of 1 ½ in. (38.1 mm), with at least $^5/_8$ in. (15.9 mm) mortar or grout cover to outside face.

3. Install adjustable anchors in accordance with the requirements of Articles 3.4 C.4.c, d, and e.
4. Provide at least one adjustable two-piece anchor, anchor of wire size W 1.7 (MW11), or 22 gage (0.8 mm) corrugated sheet-metal anchor for each 2.67 ft² (0.25 m²) of wall area.
5. Provide at least one anchor of other types for each 3.5 ft² (0.33 m²) of wall area.
6. Space anchors at a maximum of 32 in. (813 mm) horizontally and 25 in. (635 mm) vertically, but not to exceed the applicable requirement of Article 3.4 E.4 or 3.4 E.5.
7. Provide additional anchors around openings larger than 16 in. (406 mm) in either dimension. Space anchors around the perimeter of opening at a maximum of 3 ft (0.9 m) on center. Place anchors within 12 in. (305 mm) of opening.

COMMENTARY

3.4 E. *Veneer anchors* — Minimum embedment requirements have been established for each of the anchor types to ensure load resistance against push-through or pullout of the mortar joint.

2. Proper anchorage of veneer anchors into veneers using hollow masonry units can be satisfied by mortaring anchors in bed joints or on the cross-webs of the units; by grouting the cells or cores adjacent to the anchor; or by following the anchor manufacturer's requirements for installing the anchor into the cell or core above or below the bed joint and filling the cell or core containing the anchor with mortar or grout.

SPECIFICATION

3.4 F. *Glass unit masonry panel anchors* — When used instead of channel-type restraints, install panel anchors as follows:

1. Unless otherwise required, space panel anchors at 16 in. (406 mm) in both the jambs and across the head.

2. Embed panel anchors a minimum of 12 in. (305 mm), except for panels less than 2 ft (0.61 m) in the direction of embedment. When a panel dimension is less than 2 ft (0.61 m), embed panel anchors in the short direction a minimum of 6 in. (152 mm), unless otherwise required.

3. Provide two fasteners, capable of resisting the required loads, per panel anchor.

3.5 — Grout placement

3.5 A. *Placing time* — Place grout within $1^1/_2$ hr from introducing water in the mixture and prior to initial set.

1. Discard site-mixed grout that does not meet the specified slump without adding water after initial mixing.

2. For ready-mixed grout:

   a. Addition of water is permitted at the time of discharge to adjust slump.

   b. Discard ready-mixed grout that does not meet the specified slump without adding water, other than the water that was added at the time of discharge.

   The time limitation is waived as long as the ready-mixed grout meets the specified slump.

3.5 B. *Confinement* — Confine grout to the areas indicated on the Project Drawings. Use material to confine grout that permits bond between masonry units and mortar.

COMMENTARY

3.5 — Grout placement

Grout may be placed by pumping or pouring from large or small buckets. The amount of grout to be placed and contractor experience influence the choice of placement method.

The requirements of this Article do not apply to prestressing grout.

3.5 A. *Placing time* — Grout placement is often limited to 1½ hours after initial mixing, but this time period may be too long in hot weather (initial set may occur) and may be unduly restrictive in cooler weather. One indicator that the grout has not reached initial set is a stable and reasonable grout temperature. However, sophisticated equipment and experienced personnel are required to determine initial set with absolute certainty.

Article 3.5 A.2 permits water to be added to ready-mixed grout to compensate for evaporation that has occurred prior to discharge. Replacement of evaporated water is not detrimental to ready-mixed grout. However, water may not be added to ready-mixed grout after discharge.

3.5 B. *Confinement* — Certain locations in the wall may not be grouted in order to reduce dead loads or allow placement of other materials such as insulation or wiring. Cross webs adjacent to cells to be grouted can be bedded with mortar to confine the grout. Metal lath, plastic screening, or other items can be used to plug cells below bond beams.

SPECIFICATION

3.5 C. *Grout pour height* — Do not exceed the maximum grout pour height given in Table 7.

COMMENTARY

3.5 C. *Grout pour height* — Table 7 in the Specification has been developed as a guide for grouting procedures. The designer can impose more stringent requirements if so desired. The recommended maximum height of grout pour (see Figure SC-20) corresponds with the least clear dimension of the grout space. The minimum width of grout space is used when the grout is placed between wythes. The minimum cell dimensions are used when grouting cells of hollow masonry units. As the height of the pour increases, the minimum grout space increases. The grout space dimensions are clear dimensions. See the Commentary for Section 3.2.1 of the Code for additional information.

Grout pour heights and minimum dimensions that meet the requirements of Table 7 do not automatically mean that the grout space will be filled.

Grout spaces smaller than specified in Table 7 have been used successfully in some areas. When the contractor asks for acceptance of a grouting procedure that does not meet the limits in Table 7, construction of a grout demonstration panel is required. Destructive or non-destructive evaluation can confirm that filling and adequate consolidation have been achieved. The Architect/Engineer should establish criteria for the grout demonstration panel to assure that critical masonry elements included in the construction will be represented in the demonstration panel. Because a single grout demonstration panel erected prior to masonry construction cannot account for all conditions that may be encountered during construction, the Architect/Engineer should establish inspection procedures to verify grout placement during construction. These inspection procedures should include destructive or non-destructive evaluation to confirm that filling and adequate consolidation have been achieved.

Table 7 — Grout space requirements

Grout type[1]	Maximum grout pour height, ft (m)	Minimum clear width of grout space,[2,3] in. (mm)	Minimum clear grout space dimensions for grouting cells of hollow units,[3,4,5] in. x in. (mm x mm)
Fine	1 (0.30)	$^3/_4$ (19.1)	$1^1/_2$ x 2 (38.1 x 50.8)
Fine	5.33 (1.63)	2 (50.8)	2 x 3 (50.8 x 76.2)
Fine	12.67 (3.86)	$2^1/_2$ (63.5)	$2^1/_2$ x 3 (63.5 x 76.2)
Fine	24 (7.32)	3 (76.2)	3 x 3 (76.2 x 76.2)
Coarse	1 (0.30)	$1^1/_2$ (38.1)	$1^1/_2$ x 3 (38.1 x 76.2)
Coarse	5.33 (1.63)	2 (50.8)	$2^1/_2$ x 3 (63.5 x 76.2)
Coarse	12.67 (3.86)	$2^1/_2$ (63.5)	3 x 3 (76.2 x 76.2)
Coarse	24 (7.32)	3 (76.2)	3 x 4 (76.2 x 102)

[1] Fine and coarse grouts are defined in ASTM C476.

[2] For grouting between masonry wythes.

[3] Minimum clear width of grout space and minimum clear grout space dimension are the net dimension of the space determined by subtracting masonry protrusions and the diameters of horizontal bars from the as-built cross-section of the grout space. Select the grout type and maximum grout pour height based on the minimum clear space.

[4] Area of vertical reinforcement shall not exceed 6 percent of the area of the grout space.

[5] Minimum grout space dimension for AAC masonry units shall be 3 in. (76.2 mm) x 3 in. (76.2 mm) or a 3 in. (76.2 mm) diameter cell.

SPECIFICATION

3.5 D. *Grout lift height*

1. For grout conforming to Article 2.2 A:

    a. Where the following conditions are met, place grout in lifts not exceeding 12 ft 8 in. (3.86 m).

        i.   The masonry has cured for at least 4 hours.

        ii. The grout slump is maintained between 10 and 11 in. (254 and 279 mm).

        iii. No intermediate reinforced bond beams are placed between the top and the bottom of the pour height.

    b. When the conditions of Articles 3.5 D.1.a.i and 3.5 D.1.a.ii are met but there are intermediate bond beams within the grout pour, limit the grout lift height to the bottom of the lowest bond beam that is more than 5 ft 4 in. (1.63 m) above the bottom of the lift, but do not exceed a grout lift height of 12 ft 8 in. (3.86 m).

    c. When the conditions of Article 3.5 D.1.a.i or Article 3.5 D.1.a.ii are not met, place grout in lifts not exceeding 5 ft 4 in. (1.63 m).

2. For self-consolidating grout conforming to Article 2.2:

    a. When placed in masonry that has cured for at least 4 hours, place in lifts not exceeding the grout pour height.

    b. When placed in masonry that has not cured for at least 4 hours, place in lifts not exceeding 5 ft 4 in. (1.63 m) or the grout pout height, whichever is less.

3.5 E. *Consolidation*

1. Consolidate grout at the time of placement.

    a. Consolidate grout pours 12 in. (305 mm) or less in height by mechanical vibration or by puddling.

    b. Consolidate pours exceeding 12 in. (305 mm) in height by mechanical vibration, and reconsolidate by mechanical vibration after initial water loss and settlement has occurred.

2. Consolidation or reconsolidation is not required for self-consolidating grout.

COMMENTARY

3.5 D. *Grout lift height* — A lift is the height to which grout is placed into masonry in one continuous operation (see Figure SC-20). After placement of a grout lift, water is absorbed by the masonry units. Following this water loss, a subsequent lift may be placed on top of the still plastic grout.

Grouted construction develops fluid pressure in the grout space. Grout pours composed of several lifts may develop this fluid pressure for the full pour height. The faces of hollow units with unbraced ends can break out. Wythes may separate. The wire ties between wythes may not be sufficient to prevent this from occurring. Higher lifts may be used with self-consolidating grout because its fluidity and its lower initial water-cement ratio result in reduced potential for fluid pressure problems.

The 4-hour time period is stipulated for grout lifts over 5 ft 4 in. (1.63 m) to provide sufficient curing time to minimize potential displacement of units during the consolidation and reconsolidation process. The 4 hours is based on typical curing conditions and may be increased based on local climatic conditions at the time of construction. For example, during cold weather construction, consider increasing the 4-hour curing period. When a wall is to be grouted with self-consolidating grout, the grout lift height is not restricted by intermediate, reinforced bond beam locations because self-consolidating grout easily flows around reinforcing bars (NCMA MR29, 2006; NCMA MR31, 2007)

3.5 E. *Consolidation* — Except for self-consolidating grout, consolidation is necessary to achieve complete filling of the grout space. Reconsolidation returns the grout to a plastic state and eliminates the voids resulting from the water loss from the grout by the masonry units. It is possible to have a height loss of 8 in. (203 mm) in 8 ft (2.44 m).

Consolidation and reconsolidation are normally achieved with a mechanical vibrator. A low velocity vibrator with a ¾ in. (19.1 mm) head is used. The vibrator is activated for one to two seconds in each grouted cell of hollow unit masonry. When double open-end units are used, one cell is considered to be formed by the two open ends placed together. When grouting between wythes, the vibrator is placed in the grout at points spaced 12 to 16 in. (305 to 406 mm) apart. Excess vibration does not improve consolidation and may blow out the face shells of hollow units or separate the wythes when grouting between wythes.

COMMENTARY

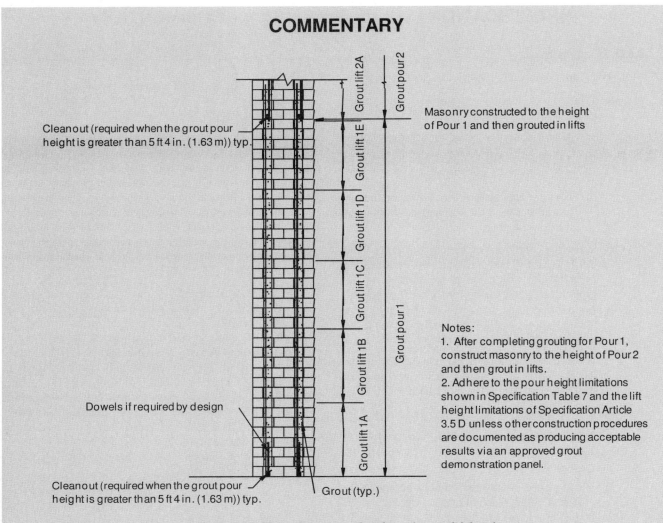

Figure SC-20 — Grout pour height and grout lift height

SPECIFICATION

3.5 F. *Grout key* — When grouting, form grout keys between grout pours. Form grout keys between grout lifts when the first lift is permitted to set prior to placement of the subsequent lift

1. Form a grout key by terminating the grout a minimum of 1½ in. (38.1 mm) below a mortar joint.

2. Do not form grout keys within beams.

3. At beams or lintels laid with closed bottom units, terminate the grout pour at the bottom of the beam or lintel without forming a grout key.

3.5 G. *Alternate grout placement* — Place masonry units and grout using construction procedures employed in the accepted grout demonstration panel.

3.5 H. *Grouting AAC masonry* — Wet AAC masonry thoroughly before grouting to ensure that the grout flows to completely fill the space to be grouted.

COMMENTARY

3.5 F. *Grout key* — The top of a grout pour should not be located at the top of a unit, but at a minimum of 1½ in. (38 mm) below the bed joint.

If a lift of grout is permitted to set prior to placing the subsequent lift, a grout key is required within the grout pour. This setting normally occurs if the grouting is stopped for more than one hour.

SPECIFICATION

3.6 — Prestressing tendon installation and stressing procedure

3.6 A. *Site tolerances*

1. Tolerance for prestressing tendon placement in the out-of-plane direction in walls shall be ± $^1/_4$ in. (6.4 mm) for masonry cross-sectional dimensions less than nominal 8 in. (203 mm) and ± $^3/_8$ in. (9.5 mm) for masonry cross-sectional dimensions equal to or greater than nominal 8 in. (203 mm).

2. Tolerance for prestressing tendon placement in the in-plane direction of walls shall be ± 1 in. (25.4 mm).

3. If prestressing tendons are moved more than one tendon diameter or a distance exceeding the tolerances stated in Articles 3.6 A.1 and 3.6 A.2 to avoid interference with other tendons, reinforcement, conduits, or embedded items, notify the Architect/Engineer for acceptance of the resulting arrangement of prestressing tendons.

3.6 B. *Application and measurement of prestressing force*

1. Determine the prestressing force by both of the following methods:

    a. Measure the prestressing tendon elongation and compare it with the required elongation based on average load-elongation curves for the prestressing tendons.

    b. Observe the jacking force on a calibrated gage or load cell or by use of a calibrated dynamometer. For prestressing tendons using bars of less than 150 ksi (1034 MPa) tensile strength, Direct Tension Indicator (DTI) washers complying with ASTM F959 or ASTM F959M are acceptable.

2. Ascertain the cause of the difference in force determined by the two methods described in Article 3.6 B.1 when the difference exceeds 5 percent for pretensioned elements or 7 percent for post-tensioned elements, and correct the cause of the difference.

3. When the total loss of prestress due to unreplaced broken prestressing tendons exceeds 2 percent of total prestress, notify the Architect/Engineer.

COMMENTARY

3.6 — Prestressing tendon installation and stressing procedure

Installation of tendons with the specified tolerances is common practice. The methods of application and measurement of prestressing force are common techniques for prestressed concrete and masonry members. Designer, contractor, and inspector should be experienced with prestressing and should consult the Post-Tensioning Institute's Field Procedures Manual for Unbonded Single Strand Tendons (PTI, 1994) or similar literature before conducting the Work. Critical aspects of the prestressing operation that require inspection include handling and storage of the prestressing tendons and anchorages, installation of the anchorage hardware into the foundation and capping members, integrity and continuity of the corrosion-protection system for the prestressing tendons and anchorages, and the prestressing tendon stressing and grouting procedures.

The design method in Code Chapter 10 is based on an accurate assessment of the level of prestress. Tendon elongation and tendon force measurements with a calibrated gauge or load cell or by use of a calibrated dynamometer have proven to provide the required accuracy. For tendons using steels of less than 150 ksi (1034 MPa) strength, Direct Tension Indicator (DTI) washers also provide adequate accuracy. These washers have dimples that are intended to compress once a predetermined force is applied on them by the prestressing force. These washers were first developed by the steel industry for use with high-strength bolts and have been modified for use with prestressed masonry. The designer should verify the actual accuracy of DTI washers and document it in the design.

Burning and welding operations in the vicinity of prestressing tendons must be carefully performed because the heat may lower the tendon strength and cause failure of the stressed tendon.

SPECIFICATION

3.6 C. *Grouting bonded tendons*

1. Mix prestressing grout in equipment capable of continuous mechanical mixing and agitation so as to produce uniform distribution of materials, pass through screens, and pump in a manner that will completely fill tendon ducts.

2. Maintain temperature of masonry above 35°F (1.7°C) at time of grouting and until field-cured 2 in. (50.8 mm) cubes of prestressing grout reach a minimum compressive strength of 800 psi (5.52 MPa).

3. Keep prestressing grout temperatures below 90°F (32.2°C) during mixing and pumping.

3.6 D. *Burning and welding operations* — Carefully perform burning and welding operations in the vicinity of prestressing tendons so that tendons and sheathings, if used, are not subjected to excessive temperatures, welding sparks, or grounding currents.

3.7 — Field quality control

3.7 A. Verify f'_m and f'_{AAC} in accordance with Article 1.6.

3.7 B. Sample and test grout as required by Articles 1.4 B and 1.6.

3.8 — Cleaning

Clean exposed masonry surfaces of stains, efflorescence, mortar and grout droppings, and debris using methods that do not damage the masonry.

COMMENTARY

3.7 — Field quality control

3.7 A. The specified frequency of testing must equal or exceed the minimum requirements of the quality assurance tables.

3.7 B. ASTM C1019 requires a mold for the grout specimens made from the masonry units that will be in contact with the grout. Thus, the water absorption from the grout by the masonry units is simulated. Sampling and testing frequency may be based on the volume of grout to be placed rather than the wall area. Alternative forming methods can also be used provided a conversion factor based on comparative testing of 10 sets of specimens has been established as required by ASTM C1019, Section 6.2

3.8 — Cleaning

Use of undiluted cleaning products, especially acids, and failing to pre-wet the masonry or to adequately rinse the masonry after cleaning can cause damage. In some situations, cleaning without chemicals may be appropriate.

FOREWORD TO SPECIFICATION CHECKLISTS

SPECIFICATION

F1. This Foreword is included for explanatory purposes only; it does not form a part of Specification TMS 602–13/ACI 530.1–13/ASCE 6–13.

F2. Specification TMS 602–13/ACI 530.1–13/ASCE 6–13 may be referenced by the Architect/Engineer in the Project Specification for any building project, together with supplementary requirements for the specific project. Responsibilities for project participants must be defined in the Project Specification.

F3. Checklists do not form a part of Specification TMS 602–13/ACI 530.1–13/ASCE 6–13. Checklists are provided to assist the Architect/Engineer in selecting and specifying project requirements in the Project Specification. The checklists identify the Sections, Parts, and Articles of the reference Specification and the action required or available to the Architect/Engineer.

F4. The Architect/Engineer must make adjustments to the Specification based on the needs of a particular project by reviewing each of the items in the checklists and including the items the Architect/Engineer selects as mandatory requirements in the Project Specification.

F5. The Mandatory Requirements Checklist indicates work requirements regarding specific qualities, procedures, materials, and performance criteria that are not defined in Specification TMS 602–13/ACI 530.1–13/ASCE 6–13 or requirements for which the Architect/Engineer must define which of the choices apply to the project.

F6. The Optional Requirements Checklist identifies Architect/Engineer choices and alternatives.

COMMENTARY

F1. No Commentary

F2. Building codes (of which this standard is a part by reference) set minimum requirements necessary to protect the public. Project specifications may stipulate requirements more restrictive than the minimum. Adjustments to the needs of a particular project are intended to be made by the Architect/Engineer by reviewing each of the items in the Checklists and then including the Architect/Engineer's decision on each item as a mandatory requirement in the project specifications.

F3. The Checklists are addressed to each item of this Specification where the Architect/Engineer must or may make a choice of alternatives; may add provisions if not indicated; or may take exceptions. The Checklists consist of two columns; the first identifies the sections, parts, and articles of the Specification, and the second column contains notes to the Architect/Engineer to indicate the type of action that may be required by the Architect/Engineer. Checklist items that are not applicable to a project should not be included in the Project Specifications.

MANDATORY REQUIREMENTS CHECKLIST

Section/Part/Article	Notes to the Architect/Engineer
PART 1 — GENERAL	
1.4 A Compressive strength requirements	Specify f'_m and f'_{AAC}, except for veneer, glass unit masonry, prescriptively designed partition walls, and empirically designed masonry. Specify f'_{mi} for prestressed masonry.
1.4 B.2 Unit strength method	Specify when strength of grout is to be determined by test.
1.5 Submittals	Define the submittal reporting and review procedure.
1.6 A.1 Testing Agency's services and duties	Specify which of Tables 3, 4, or 5 applies to the project. Specify which portions of the masonry were designed in accordance with the prescriptive partition wall, empirical, veneer, or glass unit masonry provisions of this Code and are, therefore, exempt from verification of f'_m.
1.6 B.1 Inspection Agency's services and duties	Specify which of Tables 3, 4, or 5 applies to the project. Specify which portions of the masonry were designed in accordance with the prescriptive partition wall, empirical, veneer, or glass unit masonry provisions of this Code and are, therefore, exempt from verification of f'_m.
1.6 D Sample panels	Specify requirements for sample panels.
PART 2 — PRODUCTS	
2.1 Mortar materials	Specify type, color, and cementitious materials to be used in mortar and mortar to be used for the various parts of the project and the type of mortar to be used with each type of masonry unit.
2.3 Masonry unit materials	Specify the masonry units to be used for the various parts of the projects.
2.4 Reinforcement, prestressing tendons, and metal accessories	Specify type and grade of reinforcement, tendons, connectors, and accessories.
2.4 A Reinforcing Steel	When deformed reinforcing bars conforming to ASTM A615/A615M or ASTM A996/A996M are required by strength design in accordance with Code Chapter 9 or Chapter 11, specify that the actual yield strength must not exceed the specified yield strength multiplied by 1.3.
2.4 C.1 Joint reinforcement	Specify joint reinforcement wire size and number of longitudinal wires when joint reinforcement is to be used as shear reinforcement.
2.4 C.3 Welded wire reinforcement	Specify when welded wire reinforcement is to be plain.
2.4 E Stainless steel	Specify when stainless steel joint reinforcement, anchors, ties, and/or accessories are required.
2.4 F Coating for corrosion protection	Specify the types of corrosion protection that are required for each portion of the masonry construction.
2.4 G Corrosion protection for tendons	Specify the corrosion protection method.

MANDATORY REQUIREMENTS CHECKLIST (Continued)

Section/Part/Article		Notes to the Architect/Engineer
2.4 H	Prestressing anchorages, couplers, and end blocks	Specify the anchorages and couplers and their corrosion protection.
2.5 E	Joint fillers	Specify size and shape of joint fillers.
2.7 B	Prefabricated masonry	Specify prefabricated masonry and requirements in supplement of those of ASTM C901.

PART 3 — EXECUTION

3.3 D.2-4	Pipes and conduits	Specify sleeve sizes and spacing.
3.3 D.5	Accessories	Specify accessories not indicated on the project drawings.
3.3 D.6	Movement joints	Indicate type and location of movement joints on the project drawings.
3.4 B.11	Placement tolerances	Indicate d distance for beams on drawings or as a schedule in the project specifications.
3.4 E	Veneer anchors	Specify type of anchor required.

OPTIONAL REQUIREMENTS CHECKLIST

Section/Part/Article		Notes to the Architect/Engineer
PART 1 — GENERAL		
1.5 B		Specify additional required submittals.
1.6	Quality assurance	Define who will retain the Testing Agency and Inspection Agency, if other than the Owner.
PART 2 — PRODUCTS		
2.2		Specify grout requirements at variance with TMS 602/ACI 530.1/ASCE 6. Specify admixtures.
2.5 A and 2.5 B	Movement joint	Specify requirements at variance with TMS 602/ACI 530.1/ASCE 6.
2.5 D	Masonry cleaner	Specify where acid or caustic solutions are allowed and how to neutralize them.
2.6 A	Mortar	Specify if hand mixing is allowed and the method of measurement of material.
2.6 B.2	Grout consistency	Specify requirements at variance with TMS 602/ACI 530.1/ASCE 6
PART 3 — EXECUTION		
3.2 C	Wetting masonry units	Specify when units are to be wetted.
3.3 A	Bond pattern	Specify bond pattern if not running bond.
3.3 B.2	Bed and head joints	Specify thickness and tooling differing from TMS 602/ACI 530.1/ASCE 6.
3.3 B.3	Collar joints	Specify the filling of collar joints less than $3/4$ in. (19.1 mm) thick differing from TMS 602/ACI 530.1/ASCE 6.
3.3 B.4	Hollow units	Specify when cross webs are to be mortar bedded.
3.3 B.5	Solid units	Specify mortar bedding at variance with TMS 602/ACI 530.1/ASCE 6.
3.3 B.7	Glass units	Specify mortar bedding at variance with TMS 602/ACI 530.1/ASCE 6.
3.3 B.9.b	AAC Masonry	Specify when mortar may be omitted from AAC running bond masonry head joints that are less than 8 in. (200 mm) (nominal) tall.
3.3 D.2	Embedded items and accessories	Specify locations where sleeves are required for pipes or conduits.
3.4 B.10	Joint reinforcement	When joint reinforcement is used as shear reinforcement, specify a lap length of $48d_b$ instead of 6 inches.
3.4 C.2, 3, and 4		Specify requirements at variance with TMS 602/ACI 530.1/ASCE 6.

REFERENCES FOR THE SPECIFICATION COMMENTARY

References, Part 1

ASTM E447, 1997. ASTM E447 - 97 "Test Methods for Compressive Strength of Laboratory Constructed Masonry Prisms", (Withdrawn 1998), ASTM International, West Conshohocken, Pennsylvania.

Atkinson and Kingsley, 1985. Atkinson, R.H., and Kingsley, G.R., "A Comparison of the Behavior of Clay and Concrete Masonry in Compression," Atkinson-Noland & Associates, Inc., Longmont, CO, Sept. 1985.

Bennett, 2010. Bennett, R.M., "Proposed Masonry Specified Compressive Strength Requirements." Journal of ASTM International, 7(2), Paper JAI102663, 2010

BIA, 1992. "All Weather Construction" Technical Notes on Brick Construction Number 1 Revised, Brick Industry Association (formerly the Brick Institute of America), Reston, VA, March 1992.

BIA TN 39, 2001. "Technical Notes 39, *Testing for Engineered Brick Masonry—Brick and Mortar*", Brick Industry Association, Reston, VA, Nov. 2001.

BIA TN 39B, 1988. "Technical Notes 39B, *Testing for Engineered Brick Masonry—Quality Control*", Brick Industry Association, Reston, VA, Mar. 1988.

Brown and Borchelt, 1990. Brown, R.H., and Borchelt, J.G., "Compression Tests of Hollow Brick Units and Prisms," *Masonry Components to Assemblages*, ASTM STP 1063, J.H. Matthys, editor, American Society for Testing and Materials, Philadelphia, PA, 1990, 263 - 278.

Chrysler, 2010. Chrysler, J., "Reinforced Concrete Masonry Construction Inspector's Handbook", 7th Edition, Masonry Institute of America and International Code Council, Torrance, CA, 2010.

Drysdale et al, 1999. Drysdale, R.G., Hamid, A.A., and Baker, L.R. "Masonry Structures: Behavior and Design." 2nd edition, The Masonry Society, Longmont, CO 1999.

Hegemier, 1978. Hegemier, G.A., Krishnamoorthy, G., Nunn, R.O., and Moorthy, T.V., "Prism Tests for the Compressive Strength of Concrete Masonry," *Proceedings*, North American Masonry Conference, University of Colorado, Boulder, CO, Aug. 1978, , The Masonry Society, Longmont, CO, 18-1 through 18-17.

IMI, 1973. "Recommended Practices and Guide Specifications for Cold Weather Masonry Construction," International Masonry Industry All-Weather Council, Washington, DC, 1973.

Miller et al 1979. Miller, D.E.; Noland, J.L.; and Feng, C.C., "Factors Influencing the Compressive Strength of Hollow Clay Unit Prisms," *Proceedings*, 5th International Brick Masonry Conference, Washington DC, 1979.

NCMA, 1994. "Research Evaluation of Flexural Tensile Strength of Concrete Masonry," National Concrete Masonry Association, Herndon, VA, 1994.

NCMA, 2008. "Inspection and Testing of Concrete Masonry Construction", National Concrete Masonry Association and International Code Council, Herndon, VA, 2008.

NCMA, 2012. "Recalibration of the Unit Strength Method for Verifying Compliance with the Specified Compressive Strength of Concrete Masonry" (MR37), National Concrete Masonry Association, Herndon, VA, 2012.

Noland, 1982. Noland, J.L., "Proposed Test Method for Determining Compressive Strength of Clay-Unit Prisms," Atkinson-Noland & Associates, Inc., Boulder, CO, June 1982.

Panarese et al, 1991. Panarese, W.C., S.H. Kosmatka, and F.A. Randall Jr "Concrete Masonry Handbook for Architects, Engineers, and Builders," Portland Cement Association, Skokie, IL, 1991, 121-123.

PCA, 1993. "Hot Weather Masonry Construction," Trowel Tips, Portland Cement Association, Skokie, IL, 1993.

Priestley and Elder, 1983. Priestley, M.J.N., and Elder, D.M., "Stress-Strain Curves for Unconfined and Confined Concrete Masonry," ACI JOURNAL, *Proceedings* V. 80, No. 3, Detroit, MI, May-June 1983, 192-201.

SCI and MIA, 2006(a). "CodeMaster, Special Inspection for Masonry", Structures & Codes Institute and Masonry Institute of America, Torrance, CA, 2006.

SCI and MIA, 2006(b) . "CodeMaster, Masonry Materials", Structures & Codes Institute and Masonry Institute of America, Torrance, CA, 2006.

SCPI, 1969. "Recommended Practice for Engineered Brick Masonry," Brick Industry Association (formerly Structural Clay Products Institute), Reston, VA, 1969.

Tomasetti, 1990. Tomasetti, A.A., "Problems and Cures in Masonry" ASTM STP 1063, Masonry Components to Assemblages, ASTM, Philadelphia. PA,1990, 324-338.

References, Part 2

ACI 315 (1999). "Details and Detailing of Concrete Reinforcement", ACI 315-99, American Concrete Institute, Farmington Hills, MI.

ACI-SEASC, 1982. ACI-SEASC Task Committee on Slender Walls, "Test Report on Slender Walls," ACI Southern California Chapter/Structural Engineers Association of Southern California, Los Angeles, CA, 1982.

ATL, 1981. Unpublished Field Test Report, File 80-617, B'Nai B'Rith Housing, Associated Testing Laboratories, Houston, TX, 1981.

Beall, 1989. Beall, C., "Tips on Designing, Detailing, and Specifying Glass Block Panels," The Magazine of Masonry Construction, March 1989, Addison, IL, 92 - 99.

BIA TN 18A, 2006. "Accommodating Expansion of Brickwork", *Technical Notes on Brick Construction 18A*, Brick Industry Association, Reston, VA, Oct. 2006.

BIA TN 19, 2006. "Volume Changes – Analysis and Effects of Movement," *Technical Notes on Brick Construction 18*, Brick Industry Association, Reston, VA, Oct. 2006.

Catani, 1985. Catani, M.J., "Protection of Embedded Steel in Masonry," *Construction Specifier*, V. 38, No. 1, Construction Specifications Institute, Alexandria, VA, Jan. 1985, 62.

Garrity, 1995. Garrity, S.W., "Corrosion Protection of Prestressing Tendons for Masonry," *Proceedings, Seventh Canadian Masonry Symposium*, McMaster University, Hamilton, Ontario, June 1995, 736-750.

Glashaus, 1992. "WECK Glass Blocks," Glashaus Inc., Arlington Heights, IL, 1992.

Grimm, 1985 Grimm, C.T., "Corrosion of Steel in Brick Masonry," *Masonry: Research, Application, and Problems*, STP-871, ASTM, Philadelphia, PA, 1985, 67-87.

Grimm, 1988. Grimm, C.T., "Masonry Cracks: A Review of the Literature," *Masonry: Materials, Design, Construction, and Maintenance*, STP-992, ASTM, Philadelphia, PA, 1988.

Li and Neis, 1986. Li, D., and Neis, V.V., "The Performance of Reinforced Masonry Beams Subjected to Reversal Cyclic Loadings," *Proceedings*, 4th Canadian Masonry Symposium, Fredericton, New Brunswick, Canada, June 1986, V. 1, 351-365.

NCMA TEK 10-2C, 2010. "Control Joints for Concrete Masonry Walls-Empirical Method," *NCMA TEK* 10-2C, National Concrete Masonry Association, Herndon, VA, 2010.

NCMA TEK 12-4D, 2006. "Steel Reinforcement for Concrete Masonry," *NCMA TEK* 12-4D, National Concrete Masonry Association, Herndon, VA, 2006.

Pittsburgh Corning, 1992. "PC Glass Block Products," (GB 185), Pittsburgh Corning Corp., Pittsburgh, PA, 1992.

PTI, 2006. Post-Tensioning Institute. "Chapter 4-Specifying Post-Tensioning," *Post-Tensioning Manual*, 6th Edition, Phoenix, AZ, 2006, 73-79.

Schultz and Scolforo, 1991. Schultz, A.E. and Scolforo, M.J., 'An Overview of Prestressed Masonry," *The Masonry Society Journal*, V. 10, No. 1, The Masonry Society, Longmont, CO, August 1991, 6-21.

References, Part 3

ACI 117, 1990. ACI Committee 117, "Standard Specifications for Tolerances for Concrete Construction and Materials (ACI 117-90)," American Concrete Institute, Detroit, MI, 1990.

Chrysler, 2010. Chrysler, J., "Reinforced Concrete Masonry Construction Inspector's Handbook", 7th Edition, Masonry Institute of America and International Code Council, Torrance, CA, 2010, 167-168.

MCAA, 2012. Council for Masonry Wall Bracing, *Standard Practice for Bracing Masonry Walls Under Construction*, Mason Contractors Association of America, 2012.

MIA, 2009. *Reinforced Concrete Masonry Construction Inspector's Handbook, 7th Edition*, Masonry Institute of America/International Code Council, Torrance, CA, 2009, 167-168.

NCMA MR29, 2006. "Self-Consolidating Grout Investigation: Compressive Strength, Shear Bond, Consolidation and Flow, (MR29)". National Concrete Masonry Association, 2006.

NCMA MR31, 2007. "Self-Consolidating Grout Investigation: Making and Testing Prototype SCG Mix Designs – Report of Phase II Research, (MR31)". National Concrete Masonry Association, 2007.

NCMA TEK 3-2A, 2005. "Grouting Concrete Masonry Walls", NCMA TEK 3-2A, National Concrete Masonry Association, Herndon, VA, 2005.

PTI, 1994. *Field Procedures Manual for Unbonded Single Strand Tendons, 2nd Edition*, Post-Tensioning Institute, Phoenix, AZ, 1994.

Stecich et al, 1984. Stecich, J.P, Hanson, John M. and Rice, Paul F., "Bending and Straightening of Grade 60 Reinforcing Bars" Concrete International, August 1984, Volume 6, Issue 8, 14-23.

UBC, 1985. Uniform Building Code, International Conference of Building Officials, Whittier, CA, 1985.

INDEX

---

* AAC = Autoclaved Aerated Concrete, ASD = Allowable Stress Design, MSW = Masonry Shear Wall, SD = Strength Design

* AAC = Autoclaved Aerated Concrete, ASD = Allowable Stress Design, MSW = Masonry Shear Wall, SD = Strength Design

---

* AAC = Autoclaved Aerated Concrete, ASD = Allowable Stress Design, MSW = Masonry Shear Wall, SD = Strength Design

* AAC = Autoclaved Aerated Concrete, ASD = Allowable Stress Design, MSW = Masonry Shear Wall, SD = Strength Design

* AAC = Autoclaved Aerated Concrete, ASD = Allowable Stress Design, MSW = Masonry Shear Wall, SD = Strength Design

Index, I-9

* AAC = Autoclaved Aerated Concrete, ASD = Allowable Stress Design, MSW = Masonry Shear Wall, SD = Strength Design

---

* AAC = Autoclaved Aerated Concrete, ASD = Allowable Stress Design, MSW = Masonry Shear Wall, SD = Strength Design

---

* AAC = Autoclaved Aerated Concrete, ASD = Allowable Stress Design, MSW = Masonry Shear Wall, SD = Strength Design

* AAC = Autoclaved Aerated Concrete, ASD = Allowable Stress Design, MSW = Masonry Shear Wall, SD = Strength Design